BURT FRANKLIN: RESEARCH & SOURCE WORKS SERIES 363
American Classics in History & Social Science 85

SKETCHES OF DEBATE

WILLIAM MACLAY.
FROM A MINIATURE.

SKETCHES OF DEBATE

IN THE

FIRST SENATE OF THE UNITED STATES

IN 1789–90–91,

BY

WILLIAM MACLAY

BURT FRANKLIN
NEW YORK

Published by BURT FRANKLIN
235 East 44th St., New York, N.Y. 10017
Originally Published: 1880
Reprinted: 1969
Printed in the U.S.A.

Library of Congress Card Catalog No.: 69-18609
Burt Franklin: Research and Source Works Series 363
American Classics in History and Social Science 85

PREFACE.

By act of the old Congress, the first Congress under the constitution was to convene in the city of New York on the 4th of March, 1789. A quorum of the Senate did not meet till the 6th of April, on which day the election of General Washington, as President, and John Adams, as Vice President, was announced, the former by an unanimous vote, sixty-nine being the whole number; Mr. Adams by a plurality vote, he receiving thirty-four votes, and the residue of the sixty-nine being distributed between ten other persons; and messengers were appointed to inform General Washington and Mr. Adams of their election.

The names of the members at the first session of the Senate will appear at the beginning of the journal.

The first Congress held *three* sessions. The first commenced at the city of *New York* on the 4th of March, 1789, and terminated on the 29th of September of that year. The second one was held at the same place, commencing on the first Monday of January, 1790, and terminated on the 12th day of August of that year. The third session was held at *Philadelphia*, commencing on the first Monday of December, 1790, and terminating on the 3d of March, 1791.

During those three sessions, William Maclay and Robert Morris were the Senators from Pennsylvania. In the classification of the Senate, William Maclay fell within the first class, his term expiring on the 4th of March, 1791, and he was not reëlected. His place was not supplied during the first session of the second Congress, but during the second session, viz: On the 28th of February, 1792, Albert Gallatin was elected to fill the vacancy. He was sworn, and took his seat, on the meeting of Congress in December, 1793, but, subsequently, he was declared to be ineligible for want of citizenship for nine years, as required by the third section of the first article of the constitution, and the vacancy was not supplied until James Ross was elected, the certificate of his election being submitted to the Senate on the 2d of April, 1794. He took his seat on the 24th of that month.

During the revolutionary war, the Congress sat with *closed* doors. Such was also the case during the sessions of the convention which formed our national constitution. When the first Congress held under that constitution convened, the doors of the *House of Representatives* were opened, but the Senate directed their doors to be kept closed, and were closed, except during the debate on the question of admitting Mr. Gallatin, when they were opened. The doors of the Senate were kept closed until the year 1794. Motions to have them opened were several times made, and negatived; but on 20th of February, 1794, it was resolved that after the end of that session the galleries of the Senate should be opened whilst the Senate was engaged in its legislative capacity, unless in such cases as may in the opinion of the Senate require secrecy.

In December, 1858, or January, 1859, when the Senate were about to remove from their old to their present Hall, Mr. Breckenridge, then Vice President, delivered to it an address, in the course of which he remarked, (See *Congressional Globe* of January 24, 1859:) "At the origin of the Government, the Senate seemed to be regarded chiefly as an executive council. The President often visited the Chamber, and conferred personally with this body. Most of its business was transacted with closed doors, and it took comparatively little part in the legislative debates. The rising and vigorous intellects of the country sought the arena of the House of Representatives, as the appropriate theater for the display of their powers."

It will appear hereafter that this statement was very erroneous. President Washington never visited the Senate for consultation, during its session, except on one occasion, that relating to a treaty with southern Indians, an account of which visit will hereinafter appear; and it will also appear that important questions which were debated in the House were also debated in the Senate. It was not reasonable to suppose that the distinguished men who then occupied positions in the Senate would suffer such important questions as were acted on in that body to pass without discussion. Mr. Breckenridge had not the information on the subject which we now possess.

Mr. Maclay, of Pennsylvania, it would appear, in part from the supposition that he might be called on for information, in relation to proceedings in the Senate, and quite probably in the expectation that he might be a candidate for reëlection, kept a journal; but it was not kept with a view to its publication. From this journal it appears that debates in the Senate were earnest and diffuse, referring, amongst other matters, to the following subjects, viz: the communication between the two Houses; the question of titles;

the mode of voting in the Senate, whether by ballot or *viva voce*, on nominations by the President; whether the President had the sole power to remove from office; on the first bill imposing duties on the importation of foreign goods; the organization of the judiciary; the permanent seat of the General Government; the funding bill; and other questions of national interest. Observations of Mr. Maclay, and memoranda of occurrences noted by him, are interspersed throughout the journal, which may give additional interest to it.

In the third volume of the Life and Works of John Adams, pages 408–413, there is a sketch of a debate in the Senate on the power of removal from office, and of one on the bill relating to the permanent seat of the General Government; but they are brief and of a very general character; the name of Mr. Maclay being entirely omitted in the first sketch, and but a few words being devoted to him in the other. In the History of the United States, by S. C. Hamilton, in note on page 560 of the third volume, is the following note: "Are we," Adams observed in the Senate, "the two kings of Sparta, the two consuls of Rome, or the two suffetes of Carthage?' The compiler of this volume made several efforts to ascertain from what source these remarks were obtained, but without effect.

The Writer of the Journal.

Mr. Maclay is not as generally known throughout Pennsylvania as he should be. In Lauman's Biography of Members of the U. S. Senate, he is briefly noticed as follows: " He was a Senator in Congress from Pennsylvania, from 1789 to 1791. In 1797 he was a presidential elector, and was one of those who voted for locating the seat of government on the Potomac."

The following remarks, together with his journal, will give him wider celebrity: He was a native of Franklin county, in this State, was born on the 20th of July, 1737, and was of Scotch-Irish descent. He was the son of Charles Maclay, who, with his brother, John Maclay, emigrated from the north of Ireland, and settled in Franklin county, Pennsylvania. One of the family was killed in the battle of the Boyne, fighting on the side of King James. The grandfather and father of William Maclay were Protestants; and he was a Presbyterian. He was married to a daughter of John Harris, the founder of Harrisburg, and in the latter part of his life resided within the present limits of Harrisburg, where he built the stone house on Front street, on or near the lower line of his property. He died in the year 1804. He was, in early life, a member of the bar, having been admitted to the bar in York county, in April, 1860, though he probably never practiced in that county; and it appears, from a letter of John Penn, in 1763, that Mr. Maclay had practiced law, and had acted for the prothonotary, in Cumberland county. The court-house in Carlisle having been burned, information as to his admission to the bar of that county, and practice there, cannot be obtained. Mr. Maclay was also a surveyor; and in the year 1763 he visited England, and had an interview with Thomas Penn, one of the proprietaries of the Province, relative to employment in making surveys in middle and northern Pennsylvania.

The county of Northumberland, in Pennsylvania, was organized in 1772, and in March, 1772, he was appointed, with William Plunket, to whom he was related through marriage, to administer the oaths of office to the judges and other officers in that county; and in the same year he was appointed by Richard Penn, acting under a commission from Thomas and John Penn, the proprietaries, clerk of the sessions of that county, and also register for the probate of wills in that county. He also had an appointment as deputy surveyor of lands within the Indian purchase of 1754; and in 1785 he was appointed by John Lukens, Surveyor General, deputy surveyor of lands then lately purchased from the Indians, in the district extending from the upper end of the first narrows on Lycoming creek, to the northern boundary of the State of Pennsylvania. As to his character as a surveyor, Judge Huston, one of the judges of the Supreme Court of Pennsylvania, in his book on the history and nature of land titles in Pennsylvania, remarks that when he was admitted to the bar, which was in 1795, no law book of decisions of the courts in this State had been published, except the first volume of Dallas' Reports; that he became acquainted with several persons who had been deputy surveyors, both under the proprietary and State government, and he mentions, particularly, William Maclay, from whom he observes that he acquired more information in relation to land titles than from any other one, perhaps, from all others whom he had previously consulted. As to his character as a man, I have a paper signed by several aged citizens of Harrisburg, who state that they were personally acquainted with William Maclay, then of Harrisburg, who had been a member of the first Senate of the United States, and that, "from the high character for intelligence and integrity which he possessed in this community, we consider that any statement as to fact on his journal, kept whilst he was a member of the first Senate of the United States, and made on his own observation and knowledge, is entitled to credit."

Mr. Maclay was a member of the State Legislature in 1781, and in September, 1788, was elected a Senator of the United States, in conjunction with Robert Morris. After the expiration of his term in the Senate, viz: in the year 1795–6, he was member of the Pennsylvania House of Representatives, and was again elected in 1803. He was a presidential elector in 1796, and in 1801–2–3, he was an associate judge of Dauphin county.

It also appears that in the year 1758 he served as lieutenant in the company of Captain John Montgomery, in an expedition to recover Fort Duquesne, at the present site of Pittsburgh; but the enemy had left before the troops arrived there.

Mr. Maclay was a man of strict integrity, of positive opinions; having implicit confidence in his own honesty and judgment, he was inclined to be suspicious of the integrity of others, whose sentiments or action in matters of importance, differed from his own, and his journal is evidence of the strength of his intellect. Various of his opinions on public matters agitated in his day, would not be approved of now; and if he were now alive, enjoying the lights of our experience, it is probable would not be entertained by him. But it will be seen, in the course of his journal, that he had the manliness and honesty to express them, at the hazard of his influence and popularity, a virtue not possessed by all of the public men of our day.

As respects his personal appearance, Mr. Maclay is said to have been six feet three inches in height, and stout and muscular. His complexion was light, and his hair, in middle age, appears to have been brown, and was worn tied behind, or clubbed. On the first page of a book of surveys of land belonging to him, of which he had large bodies, is a statement of his marriage, and of the dates of the birth of his children, which terminates in the following beautiful expression: "As to our three dear, departed babes, Faith, Hope, and Charity, too, must conspire to place them in celestial mansions, and their names, of course, will be found in the registry of Heaven."

He was in advance of public sentiment in Pennsylvania, on the subject of imprisonment for debt, an essay, by him, in favor of its abolition, being left among his papers.

He was very decidedly opposed to bestowing on the President and Vice President, any other title than that given in the Constitution.

The matter of titles was suggested by Mr. Adams, on the second day after his installation. Mr. Maclay attacked the proposition at once, resting his objections on the Constitution. He was instrumental in defeating the measure in the House, which, after deciding against titles, addressed the President, as suggested by Mr. Maclay, by his constitutional title. Thus, in effect, settling the question between the Houses, as the Senate at length pursued the same course.

It is intimated in the life of General Peter Muhlenberg, pages 315–318, that General Washington was in favor of an additional title to be bestowed on the President, and that he was supposed to favor that of High Mightiness, a title applied to the Stadtholders of Holland. This opinion of Mr. Muhlenburg, was grounded merely on an inference on his part; for on the occasion referred to, General Washington expressed no opinion on the subject. In a letter of General Washington's, to Doctor Stuart, of Virginia, written in July, 1789, and published in the tenth volume of Sparks' publications, it is stated by him that he was opposed to an additional title; and he further stated that the truth is, the question was moved before I arrived, (at New York,) without any privity or knowledge on my part, and urged, after I was apprised of it, contrary to my opinion. (See note as to his letter.)

In the fourth volume of the life of Washington, by Washington Irving, it is stated that Washington was opposed to conferring on the President an additional title; but it is added, that the *inauguration* was delayed on account of the difficulty or contention on the subject. This is a mistake. See the subject of titles treated of in the journal.

It may be remarked that the letter of Mr. Adams, written in January, 1792, and printed in the eighth volume of his works pages 512–13, presents but a partial view of his course on the subject of titles. It does not appear that the opinion of General Washington *in opposition to titles* was generally known in the Senate whilst the matter was pending before the Senate; for after the debate in that body was concluded, Mr. Maclay made a memorandum to the effect that he had endeavored to ascertain the sentiments of the President on the subject, but had not succeeded.

Mr. Maclay felt a strong desire to have the seat of government on the Susquehanna. This measure appears to have failed in the

NOTE.—It is to be lamented that he (meaning Mr. Adams) and some others have stirred a question which has given rise to so much animadversion, and which, I confess, has given me much uneasiness, lest it should be supposed by some, unacquainted with facts, that the object they had in view was not displeasing to me. The truth is, the question was moved before I arrived, without any privity or knowledge of it on my part, and urged, after I was apprized of it, contrary to my opinion; for I foresaw and predicted the reception it has met with, and the use that would be made of it by the adversaries of the Government. Happily, this matter is now done with, I hope never to be revived.

Senate by reason of opposition by Robert Morris. He was at first desirous for its location at the Falls of the Delaware; but failing in that, he endeavored to have it established in a district around Germantown, contending that it ought to be near to a commercial place. The Susquehanna measure passed the House of Representatives and was agreed to in the Senate, but Germantown was afterwards substituted in the Senate, through the pertinaceous efforts of Mr. Morris. It was agreed to in the House, but at the instance of Mr. Madison an amendment, perhaps immaterial, was made in the House, providing for the operation of the laws of Pennsylvania in the district until supplied or altered by Congress. This amendment rendered necessary the return of the bill to the Senate, where, it would appear, there was a majority opposed to Germantown; and on the 28th of September, 1789, the bill was postponed.

In relation to this measure, Mr. Maclay raised his warning voice against yielding the Susquehanna, intimating that at the next session of Congress the seat of government would be fixed on the Potomac. His voice was prophetic; and at the next session, through an arrangement between Mr. Hamilton and certain members from Virginia and Pennsylvania, the funding bill was passed, and also the bill fixing the permanent seat of government in the District of Columbia. It does not certainly appear from the journal of Mr. Maclay that General Washington, as has been elsewhere intimated, interposed his influence in favor of the Potomac whilst the bill was pending before the first Congress; but it is not improbable that he expressed a preference for its location on the Potomac during the *second* session. Mr. Madison, however, appears to have been decided in favor of its location on the Potomac, before General Washington was inaugurated. In relation to members from Pennsylvania supporting the measure which passed for the removal from New York, it was said that certain of them supposed it probable, if the Government were settled at *Philadelphia* for the period of ten years, that Congress would be so pleased with the city as to be disinclined to remove from it. It may also be remarked that if Mr. Morris had acceded to the vote in favor of locating the seat of Government on the Susquehanna, after the designating of that position by a majority vote in both Houses, it would probably have received the official approval of the President. And if Mr. Maclay had agreed to Germantown as its seat, it might have been carried by his vote and influence after the return of the bill, with the amendment made on motion of Mr. Madison. Thus it is probable that Pennsylvania lost the permanent seat through the disagreement between her Senators. Harrisburg was not formally proposed in the Senate as the permanent seat by Mr. Maclay, but it was most probably much desired by him for its position, he having there about one hundred and eighty acres of land, on part of which the present State Capitol is now built.

The first bill passed by the Senate related to the administration of oaths.

The second bill introduced into Congress was a bill for levying imposts on imported goods. It is stated by Mr. Benton, in his abridgment of the debates of Congress, that Congress in its passage of that act had no positive reference to the encouragement of domestic manufactures; that the object of Congress was *revenue* only, and that the encouragement of manufactures was merely incidental to the revenue object. Let the matter be examined. The subject of the collection of duties on foreign importations was introduced into the House of Representatives by Mr. Madison on the 8th of April, 1789. The bill eventually agreed on was passed in the House on the 16th of May, and was received in the Senate on the 18th of that month, and was passed by that body on the 11th of June, with amendments. Under that date, after the action of the Senate on that bill, Mr. Maclay made the following memorandum : " The Senators from Jersey, Pennsylvania, Delaware, and Maryland in every act seemed desirous of making the impost productive, both as to revenue and effective *for the encouragement of manufactures;* and seemed to consider the whole of the impost (salt excepted) much too low. Articles of luxury many of them would have raised one half. But the members both from the North and—still more particularly from the South. were ever in a flame when any articles were brought forward that were in any considerable use among them."

It will also appear from the extract of debates in the *House of Representatives* that a majority of the House were favorable to the encouragement and protection of such establishments.

As to Protection.

On the 8th April, 1789, Mr. Madison introduced into the House of Representatives a proposition declaring it as the opinion of the Committee of the Whole that duties should be laid on certain importations, viz : On rum and other spirituous liquors ; on molasses; on wines, a specific duty per gallon ; on teas ; on pepper ; on sugar ; on cocoa and coffee, a specific duty per pound ; and on all other articles a per centum duty on their value at the time and place of importation.

The object of the measure was *revenue* only, and it was to be of a merely temporary character, and was intended to affect the spring importations.

After he and others had addressed the House, Mr. Fitzsimmons, of Pennsylvania, remarked that he observed from what had been said that the proposed plan of revenue is viewed by them as a temporary system, to be continued only until proper materials are brought forward, and arranged in more perfect form. But that he carried his views on the subject much further, and earnestly wished such a one as, in its operation, would be in some way adequate to the present situation as respects *our agriculture, our manufactures,* and *our commerce.* He offered an amendment that duties ought to be imposed on certain enumerated articles, including beer, ale, porter, steel, writing and wrapping paper, castings of iron, and on slit or rolled iron.

After others had spoken, *Mr. Madison* remarked that from what had been suggested he was led to apprehend that they should be under the necessity of traveling further into the investigation of principles than he had supposed to be necessary, and had in contemplation, when he offered the propositions to the House. . . . . He perceived that however much we may be disposed to promote domestic manufactures, we ought to pay some regard to the present policy of obtaining revenue. It may be remarked, also, that by fixing on a temporary expedient for this purpose, we may gain more than we shall lose by suspending the consideration of the other subjects until we obtain fuller information of the state of our manufactures. He further remarked that notwithstanding the deference and respect paid to the interests of different sections of the United States, we must limit our consideration on this head, and consider the general interest of the Union, for this is as much every gentleman's interest to consider as is the local or State interest; and any system of impost that this committee may adopt must be founded on the principles of mutual concession. Gentlemen will be pleased to recollect that those parts of the Union which contribute more under one system than the others, are also those parts more thinly planted, and consequently stand more in need of national protection. He further observed that there is another consideration. The States that are most advanced in population, and ripe for manufactures, ought to have their particular interests attended to, in some degree. While these States retained the power of making regulations of trade, they had the power to protect and cherish such institutions. By adopting the present constitution, they have thrown the exercise of this power into other hands. They must have done this with an expectation that those interests would not be neglected here.

In the course of the proceeding on the bill, Mr. Lee, of Virginia, moved to strike out the proposed duty on *steel;* observing that the consumption was very great, and essentially necessary to agricultural improvements.

Mr. Tucker, of South Carolina, joined in this.

Mr. Clymer, of Pennsylvania, replied that the manufacture of steel in America was rather in its infancy; but as all the materials necessary to make it were the produce of almost every State in the Union, and as the manufacture was already established and attended with considerable success, he deemed it prudent to emancipate our country from the manacles in which she was held by foreign manufacturers.

Mr. Madison thought the object of selecting this article to be solely the encouragement of manufacture, and not revenue; for on any other consideration it would be more proper, as observed by the gentleman from Carolina, Mr. Tucker, to give *a bounty* on the importation. He thought it best to reserve this article to the non-enumerated ones, where it would be subject to a five per cent. *ad valorem.*

Mr. Fitzsimmons thought if gentlemen would not get rid of local considerations, the committee would make little progress, &c. The matter was further debated.

Mr. Moore, from Virginia, declared the southern States well calculated for the cultivation of hemp, and from certain circumstances well inclined thereto. He conceived it the duty of the committee to pay as much respect to the encouragement and protection of *husbandry,* (the most important of all the interests of the United States,) as they did to *manufactures.*

Next, Mr. Burke, of South Carolina, thought it proper to suggest to the committee what might be the probable effect of the proposed measure in the State he represented, and the adjoining one—Georgia. The staple products of that part of the Union were hardly worth cultivating, on account of their fall in price. The planters were, therefore, disposed to pursue some other. The lands are certainly well adapted to the growth of hemp, and he had no doubt but its culture would be practiced with attention. *Cotton is likewise in contemplation* among them; and if good seed could be procured, he hoped it might succeed. But the low, strong, rich lands would produce hemp in abundance—many thousand tons even this year, if it was not so late in the season. He liked the idea of laying a low duty *now,* and *encouraged* against the time when a supply might be had from our own cultivation.

A duty of six cents was imposed on *manufactured tobacco.* This was on motion of Mr. Sherman, who said he thought the duty ought to amount to a *prohibition.* On *cotton* a duty of three cents a pound was laid, and on coal a duty of two cents a bushel was imposed. Mr. Bland, of Virginia, had moved *three* cents, observing that the mines open in Virginia were capable of supplying the whole United States, and if some restraint were laid upon the importation of *foreign coal* these mines might be worked to advantage. He thought it needless to insist upon the advantages resulting from a colliery as a supply for culinary and mechanical purposes, and as a nursery to train up seamen for a navy.

In debate on May 12, 1789, (See Annals of Congress, vol. I, p. 345,) in the discussion relative to the duty on molasses, Mr. *Madison* remarked that the long list of enumerated articles subject to a high duty were pretty generally for the benefit of the manufacturing part of the northern community. See loaf sugar, candles, cheese, &c. He hoped gentlemen would not infer from this observation that he thought the encouragement held out by the bill to the *manufacturers* improper. Far from it; he was glad to see their growing consequence, and was disposed to give them every aid in his power. From this view of the subject, he was inclined to adhere to the bill, and not make any reduction.

It thus appears that duties were laid on importations of steel, hemp, tobacco, and coal, for the purpose of encouraging their manufacture and production in this country ; and as to the action or opinion of Senators, reference is made to the remarks of Mr. Maclay, before quoted. And it may be remarked that it is declared *in the preamble to the act,* that " it is necessary for the support of Government, for the discharge of the debts of the United States, and the encouragement and protection of *manufactures,* that duties be laid on goods, wares, and merchandise imported."—*See second vol. Annals of Congress, p. 2183.*

It may be further remarked that certain usages practiced in the early life of the Government, have been changed. During the administration of Washington and of Mr. Adams, the President delivered his message in person, in the presence of Congress, and members of each of the Houses returned its address by waiting on the President in carriages. This practice was spoken against by Mr. Maclay, and it is now discontinued. The message of the President is sent to Congress, and referred to committees.

The constitution providing that Congress shall have power " to lay and collect taxes, duties, imposts, and excises to pay the debts and provide for the common defense and *general welfare* of the

United States," a question has arisen whether Congress had the power to appropriate portions of the money thus collected to promote what, in the discretion of Congress, was considered the promotion of the *general welfare.*

Mr. Hamilton supported the affirmative of the proposition in his celebrated report on manufactures, submitted to the House of Representatives, in December, 1791. See Annals of Congress. This view was earnestly combatted by Mr. Jefferson.

Mr. Bayard, of Delaware, in April, 1874, called the same clause into requisition in support of an appropriation by Congress for the Centennial Exhibition, in which he declared that the preamble to the Constitution declares that "to provide for the common defense and general welfare," was one of the objects of creating the Government; that he considered that the plain words of the clause should not be stripped of all natural meaning, and denied all effect; but that they do contain a grant of power, and impose the duty of its execution—not an unlimited, distinct, independent power, but like all other grants in the Constitution—a qualified power, checked and balanced by other provisions, together with which it is to be construed.

Mr. Thurman combatted this construction of the constitution, but the Senate passed a bill for an advance of money in support of the exhibition, with a provision that the amount of the appropriation or a portion of it, be returned to the national treasury.

In the preamble to the constitution it is declared that " We, the people of the United States, in order to form a more perfect union, establish justice, insure domestic tranquillity, provide for the common defense, promote the general welfare, and secure the blessings of liberty to ourselves and our posterity, do ordain and establish this constitution for the United States of America."

Whilst politicians have been contending as to whether the Constitution authorized the Government to sustain and protect domestic manufactures, the people of the north and western part of the Union have, under the influence of their good sense and energies, and the protection actually afforded to them, made our country distinguished amongst the nations of the earth for its manufacturing operations, and made it ready to contend with other nations in that great and diversified department; whilst the southern section of the country, confining itself to one branch of industry, has fallen to the rear in point of prosperity and material advancement.

But a little over a century of time has elapsed since our nation, as such, began its existence. After the revolutionary war, when its national existence was acknowledged, it started with a population of about three millions, and a debt about eighty. The amount of this debt excited the fears of many; but the nation has since mastered a debt of over three thousand millions of dollars, and its population has increased to over forty millions. Our national boundaries, in revolutionary times, did not reach westward to the Father of Waters. Now they have ascended that stream above two thousand miles—have crossed the great mountain barrier, and been stopped only by the ocean in their march towards the setting sun, and our people are there, in position to enter into communication with the immense population of the eastern part of the world. " Our country—a Hercules in its infancy!"—who could have foretold so speedy a manhood. Our national progress, moreover, is not marked, as has been the course of other nations, by ravage or desolation; but has been attended with the olive branch of peace and kindness, with the offer to share with ourselves in all the privileges afforded by our Government, which we ourselves enjoy, and with the right essential to their comfort, to regulate their local interests in their own way. Let England and other nations take heed of our example, and treat their subordinate or dependent dominions in the same way.

As to Cotton.

In 1784 an American ship landed eight bags of cotton at Liverpool, and the custom-house officers seized them on the ground that cotton was not a product of the United States. Fifty years later (in 1832) England received two hundred and twenty million pounds of cotton from America.

In Relation to the Matter of Titles.

Mr. Maclay has elsewhere remarked : I, however, will endeavor (as I have hitherto done) to use the resentment of the Representatives to defeat Mr. Adams, &c., on the subject of titles. The pompous and lordly distinctions which the Senate have manifested a disposition to establish between the two Houses has nettled the Repre sentatives ; and this business of titles may be considered as part of the same tune. While we are debating on titles, I will, through the Speaker, Muhlenberg, and other friends, get the idea suggested of answering the President's address without any title, in contempt of our deliberations which still continue on that subject. This once effected, will confound them completely, and establish a precedent they will not dare to violate. (See postea, p. 46.)

A Brief Report made by the Librarian of Congress upon Maclay's Journal, 3 vols.

THE Journal of WILLIAM MACLAY, a Senator in Congress from the State of Pennsylvania, covers a period of about two years, viz: From April 24, 1789, to March 3, 1791. Its chief value consists in the fact that it records with some fullness, the proceedings of the first Senate organized under the Constitution, and at a period when the sessions were held with closed doors. It is well known that no report of the debates in the Senate exists for the period embraced by the 1st to the 5th Congress inclusive. During the ten years from 1789 to 1799, only a bare outline of the business transacted is found in the Annals of Congress, or elsewhere, altho' the debates in the House of Representatives were reported with considerable fullness. The few notices of the business and debates in the Senate during this period, preserved in the published writings of JOHN ADAMS, JEFFERSON, MADISON, WALCOTT, and others, are of high interest and value. Yet in none of them is there any continuous journal purporting to give a record of the debates in the Senate. This vacuum is to a certain extent supplied by this *MS.* Journal of Senator MACLAY. Although not a formal report of debates, as to the language used, it gives the sentiments expressed by the leading speakers on both sides, on most of the important questions discussed at length. Among these were the questions of the official title for the President of the U. S., the power of removal from office, the doctrine of a protective tariff, the location of the permanent seat of Government, the jurisdiction of the Federal Courts, etc.

Besides these, the Journal contains Mr. MACLAY's account of the inauguration of President WASHINGTON at N. Y. in 1789, of various Presidential dinners and state ceremonies in the early days of the Government, and some criticisms of the President, Vice President ADAMS, and other public men of the time. As a whole, this MS. record, which has never been published, would add a contribution of considerable interest and value to the stores of information we possess regarding the early politics of the country. The period it embraces, covering as it does the very origin of the Government under the Constitution, is continually enhanced in interest with the growth of the historical spirit in the country.

A. R. SPOFFORD.

Presented to Committee on the Library, Washington, March, 1869.

MEMORANDA.

In December, 1858, or in the early part of January, 1859, Mr. Breckenridge, Vice President, delivered an address to the Senate when it was about taking possession, or had taken possession, of its new hall.

In the course of this he observed: "At the origin of the Government, the Senate seemed to be regarded chiefly as an executive council. The President often visited the Chamber and conferred personally with this body. Most of its business was transacted with closed doors, and it took comparatively little part in the legislative debates. The rising and vigorous intellects of the country sought the arena of the House of Representatives as the appropriate theater for the display of their powers," &c.

Now, it appears from the journal of Mr. Maclay, that there was debated in the Senate the question of titles to the President and Vice President; the question whether nominations by the President were to be acted on by ballot or *viva voce;* the question whether the President had the sole power to remove from office; the tariff bill; debate as to the seat of government; the judiciary bill, and other matters.

The members of the first Senate were not men of inferior minds, and a number of them were of distinguished ability. Was it a reasonable supposition that they would pass upon the important subjects submitted to their consideration without discussion; and is it not reasonable now to entertain a desire to know something of their action within the Chamber of the Senate, at the organization of the Government, when the constitution was being put into action?

The members of the Senate were as follows:

From New Hampshire—John Langdon*, Paine Wingate; Massachusetts—Caleb Strong*, Tristram Dalton; Connecticut—Oliver Ellsworth*, William S. Johnson*; New York—Rufus King*, Philip Schuyler; New Jersey—William Paterson*, Jonathan Elmer; Pennsylvania—William Maclay, Robert Morris*; Delaware—Richard Bassett*, George Read*; Maryland—Charles Carroll, John Henry; Virginia—Richard Henry Lee, William Grayson; South Carolina—Ralph Izard, Pierce Butler*; Georgia—William Few*, James Gunn.

North Carolina and Rhode Island not having adopted the Constitution, had no members in the Senate during the first session, but subsequently, from North Carolina appeared Samuel Johnston and Benjamin Hawkins; from Rhode Island appeared Theodore Foster and Joseph Stanton; from New Jersey, Philemon Dickinson appeared in place of Mr. Paterson; and from Virginia, James Monroe, in place of William Grayson, deceased.

Those above named marked * were members of the convention which framed the constitution of the United States.

Further, it was not customary or usual in the President to visit the Senate Chamber to confer with Senators relative to legislation. He visited the Chamber in August, 1789, in relation to arrangements with northern Indians; but as to no other deliberative business before the Senate. As to the occasion of his being there in August, 1789, and for further particulars on that occasion, see the statement of Mr. Maclay.

SKETCHES OF DEBATES.

By an act of Congress of 13th September, 1788, electors of President and Vice President were to be selected on the first Wednesday of January, 1789, and to give their votes on the first Wednesday of February. The first Wednesday of March, 1789, being the 4th day of March, was fixed upon as the time, and the city of New York as the place, for commencing proceedings under the Constitution. The ratification of the Constitution by New Hampshire was the ninth in order, and a committee of arrangements was appointed for carrying the new system into operation.

A quorum of the House of Representatives was not formed till the 1st of April, 1789, and of the Senate not until the 6th.

The members of the Senate were as follows:
New Hampshire—John Langdon*, Paine Wingate.
Massachusetts—Caleb Strong*, Tristram Dalton.
Connecticut—Oliver Ellsworth*, William S. Johnson*.
New York—Rufus King*, Philip Schuyler.
New Jersey—William Paterson*, Jonathan Elmer.
Pennsylvania—William Maclay, Robert Morris.*
Delaware—Richard Bassett*, George Read.*
Maryland—Charles Carroll, John Henry.
Virginia—Richard Henry Lee, William Grayson.
South Carolina—Ralph Izard, Pierce Butler.*
Georgia—William Few*, James Gunn.

North Carolina and Rhode Island not having adopted the Constitution, had no members in the Senate during its first session.

On the day on which the Senate was organized by the members from eleven States, the election of General Washington as President, and of John Adams as Vice President, was announced, the former by an unanimous vote, sixty-nine being the whole number; Mr. Adams by a plurality vote, he receiving thirty-four votes, the residue of the votes being distributed between ten other persons; and messengers

---

* Those whose names are marked * were members of the convention which framed the Constitution of the United States.

were appointed to notify them of their election, Charles Thompson being sent to inform General Washington, and Sylvanus Bourn to notify Mr. Adams.

On the 8th of April, Samuel Alyne Otis was elected Secretary of the Senate.

It was subsequently determined that the terms for which the President, Vice President, and Senators were respectively chosen, did, according to the Constitution, commence on the 4th of March, 1789.

The Senators were classified into three classes—one class to hold for two years, one for four years, and the other for six years; and on the 15th of May the classes were determined by lot. In the first class, fell William Maclay, the compiler of the subsequent journal, and his term expired on the 4th of March, 1791.

It was also determined that whenever a vacancy shall happen in the Senate or House of Representatives, and an election be held to fill the vacancy, the person elected shall not be entitled to hold his seat beyond the term for which the Senator or Representative, in whose stead he was elected, would, if the vacancy had not happened, have been entitled to hold a seat.

The Mayor of the city of New York offered the City Hall as the place of meeting of the Senate, and it was accepted. On the 16th of April, on the part of the Senate, Mr. Langdon, Mr. Carroll, and Mr. Johnson were appointed to wait on the President, and Mr. Ellsworth and Mr. Dalton to wait on the Vice President. A committee was appointed to report on the mode of communication between the two Houses, and to confer with such committee as may be appointed by the House for the purpose.

In relation to the installation of the *Vice President*, the Senate Journal of April 21, is as follows:

The committee appointed to conduct the Vice President to the Senate Chamber, executed their commission, and Mr. Langdon, *the Vice President pro tempore*, meeting the Vice President on the floor of the Senate Chamber, addressed him as follows:

Sir: I have it in charge from the Senate, to introduce you to the chair of this House; and also to congratulate you on your appointment to the office of Vice President of the United States of America.

After which Mr. Langdon conducted the Vice President to the chair, when the Vice President addressed the Senate as follows:

Gentlemen of the Senate: Invited to this respectable situation by the suffrages of our fellow-citizens, according to the Constitution, I have thought it my duty, cheerfully and readily, to accept it. Unaccustomed to refuse any public service, however dangerous to my reputation, or disproportioned to my talents, it would have been inconsistent to have adopted another maxim of conduct at this time, when the prosperity of the country and the liberties of the people require, perhaps, as much as ever, the attention of those who possess any share of the public confidence.

I should be destitute of sensibility, if, upon my arrival in this city, and presentation to this Legislature, and especially to this Senate, I could see, without emotion, so many of those characters of whose virtuous exertions I have so often been a witness; from whose countenances and examples I have ever derived encouragement and animation; whose disinterested friendship has supported me in many interesting conjunctures of public affairs, at home and abroad; those celebrated defenders of the liberties of this country, whom menaces could not intimidate, corruption seduce, or flattery allure; those intrepid assertors of the rights of mankind, whose philosophy and policy have enlightened the world in twenty years more than it was ever before enlightened in many centuries by ancient schools or modern universities.

I must have been inattentive to the course of events, if I were ignorant of the fame, or insensible to the merit of those other characters in the Senate to whom it has been my misfortune to have been hitherto personally unknown.

It is with satisfaction that I congratulate the people of America on the formation of a National Constitution, and the fair prospect of a consistent administration of a government of laws; on the acquisition of a House of Representatives chosen by themselves, of a Senate thus composed by their own State Legislatures, and on the prospect of an executive authority in the hands of one whose portrait I shall not presume to draw. Were I blessed with powers to do justice to his character, it would be impossible to increase the confidence or affection of his country, or make the smallest addition to his glory. This can only be effected by a discharge of the present exalted trust on the same principles, with the same abilities and virtues, which have uniformly appeared in all his former conduct, public or private.

May I, nevertheless, be indulged to inquire, if we look over the catalogue of the first magistrates of nations, whether they have been denominated presidents or consuls, kings or princes, where shall we find one whose commanding talents and virtues, whose overruling good fortune, have so completely united all hearts and voices in his favor, who enjoyed the esteem and admiration of foreign nations and fellow-citizens with equal unanimity? Qualities so uncommon are no common blessings to the country that possesses them. By those great qualities and their benign effects, has Providence marked

out the head of the nation, with a hand so distinctly visible as to
have been seen by all men, and mistaken by none.

It is not for me to interrupt your deliberations by any general
observations on the state of the nation, or by recommending or proposing any particular measure. It would be superfluous to gentlemen of your great experience, to urge the necessity of order. It is
only necessary to make an apology for myself. Not wholly without
experience in public assemblies, I have been more accustomed to
take a share in their debates, than to preside in their deliberations.
It shall be my constant endeavor to behave toward every member
of this most honorable body with all that consideration, delicacy,
and decorum, which becomes the dignity of his station and character ; but if, from inexperience or inadvertency, anything should ever
escape me inconsistent with propriety, I must entreat you, by im-
puting it to its true cause, and not to any want of respect, to pardon
and excuse it.

A trust of the greatest magnitude is committed to this Legislature ; and the eyes of the world are upon you. Your country
expects from the results of your deliberations, in concurrence with
the other branches of Government, consideration abroad, and con-
tentment at home—prosperity, order, justice, peace, and liberty.
And may God Almighty's providence assist you to answer their
just expectations.

On the 23d of April the committee. who consisted of Mr. Strong,
Mr. Izard, and Mr. Lee, appointed on the 16th to report a mode of
communication between the two Houses with respect to papers, bills,
and messages, reported that they had conferred with a committee
of the House, and had agreed to the following report :

When a bill or other message shall be sent from the Senate to the
House of Representatives, it shall be carried by the Secretary, who
shall make one obeisance to the Chair on entering the door of the
House of Representatives, and another on delivering it at the table
into the hands of the Speaker. After he shall have delivered it, he
shall make an obeisance to the Speaker, and repeat it as he retires
from the House.

When a bill shall be sent up by the House of Representatives to
the Senate, it shall be carried by two members, who, at the bar of
the Senate, shall make their obeisance to the President, and thence,
advancing to the Chair, make a second obeisance, and deliver it into
the hands of the President. After having delivered the bill they
shall make their obeisance to the President, and repeat it as they
retire from the bar. The Senate shall rise on the entrance of the
members within the bar, and continue standing until they retire.

All other messages from the House of Representatives shall be carried by one member, who shall make his obeisance, as above mentioned; but the President of the Senate alone shall rise.

Read and accepted.

The report of the joint committee was not adopted *in the House of Representatives.* It appears from the Journal of the House of the 23d of April, that the report of the committee was ordered to lie on the table, and on the 24th was recommitted to the same committee; and that on the 28th of April Mr. Richard Bland Lee, from that committee, reported as follows:

When a message shall be sent from the Senate to the House of Representatives, it shall be announced at the door of theHouse by the Doorkeeper, and shall be respectfully communicated to the Chair by the person by whom it may be sent.

The same ceremony shall be observed when a message shall be sent from the House of Representatives to the Senate.

Messages shall be sent by such persons as a sense of propriety in each House may determine to be proper.

The said report was twice read; and on the question put thereupon, agreed to by the House.

On the 23d of April, on motion in the Senate, it was

"*Resolved,* That a committee, consisting of three members, be appointed to consider and report what *style or titles* it will be proper to annex to the office of President and Vice President of the United States, if any other than those given in the Constitution. Also to consider of the time, place, and manner in which, and the person by whom the oath prescribed by the Constitution shall be administered to the President, and to confer thereon with such committee as the House of Representatives shall appoint for that purpose."

Mr. Lee, Mr. Izard, and Mr. Dalton were chosen.

It would appear from the memorandum of Mr. Maclay, under date of the 8th May, that on the 23d of April, the day on which the resolution on the subject of *titles* was proposed, Mr. Adams, the Vice President, (this being the second day after his installation as President of the Senate,) addressed the Senate in favor of titles, and that Mr. Maclay replied, resting his objections on the Constitution.

General Washington was met at Elizabethtown, in New Jersey, on the 23d day of April, by the committees of the Senate and House, and was escorted to the city of New York, where he arrived about three o'clock in the afternoon of that day, and was conducted to the house appointed for his residence.

On the 24th of April, the commission of the committee with regard to titles was *re-considered* in the Senate; and a motion was made that the words "what titles it will be proper to annex to the offices of President and Vice President of the United States, if any, other than those given in the Constitution," be struck out; but it was *negatived.* On motion, the words "style or," before title, were added.

On the Journal of the *House of Representatives*, under date of April 24, it is stated, that "the Speaker laid before House a letter from the Vice President of the United States, enclosing a resolution of the Senate, appointing a committee to consider and report what style or titles it will be proper to annex to the office of President and Vice President of the United States, if any other than those given in the Constitution; also to consider of the time, place and manner in which, and the person by whom the oath prescribed by the Constitution shall be administered to the President; and to confer thereon with such committee as this House should appoint for 'hat purpose. Whereupon, ordered that a committee, to consist of five members, be appointed for the purpose expressed in the resolution of the Senate. The members elected were Messrs. Benson, Ames, Madison, Carroll, and Sherman.

On the 25th the Right Reverend Samuel Provost was elected Chaplain of the Senate.

A letter from Charles Thomson, Esq., dated the 24th of April, 1789, directed to the President of the Senate, purporting his having delivered to Gen. Washington the certificate of his being elected President of the United States, was read, and ordered to be filed.

On the same day the committee appointed to consider of the time, and place, and manner in which, and of the person by whom the oath prescribed by the Constitution shall be administered to the President of the United States, and to confer with a committee of the House appointed for that purpose, report:

That the President has been pleased to signify to them, that any time or place which both Houses may think proper to appoint, and any manner which shall appear most eligible to them, will be convenient and acceptable to him. They further reported that requisite preparation cannot probably be made before Thursday next; that the President be, on that day, formally received by both Houses in the Senate chamber; that the Representatives' chamber being capable of receiving the greater number of persons, that, therefore, the President do take the oath in that place, and in the presence of both Houses. That after the formal reeception of the President in the Senate chamber, he be attended by both Houses to the Representatives' chamber, and that the oath be administered by the chancellor of the State of New York.

The committee further report it, as their opinion, that it will be proper that a committee of both Houses be appointed to take order for conducting the business. This was read and accepted. Whereupon Mr. Lee, Mr. Izard, and Mr. Dalton, on the part of the Senate, together with a committee that may be appointed on the part of the House of Representatives, were empowered to take order for conducting the business.

On the same day was read an order of the House of Representatives, concurring in the appointment of a committee on their part, to confer with a committee appointed on the 24th instant, on the part of the Senate, to consider and report "what style, &c., it will be proper to annex to the offices of President and Vice President." From it it appeared, as before stated, that Mr. Benson, Mr. Ames, Mr. Madison, Mr. Carroll, and Mr. Sherman were appointed on the part of the House.

On the Senate Journal, under date of Monday, April 27, it is stated that "the committee appointed to take order for conducting the ceremonial of the formal reception, &c., of the President, reported :

" That it appears to them more eligible that the oath should be administered to the President in the outer gallery, adjoining the Senate chamber, than in the Representatives' chamber ; and, therefore, submit to the respective houses the propriety of authorizing their committee to take order as to the place where the oath shall be administered to the President, the resolution of Saturday, assigning the Representatives' chamber as the place, notwithstanding. Read and accepted.

"*Resolved,* That after the oath shall have been administered to the President, he, attended by the Vice President and members of the Senate and House of Representatives, proceed to St. Paul's Chapel, to hear divine service, to be performed by the Chaplain of Congress, already appointed. Sent to the House of Representatives for concurrence."

Before proceeding further, we remark that on the 5th of March, 1789, the General Assembly of Pennsylvania passed resolutions offering the use of the public buildings *in the city of Philadelphia*, for the temporary use of Congress ; and that a design existed with some members of Congress to make an early effort to remove the Congress from New York to Philadelphia, which effort, however, failed, as stated in the following extract of a letter dated New York, 16th April, 1789, addressed by William Maclay to Judge Peters, of Philadelphia, viz :

" Dear Sir : I have received yours of the 12th, and will, with my own hand, deliver Mr. Adams' letter, as he is now expected daily. The messenger that went for him took a passage by water, and was at Rhode Island in nineteen hours; so that in all probability Mr. Adams received official information of his election in two days after the ballots were opened. *Fortune* has now fixed us here for the present session. The Romans, you know, made a goddess of her; and although she is not now worshiped, yet her power seems not to be diminished. The critical moment to have been embraced, was just after the ballots were opened, and before the messengers were sent off for the President and Vice President. An adjournment to Philadelphia was the point to be carried. What we most wanted was a bold, determined leader in the lower House, of a different State from our own. We wanted to make Madison the man, but his darling Potomac kept uppermost with him, in spite of all our efforts. We greatly regretted the absence of Fitzsimmons.

On the other hand, not greater consternation seized the city when the British left them. Beaux, belles, macaronis, clergy, and all, went to work, and such a running from house to house was hardly ever heard of. Our friends of New England gave way, and declared for removal to the *permanent* residence only. In the meanwhile the irrevocable hour was passed, the messengers were sent off, and our scheme sunk in abortion. It now remains that we lay in a sufficient stock of materials for the end of the session, and that proper attention be paid to the word *adjournment*, when, I hope, madam, the Roman Goddess, will be more propitious to our wishes.

Thank you for the mention of your *plough*. Never word brought a more endearing assemblage of ideas in its train. All the joys and blessings of domestic life seemed to start into existence at the very mention of this first of human inventions. There is not even the *sign* of such an implement in this vile place, keen and attentive as they are to their interests. I wonder none of them have thought of such a thing, for even an ale-house with such a symbol at the door would command custom. Our Pennsylvanians, at least, would venerate the plough. Somebody brought a report into town that there was a green field two or three miles off. Mr. Clymer and a party immediately set off in quest of it. I could not be of their company, as I have been confined, for some days, by a violent rheumatism in my right knee—a complaint for which, I am told, this place is remarkable. I am, however, much better, and hope for health in a few days—a blessing which I have, in a great degree, been a stranger to since I came to this place.

Am, with much respect, your obedient, humble servant,

WILLIAM MACLAY.

Honorable RICHARD PETERS.

It has been before stated that General Washington arrived at New York on the 23d of April. The Journal of Mr. Maclay commences on the next day, the 24th of April, and he, *inter alia*, remarks :

I understood that it was agreed among the Senators yesterday, that they would meet at the hall this morning, and go in a body to pay their respects to General Washington. I went, about ten o'clock, to the hall, accordingly. There was, however, no person there. After staying some time, Ellsworth came in. I repeated the conversation of last night, and asked him whether he had been to wait on the General. Yes, he had been, and a number more with him. Some went last night, and some this morning. * * * *
I whipped down stairs, and joined the Speaker and a number more of the Pennsylvanians, who were collecting for that purpose; went and paid my respects, &c.

Mr. Izard had yesterday been very anxious to get a report adopted, respecting the communications between the Houses. It was so. But now we hear the House below laugh at it. Mr. Izard moved to have the adoption taken from the minutes. This could not be done. But now a curious scene opened. Mr. Lee, being of the *Title* Committee of yesterday, produced a copy of the resolution for appointing that committee, and moved that the House should pass a vote for the transmitting it down to the other House. This was truly ridiculous; but mind, this business had been (gone) into yesterday solely on the motion of our President, (Mr. Adams); but, now, (he continues,) Lee wanted to bring it on again, when the President would not appear in it." " I showed the absurdity of his motion plainly enough ; but it seemed to me, that by getting a division of the resolution, I could, perhaps, throw out the part about *titles* altogether. Mr. Carroll, of Maryland, showed he was against titles. I wrought so far, that I got a question, whether we should throw out the part about titles altogether. We lost the question." However, I could plainly see that we gained ground in the House.

Now, a most curious question arose. The President (Mr. Adams) knew not how to direct the letter to the Speaker. He called on the House to know how it should be directed. The House showed a manifest disinclination to interfere. The President urged, and ceased not until a question was pointedly put, whether the Speaker should be styled *honorable.* It passed in the *negative ;* and from this omen, I think our President may go and dream about titles for none will he get.

25th April, Saturday. Attended the House. Ceremonies, endless ceremonies, the whole business of the day. I did not embark warmly this day. " Otis, our Secretary, makes the grossest mistakes in our minutes, and it cost us an hour or two to rectify them. I was up as often, I believe, as was necessary, and certainly threw so much light on two subjects, that the debate ended on each."

The President, as usual, made us two or three speeches from the chair. I will endeavor to recollect one of them. It was on the reading of a report, which mentioned that the President should be received in the Senate chamber, and proceed thence to the House of Representatives, to be sworn.

" GENTLEMEN : I do not know whether the framers of the Constitution had in view the two Kings of Sparta, or the two consuls of Rome, when they formed it—one to have *all* the power while he held it ; and the other to be nothing. Nor do I know whether the architect that formed our room, and the wide chair in it, (to hold two, I suppose,) had the Constitution before him. Gentlemen, I feel great difficulty, how to act. I am possessed of two separate powers—the one in *esse*, the other in *passe*. I am *Vice President*. In this, I am nothing ; but I may be everything. But I am President, also, of the Senate. When the President comes into the Senate, what shall I be ? I wish, gentlemen, to think what I shall be."

A solemn silence ensued. God forgive me, for it was involuntary, but the profane muscles of my face were in tune for laughter, in spite of my indisposition.

Ellsworth thumbed over the sheet Constitution, and turned it for some time. At length he rose, and addressed the Chair, with the most profound gravity :

" Mr. PRESIDENT : I have looked over the Constitution, (paused,) and I find, sir—it is evident and clear, sir—that wherever the Senate is to be, there, sir, you must be at the head of them ; but, further, sir, (there he looked aghast, as if some tremendous gulf had yawned before him,) I shall not pretend to say."

" Thursday next is appointed for swearing in the President. I am worse of my rheumatism, and perhaps it is owing to the change of weather, for the wind is at northwest, and cold.

" Sunday, 26th April. Went out half after nine o'clock ; visited Governor St. Clair, General Butler, Delany, McPherson. At Ellsworth's called on Mr. Clymer and Mr. Fitzsimmons. The very end of this visit was to concert some measures with them for the re-

NOTE.—The following is a note to third volume of J. C. Hamilton's history. I have endeavored to ascertain where it was obtained by him, but I have not succeeded :

"Are we," Adams observed in the Senate, "the two Kings of Sparta, the two Consuls of Rome, or the two Suffetes of Carthage."—*See 3d vol., p. 560, of His. U. S., by John C. Hamilton.*

moval of Congress, but they kept me off. I mentioned a favorable disposition in some of the Maryland gentlemen to be in unison with the Pennsylvania delegation. They seem not to credit me.

"Monday, 27th April, 1789. Attended the hall. We had prayers this day by the Chaplain, Doctor Provost. A new arrangment was reported from the joint committee of ceremonies. This is an endless business. Lee offered a motion to the Chair that after the President was sworn, (which now is to be in the gallery opposite the Senate Chamber,) the Congress should accompany him to Saint Paul's church and attend divine service. This had been agitated in the joint committee; but Lee said expressly *that they would not agree to it.* I opposed it as an improper business, after it had been in the hands of the joint committee and rejected, as I thought this certain method of creating a dissension between the Houses."

As to Duties on Importations.

th of April, the House of Representatives being in Committee of the Whole, Mr. Madison addressed it on the subject of duties on imports, and having in view to embrace the spring importations, introduced a resolution as follows:

Resolved, in opinion of this committee, that the following duties ought to be laid on goods, wares, and merchandise imported into the United States, viz: On rum, per gallon, —— of a dollar; on all other spirituous liquors, ——; on molasses, ——; on Madeira wine, ——; on all other wines, ——; on common Bohea teas, per lb., —— on all other teas, ——; on paper, ——; on brown sugars, —— on loaf sugars, ——; on all other sugars, ——; on cocoa and coffee, ——; on all other articles, —— per cent. on the value, at the time and place of importation.

That there ought, moreover, to be a duty on all vessels in which goods, wares, or merchandise shall be imported, the duties following, viz: On all vessels built within the United States and belonging wholly to citizens thereof, at the rate of ——. On all vessels belonging wholly to the subjects of Powers with whom the United States have formed treaties, &c., &c.; and on all others belonging wholly or in part to the subjects of other Powers, the rate of ——.

Some debate ensued, and the committee rose, and the subject was subsequently before the House and was debated, as stated in part, in the preface to this book.

It is now four o'clock, and I will take a walk. In my walk I fell in with Mr. Sturgis, Mr. Wyngate, Mr. Goodhue. We took a circuit on the island and came into town. On the way we talked of the permanent residence. They all allowed that New York was not the place. One of them said it ought to be in Pennsylvania. I said little, but remarked that although we would be better accommodated in Philadelphia, I thought we should think of the *permanent* residence. New houses should be built for the members from each State, when they should not be degraded to the humiliating necessity of begging for lodgings from house to house. I, however, remarked coolly that Virginia affected acquiescence in this place, expecting the Pennsylvanians would be fretted into an acceptance of their measures for the *Potomac;* that the Potomac was convenient for a great part of Pennsylvania; that by our joining our votes to those of Virginia and Maryland and the more southerly States, we could go to the Potomac any time. One of them remarked, the numerous votes of Virginia would not avail. I did not get time to answer, for another replied that we had members on our side in the Senate also.

The Vice President's speech is now in the hands of every one, and is received with merited applause. A thought as to the composition of it. But first I will lay down my own rule for judging in cases of this kind. When every word conveys an idea, and sentiment follows expression, the composition is good. But where the words and expressions are so happily arranged that every corresponding idea and sentiment brings a kindred group in its train, the composition rises to excellent, grand, sublime.

Now for the sinking scale. When ideas follow slowly, with difficulty, or not at all, the composition may be termed heavy, dull, stupid. I will read it again, but I am inclined to place it under the *heavy* head.

Visit by Washington.

Next Thursday, I ought to note with some extraordinary mark. I had dressed, and was about to set out, when General Washington, the greatest man in the world, paid me a visit. I met him at the foot of the stairs. Mr. Wynkoop just came in. We asked him to take a seat. He excused himself, on account of the number of his visits. We accompanied him to the door. He made us complacent bows—one, before he mounted, and the other, as he went away, on horseback. I attended at the Hall; just nothing at all done. I, however, paid very formal visit to the Vice President. It began to rain, and I came home. I may as well minute a remark here as any where else; and, indeed, I wish it were otherwise—not for what we have, but for what others want. But we have really more republican plainness and sincere openness of behavior in Pennsylvania than in any other place I have ever been in. I was impressed with a different opinion, until I have had full opportunity of observing the gentlemen of New England; and sorry am I to say it, but no people in the Union dwell more on trivial distinctions and matters of mere form. They really seem to show a readiness to stand on punctilio and ceremony. A little learning is a dangerous thing, ('tis said.) May not the same be said of breeding. It is certainly true, that people little used with company are more apt to take offense and are less easy than men much versant in public life. They are an unmixed people in New England, and used only to see neighbors, like themselves; and when once an error of behavior is crept in among them, there is small chance of its being cured; for should they go abroad, being early used to a ceremonious and reserved behavior, and believing that good manners consist entirely in punctilios, they only add a few more stiffened airs to their deportment, excluding good humor, affability of conversation, and accommodation of temper and sentiment, as qualities too vulgar for a gentleman. Mr. Strong gave us, this morning, a story which, with many others of a similar nature, which I have heard, places this in a clear point of light.

By the Constitution of Massachusetts, the Senate have a right of communicating bills to their Lower House. Some singular business made them shut their doors. At this time, called Samuel Adams, of the Senate, to communicate a bill. The Doorkeeper told him his orders. Back returned the enraged Senator. The whole Senate took flame, and blazed forth in furious memorial against the Lower House for breach of privilege. A violent contest ensued, and the whole State was convulsed with litigation.

April 29. Attended the Hall. This day a bill was read the second time, respecting the administering the oath for the support of the new Government. A diversity of opinion arose, whether the law should be extended so as to oblige the officers of the *State* Governments to take the oaths. The power of Congress to do this was asserted by some, and denied by others, in pointed terms. I did not enter into the merits on either side; but before the question was put, gave my opinion, that the first step towards doing *good*, was to was to be sure of doing *no harm*. Gentlemen had been very pointed for and against the power. If *we* divided here, what must we expect the people out of doors to be. That in the exercise of powers given us by Congress, we should deal in no uncertainties; that while we had the Constitution plainly before us, all was safe and certain; but if we took on us to deal in doubtful matters, we trod on hollow ground, and might be charged with an assumption of powers not delegated. I, therefore, on this ground, was against the commitment. The bill, however, was committed, and with it closed the business of the day.

I have observed, ever since we began to do business, that a Jehu-like spirit has prevailed with a number of gentlemen, and with none more than with the member from the ancient dominion, who is said to be a notorious anti-Federalist—a most expensive and enormous machine of a Federal judiciary—pompous titles, strong efforts after religious distinctions, coercive laws for taking the oaths, &c., &c. I have uniformly opposed, as far as I was able, everything of this kind, and, I believe, have sacrificed every chance of being popular, and every grain of influence in the Senate by so doing. But, be it so. I have the testimony of my own conscience, that I am right. High-handed measures are at no time justifiable; but now they are highly impolitic. Never will I consent to straining the Constitution; nor never will I consent to the exercise of a doubtful power. We come here the servants—not the lords—of our constituents. The new Government, instead of being a powerful machine, whose authority would support any measure, needs helps and props on all sides, and must be supported by the ablest names and the most shining characters which we can select. The President's amiable deportment, however, smoothes and sweetens everything. Charles Thompson has, however, been ill-used by the Committee of Arrangements of the ceremonial. This is wrong. His name had been left out of the arrangement for to-morrow.

The journal of *Mr. Maclay* proceeds:

Thursday, 30th April. This is a great, important day. Goddess of Etiquette assist me while I describe it. The Senate stood adjourned to half after eleven o'clock. About ten, dressed in my best clothes. Went for Mr. Morris' lodgings; but met his son, who told me that his father would not be in town until Saturday. About ten, turned into the Hall. The crowd already great. The Senate met. The President (Mr. Adams) rose in the most solemn manner:

GENTLEMEN: I wish for the direction of the Senate. The President will, I suppose, address the Congress. How shall I behave? How shall we receive it? Shall it be standing or sitting?

Here followed a considerable talk from him, which I could make nothing of. Mr. *Lee* began with the House of Commons, as is usual with him; then the House of Lords; then the King, and then back again. The result of his information was, that the Lords sat, and the Commons stood, on the delivery of the King's speech.

Mr. Izard got up and told how often he had been in the House of Parliament. He said a great deal of what he had seen there; made, however, this sagacious discovery, that the Commons stood because they had no seats to sit, on being arrived at the House of Lords. It was discovered, after some time, that the King sat too, and had his robes and crown on.

The President got up again, and said he had been very often, indeed, at the Parliament on those occasions, but there always was such a crowd, and *ladies along*, he could not say how it was.

Mr. Carroll got up to declare that he thought it of no consequence how it was in Great Britain—they were no rule to us, &c. But all at once the Secretary, who had been out, whispered to the Chair that the Clerk from the Representatives was at the door with a communication. Gentlemen of the Senate, how shall he be received? A silly kind of resolution of the committee on that business had been laid on the table some days ago. *The amount* of it was, that each House should communicate to the other what and how they chose. It concluded, however, something in this way—that everything should be done with all the *propriety* that was *proper*. The question was, Shall this be adopted, that we may know how to receive the Clerk? It was objected; this will throw no light on the subject; it will leave you where you are.

Mr. Lee brought the House of Commons before us again. He reprobated the rule—declared that the Clerk should not come within the bar of the House; that the proper mode was for the Sergeant-at-Arms, with the mace on his shoulder, to meet the Clerk at the door and receive his communication. We are not, however, provided for this ceremonious way of doing business, having neither mace nor Sergeant, nor masters in chancery, who carry down bills from the English Lords.

Mr. Izard got up and labored unintelligibly to show the great distinction between a communication and a delivery of a thing; but he was not minded.

Mr. Ellsworth showed plainly enough that if the Clerk was not permitted to deliver the communication, the Speaker might as well send it enclosed. Repeated accounts came that the Speaker and Representatives were at the door. Confusion ensued; the members left their seats. Mr. Reed rose and called the attention of the Senate to the neglect that had been shown to Mr. Thomson, late Secretary. Mr. Lee rose to answer him; but I could not hear one word he said.

The Speaker was introduced, followed by the Representatives. Here we sat an hour and ten minutes before the President arrived. This delay was owing to Lee, Izard, and Dalton, who had stayed with us until the Speaker came in, instead of going to attend the President.

The President advanced betweeen the Senate and Representatives, bowing to each. He was placed in the chair by the President of the Senate; the Senate, with their President, on the right, the Speaker and Representatives on his left. The President of the Senate rose, and addressed a short sentence to him. The import of it was, that he should now take the oath of office as President. He seemed to have forgot half of what he was to say, for he made a dead pause and stood for some time to appearance in a vacant mood. He finished with a formal bow, and the President was conducted out of the middle window into the gallery, and the oath administered by the Chancellor.* Notice that the business was done was communicated to the crowd, who gave three cheers, and repeated it on the President's bowing to them. As the company returned into the chamber, the President took the chair and the Senate and Representatives their seats. He rose and all arose, and he addressed them. (See the address.)

This great man was agitated and embarrassed more than ever he was by the leveled cannon or pointed musket. He trembled, and several times could scarce make out to read, though it must be supposed he had often read it before. He made a flourish with his right hand which left rather an ungainly impression. I sincerely, for my part, wished all set ceremony in the hands of the dancing masters, and that this first of men had read off his address in the plainest manner, without ever taking his eyes from the paper; for I felt hurt that he was not first in everything. He was dressed in deep brown, with metal buttons with an eagle on them, white stockings, a bag, and sword.†

---

* Congress sat in the city hall, called Federal Hall, situate on Wall street, opposite the head of Broad street. To gratify the public curiosity, an open gallery adjoining the Senate Chamber had been selected as the place where the ceremony should take place.—*Presidents of the U. S., by Edwin Williams.*

† In the *Pennsylvania Packet*, under date of Tuesday, April 28, 1789, relative to the inauguration it is stated : In the evening was exhibited, under the direction of Col. Bauman, a very ingenious and splendid show of fireworks. The Count de Moustier's house was elegantly illuminated, and a variety of transparent paintings were exhibited. His Excellency Don Diego de Gardoqui's house also displayed a great assemblage of beautiful figures, executed in the most masterly and striking manner, and which attracted considerable attention from the vast multitude of citizens assembled to view the various scenes of the evening. The ceremony of this remarkable day completed the organization of the Federal body. Every honest man must feel a singular felicity in contemplating this day. Good government, the best of blessings, now commences under favorable auspices. We beg leave to congratulate our readers on the great event.

A writer in the same, under date of May 7, remarks that "the fire-works exhibited in the evening were truly brilliant, and the illuminations and transparent paintings of the French and Spanish ambassadors surpassed even conception itself."

From the Hall there was a grand procession to St. Paul's church, where prayers were said by the Bishop. The procession was well conducted and without accident, as far as I have heard. The militia were under arms, lined the street near the church, made a good figure, and behaved well.

The inaugural address was as follows:

Fellow-citizens of the Senate and of the House of Represent-atives: Among the vicissitudes incident to life, no event could have filled me with greater anxieties than that of which the notification was transmitted by your order, and received on the 14th day of the present month. On the one hand, I was summoned by my country—whose voice I can never hear but with veneration and love—from a retreat which I had chosen, with the fondest predilection; and in my flattering hopes, with an immutable decision, as the asylum of my declining years—a retreat which was rendered every day more necessary, as well as more dear to me, by the addition of habit to inclination, and of frequent interruptions in my health, to the gradual waste committed on it by time. On the other hand, the magnitude and difficulty of the trust to which the voice of my country called me, being sufficient to awaken, in the wisest and most experienced of her citizens, a distrustful scrutiny into his qualifications, could not but overwhelm with despondence, one who, inheriting inferior endowments from nature, and unpracticed in the duties of civil administration, ought to be peculiarly conscious of his own deficiencies. In this conflict of emotions, all I dare aver is, that it has been my faithful study to collect my duty from a just appreciation of every circumstance by which it might be effected. All I dare hope is, that if, in executing this task, I have been too much swayed by a grateful remembrance of former instances, or by an affectionate sensibility to this transcendent proof of the confidence of my fellow-citizens, and have thence too little consulted my incapacity, as well as disinclination, for the weighty and untried cares before me, my error will be palliated by the motives which misled me, and its consequences be judged by my country, with some share of the partiality in which they originated.

Such being the impressions under which I have, in obedience to the public summons, repaired to the present station, it would be pe-

---

In relation to the inaugural address of Washington, Fisher Ames, who was possessed of a more poetic temperament than that of Mr. Maclay, wrote: "It was a touching scene, and quite solemn kind. His aspect, grave, almost to sadness; his modesty, actually shaking; his voice, deep, a little tremulous, and so low as to call for close attention; added to the sense of objects presented to the mind and overwhelming it, produced emotions of the most affecting kind upon the members."—*Works of Fisher Ames, Vol. I, p. 34.*

culiarly improper to omit, in this first official act, my fervent supplication to that Almighty Being who rules over the universe, who presides in the councils of nations, and whose providential aids can supply every human defect, that His benediction may consecrate to the liberties and happiness of the people of the United States, a Government instituted by themselves, for these essential purposes ; and may enable every instrument employed in its administration to execute, with success, the functions allotted to his charge.   In tendering this homage to the Great Author of every public and private good, I assure myself that it expresses your sentiments not less than my own, nor those of my fellow-citizens at large less than either. No people can be bound to acknowledge and adore the invisible hand which conducts the affairs of men more than the people of the United States.   Every step by which they have advanced to the character of an independent nation, seems to have been distinguished by some token of providential agency ; and in the important revolution just accomplished in the system of their united Government, the tranquil deliberations and voluntary consent of so many distinct communities from which the event has resulted, cannot be compared with the means by which most Governments have been established, without some return of pious gratitude, along with an humble anticipation of the future blessings which the past seems to presage. These reflections, arising out of the present crisis, have forced themselves too strongly on my mind to be suppressed.   You will join with me, I trust, in thinking that there are none under the influence of which the proceedings of a new and free Government can more auspiciously commence.

By the article establishing the executive department, it is made the duty of the President " to recommend to your consideration such measures as he shall judge necessary and expedient."   The circumstances under which I now meet you will acquit me from entering into that subject, further than to refer to the great constitutional charter under which you are assembled ; and which, in defining your powers, designates the objects to which your attention is to be given.   It will be more consistent with those circumstances, and far more congenial with the feelings which actuate me, to substitute, in place of a recommendation of particular measures, the tribute that is due to the talents, the rectitude, and the patriotism, which adorn the characters selected to devise and adopt them.   In these honorable qualifications, I behold the surest pledges, that, as on one side, no local prejudices or attachments, no separate views, nor party animosities, will misdirect the comprehensive and equal eye which ought to watch over this great assemblage of communities and interests; so, on another, that the foundations of our national policy will be laid in the pure and immutable principles of private morality; and the preëminence of free government be exemplified by all the attributes which can win the affections of its citizens, and command the respect of the world. I dwell on this prospect with every satisfaction which an ardent love for my country can inspire. Since there is no truth more thoroughly established than that there exists, in the economy and course of nature, an indissoluble union between virtue and happiness; between duty and advantage; between the genuine maxims of an honest and magnanimous policy, and the solid rewards of public prosperity and felicity; since we ought to be no less persuaded that the propitious smiles of heaven can never be expected on a nation that disregards the eternal rules of order and right, which heaven itself has ordained; and since the preservation of the sacred fire of liberty, and the destiny of the republican model of government, are justly considered as deeply, perhaps as finally, started on the experiment entrusted to the hands of the American people.

Besides the ordinary objects submitted to your care, it will remain with your judgment to decide how far an exercise of the occasional power delegated by the fifth article of the Constitution, is rendered expedient at the present juncture, by the nature of objections which have been urged against the system, or by the degree of inquietude which has given birth to them. Instead of undertaking particular recommendations on this subject, in which I could be guided by no light derived from official opportunities, I shall again give way to my entire confidence in your discernment and pursuit of the public good; for, I assure myself, that while you carefully avoid every alteration which might endanger the benefits of a united and effective government, or which ought to await the future lessons of experience, a reverence for the characteristic rights of freemen, and a regard for the public harmony, will sufficiently influence your deliberations on the question, how far the former can be more impregnably fortified, or the latter be safely and advantageously promoted.

To the preceding observations I have one to add, which will be more properly addressed to the House of Representatives. It concerns myself, and will, therefore, be as brief as possible.

When I was first honored with a call into the service of my country, then on the eve of an arduous struggle for its liberties, the light in which I contemplated my duty required that I should renounce every pecuniary compensation. From this resolution I have in no instance departed. And being still under the impression which produced it, I must decline, as inapplicable to myself, any share in the personal emoluments which may be indispensably included in a permanent provision for the executive department; and must accordingly pray that the pecuniary estimates for the station in which I am placed, may, during my continuance in it, be limited to such actual expenditures as the public good may be thought to require.

Having thus imparted to you my sentiments, as they have been awakened by the occasion which brings us together, I shall take my present leave; but not without resorting once more to the benign Parent of the human race, in humble supplication, that since He has been pleased to favor the American people with opportunities for deliberating in perfect tranquillity, and dispositions for deciding with unparalleled unanimity on a form of Government for the security of their union, and the advancement of their happiness, so His divine blessing may be equally conspicuous in the enlarged views, the temperate consultations, and the wise measures, on which the success of this Government must depend.

G. WASHINGTON.

April 30, 1789.

The Senate returned to their chamber after service, formed, and took up the address. Our President called it *his most gracious speech.* I cannot approve of this. A committee was appointed on it—Johnson, Carroll, Patterson. Adjourned.

In the evening, there were grand fire-works. The Spanish ambassador's house was adorned with transparent paintings; the French minister's house was illuminated; the Hall was grandly illuminated, and after all this the people went to bed.

The journal of Mr. Maclay proceeds as follows:

May 1. Attended at the Hall at eleven. The prayers were over and the minutes reading. When we came to the minute of the speech, it stood, *His most gracious speech.* I looked all round the Senate. Every countenance seemed to wear a blank. The Secretary was going on. *I* must speak or nobody would.

Mr. President, we have lately had a hard struggle for our liberty, against kingly authority. The minds of men are still heated. Everything related to that species of government is odious to the people. The words prefixed to the President's speech are the same that are usually placed before the speech of his Britannic Majesty. I know they will give offense. I consider them as improper. I therefore move that they be struck out, and that it stand simply *address* or *speech*, as may be judged most suitable.

Mr. President rose in his chair, and expressed the greatest surprise that anything should be objected to on account of its being taken from the practice of that government under which we had lived so long and so happily, formerly. That he was for a dignified and respectable government, and as far as he knew the sentiments of the people, they thought as he did.

Painful as it was, I had to contend with the Chair. I admitted that the people of the Colonies (now States) had enjoyed formerly great happiness under that species of government; but the abuses of that government, under which they smarted, had taught them what they had to fear from that kind of government. That there had been a revolution in the sentiments of people respecting government, equally as great as that which had happened in the Government itself. That even the modes of it were now abhorred. The enemies of the Constitution had objected to it the facility there would be of transition from it to kingly government, and all the trappings and splendor of royalty. That if such a thing as this appeared on our minutes, they would not fail to represent it as the first step of the ladder in the ascent to royalty.

The President rose a second time, and declared that *he* had mentioned it to the Secretary. That he could not possibly conceive that any person could take offense at it.

I had to get up again, and declare that though I knew of its being mentioned from the Chair, yet my opposition did not proceed from any motive of contempt—that although it was a painful task, it was solely a sense of duty that raised me.

The President stood during this time. Said he had been long abroad, and did not know how the tempers of people might be now.

Up now rose Mr. Reed, and declared for the paragraph. He saw no reason to object to it because the British speeches were styled *most gracious.* If we chose to object to *words* because they had been used in the same sense in Britain, we should soon be at a loss to do business.

I had to reply. It is time enough to submit to *necessity* when it exists. At present there is no loss for words. The words speech or address, without any addition, will suit us well enough.

The first time I was up, Mr. Lee followed me with a word or two by way of seconding me; but when the President, on being last up, declared that *he* was the person from whom the words were taken, Mr. Lee got up and informed the Chair that he did not know that circumstance, as he had been absent when it happened.

The question was put and carried for erasing the words, without a division.

After the house adjourned, the President took me to one side, declared how much he was for an efficient Government, how much he respected General Washington, and much of that kind.

I told him I would yield to no person in respect to General Washington; that our common friends would, perhaps, one day inform him that I was not wanting in respect to himself; that my wishes for an efficient Government were as high as any man's, and begged him to believe that I did myself great violence when I opposed him in the chair, and nothing but a sense of duty would force me to it. He got upon the subject of checks to Government and the balances of power. His tale was long—he seemed to expect some answer. I caught at the last word, and said, undoubtedly, without a balance there could be no equilibrium, and so I left him hanging in geometry.

May 2. Attended Senate. This a day of no business whatever. Langdon came and shook hands very heartily with me. Some of the other New England men shy. Patterson only was at the Senate chamber before me. He passed censure on the conduct of the President; said he made himself too busy. He hinted as if some of the Senate would have taken notice of the *gracious* officer, if I had not. I told him I was no courtier, and had no occasion to trim; but said it was a most disagreeable thing to contend with the Chair, and I had already held that disagreeable post more than once.

Monday, 4th May. Went early to the post office. As I came back, met General St. Clair. He seemed desirous of speaking with me. Said he had been to my lodgings, and asked me what I thought of the President's new arrangements. It was the first I had heard of them.

The President is neither to entertain or receive invitations. He is to have levee days on Tuesdays and Fridays, when only he is to be seen.

I told the General, that General Washington stood on as difficult ground as he had ever done in his life. That to suffer himself to be run down, on the one hand, by a crowd of visitants, so as to engross his time, would never do, as it would render his doing business impracticable. But, on the other hand, for him to be seen only in public, on stated times, like an Eastern Lama, would be equally offensive. If he was not to be seen but *in public*, where nothing confidential could pass between him and any individual, business would, to all appearance, be done without him, and he could not escape the charge of favoritism; all court would be paid to the supposed favorite, weakness and insignificance would be considered as characteristic of the President, and he would not escape contempt; that it was not thus—the General gained the universal plaudits of his admiring fellow-citizens. I reiterated these ideas in every shape and in every different light I could place them, for nearly half an hour, that we walked in front of St. Paul's church. The General said he wished to collect men's sentiments, and the design was to communicate them to the General. I told him my late conduct in the Senate had been such as would render any opinion of mine very ungracious at court, and, perhaps, he had better never make mention of my name. Much more was said, but not worth committing to paper.

Washington to Hamilton.

NEW YORK, *May 5, 1789.*

DEAR SIR: I beg you to accept my unfeigned thanks for your friendly communications of this date, and that you will permit me to entreat a continuation of them, as occasions may arise.

The manner chosen for doing it is most agreeable to me. It is my wish to act right; if I err, the head and not the heart shall, with justice, be chargeable.

With sentiments of sincere esteem and regard,

I am, dear sir,

Your obedient servant,

GEO. WASHINGTON.

In 4th Hamilton's works, p. 1, is the following letter of Hamilton to Washington :

NEW YORK, *May 5, 1789.*

SIR: In conformity to the intimation you were pleased to honor me with on . . . . . . evening last, I have reflected upon the etiquette proper to be observed by the President, and now submit the ideas which have occurred to me on the subject. The public good requires, as a primary object, that the dignity of the office should be supported.

Whatever is essential, that ought to be pursued, though at the risk of partial or momentary dissatisfaction. But care will be necessary to avoid extensive disgust or discontent. Men's minds are prepared for a pretty high tone in the demeanor of the executive, but I doubt whether for so high a tone as in the abstract might be desirable. The notions of equality are yet, in my opinion, too general and too strong to admit of such a distance being placed between the President and other branches of the Government as might even be consistent with a due proportion. The following plan will, I think, steer clear of extremes, and involve no very material inconveniences :

1. The President to have a levee day once a week for receiving

visits; an hour to be fixed at which it shall be understood that he will appear, and consequently that visitors are to be previously assembled.

The President to remain half an hour, in which time he may converse cursorily on indifferent subjects, with such persons as shall invite his attention, and at the end of that half hour disappear. Some regulation will be hereafter necessary to designate those who may visit.

A mode of introduction, through particular officers, will be indispensible. No visits to be returned.

2. The President to accept no invitations, and to give formal entertainments only twice or four times a year—the anniversaries of important events in the Revolution. If twice, the day of the declaration of independence and that of the inauguration of the President—which completed the organization of the Constitution—to be preferred. If four times, the day of the treaty of alliance with France, and that of the definitive treaty with Britain, to be added. The members of the two Houses of the Legislature, principal officers of the Government, foreign ministers, and other distingnished strangers only to be invited. The numbers form, in my mind, an objection; but there may be separate tables, in separate rooms. This is practiced in some European courts. I see no other method in which foreign ministers can, with propriety, be included in any attentions of the table, which the President may think fit to pay.

3. The President, on the levee days, either by himself or some gentleman of his household, to give informal invitations to family dinners on the days of invitation. Not more than six or eight to be invited at a time, and the matter to be confined essentially to members of the Legislature and other official characters. The President never to remain long at table.

I think it probable that the last article will not correspond with the ideas of most of those with whom your Excellency may converse; but, on further mature reflection, I believe it will be necessary to remove the idea of too immense an inequality, which, I fear, would excite dissatisfaction and cabal. The thing may be so managed as neither to occasion much waste of time nor to infringe on dignity.

It is an important point to consider what persons may have access to your Excellency on business. The heads of departments will, of course, have this privilege. Foreign ministers of some descriptions will also be entitled to it. In Europe, I am informed, ambassadors only have direct access to the chief magistrate. Something very near what prevails there would, in my opinion, be right.

The distinction of rank between diplomatic characters requires attention, and the door of access ought not to be too wide to that class of persons. I have thought that the members of the Senate should also have a right of *individual* access on matters relative to the *public administration.* In England and France, peers of the realm have this right. We have none such in this country, but I believe that it will be satisfactory to the people to know that there is some body of men in the State who have a right of continual communication with the President. It will be considered a safe-guard against secret combination to deceive him.

I have also asked myself, will not the Representatives expect the same privilege, and be offended if they are not allowed to participate with the Senate? There is sufficient danger of this to merit consideration, but there is a reason for the distinction in the Constitution. The Senate are coupled with the President in certain executive functions, treaties, and appointments. This makes them in a degree his constitutional counselors, and gives them a *peculiar* claim to the right of access. On the whole, I think the discrimination will be proper, and may be hazarded.

I have chosen this method of communication, because I understood your Excellency that it would be most convenient to you. The unstudied and uncermonious manner of it will, I hope, not render it less acceptable. And if, in the execution of your commands, at any time, I consult frankness and simplicity more than ceremony or profession, I flatter myself you will not, on that account, distrust the sincerity of my cordial wishes for your personal happiness, and the success of your administration.

I have the honor to be, with the highest respect,

Your Excellency's most obedient and humble servant,

Though out of order, as to date, the letter of President Washington to John Adams, and the reply of Mr. Adams, is here given :

17th May, 1789.

The President of the United States wishes to avail himself of your sentiments on the following points :

1. Whether a line of conduct equally distant from an association with all kinds of company on the one hand, and from a total seclusion from society on the other, ought to be adopted by him? And in that case, how is it to be done ?

2. What will be the least exceptionable method of bringing any system which may be adopted on this subject before the public and into use ?

3. Whether, after a little time, one day in every week will not be sufficient for receiving visits of compliment?

4. Whether it would tend to prompt impertinent applications, and involve disagreeable consequences, to have it known that the President will, every morning, at eight o'clock, be at leisure to give audience to persons who may have business with him?

5. Whether, when it shall have been understood that the President is not to give general entertainments, in the manner the Presidents of Congress have formerly done, it will be practicable to draw such a line of discrimination, in regard to persons, as that six, eight, or ten official characters, including in rotation the members of both Houses of Congress, may be invited, personally or otherwise, to dine with him on the day fixed for receiving company, without exciting clamors in the rest of the community?

6. Whether it would be satisfactory to the public for the President to make about four great entertainments in a year, on such great occasions as the anniversary of the Declaration of Independence, the alliance with France, the peace with Great Britain, the organization of the General Government; and whether arrangements of these two last kinds could be in danger of diverting too much of the President's time from business, or of producing the evils which it was intended to avoid by his living more recluse than the Presidents of Congress have hitherto lived?

7. Whether there would be any impropriety in the President's making informal visits; that is to say, in his calling upon his acquaintances or public characters, for the purpose of sociability or civility? And what as to the form of doing it, might evince these visits to have been made in his private character, so as that they may not be construed into visits from the President of the United States? And in what light would his visits rarely at tea-parties be considered?

8. Whether, during the recess of Congress, it would not be advantageous to the interests of the Union for the President to make the tour of the United States, in order to become better acquainted with their principal characters and internal circumstances, as well as to be more accessible to numbers of well-informed persons who might give him useful information and advice on political subjects?

9. If there is a probability that either of the arrangements may take place, which will eventually cause additional expenses, whether it would not be proper that these ideas should come into contemplation at the time when Congress shall make a permanent provision for the support of the Executive?

Remarks

On the one side no augmentation can be effected in the pecuniary establishment, which shall be made in the first instance for the support of the Executive. On the other, all moneys destined to that purpose, beyond the actual expenditure, will be left in the treasury of the United States, or sacredly applied to the promotion of some national objects.

Many things which appear of little importance in themselves and at the beginning, may have great and durable consequences from their having been established at the commencement of a new General Government. It will be much easier to commence the administration upon a well adjusted system, built on tenable grounds, than to correct errors or alter inconveniences after they shall have been confirmed by habit. The President, in all matters of business and etiquette, can have no object but to demean himself in his public character in such a manner as to maintain the dignity of his office, without subjecting himself to the imputation of superciliousness or unnecessary reserve. Under these impressions, he asks for your candid and undisguised opinion.

Vice President's Answer.

New York, *17th May, 1789.*

The Vice President has the honor to present his humble opinion, on the points proposed for his consideration.

1. That an association with all kinds of company, and a total seclusion from society, are extremes which, in the actual circumstances of this country, and under our form of government, may be properly avoided.

2. The system of the President will gradually develop itself in practice, without any formal communication to the Legislature, or publication from the press. Paragraphs in the public prints may, however, appear from time to time, without any formal authority, that may lead and reconcile the public mind.

3. Considering the number of strangers from many countries, and of citizens from various states, who will resort to the seat of government, it is doubted whether two days in the week will not be indispensable for visits of compliment. A little experience, however, will elucidate this point.

4. Under the fourth head, it is submitted to consideration whether all personal applications ought not to be made, in the first instance, to a minister of state. Yet an appeal should be open, by petition, to the President, who, if he judges the subject worthy of it, may admit the party to a personal interview. Access to the Supreme

Magistrate ought not to be rigorously denied in any case that is worthy of his consideration. Nevertheless, in every case, the name, quality, and, when these are not sufficient to raise a presumption in their favor, their business, ought to be communicated to a chamberlain or gentleman in waiting, who should judge whom to admit and whom to exclude. Some limitation of time may be necessary, too, as, for example, from eight to nine or ten; for, without it, the whole forenoon, or the whole day, may be taken up.

5. There is no doubt that the President may invite what official characters, members of Congress, strangers, or citizens of distinction he pleases, in small parties, without exciting clamors; but this should always be done without formality.

6. The entertainments mentioned in this article would much more properly be made by a minister of state for foreign or domestic affairs, or some other minister of state, or the Vice President, whom, upon such occasions, the President, in his private character, might honor with his presence. But in no case whatever can I conceive it proper for the President to make any formal public entertainment.

7. There can be no impropriety in the President's making or receiving informal visits among his friends or acquaintances at his pleasure. Undress, and few attendants, will sufficiently show that such visits are made as a man, a citizen, a friend, or acquaintance. But in no case whatever should a visit be made or returned in form by the President; at least, unless an Emperor of Germany, or some other sovereign, should travel to this country. The President's pleasure should absolutely decide concerning his attendance at tea-parties in a private character, and no gentleman or lady ought ever to complain if he never or rarely attends. The President's private life should be at his own discretion, and the world should respectfully acquiesce. As President, he should have no intercourse with society, but upon public business, or at his levees. This distinction it is, with submission, apprehended, ought to govern the whole conduct.

8. A tour might, no doubt, be made with great advantage to the public, if the time can be spared; but it will naturally be considered, as foreign affairs arrive every day, and the business of the executive and judicial departments will require constant attention, whether the President's residence will not necessarily be confined to one place.

Observations.

The civil list ought to provide for the President's household. What number of chamberlains, aides-de-camp, secretaries, masters of ceremonies, &c., will become necessary, it is difficult to foresee.

But should not all such establishments be distinct from the allowance to the President for his services, which is mentioned in the Constitution? In all events, the provision for the President and his household ought to be large and ample. The office, by its legal authority, defined in the Constitution, has no equal in the world, excepting those only which are held by crowned heads; nor is the royal authority in all cases to be compared to it. The royal office in Poland is a mere shadow in comparison with it. The Dogeship in Venice, and the Stadtholdership in Holland, are not so much. Neither dignity nor authority can be supported in human minds, collected into nations or any great numbers, without a splendor and majesty in some degree proportioned to them. The sending and receiving ambassadors is one of the most splendid and important prerogatives of sovereigns, absolute or limited; and this, in our Constitution, is wholly in the President. If the state and pomp essential to this great department are not in a good degree preserved, it will be in vain for America to hope for consideration with foreign powers.

These observations are submitted, after all, with diffidence, conscious that my long residence abroad may have impressed me with views of things incompatible with the present temper and feelings of our fellow-citizens, and with a perfect disposition to acquiesce in whatever may be the result of the superior wisdom of the President.

Attended Senate. Soon after the bill prescribing the oath, &c., was taken up, and the amendments.

On the Senate journal, under date of May 2, it is stated that Mr. Strong, from the committee to whom the bill from the House of Representatives was referred, to regulate the time and manner of administering certain oaths, reported sundry amendments thereto, which were assigned for consideration on Monday next.

Monday, May 4. The Senate proceeded to the consideration of the report of the committee on the bill to regulate the time and manner of administering certain oaths.

In line one, strike out the words " Congress of the United States," and insert, " Senate and Representatives of the United States of

---

NOTE.—It is a singular fact that this should be the only answer to the President's queries on this delicate subject which has been found among Washington's papers. It is certain that he submitted them to Mr. Madison and Mr. Jay, and it is likely to several other persons in whose judgment he trusted. Mr. Hamilton's answer, which is informal, has been published, for the first time, in the late collection made of his works, vol. 4, page 1.

America, in Congress assembled." At the end of the second paragraph, add the words " of the Senate," and insert the following clause :

"And be it further enacted, that the members of the several State Legislatures, and all executive and judicial officers of the several States, who have been heretofore chosen or appointed, or who shall be chosen or appointed before the first day of August next, and who shall then be in office, shall, within one month thereafter, take the same oath or affirmation, except where they shall have taken it before ; which may be administered by any person authorized by the law of the State in which such office shall be holden to administer oaths. And the members of the several State Legislatures, and all executive and judicial officers of the several States, who shall be chosen or appointed after the said first day of August next, shall, before they proceed to execute the duties of their respective offices, take the foregoing oath or affirmation, which shall be administered by person or persons, who, by the law of the State, shall be authorized to administer the oath of office ; and the person or persons so administering the oath hereby required to be taken, shall cause a record or certificate thereof to be made, in the same manner as by the law of the State, he or they shall be directed to record or certify the oath of office."

In the last paragraph, strike out the words " of the United States of America," in the third and fourth lines, and insert the same words in the fourth line, next after the words " as the case may be ; " and which being accepted, Tuesday morning, eleven o'clock, was assigned for the third reading of the bill.

Mr. Maclay, in his journal, remarks :

The first amendment was on the enacting clause. It stood *by the Congress of the United States.* The amendment, *by the Senate and Representatives.*

It was openly avowed by Mr. Izard that the dignity and preëminence of *the Senate* was the object aimed at by the amendment. But the words of the Constitution are, All legislative power herein granted, shall be vested in a *Congress* of the United States. Again, section eight. The *Congress* shall have power, &c. The amount of all I said resolved itself into this. The legislative authority (the power of making laws in certain cases) is given to *Congress.* Let Congress execute this trust under the same name. In other words, it is under the *firm of Congress*, that we have received our authority and power. Let us execute it under the same firm.

Ellsworth, who is a vastly better speaker than I am, was in sentiment with me this time. He placed the subject in various lights, and said enough, I thought, to convince any one who was not determined to be otherwise. But the fact with us is, that the point sought after is to find what will be most agreeable; or, in other words, where will the majority be; for never was a text more practiced on than that, in a multitude of counselors (say Senators) there is safety. Indeed, it seems the governing principle.

Mr. Izard gave us a kind of dissenting speech from both original and amendment. He wanted the *President's* name in it.

The President rose in the chair to deliver sentiments to the same purpose; and upon this principal he was rather against the amendment, because it did not mention the President. *The amendment carried.*

The next amendment was a clause obliging the officers of the State Legislatures to take the oath within a month after the 1st of August.

Mr. Ellsworth argued on the inaccuracy of the language of the amendment—that it was doubtful as to the intent of it every way. I thought he nearly exhausted the subject.

Before the vote was put I chose to say something. It amounted to this—that the subject was a doubtful one every way—the power of Congress at any time; or the propriety of exercising it at this time, if admitted. The words of the amendment were also doubtful and doubted. I would, therefore, deal in no doubtful matters.

Izard rose in a flame; declared he knew not what gentlemen meant by talking of doubts—he never heard of any. He was very angry.

Mr. Langdon followed him. Read the Constitution, that all *officers, both of the United States and several States*, shall be bound by oath, &c.

I had to get up in my own defense. I observed that gentlemen mistook the point. The question was not whether the officers should take the oath, but was it our business to interfere in it. It was equally clear that Senators, Representatives, and electors were to be chosen by the State, but who ever thought of a law to oblige them to do these things. The adopting States, by the terms of their adoption, had pledged themselves to conform to the Constitution, which contained these things among its fundamental rules. Among the powers delegated to Congress this was not mentioned, nor was it necessary, being already provided for in the Constitution.

As to *doubts*, individuals had doubted, and States had doubted. Massachusetts, it appeared, considered the power of making a law to be with *Congress*. Connecticut thought so differently that they had passed a State law for the purpose. For *my* part, I greatly doubted, at least, the propriety of meddling with it, unless the

States should be guilty of neglect. But I was not so uncharitable as to damn him that doubted not.

Up rose Lee. He was for the amendment, but had more doubts than anybody.

The rage of speaking caught hold of half the Senate at least. Some sensible things were said, but a great many foolish ones. Ellsworth rose a second time. He took nearly the track I had been on; but he explained everything with a clearness and perspicuity which I was quite incapable of. I was highly pleased with him. How readily the sentimental strings sound unisons when both are touched by the same agreeable motive. But enough; the amendment was carried against us.

I learned this day that the *title* selected from all the potentates of the earth for our President was to have been taken from Poland, viz: Elective majesty. What a royal escape.

Dined this day with the French minister. The first place I have been at since my illness. But I have minuted enough for this day; so stop.

The Senate journal is as follows :

Thursday, May 5. The bill to regulate the time and manner of administering certain oaths was read the third time and passed, with amendments.

Ordered, That the Secretary carry the aforementioned bill to the House of Representatives, together with the amendments, and address the Speaker in the words following :

SIR : The Senate have passed the bill, entitled "An act to regulate the time and manner of administering certain oaths," with amendments, to which they desire the concurrence of your House.

Ordered, That when a bill has passed the Senate, the Secretary shall indorse the final determination thereon, and the day when such final question was taken, previous to its being transmitted to the House of Representatives :

Mr. Maclay, in his journal, remarks :

May 5. The bill of yesterday had a third reading. But now how is it to be sent to the other House. A motion was made and seconded, that it go *by the Secretary*. From half after eleven to half after one, was this important question agitated. The other House had effronted the Senate by sending up the bill in a letter ; and now we would not send it down by a member. The dignity of the House was much insisted on. We were plagued with the Houses of Lords and Commons, and *parliamentary* was the supplementary word to every sentence. I doubted much whether I should rise or not. However, where everybody had something to say, I scorned to be silent. I remarked that I rose with reluctance on a subject when I had not been able to draw any information from experience, as the State I had the honor to represent had but one House. Yet from what I could learn, the States in the Union, which had two Houses, carried on their communications by their members. That this I considered the most cordial and friendly mode of intercourse ; and that I would much rather take example from our own States than from Great Britain. That this intercourse, therefore, was the one which I most sincerely wished, and thought the sooner it was adopted the better. If our members should be ill-treated below, as had been alleged by some gentlemen, the fault would not be ours ; and then we would be fully justified by adopting some other mode. A communication by our Secretary was a bad one—it interrupted business, as we could not proceed without him. If we meant it by way of returning the affront that had been offered us, this was wrong. We should send the bill by letter ; and this would be treating them in kind.

I was answered—at least, an attempt was made ; but I was not convinced. Mr. Langdon got up soon after, and seemed to adopt all I had said ; but the motion was carried against us. Mr. Ellsworth was with us, and so was Mr. Carroll ; but he concluded, with saying, he would, this time, vote for the Secretary to go down with the bill.

I forgot to minute a very long speech of Mr. Ellsworth, when the bill was on the third reading. He prefaced his discourse by saying he would make no motion, but gentlemen might do as they pleased after he had delivered his sentiments. The whole amounted to this, that the great and dignified station of the President, and the conspicuous part which he would act in the field of legislation, as all laws must pass in review before him, and were subject to his revision and correction, &c., &c., entitled him to have his name or place marked in the enacting clause of the laws ; or, at least, he should be brought into view among the conspicuous parts of Congress.

Ideas of the above kind were dwelt on, and varied with agreeable enough diction, for near a quarter of an hour. I was confident he neither wished nor expected to have any serious motion made on such untenable ground. What, then, could be his motive, solely to play the courtier. Something of this kind had been hinted from the Chair. Mr. Izard had been explicit on the subject. Mr. Ellsworth now plays the middle game. He knows the thing cannot take place, but he will bring it fully into view, so that he can say it was not my fault, and thus secure his interest with the high-toned courtiers. No motion was made. Indeed, the spirit of his address was reducible to this: I will make no motion. If any of you are foolish enough to do it you may.

May 6. No Senate this day. There was a Commencement at St. Paul's church. The Senate were served with tickets. Dr. Johnson, the principal of the college, could not attend with us. I had heard that Mr. Morris was come to town. I went for his lodging. This, another useless journey, for he has not come. I would have been very glad of Mr. Morris' company. It has happened otherwise, I have been alone. I have had to bear the chilling cold of the North and the intemperate warmth of the South, neither of which are favorable to the middle States, from which I come. Lee and Izard, hot as the burning sand of Carolina, hate us. Adams, with all his frigid friends, cool and wary, bear us no good will. I could not find a confidant in one of them; or say, to my heart, here is the man I can trust. What has been my conduct then—spirit of rectitude bear witness for me—have I trimmed to one of them? Or have I once withheld a single sentiment that my judgment approved of? I trust I have not. Regardless of consequences, with no eye to emolument, without desire for reappointment, I mean to act as if I were immortal, and yet I wish to give satisfaction and content to the State that sent me here. Never, however, will I purchase that with discontent in my own bosom; nor does my dear country demand such a sacrifice at my hand.

The journal, under date of the 7th May, proceeds:

The committee reported an answer to the President's speech. It was read. One part was objected to, which stated the United States to have been in anarchy and confusion, and the President stepping in and rescuing them. A very long debate. The words were struck out. Mr. Lee offered a part of a sentence which I thought filled the sentence with propriety. It was, however, lost. Mr. Patterson offered a clause, " rescued us from evils impending over us." This was carried; but nearly half the Senate made sour faces at it. Mr. Ellsworth said it was tautological; but seemed at a loss as to mending it. I rose, more in consequence of a kind of determination that I have adopted of saying something every day than from any fondness of the subject. I admitted that there appeared something

NOTE.—It is said that the celebrated Charles Fox, in his early service in Parliament, was in the habit of speaking as frequently as a suitable opportunity was offered him. One object in his course was to advance his reputation as an orator; and to this practice, it is said that he attributed, in a considerable degree, his proficiency as a debater. Of him Burke said that he was "the greatest debater the world ever saw." Pitt observed that "whenever I have made a better speech than usual, I observe that Fox, in his reply, surpasses himself."—See *Earl Russell's Recollections*, 219, 220.

tautological in the words, and it was not easy to mend them consistent with elegant diction ; but if the first syllable was taken from the word *impending*, it would then stand, " evils pending over us." The objection would be obviated, but I would not say the language would be eloquent. But since I was up, I could not help remarking that I thought the whole clause improper. That to state the whole Union as being in anarchy, or under impending ruin, was to sanctify the calumnies of our enemies, who had long labored in the foreign gazettes to represent us as a people void of government. It was fixing a stain on the annals of America ; for future historians would appeal to the transactions of this very day as a proof of our disordered circumstances. I, therefore, was against the whole clause.

Mr. Wyngate followed me, and was for having the clause struck out. This could not well be done, consistent with order. I mentioned that if a reconsideration was moved, I would second it. It was reconsidered and amended, and afterwards recommitted to the same committee. They retired for the purpose of dressing it.

Now, the President rose, to draw the attention of the Senate to the manner of returning the answer to the President. A committee was appointed to confer, on this and other subjects, with a committee of the Representatives.

There are three ways, gentlemen, (said our President,) by which the President may communicate with us. One is, personally. If he comes here, we must have a seat for him. *In England*, it is called a *throne*. To be sure, it is behind that seat we must seek for shelter and protection. The second is by a Minister of State. The third is by his chamberlain, or one of his *aids-de-camp*, I had almost said ; but that is a military phrase. It may become a great constitutional question.

Seeing the House look blank, he said, I throw these things out for gentlemen to think of.

Mr. Lee got up, and said something on the propriety of having a seat, with a canopy, for the President.

Mr. Langdon said something, but did not seem well collected, and spoke so low, I did not hear him. The time was trifled till near eight o'clock. The day was cold, and the members collected near the fire, leaving their seats. The committee returned with the message, and it really read vastly better, and was altered in the exceptionable phrases. In one place, speaking of the Government, it mentioned *dignity and splendor*. I submitted it to the gentlemen who had the amending of it, whether *respectability* was not better than *splendor*. Mr. Carroll, of the committee, did not defend the word splendor; but said respectability had been used before, if he recollected right. Mr. Patterson said it sounded much better than respectability, and rounded the period. Doctor Johnson said *splendor* signified, in this place, the highest perfection of government. These were the three members of the committee.

I mentioned that if the word respectability had been used immediately before, it would be improper; that dignity alone, I thought, expressed all that was wanted. As to the seeking of sounding names and pompous expressions, I thought them exceptionable on that very account, and that no argument was necessary to show it. Different men had a train of different ideas raised by the same word. Splendor, when applied to government, brought into my mind, instead of the highest perfection, all the faulty finery, brilliant scenes, and expensive trappings of royal government, and impressed my mind with an idea quite the reverse of republican respectability, which, I thought, consisted in firm and prudent councils, frugality, and economy. I found I was well seconded, and concluded that my motion went to recommend a reconsideration of the word *splendor* to the committee. They did not alter it, and the answer was agreed to.

The President rose in the chair, and repeated twice, with more joy on his face than I had ever seen him assume before, that he hoped the Government would be supported with *dignity and splendor*. I thought he did it by way of triumph over me for a former defeat I gave him, but it may be I was mistaken.

The following is the answer to the President's speech, reported by the committee:

SIR: We, the Senate of the United States, return you our sincere thanks for your excellent speech delivered to both Houses of Congress; congratulate you on the complete organization of the Federal Government; and felicitate ourselves and our fellow-citizens on your elevation to the office of President; an office highly important by the powers constitutionally annexed to it, and extremely honorable from the manner in which the appointment is made. The unanimous suffrage of the elective body in your favor, is peculiarly expressive of the gratitude, confidence, and affection of the citizens of America, and is the highest testimonial at once of your merit and their esteem. We are sensible, sir, that nothing but the voice of your fellow-citizens could have called you from a retreat, chosen with the fondest predilection, endeared by habit, and consecrated by the repose of declining years. We rejoice, and with us all America, that, in obedience to the call of our common country, you have returned once more to public life. In you all parties confide; in you all interests unite; and we have no doubt that your past services, great as they have been, will be equaled by your future exertions; and that your prudence and sagacity as a statesman will tend to avert the dangers to which we are exposed, to give stability to the present government, and dignity and splendor to that country which your skill and valor as a soldier so eminently contributed to raise to independence and empire.

When we contemplate the coincidence of circumstances and wonderful combinations of causes, which gradually prepared the people of this country for independence—when we contemplate the rise, progress, and termination of the late war, which gave them a name among the nations of the earth, we are, with you, unavoidably led to acknowledge and adore the great Arbiter of the universe, by whom empires rise and fall. A review of the many signal instances of divine interposition, in favor of this country, claims our most pious gratitude; and, permit us, sir, to observe, that, among the great events which have led to the formation and establishment of a Federal Government, we esteem your acceptance of the office of President as one of the most propitious and important.

In the execution of the trust reposed in us, we shall endeavor to pursue that enlarged and liberal policy to which your speech so happily directs. We are conscious that the prosperity of each State is inseparably connected with the welfare of all, and that, in promoting the latter, we shall effectually advance the former. In full persuasion of this truth, it shall be our invariable aim to divest ourselves of local prejudices and attachments, and to view the great assemblage of communities and interests committed to our charge with an equal eye. We feel, sir, the force, and acknowledge the justness of the observation, that the foundation of our National policy should be laid in private morality. If individuals be not influenced by moral principles, it is in vain to look for public virtue: it is, therefore, the duty of Legislators to enforce, both by precept and example, the ultility, as well as the necessity, of a strict adherence to the rules of distributive justice. We beg you to be assured that the Senate will, at all times, cheerfully coöperate in every measure which may strengthen the Union, conduce to the happiness, or secure and perpetuate the liberties of this great confederated Republic.

We commend you, sir, to the protection of Almighty God, earnestly beseeching Him long to preserve a life so valuable and dear to the people of the United States; and that your administration may be prosperous to the nation and glorious to yourself.

Read and accepted; and ordered that the Vice President should affix his signature to the address, in behalf of the Senate.

As to the Subject of Titles.

May 8. Senate formed. Mr. Ellsworth moved for the report of the joint committee on the subject of *Titles* to be taken up; and it was accordingly done. Mr. Lee led the business. He took his old ground—all the world, civilized and savage, called for titles. There must be something in human nature that occasioned this general consent; therefore he conceived it was right. Here he began to enumerate many nations who gave titles—such as Venice, Genoa, &c. The Greeks and Romans, it was said, had no titles; but, making a profound bow to the Chair, you were pleased to set us right in this, with respect to the Conscript Fathers, the other day. Here he repeated the President's speech, of the 23d ultimo, all over, almost verbatim.

Mr. Ellsworth rose. He had a paper in his hat, which he looked constantly at. He repeated almost all that Mr. Lee had said, but got on the subject of *Kings*—declared that the sentence, in the primer, of "*fear God and honor the King*," was of great importance—that kings were of divine appointment. Saul, the head and shoulders taller than the rest of the people, was elected by God and anointed by His appointment.

I sat after he had done for a considerable time to see if anybody would rise. At last I got up, and first answered Lee, as well as I could, with nearly the same arguments, drawn from the Constitution, as I had used on the 23d ultimo. I mentioned that within the space of the last twenty years, more light had been thrown on the subject of government, and on human affairs in general, than for several generations before. This light of knowledge had diminished the veneration for titles; and that mankind now considered themselves as little bound to imitate the follies of civilized nations as the brutalities of savages. The abuse of power and the fear of bloody masters had extorted titles, as well as adoration, in some instances, from the trembling crowd. The impresson now on the minds of the citizens of these States, was that of horror for kingly authority.

Izard got up. He dwelt almost entirely on the antiquity of *kingly* government. He could not, however, well get further back than Philip of Macedon. He seemed to have forgotten both Homer and the Bible. He urged for something equivalent to nobility having been common among the Romans; for they had three names that seemed to answer to *Honorable*, or something like it before and something like it behind. He did not say *Esquire*.

Mr. Carroll rose, and took my side of the question. He followed nearly the track I had been in, and dwelt much on the information that was now abroad in the world. He spoke against *Kings*.

Mr. Lee and Mr. Izard were both up again. Langdon was up several times, but spoke short each time. Patterson was up, but there was no knowing which he was of. Lee considered him against him, and answered him; but Patterson finally voted with Lee. Ellsworth was enumerating how *common* the appellation of *President* was. The President put him in mind that there were presidents of fire companies and of a cricket club. Mr. Lee, at another time, was saying he believed that some of the States authorized titles by their constitution. The President, from the chair, told him that Connecticut did it. At sundry other times, he interfered in a like manner. I had been frequently up, to answer new points, during the debate. I collected myself for a last effort.

I read the clause in the Constitution against titles of nobility— showed that the spirit of it was against not only granting titles by *Congress*, but against the permission of foreign potentates granting any titles whatever. As to *kingly* government, it was equally out of the question, as a republican government was guaranteed to every State in the Union; that they were both equally the forbidden fruit of the Constitution. I called the attention of the House to the consequences that were likely to follow. Gentlemen seemed to court a rupture with the other House. The Representatives had adopted the report, and were this day acting on it, or, according to the spirit of the report. We were proposing a title. Our conduct would mark us to the world as actuated with the spirit of dissention, and the characters of the Houses would be as aristocratic and democratical. The report was, however, *rejected*.

Excellency was moved for as a title by Mr. Izard. It was withdrawn by Mr. Izard, and *highness*, with some prefatory word, proposed by Mr. Lee. Now long harrangues were made in favor of this title. Elective was placed before. It was insisted that such a dignified title would add greatly to the weight and authority of the Government, both at home and abroad. I declared myself totally of a different opinion. That at present it was impossible to add to the respect entertained for General Washington. If you gave him the title of any foreign prince or potentate a belief would follow that the manners of that prince and his modes of government would be adopted by the President. (Mr. Lee had just before I got up read over a list of the titles of all the princes and potentates of the earth, marking where the word highness occurred. The grand Turk had it. All the princes of Germany had it. The sons and daughters of crowned heads, &c.) That particularly elective highness which, sounded nearly like *electoral* highness, would have a most ungrateful sound to many thousands of industrious citizens who had fled from German oppression. Highness was part of the title of a prince or princes of the blood, and was often given to *dukes*. It was degrading our President to place him on a par with any prince of any blood in Europe; nor was there one of them that could enter the lists of true glory with him. But I will minute no more. The debate lasted till half after three o'clock, and it ended in appointing a committee to consider of a title to be given to the President.

This whole silly business is the work of Mr. Adams and Mr. Lee. Izard follows Lee, and the New England men, who always herd together, follow Mr. Adams. Mr. Thompson says this used to be the case in the old Congress. *I* had, to be sure, the greatest share in this debate, and must now have completely *sold* (no, *sold* is a bad word, for I have got nothing for it) every particle of Court favor, for a *Court* our House seems determined on, and to run into all the fooleries, fopperies, and pomp of Royal etiquette.

May 9. Attended the Hall, at ten o'clock, to go on the Judicial Committee. Met many of the members. I know not the motive; but I never was received with more familiarity, nor quite as much, before, by the members. Ellsworth, in particular, seemed to show a kind of fondness. The Judicial Committee did no business. Senate formed—it took a long time to correct the minutes. At length the committee came in and reported a title—*His Highness, the President of the United States of America and Protector of the Rights of the Same.*

Mr. Few had spoke a word or two with me, and signified his unwillingness to do anything hastily. He got up and spoke a great deal against hasty measures. He did not pointedly move for postponement, but it amounted nearly to it. The clerk of the other House, in the meantime, appeared at the bar, and announced the adoption of the report of the joint committee, (rejecting titles.)

I got up and expressed my opinion that what had fallen from the honorable gentleman from Georgia amounted to a motion for a postponement, and asked leave to second him. I then pointed out the rupture that was likely to ensue with the other House—that this was matter of very serious import; and I thought it our indispensible duty to avoid any inconvenience of that kind—that by the arrangement between the Houses, in case of disagreement, a conference might be requested—that my intention was, if a postponement was carried, to move, immediately, for a committee of conference to be appointed, on the difference between the two Houses; and I had hopes that, by these means, all subject of debate would be done away.

Mr. Reed got up and moved that the report might be adopted. He was not seconded; but the motion was in itself idle. *Mr. Strong* spoke in favor of the postponement, and was interrupted from the Chair. Mr. Dalton, after some time, spoke in favor of it. I could now see a visible anxiety in the Chair. I had a fine, slack, and easy time of it to-day. Friends seemed to rise in succession. Lee went over his old ground twice, but owned, at last, there was great difficulty every way; but said, plainly, the best mode was for the House (Senate) to adopt the report, and then the other House would follow. He found, however, the current begin to turn against him, and he laid his head on his hand, as if he would have slept. Mr. Strong was up again. He said, among other things, that he thought the other House would follow; but there was a risk in it.

Mr. Izard got up at last. He, too, was for a *postponement.* I could see that the President kindled at him. Mr. Izard said we *knew* the other House had adopted the report. The President interrupted him, and said *no*, we had no right to know it, nor could we know it until after the clerk had, this morning, given official information. The members fixed themselves, and the question was called for.

Up now got the President, and for forty minutes did he harangue us from the chair. He began first on the subject of *order*, and found fault with everything almost; but down he came to particulars, and pointedly blamed a member for disorderly behavior. The member had mentioned the appearance of a captious disposition in the other House. This was disorderly, and spoke with asperity. The member meant was Mr. Izard. All this was only prefatory. On he got on his favorite topic of titles, and over the old ground of the immense advantage, of the absolute necessity of them.

When he had exhausted this subject, he turned a new leaf. I believe, on a conviction, that the postponement would be carried, and perhaps the business lost, by an attention to the other House.

Gentlemen, I must tell you that it is *you* and the *President* that have the making of titles. Suppose the President to have the appointment of Mr. Jefferson at the Court of France. Mr. Jefferson is, in virtue of that appointment, the most illustrious, the most powerful, and what not. But the President himself must be something that includes all the dignities of the diplomatic corps, and something greater still. What will the common people of foreign countries—what will the sailors and soldiers say, George Washington, President of the United States, they will despise him. This is all nonsense to the philosopher; but so is all government, whatever.

The above I recollect with great precision; but he said fifty more things, equally injudicious, which I do not think worth mentioning. It is evident that he begins to despair of getting the article of titles through the House of Representatives, and he has turned his eye to get it done solely by the Senate.

Having experienced relief, by the interference of sundry members, I had determined not to say another word, but his *new leaf* appeared so absurd, I could not help some animadversions on it.

The Constitution of the United States has designated our chief magistrate by the appellation of the President of the United States of America. This is his title of office, nor can we alter, add to, or diminish it, without infringing the Constitution. In like manner, persons authorized to transact business with foreign powers are styled embassadors, public ministers, &c. To give them any other appellation would be an equal infringement. As to grades of orders or titles of nobility, nothing of this kind can be established by Congress.

Can then the President and Senate do that which is prohibited to the United States at large? Certainly not. Let us read the Constitution: " No title of nobility shall be granted by the United States." The Constitution goes further. The servants of the public are prohibited from accepting them from any foreign State, king, or prince. So that the appellations and terms given to nobility in the Old World, are contraband language in the United States; nor can we apply them to our citizens, consistent with the constitution.

As to what the common people, soldiers, and sailors of foreign countries may think of us, I do not think it imports us much. Perhaps the less they think, or have occasion to think of us, the better.

But suppose this a desirable point, how is it to be gained?
The English excepted, foreigners do not understand our language. We must use Hohen Mogende to a Dutchman; be . . . . . . to a Turk or Algerine; and so of the rest. From the *English*, indeed, we may borrow terms that would not be wholly unintelligible to our own citizens. But will they thank us for the compliment? Would not the plagiarism be more likely to be attended with contempt than respect among all of them. It has been admitted that all this is nonsense to the philosopher. I am ready to admit that every high-sounding, pompous appellation, descriptive of qualities which the object does not possess, must appear bombastic nonsense in the eye of every wise man. But I cannot admit such an idea with respect to government itself. Philosophers have admitted not only the utility but the necessity of it. Their labors have been directed to correct the views and expose the follies which have been

engrafted upon it, and to reduce the practice of it to the principles of common sense, such as we see exemplified by the merchant, the mechanic, and the farmer, whose every act or opinion tends to a productive or beneficial effect, and above all, to illustrate this fact, that Government was instituted for the benefit of the people, and that no act of Government is justifiable that has not this for its object. Such has been the labor of the philosophers with respect to Government, and sorry, indeed, would I be if their labors should be in vain.

After all this, he had to put the question, and the postponement was carried. I kept my word, and offered the resolution for a conference, &c. It was carried, and the committee appointed.

Ellsworth drew up a new resolution. It was to keep the difference out of sight, and to proceed, *de novo*, on a title for the President.

I did not care to enter into debate, but expressed my fear that the House of Representatives would be invited, and would not meet us on that ground. As if they meant to provoke the other House, they insisted that the minute of rejection should go down with the appointment of the committee. Little good can come of it thus circumstanced, more especially as the old committee were reappointed.

From the Senate Journal, it appears that Mr. Lee, Mr. Ellsworth, and Mr. Johnson were the committee, and the instruction to the committee was as follows: " That they consider and report under what title it will be proper for the President of the United States in future to be addressed; and confer thereon with such committee as the House of Representatives may appoint for that purpose." It is further stated that the Secretary carried to the House of Representatives the " rejection of the report of the committee appointed to consider what style, &c., it will be proper to annex to the offices of President and Vice President; and the appointment of a committee on the part of the Senate to confer on a title under which it will be proper to address the President of the United States."

The committee of conference on the part of *the House* were Mr. Madison, Mr. Trumbull, Mr. Page, Mr. Benson, and Mr. Sherman.

In his memorandum of May 10, Mr. Maclay complains of the delay of the impost bill, to the great loss of the revenue.

The President at the Theater.

I received a ticket from the President United States, to use his box this evening at the theater, being the first of his appearance at the play-house since his entering on his office. Went. The President, Governor of the State, Foreign Ministers, Senators from New Hampshire, Connecticut, Pennsylvania, Maryland, and South Carolina, and some ladies in the same box. I am old, and notices or attentions are lost on me. I could have wished some of my dear children in my place. They are young, and would have enjoyed it. Long might one of them live to boast of their having been seated in the same box with the first character in the world. The play was The School for Scandal. I never liked it. Indeed, I think it an indecent representation before ladies of character and virtue. Farce, The Old Soldier. The house greatly crowded, and I thought the players acted well; but I wish we had seen the Conscious Lovers, or some one that inculcated more prudential manners.

12th May. Went early this morning to wait on Mr. Fitzsimmons. Was informed that Mr. Morris had called to see him this morning. Took no notice of this, but went in quest of Mr. Morris. Found him at the door, where he kept his office. Took a long walk with him, and gave him a detail of all that had happened in the Senate since he left it, as exactly as I could. He seemed to listen to me in a friendly way. Came to the House at eleven, Senate met, but there really was nothing happened worth mentioning. The business of considering the title which was laid on the table was postponed, to see what would be the result of the conference of the joint committee on that business. Adjourned.

Went to hear the debates of the House of Representatives from the gallery. From there, went with Mr. Morris to the President's levee. Stayed until the company began to withdraw. Felt, I believe, a little awkward, for my knee pained me, and the business of standing was not very agreeable to me. Left Mr. Morris at the levee, came home. Stayed till four o'clock, and went and dined with the Speaker.

This day the President gave us no set speech from the chair; but I know not whether it was want of memory or design, but a motion made by me and seconded by Lee was passed by by him, and a second motion put. He, however, seemed confused. The speech which he made yesterday was on the subject of our having a sergeant-at-arms. He seemed to wish that the officer should be *Usher of the Black Rod.* He described this office as appurtenant to the House of Lords, and concluded by telling us that Sir Francis Mollineaux was the officer, and *that he had the honor of being introduced by him to the House of Lords.*

My business with Mr. Fitzsimmons this morning was to inform him how much I feared the cabal of the New England members in the Senate, and that if they were not gratified in some measure, as to their favorite article of molasses, they would join with every member who objected to any single article, and promise him gratification in his particular humor, if he would join them. By these means, all the discontents being invited and indulgence given, even to caprice and whim, the bill would be lost. He laughed at my fears. The molasses affair was to be called up again. I asked him if he was sure of a majority in the House for continuing the duty at *six* cents. Very confident of it, yet he was mistaken, and it was reduced to five.

I felt great joy on the coming of Mr. Morris to town; for now I shall have one in whom I can confide.

May 13. Paid some visits this morning. Senate met. The title lay on the table. Mr. Lee informed the House that the committee on that business had met, but being in the Senate chamber, were dispersed on the meeting of the Senate, and had agreed to meet tomorrow morning.

Report for classing the Senate permitted to lie on the table. Moved and a committee appointed to confer on the subject of newspapers. A committee of nine appointed for the penal federal laws. I can observe a total change of behavior, or at least a considerable one, in our President. Instead of directing two Senators to read the ballots for committee men, as he did heretofore, he this day read them aloud from the chair, and the clerk tallied. This is the first step towards reformation, and I hope it will be *progressive.*

May 14. Senate met. The President reminded us of the title report. The committee were out on that business. The classing report adopted. A motion of yesterday was on the table for the regulating joint committees. Ellsworth, according to his custom, drew another one. Mr. Langdon withdrew his in complaisance to Ellsworth. Lee moved to strike out the latter part of Ellsworth's. Ellsworth, in complaisance to Lee, seconded him. This spoiled the motion; and all complaisance being at an end, the rest was rejected by the House. It was here the President made us his speech for the day. He said parliamentary customs, when found convenient, should be followed as good examples; (this is the first time ever I heard him guard his parliamentary lessons, but I observed yesterday that there was a change;) that conferences were very seldom used by the Houses in Great Britain; that little benefit was obtained from them; they could be but of little use only in case of difference of opinion with respect to bills.

The whole seemed to aim at lessening the intercourse between the two Houses. I could not help thinking of his speech of the 9th instant. It seemed the second part of it.

May 14. Now rose Mr. Lee to report on *Titles*, from the joint committee. He reported that the committee from the other House had adhered in the strictest manner to their former resolution. He moved that the report, which had been laid on the table, in favor of titles, should be entered on the files of the House; and that a motion which he had in his hand should be adopted. The spirit of the motion was, that to keep up a proper respect for our chief magistrate, attention should be paid to the customs of civilized nations. That the appearance of the affectation of simplicity would be injurious—that the Senate had decided in favor of titles from these motives; but that, in conformity to the practice of the other House, *for the present* they resolve to address the President *without* title.

It is stated, on the Senate Journal, that the committee of conference reported their inability to agree with the committee of the House, and, also, that the committee appointed on the 9th instant, to consider and report under what title it will be proper for the Senate to address the President of the United States of America, reported that, in the opinion of the committee, it will be proper to address the President : " His Highness, the President of the United States of America, and Protector of their Liberties." Which report was *postponed ;* and the following resolve was agreed to, to wit :

From a decent respect for the opinion and practice of civilized nations, whether under monarchical or republican forms of government, whose custom is to annex titles of respectability to the office of their chief magistrate; and that, on intercourse with foreign nations, a due respect for the majesty of the people of the United States may not be hazarded by an appearance of singularity, the Senate have been induced to be of opinion that it would be proper to annex a respectable title to the office of President of the United States ; but the Senate, desirous of preserving harmony with the House of Representatives, where the practice lately observed in presenting an address to the President was without the addition of titles, think it proper, for the present, to act in conformity with the practice of that House ; therefore,

Resolved, That the present address be, " To the President of the United States," without addition of title. (See antea, end Preface.)

A motion was made to strike out the preamble as far as the words " but the Senate ;" which passed in the negative ;

And, on motion for the main question, it passed in the affirmative.

Yesterday Mr. Muhlenberg accosted me with " your Highness of the Senate." On my pausing, he said Wynkoop had been christened by them his Highness of the Lower House, and he thought I was entitled to the same distinction in the Senate.

The journal proceeds, (and this appears to refer to the proceedings in the Senate,) As we had the business all over again, I determined to try what ridicule could do. If all men were of our stature, there would be neither high nor low. *Highness*, when applied to individuals, must naturally denote the excess of stature which he possesses over other men. An honorable member told us, the other day, of a certain king who was the head and shoulders taller than anybody else. This, more especially when he was greased with a great horn of oil, must render him *highly* conspicuous. History, too, if I mistake not, will furnish us with an example where a great Thracian obtained the empire of the world from no other circumstance. But if this antiquated principle is to be adopted, give us fair play. Let *America* be searched, and it is most probable that the honor will be found to belong to some huge *Patagonian*. This, indeed, is putting one sadly over the head of another. True, but *Nature* has done it, and men should see where she leads before they adopt her as a guide.

It may be said that this business is metaphorical, and the high station of the President entitled him to it. Nothing can be true metaphorically which is not so naturally, and under this view of the proposed title, it belongs with more propriety to the *Man in the Moon*, than anybody else, as his station (when we have the honor of seeing him) is certainly the most exalted of any that we know of.

Gentlemen may say this is fanciful. Would they wish to see the subject in the most serious point of view that it is possible to place it. Rome, after being benighted for ages in the darkest gloom of ecclesiastic and aristocratic tyrrany, beheld a reformer, in the fourteenth century, who, preaching from stocks and stones, and the busts and fragments of ancient heroes, lighted up the lamp of liberty to meridian splendor. Intoxicated with success, he assumed a string of titles, none of which, in my recollection, was equally absurd with the one before you. In consequence of which, and of his aping some other symbols of nobility and royalty, he fell, and pulled down the whole republican structure along with him, marking particularly the subject of titles as one of the principal rocks on which he was shipwrecked.

As to the latter part of the title, I would only observe that the power of war is the organ of protection. This is placed in Congress by the Constitution. Any attempt to divest them of it and place it elsewhere, even with General Washington, is *treason* against the United States, or, at least, a violation of the Constitution.

In order to get out of the kind of puzzle which Lee had engaged us in, we moved a general postponement of the report on the title, hoping this would cut up the whole matter by the roots. It was carried. And even after this, Lee hung with obstinacy to the idea of putting it on the files of thé House.

" Through the whole of this business, I have endeavored to mark the conduct of General Washington. I have no clue that will lead me fairly to any just conclusion as to his sentiments. I think it scarce possible but he must have dropped something on a subject which has excited so much warmth. If he did, it was not on our side, or I would have heard it. But no matter, I have by plowing with the heifer of the other House completely defeated them."

Mr. Carroll rose and opposed the imperfect resolution being put on the files by the order of the House. I seconded him in opposing this, as putting such a thing on the files by special order of the House was giving it an authority which no postponed paper should have, and carried the air of an adoption. Papers were never specially ordered on the files but with a view of perpetuating information. A special order for putting on the files would hereafter be considered as an adoption, this part of this motion being lost by a general postponement of the report.

The journal of Mr. Maclay proceeds·

" Mr. Morris rose after the question had been carried, and expressed his dislike of the title, viz : *Highness and protector of the rights of America.* He said the protection lay with the whole Congress. He was right in his remarks, but he was told the question was carried."

" Mr. Carroll expressed great dislike at the forepart of the motion, which stated the acts of the Senate to be in favor of titles, when, in fact, no such resolution ever had passed the Senate."

" I rose and moved a division of the motion. Was immediately seconded by Mr. Carroll."

" Now a long debate ensued. Mr. Ellsworth traversed the whole field of titles over again. Doctor Johnson spoke much more to the point. Mr. Patterson, after reading over the motion, was of opinion that a division should take place at the word *Senate.* I was also, with Mr. Morris, of opinion that the division would stand best at this place. I withdrew my motion, and seconded his for the division from the word Senate. The division was full enough to answer all the purposes which they avowed, taking it at this place. But it is evident they have not given up the idea of titles, and seem insultingly to say so to the House of Representatives. Affectation of simplicity is directly charged on the other House. This they amended by putting in the word *appearance.* I endeavored to draw my principal argument, when last up, from the unfairness of the forepart. It expressly recited a determination of the Senate to grant titles. No such resolution had ever passed. It might be implied that the Senate were in favor of titles, but why refer to a resolution that did not exist. *Accommodation* was the principle held out. But was ever thing done with so ill a grace? It was saying we meet you on the principles of accommodation, but you are completely wrong, and we are perfectly right. Can any good come of such accommodation? Mr. Carroll declared that the idea held forth was that the Senate were for titles, but it was well known they were not all for titles. He was opposed, and so were sundry other gentlemen. He wished only for a fair question, that it might be seen who were for them, and who were not. He wished the yeas and nays, and let the world judge.

Mr. Few declared the gentleman had missed the opportunity of the yeas and nays. They should have been called when the report against titles was rejected. Mr. Few was much out in this; for there were but *three* of us, and he need not have made his remarks. It was evident that they wished to prevent the yeas and nays. The question was put. The House divided. Eight with us. Ten against us. *Mr. Caroll* called for the yeas and nays. None rose with him but Mr. Henry and myself, and for want of another man, we lost them.

The committee was now ordered to wait on *the President* to know the time when he will be pleased to receive the address of the Senate.

The report of the joint committee on the enrollment of papers was read, and the House adjourned. And now I hope we have disposed of a business (viz: relating to titles,) which in one shape or other has engaged almost the whole time of the Senate from the 23d of April, the day that our President began it. Had it not been for Mr. Lee, I am firmly convinced no other man would have ventured to have followed our President. But Lee led, Ellsworth seconded him, the New England men followed, and Izard joined them; but really *haud equis possibus,* for he was only for the title of *Excellency,* which had been sanctified by use. Lee has a cultivated understanding, great practice in public business, with a factious, restless disposition. He has acted as high priest through the whole of this idolatrous business. It is easy to see what his aim is.

By following the President of the Senate, he hopes to govern all the members from New England, and with a little assistance from Carolina or Georgia, to be absolute in the Senate. Ellsworth, and some more of the New England men, flatter him in turn, expecting he will be with them on the subject of *residence.* Had it not been for our President and Lee, I am convinced the Senate would have been as averse to titles as the House of Representatives. The game that our President and Mr. Lee appear to have now in view is to separate the Senate as much as possible from the House of Representatives. Our President's doctrine is that all honors and titles should flow from the President and Senate only. But once more, subject of titles, farewell! May I never hear motion or debate on thee more! Mem. The fall of Rienzi, the Roman reformer, who split on the rock of titles, was completely in point.

In connection with this subject, I give the following extract from a letter dated 16th May, 1789, addressed by William Maclay to Tench Coxe, of Philadelphia :

You will readily gather from the public papers that there has been some difference of sentiment between the Houses on the subject of *titles.* This business, after having agitated us for near three weeks, is, I expect, blown over. I sincerely hope it never will again be blown up so as to kindle the fire of contention. The minority in this business was so small as to be unable to obtain the yeas and nays in our House, except on one question, when the greater part declined calling them ; and yet they were firm to the last, and with the assistance derived from the countenance and determinations of the other House, have really obtained a temporary victory. They had some other difficulties to contend with, which at present shall be nameless. Mr. Morris was absent during this troublesome business.

The impost bill will be with us on Monday next. It is limited to seven years, and a variety of opinions are held on this point. I will be happy to have yours on this or any other subject.

May 15. Senate met. On the reading of the minutes, Mr. Few got up and moved warmly that the minute of yesterday on the division of Mr. Lee's motion should be struck out. Lee was for it in a moment. By these means, the vote of yesterday, which respected titles, would have the appearance of unanimity. It was opposed by Mr. Carroll, Ellsworth, and myself. The minute, however, remained.

The committee reported that the President of the (United) States would receive our address a quarter after twelve, on Monday. It was said we should go in carriages.

The classing report was called for; the ballots were drawn. I fell in the first class with Mr. Dalton, Mr. Ellsworth, Mr. Elmer, Mr. Carroll, and Mr. Grayson.

The President now informed the Senate that a letter had come to his hand, which he supposed was intended for him; but it was most improperly directed. It was directed to his Excellency the Vice President. He asked the opinion of the Senate laughingly, and concluded it was against all rule.

I said that until we had a rule obliging people to be regular, we must submit to their irregularities, more especially of this kind.

Mr. Morris said the majesty of the people would do as they pleased.

All this I considered *sportive*. But he put a serious question, should the letter, so directed, be read. Langdon and sundry others said yes; and read it was. From Loudon, the printer, offering to print for us. Adjourned.

May 16. A message came from the House of Representatives. It was on the affair of a joint committee on newspapers and employing printers. Sundry petitions had come in from different printers. One was just now read from one Fenno I moved that Fenno's, and all petitions of a similar nature, should be referred, for information, to the committee on newspapers and employing printers. It was seconded. Ellsworth rose in great warmth, and opposed it violently. Some more of the New England men joined him. It really seemed to me as if he wished to try whether he could not carry anything. He was, however, disappointed. A report of a committee for revising the minutes was read. The petition of one Duncan Campbell was read, and occasioned sundry remarks. Laid on the table.

The address (to the President) was now produced, engrossed. The word *To* disobliged Ellsworth, and a long debate ensued about it. I did not touch this trite subject. But it was to be signed; and here a mighty difficulty was signified from the chair, and the wisdom of the House called on to determine if the chair had done right. Every act had been signed J. A., *Vice President.* The President gave this information in such a way as left nobody in doubt that his opinion went with the practice. Mr. Carroll got up, and said he thought it a matter of indifference, and concluded that he agreed it should be signed *Vice President.* His looks, thought, betrayed dissent. But the goddess of good nature apologize for this slight aberration from sentimental rectitude. He has, for some time past, been equally, with myself, opposed to the opinions of the Chair, and this was his peace offering. Two weeks ago, I was with Mr. Reed, of the Delaware State, in the upper gallery of the House of Representatives. A message came from the Senate. The signature was read aloud, John Adams, Vice President. Mr. Reed turned to me, and said " that is wrong." Yet Mr. Reed now made a very long speech, declaring there was no impropriety in it. Mr. Lee hinted, very diffidently, his disapprobation of it. Mr. Morris said our acts should be signed by our own President. Mr. Ellsworth showed some inconvenience that would attend this practice.

I rose. Said the very term Vice President carried on the face of it the idea of holding the place of the President in his absence. That every act done by the Vice President, as such, implied that when so acting he held the place of President. In this point of view, nothing could be more improper than the Vice President signing an address to the President. It was like a man signing an address to himself. The business of the Vice President was when he acted exactly the same with that of President, and could not mix itself with us as a Senate.

Here the President tried very hard to raise a laugh. Seeing him willing to bear me down, I continued : Sir, we know you not as *Vice President* within this House. As *President of the Senate* only do we know you. As President of the Senate only can you sign or authenticate any act of this body.

He said, after I sat down, that he believed he need not put the question, a majority of those who had spoken seemed to be in favor of his signing as President of the Senate. Mr. Carroll said he need not put the question, and none was put. Adjourned.

Sunday, 17th May. Stayed at home this day. Wrote letters to sundry persons. Did not go out until four o'clock, when I thought it warm enough. Called at the lodgings of Mr. Fitzsimmons and Clymer. They had gone to Brunswick. Walked to the Speaker's. We walked to Cuyler's Hook. The east wind blew raw and cold. I left them, and came home. Found myself rather indisposed. Caught some cold in my walk, and was the worse for it. I never have been in a place remarkable for such variable weather. Set out when one will with ever such agreeable sunshine, I never have been able to go two miles and return without a change of air. The wind which crosses the North river is cold. But there is a rawness in the east wind that, with me, seems to clog the springs of life. Mr. Scott, however, from Washington county, has experienced a favorabie revolution in his health since he came here.

Address to the President.

Monday 18th. Senate met. The address (to the President) was read over, and we proceeded in carriages to the President's to present it. Having no part to act but that of a mute, I had nothing to embarrass me. We were received in an ante-chamber. Had some little difficulty about seats, as there were several wanting; from whence may be inferred that the President's *major domo* is not the most provident, as our numbers were well enough known. We had not been seated more than three minutes, when it was signified to us to wait on the President in his levee room. Our President went foremost, and the Senators followed, without any particular order. We made our bows as we entered; and our President. having made a bow, began to read an address. He was much confused. The paper trembled in his hand, though he had the aid of both by resting it on his hat, which he held in his left hand. He read very badly all that was on the front pages. The turning of the page seemed to restore him, and he read the rest with more propriety. This agitation was the more remarkable as there were but twenty-two persons present, and none of them strangers.

The President took his reply out of his pocket. He had his spectacles in his jacket pocket; having his hat in his left hand and the paper in his right. He had too many objects for his hands. He shifted his hat between his forearm and the left side of his breast. But taking his spectacles from the case embarrassed him. He got rid of this small distress by laying the spectacle case on the chimney-piece. Colonel Humphreys stood on his right, Mr. Lear on his left. Having adjusted his spectacles, which was not very easy, considering the engagements on his hands, he read the reply with tolerable exactness, and without much emotion.

I thought he should have received us with his spectacles on, which would have saved the making of some uncouth motions. Yet, on the whole, he did nearly as well as anybody else could have done the same motions. Could the laws of etiquette have permitted him to have been disencumbered of his hat, it would have relieved him much.

After having read his reply, he delivered the paper to our President, with an easy inclination, bowed round to the company, and desired them to be seated. This politeness seems founded in reason, for men, after standing quite still some time, want to sit, if it were for only a minute or two. Our President did not comply, nor did he refuse, but stood so long that the President repeated the request. He declined it by a low bow, and retired. We made our bows, came out to the door, and waited till our carriages took us up. Colonel Humphreys waited on us to the door. Returned.

Senate formed. The address and reply were ordered on the minutes. The reply was as follows :

GENTLEMEN : I thank you for your address, in which the most affectionate sentiments are expressed in the most obliging terms. The coincidence of circumstances which led to this auspicious crisis, the confidence reposed in me by my fellow-citizens, and the assistance I may expect from councils which will be dictated by an enlarged and liberal policy, seem to presage a more prosperous issue to my administration than a diffidence of my abilities had taught me to anticipate. I now feel myself inexpressibly happy in a belief that Heaven, which has done so much for our infant nation, will not withdraw its providential influence before our political felicity shall have been completed ; and in a conviction that the Senate will at all times coöperate in every measure which may tend to promote the welfare of this confederated Republic. Thus supported by a firm trust on the Great Arbiter of the universe, aided by the collective wisdom of the Union, and imploring the divine benediction on our joint exertions in the service of our country, I readily engage with you in the arduous but pleasing task of attempting to make a nation happy.

G. WASHINGTON.

The Clerk of the House brought up the *impost* bill. Thursday was assigned for it. Some petitions were read, and the House adjourned.

May 19. Senate met at eleven. A report was taken up regulating the mode of keeping the journals, and directing them to be published monthly. Agreed to, and the committee appointed to prepare them for the press. Adjourned. Had agreed with sundry of our Pennsylvania friends to go to the levee. General Muhlenberg came to me, and told me they would meet me in the committee-room. We did so, and we went to the levee. I went foremost, and left them to follow, and do as well as they could. Indeed, they had no great thing of a pattern, for I am but a poor courtier. The company was large for the room. The foreign Ministers were there. Van Berkel, the Dutch Minister, (for the first time, I suppose,) gaudy as a peacock. Our Pennsylvanians withdrew before me. The President honored me with a particular *tête-a-tête*. How will this weather suit your farming ? Poorly, sir; the season is the most backward I have ever known. It is remarkably so here, but, by letters from Pennsylvania, vegetation is slow in proportion there. The fruit, it is to be expected, will be safe, and backward seasons are in favor of it; but in Virginia it was lost before I left that place. . . . Much depends on the exposure of the orchard. Those with a northern aspect have been found by us to be the most certain in producing fruit. . . . Yes; that is a good observation, and should be attended to. Made my bow, and retired.

May 20. I attended at the Hall about half after ten o'clock. The committee did not meet me. Senate met, but there was no business done. Adjourned, that the committees might go to work. I thought I got cold yesterday in the House of Representatives, and set off to come home. Colonel Few overtook me, and we took a long walk to view the garden of a Dutchman, who lives beyond the Bowery. Spent some time, with a degree of satisfaction, viewing his harmless and silent little beauties of the garden. On the road, Mr. Few threw out many generous sentiments on the subject of the temporary residence. The general belief is, however, that he is favorable to this place.

May 21. Went about half after nine to Mr. Morris' lodging. He was out, but expected in. Stayed until ten, and then went to the Hall and stayed till the Senate met. Our President is progressive in reformation. He used to keep us until half after eleven, or a quarter, at least. He was here this day at eight or ten minutes before eleven, and, strange to tell, *he was without a sword.*

The *impost* bill, being the order of the day, was taken up, and postponed until Monday. A resolution was handed to the Chair by Ellsworth. It was for the Senate forming something like a committee of the whole. However, it seemed to amount to nothing more than a suspension of our rules for the time mentioned or alluded to in it. Adjourned. I returned home to write letters.

An idea has gone abroad that the mercantile interest has been exerted to delay this bill. The merchants have undoubtedly regulated the prices of their goods agreeable to the proposed duties, so that the consumers of dutied articles really now pay the whole of the impost; and whatever the proposed duties exceed the State duties now paid is clear gain to the merchant. Some of them, indeed, dispute the payment of *the State impost.*

Note.—The resolution adopted on this day appears from the journal to have been:

Resolved, That all bills on a second reading shall be considered by the Senate in the same manner as if the Senate were in a committee of the whole, before they shall be taken up and proceeded on by the Senate, agreeably to the standing rules, unless otherwise ordered.

On this day, William Grayson, from Virginia, appeared and took his seat. He was added to the committee appointed on the 13th May, to define the crimes and offenses that shall be cognizable under the authority of the United States, and their punishment.

The interim collection bill is rejected in the lower House; and the reason given is the most loose I ever heard assigned, viz: It was said a better one was forming. Surely this was no parliamentary reason. Had any new bill been offered to the House—had any been in the hands of a committee, the reason would have justified the measure; but because it is said Mr. Williams, of Baltimore, is making one, of his own motion, and without any order of the House, it is not so proper. Perhaps it may turn out best.

May 22. Attended at the Hall at ten o'clock, and waited a whole hour for the committee for arranging the rooms. They did not meet. The Senate met. Soon after, the clerk of the lower House attended with the bill for taking the *oaths*, which was presented to the Chair.

The President rose and addressed the House:

I have, since the other day when the matter of my signing was talked of in the Senate, examined the Constitution. I am placed here by the people. To part with the style given me is a dereliction of my right. It is being false to my trust. *Vice President* is my title, and it is a point I will insist upon.

He said several other things; then paused and looked over the bill. He then addressed the Senate again, and, with great positiveness, told them that he would sign it as Vice President of the United States and President of the Senate.

He asked Mr. Lee if it had been compared, and handed it to Mr. Lee. I cannot say whether he signed it before he spoke to Mr. Lee or after; but it was not read, nor was any question whatever put upon it—whether it should be read, whether it should be signed, or any other motion whatever.

Mr. Ellsworth got up and declared himself satisfied with that way of signing it. Mr. Strong got up and thought it should be Vice President alone. This is certainly a most egregious insult to any deliberative body; but as Patterson told me a day or two after the *gracious affair*, that if I had not opposed that measure somebody else would, I determined to see who would oppose this—and all was sile e. Adjourned till Monday, at eleven o'clock.

Called on Mr. Morris this afternoon. Told him that murmurs were abroad against the conduct of the Congress. That although the duty was not collected for the use of the public, yet, as the rates were in the possession of everybody, the merchants had raised their goods in proportion. That the public was now in the act of paying, and the merchants gainers, for the public treasury got nothing. That commercial influence was blamed for the delay. He replied, " I suppose they blame me." I answered, these things were said before you came to town. I desired him to appoint some time when I could wait on him in order to examine the impost bill, that we might be prepared for any amendment which we would offer. I asked his opinion as to the height of the duties generally. He said he wished to see the bill for collection, and to know under what penalties smuggling would be prohibited. That from them he would form an opinion whether they were too high or not. I replied that they would not be too high with regard to the revenue raised, and I would have the penalties and prohibitions against smuggling as severe as possible; and if, under the circumstances, the depravity and villainy of people would render the impost unproductive, it would, at least, demonstrate the necessity of adopting some other mode of supplying the treasury.

Saturday, 23d. This is a fine day, and all the world are run a gadding. Mr. Dennis called this morning. He says the ship Chesapeake, from Bengal, is unloading at Amboy. The duties on this ship would, by this act, have been about £8,000—some say ten. I am much distressed with the delay of Congress. The reputation of our administration will be ruined. The merchants have already added the amount of the duties to the price of their goods. In this point of view the impost is levied, but not a farthing goes into the treasury of the United States; and all the difference between the State duties levied and the proposed duties, is clear gain to the merchants. In the Jerseys, it is all clear gain, for they have no duties; and vessels are daily crowding there to store their goods until the impost takes place. Delany's estimate of the impost for Pennsylvania for a year was $863,623=323,858:12:6. Half of this taken for the spring importation, is 161,929:6:6; as Pennsylvania is supposed one half of the Union, if we were adopting States, the loss would be 1,2954,34:10; and the devil of it is, that the sum will actually be paid by the consumers. I could not bear my own thoughts on this subject any longer. I considered it my duty to go and rouse our Pennsylvania members. I called on the Speaker and his brother first. They admitted all I said. From there, I went to Mr. Scott. He said it was undeniable. I endeavored to rouse all of them. From there, I went to the lodgings of Fitzsimmons and Ellsworth. Found Mr. Fitzsimmons. Declared my mind with great freedom, and he heard me with more patience than ever I remember. He said he wished he had stuck to this business from the beginning. That he had brought this draft of a bill, which was committed to Gerry, Lawrence, and himself. He left it with Lawrence, being an official man, to correct. That Lawrence kept it three weeks, and did nothing. That then Gerry took it, and kept it two weeks, and put it in the hands of Mr. Williams, of Baltimore, who had kept it until within three or four days. That it came from Williams a most voluminous thing of more than forty pages. That he would now stick to it until it was finished.

The foregoing calculation, founded on Delaney's estimate, is certainly much too high. But if we suppose the port of Philadelphia to receive one fifth only of the importations, and throw one half off for error and accidents, yet still the loss sustained will be near a million and a half of dollars, and the greater part of this sum actually remains as profit to the merchants. Mr. Fitzsimmons has promised that the bill shall be reported on Monday. The Speaker has promised to go among the members, and rouse them all in his power. For my part, think what they will of me, I will not be silent.

Sunday, 24th. I attended Mr. Morris, agreeable to appointment. We did not perfectly agree about the preamble of the bill, but there was no difference of consequence. It was verbal only. We came to the discrimination between nations in treaty and those not. Here we differed. He was totally against it. He used arguments. I made some reply, but each retained his opinion. Mr. Morris said that teas would bear more. He said double, and I agreed to it. I alleged that all seven and a half *ad valorem* articles should be raised at least to ten per cent. Mr. Morris seemed of the same way of thinking. Mr. Morris, however, suddenly exclaimed, " Let us go to Fitzsimmons ; he knows all about it—he has been thinking on the subject. I want to go and take a stroll somewhere." I thought by this, he did not like close thinking. I have been of this opinion before now. He has, however, a strong and vigorous mind, when it does act. To Fitzsimmons we went, and found him very busy at the bill. Mr. Carroll, of House of Representatives, came in. We got on the discrimination. We were all of a different opinion from Mr. Morris. We asked Mr. Fitzsimmons the reason of so many articles being at seven and a half, which we thought should be ten, along with glass and china. He said there really was no reason for it, but the House would not agree to it.

Mr. Morris proposed a jaunt to the Narrows, but no boat could be got. We then walked up the North river to one Brannan's, who has the green-house and garden. Here we dined. Mr. Morris often touched me on the subject of my dislike to the Vice President. We got on the subject of their salaries. Mr. Morris mentioned $20,000 for the President, and $8,000 for the Vice President. I opposed both, but it was in the funny way, all of it. Mr. Morris had alleged that the Vice President must see the foreign ministers, &c., as the

President could not, and the salary was to enable him to do so ; and what obligation is he under to do so. Some of the Presidents of Pennsylvania have had £1,250 to enable them to see strangers. Some have not spent ten pounds per annum in that way. Strolled, after dinner, about the house taken by the Vice President. Sat in the shade. Crossed the fields, and came, at length, to Baron Polnitz. This man we found sensible, and well informed. He has studied agreeableness, and has more   .   in that way than I have seen before. I have heard him spoken rather disrespectfully of. This, however, I suppose flowed from the force of our old habits, derived from the English, who seldom ever speak well of a foreigner. I will see him again. It is said he has moved in the highest stations of life, and seen much. But I intend to hear from him, and perhaps will hear more of him in the meanwhile.

May 25. Went early to the Hall. The Senate met. The impost bill was taken up, and, according to Ellsworth's resolution, we were to act as if in a committee of the whole. *But the President kept the chair*, and I thought it made Mr. Ellsworth look foolish. A message was announced from the President by General Knox. According to the resolution, we were *in committee ;* but the President kept the chair, and the General advanced and laid the papers (being very bulky) on the table. Our President had given us a speech, before the minutes were read, on the subject of receiving a message from the President. His supreme delight seems to be in etiquette.

We sat on the impost bill, and debated long on the style of *the enacting clause.* It was an old field, and the same arguments were used which had formerly been advanced ; but the style of the law, which had already passed, was adopted.

Now came the first duty of twelve cents on spirits of Jamaica proof. We debated until a quarter past three ; and it was reduced to eight. Adjourned.

When I came home in the evening, I told Mr. Wynkoop the business of the day. He said things of this kind made him think whether our style government in Pennsylvania was not best. Certain it is that a government with so many branches affords a large field for caballing ; first in the lower House, and, the moment a party finds a measure lost, or likely to be lost, all engines are set to work, in the upper House. If they are likely to fail here, the last attempt is made with the President ; and as most pains are always taken by bad men to support bad measures, the calculation seems in favor of the exertions and endeavors that are used more than in the justness of the measure.

On the other hand, a fuller field is opened for investigation, but unfortunately, intrigue and cabal takes place of fair inquiry. Here an observation forces itself upon me : That, in general, the further any measure is carried from the people, the less their interests are attended to.

I fear that our impost bill will be rendered in a great measure unproductive. This business is the work of the New England men. They want the article of molasses quite struck out, or, at least, greatly reduced ; therefore, they will strike at everything ; or, to place it in a different point of view, almost every part will be proscribed either by one or other of those who choose to be opponents, for every conspirator must be indulged in the sacrifice of his particular enemy. I called on Mr. Fitzsimmons sometime ago to express my fears on this very head, and I wished him to consent to a reduction of the molasses duty to four cents to avoid a thing of this kind, but I was not attended to. Indeed, I thought he had the best right to know. I felt too much confidence about that time in the return of Mr. Morris.

May 26. Attended the Hall early. Was the first. Mr. Morris came next, the President next. I made an apology to the President for the absence of our Chaplain, Mr. Linn. There had been some conversation yesterday in the Senate, about the style of the Bishop. It had been entered on the minutes *right reverend.* The President revived this discourse, and got at me about titles. I really never had opened my mouth on the affair of yesterday. He, however, addressed to me all he said, concluding, you are against titles. But there are no people in the world so much in favor of titles, as the people of America ; and the government never will be properly administered, until they are adopted in the fullest manner. We think differently, indeed, on the same subject. I am convinced that were we to adopt them in fashion of Europe, we would ruin all. You have told us, sir, that they are idle, in a philosophic point of view. Governments have long been at odds with common sense. I hope the conduct of America will reconcile them. Instead of adding respect to government, I consider that they would bring the personages who assumed them into contempt and ridicule.

Senate met. After some motions as to the business which should be taken up, and the appointment of a committee of conference on the mode of receiving communications from the President, the *impost* was taken up.

There was a discrimination of five cents, in favor of nations having commercial treaties with us, per gallon on Jamaica spirits. Then rose against all discrimination, Mr. Lee, Mr. Dalton, Mr. Izard, Mr. Morris, Mr. Wingate, Mr. Strong. At first, they rather gave opinions than any arguments.   I declared for discrimination.   That if commercial treaties were of any use at all, nations in treaty should stand on better terms than those who had kept at a sulky distance. But if we now treated all alike, we need never, hereafter, propose a commercial treaty.   I asked, if we were not called on by gratitude, to treat with discrimination those nations who had given us a helping hand in the time of distress.   Mr. Carroll rose on the same side with me.

I was, however, answered from all sides.   All commercial treaties were condemned.   It was echoed from all parts of the house that nothing but *interest* governed all nations.   My very words were repeated, and contradicted in the most pointed terms.   I never had delivered anything in the speaking way on which I was so hard run. Strong, who is but a poor speaker, showed ill-nature.   Said nothing like reason or argument had been offered.   It was insisted that this discrimination was showing an inimical disposition to Great Britain ; it was declaring commercial war with her.

I had to reply as well as I could.   I alleged that these arguments were against the whole system of administration under the old Congress, and, in some measure, against the engagements entered into by that body, although these engagements were sanctified by the Constitution ; that Great Britain had nothing to do in this business ; that nations in treaty were on terms of friendship.   Strangers had no right to be offended at acts of kindness between friends. She might be a friend if she pleased, and enjoy these favors.   On the contrary, I thought our *friends* were the people who had a right to be offended if no discrimination took place.

It had been asserted that *interest* solely governed nations.   I was sorry it was so much the case, but I hoped *we* would not in every point be governed by that principle.   The conduct of *France* to us in our distress, I thought was founded, in part, on more generous principles.   Had the principle of *interest* solely governed, she would have taken advantage of our distress, when we were in abject circumstances, and would have imposed hard terms on us, instead of treating on the terms of mutual reciprocity.   She likewise remitted large sums of money.   Was this from the principle of interest only ?   What had been the conduct of the two nations since the peace ?   Civility on the part of the French, and very different treatment by the British.   Our newspapers teemed with these accounts.   (Ellsworth had said, it has been asked if we are not called on by gratitude, &c.   I answered, no.)   The answer no has been given to the calls of gratitude in this business ; but the great voice of the people at large would give a very different answer.   So far as my sphere of knowledge extended, I had a right to say so. But the sense of the people at large expressed by their representatives in the clause before us, holds a different language.

Mr. Langdon spoke, and seemed to be of our opinion. I did not hear a no, however, on the question, but Mr. Carroll's and my own.

All ran smooth now till we came to molasses. Till quarter after three did the New Englanders beat this ground, even to the baiting of the hook that caught the fish that went to buy the molasses. The motion was to reduce it to four cents, from five. I had prepared notes, but there was such an eagerness to speak, and finding that we should carry it, I let them fight it out. The votes for four carried. All the arguments of the other House were repeated over and over.

May 27. Attended Senate. The minutes were read. I was astonished to hear Strong immediately get up and begin a long harrangue on the subject of molasses. One looked at another. Mr. Carroll had taken his seat next to me. Several of the gentlemen murmured. At last Mr. Carroll rose, and asked pardon for interrupting any gentleman ; but said that matter had been determined yesterday. The President said the question had been taken on four cents being put instead of five ; but no question had been taken on the paragraph after it was amended. The whole sentence was on molasses per gallon, four cents. That a second question should be put on it was idle ; but it was plain that the matter had been agreed on between the President and the New England men ; and, in all probability, they had got some people, who voted for *four* yesterday, to promise to vote for less to-day.

Dalton, however, got up, and made a long speech that some of the gentlemen are absent, and particularly the gentlemen who moved for the four cents ; and desired it might be put off until to-morrow.

Now came on wine of Madeira. All the arguments of yesterday were had over again, and it was voted at eighteen cents. When we came to *loaf sugar*, it was postponed. When we came to *cables*, the New England men moved to postpone everything of that kind—Mr. Langdon being absent—until we came to *steel*. I then moved an adjournment, as it was near the time, for I wished Mr. Morris to be here, as I expect a pointed opposition on that business, and as he has got all the information on the most of subjects. I have been as attentive as possible to get information, as far as my sphere of influence extended ; but the private communications of the citizens of Philadelphia have, generally, been by letter to Mr. Morris, Mr. Fitzsimmons, or Mr. Clymer. I regret that they furnish me with none of this information. I must, however, serve my country as well as I can.

The *collection bill* is at last reported. I cannot think but that there has been studied delay in this business. The bill itself is said to be a volume. It is ordered to be printed.

May 28. Having found the opposition to run hard yesterday against the impost, I determined to go this morning among all my Pennsylvania friends, and call on them for any information which they could give me in the way of their private letters, or otherwise. I got an account of all the sugar-houses in Philadelphia from the Speaker. Called on Mr. Morris. Told him the war on molasses was to be waged again. Called on Mr. Clymer and Mr. Fitzsimmons. Got from Mr. Fitzsimmons a list of the Pennsylvania protecting duties. Then went to the Hall. I was here over an hour before any person came. Langdon, Carroll, and the President came. The discourse was general on the subject of government. If our new government does well, (said our President,) I shall be more surprised than ever I was in my life. Mr. Carroll said he hoped well of it—it would be sufficiently powerful. If it is, said he, I know not from whence it is to arise. It cannot have energy. It has neither rewards nor punishments. Mr. Carroll replied the people of America were enlightened. Information and knowledge would be the support of it. Mr. Adams replied information and knowledge were not the sources of obedience. That ignorance was a much better source. Somebody replied that it had formerly been considered as the mother of devotion, but the doctrine of late was considered rather stale.

I began now to think of what Mr. Morris had told me, that it was necessary to make Mr. Adams Vice President, to keep him quiet. He is anti-federal, but one of a very different turn from the general cast. A mark may be missed as well above as below.

Senate met. Cables, cordage, &c., came up. They stood at seventy-five. Mr. Langdon spoke warmly against this. Mr. Morris moved a reduction to fifty. I urged him so much that he said sixty. This was seconded. I had to show some pointed reason why I urged sixty. Indeed, it was very much against my will that any reduction took place. The protecting duties of Pennsylvania were 4/2—about fifty-six cents. To place the manufacturers of Pennsylvania, who had a claim on the faith of the State, on a worse ground than they stood before, would be injurious, in a degree, to their private property, and break the engagement the State had made with them. This argument went to all the protecting duties of Pennsylvania. Gentlemen had complained that they had no *hemp* in the Western States. This was the case of Pennsylvania. At the close of the war, the protecting duties on cordage called for the manufacturing of it. The manufacture called for the hemp. It was, in fact, a bounty on the raising of that article. The effect of the protecting duty in Pennsylvania, was at first felt by the importers. It was, for a time, an unproductive expense. It is thus, almost, with every distant prospect. He that plants an orchard, cannot immediately eat the fruit of it. But the fruit had already ripened in Pennsylvania, and so it would in other places. I was up four times in all. We carried it, however, at sixty.

We passed on, with little interruption, until we got to *twine*. Mr. Lee kept us an hour and a quarter on this business, because the Virginians had hitherto imported their nets from Britain. Once for all, I may remark of him, that he has given opposition to every article, especially the protecting duties. He declares openly against the principle of them. Grayson declared against all impost, as the most unjust and oppressive mode of taxation. It was in vain Lee was told he could be supplied with all the nets Virginia wanted, from any part of New England. That what could be supplied from any one part of the Union, should be protected by duties on the importations of the same articles from foreign parts. It was lowered to one dollar and fifty cents.

And now for the article of molasses.

Lee declared the second question totally out of order.

It is true, parliamentary precedent might be alleged in favor of such second question; but in the present case I guessed some parties had changed sides. From the discourse, it appeared to me that Few, of Georgia, had changed.

The President made a harangue on the subject of order. The facts were all agreed to, viz: That it was agreed to strike out *five* cents. That the first motion seconded was to insert *two* cents. The second motion seconded was for *three* cents. The third motion seconded was for *four* cents. That a very long and tedious discussion took place with all the three motions before the Chair. That adjournment had been called for and negatived, expressly on the avowed reason that the committee would first get rid of the article. That the President mentioned from the chair that he would put the question on *four* first, being the highest sum. The question was put and carried, and the Senate afterwards adjourned.

The President made a speech, which really was to me unintelligible. He seemed willing to persuade the members that the above was a very unfair mode of doing business, and that they had not an opportunity of declaring their sentiments freely in the above way. He concluded, however, *that after the four had been carried, it was in order to move for any lower sum.*

Mr. Morris rose, and declared it was with reluctance that he differed with the Chair on a question of order, and was beginning to argue on the subject. But the New England men, seeing their darling President likely to be involved in embarrassment for the unguarded steps he had taken in their favor, with one consent declared they were satisfied to pass the article at present, and take it up in *the Senate.*

Now came the postponed article of *loaf sugar.* Lee labored with spite and acrimony in the business. He said the loaf sugar of America was bad. It was *lime* and other vile compositions. He had broke a spoon in trying to dissolve and separate it; and so I must go on breaking my spoons, and the three millions of people must be taxed to support half a dozen people in Philadelphia. He pronounced this sentence, especially the part about the spoon, with so tremulous an accent, and so forlorn an aspect, as would have excited even stoics to laughter. There was a laugh, but no retort on him.

I supported the motion by showing that the sugar *baking* business was of importance, as it gave employment to many other artificers—the mason, brick-maker, layer, carpenter, and all the artificers employed in building; for they had to build largely. The coppersmith, potter, and cooper were in much employ with them. The business was in a declining state, and some sugar-houses discontinued. In Pennsylvania, the old protecting duty was 9/10 per hundred weight, and the raw sugar was 1/ per cent. *Now* there was no protecting duty whatever, for one cent on the pound of brown was in proportion to three on the loaf. The sugar baker of Pennsylvania was, therefore, undeniably on a worse footing than formerly, at least by the whole amount of the Pennsylvania protecting duty; and as he paid 6/6 per hundred weight more on the importation of the raw material. The British, too, aimed at a monopoly of this business, and gave a bounty of 26/ sterling on exportation; so that it became us to counteract them or lose the manufacture. Mr. Morris and Mr. Dalton satisfied some gentlemen as to the manner of importing sugars. I thought this as plain a subject as could come before the House, and yet we divided, and the President gave us the casting vote. He desired leave to give us the reasons of his vote. This seemed to imply a degree of vanity, as if among us all we had not placed the matter in a right point of view. For my part, I was satisfied with his vote. It was now near four o'clock. Adjourned.

May 29. The article of *steel* was passed over with little difficulty, and here, I confess, I expected a considerable opposition. *Nails* and *spikes* were next. Here an opposition from the Carolina and Georgia men led to an increase of the duty. Now came *salt.* Up rose Lee, of the ancient Dominion. He gave us an account of the great revenue derived from salt in France, England, and all the world. Condemned the general system of the bill. Said this was almost the only article in it that would reach the interior parts of the State. The interior parts of the country, with their new lands, could much better afford to pay high taxes than the settlers of the exhausted lands. The carriage of it was nothing, for they all had teams and fine horses. He concluded a lengthy harangue with a motion for *twelve* cents, which, in his opinion, was vastly too low. He was seconded by Mr. Carroll.

Ellsworth rose for an augmentation ; but said if twelve was lost, he would move for nine. Lee, Carroll, Ellsworth, and Morris, speakers in favor of the augmentation. Any *reduction* seemed out of the question with everybody. Against the augmentation, speakers, Izard, Few, and self. I thought my friends on our side of the question, were rather warm, and used some arguments that did not apply well. They, perhaps, with equal justice, thought the same of me. I advocated the new settlers. Endeavored to show that their superior crops were justly due to superior labor ; that every acre of new land cost from five to ten dollars per acre, clearing and fencing. The expenses of new buildings were immense. Men spent an active life often on a farm, and died with the farm in debt to them. New settlers labored for posterity—for the public. They were the real benefactors to the community, and deserved exemption, if any did. It had been said it was their *choice.* No ; necessity, dire necessity, compelled many. But, were they exempted from the effects of the other part of the bill ? No. They could raise no sheep ; of course, no *wool.* Coarse duffels, blankets swan-skins, in a word, all their woolens were imported, and they would, of course, pay the impost on these articles from *necessity ;* which was not the case in general with other citizens, who might either manufacture or buy, as they had the materials.

But over and above this, *luxuries* would find their way among them. All people down to the savage were fond of finery ; the rudest, the most so. And I was convinced that the poor, the amount of their several stocks taken into consideration, spent more in superfluities than the rich. All these arguments apart, the article of *salt* was the most necessary of any in the bill, and, in proportion to the original cost, was the highest taxed. It was a new and untried source of revenue in many of the States. It ought, therefore, to be touched with a gentle hand, if at all. I knew not whether the discontents would follow that had been predicted, and I hoped they would not, but wished we could avoid giving occasion for any. For these reasons, I should at present be for leaving it where the wisdom of the other House had placed it.

The question was put. The House divided, and the President gave it in our favor.

May 30. The Speaker called. He dined yesterday with the President. A number of the Senators were present. The Pennsylvanians had agreed to call on Mr. Morris between ten and eleven. Mr. Morris had yesterday mentioned that time as a convenient time to him. The gentlemen of Congress have, it seems, called on Mrs. Washington and all the congressional ladies. Speaker, Wynkoop, and myself called on Mrs. Morris half after ten. Not at home. Left our card. Being in the lady way, we called to see Mrs. Langdon and Mrs. Dalton.

June 1. The impost bill was taken up, and a number of articles passed over. When we came to *tea*, the impost proceeded on a discrimination in favor of our own ships. Here a motion was made by Ellsworth, seconded by Lee, that went against all discrimination in favor of our own shipping; or, in other words, against any protecting duty for the East India trade; and, indeed, the arguments went against the East India trade altogether.

I got up early in the business. I laid it down that the use of *tea* was now so general that any interdiction of it was impossible; that have it, the people would. If this was the case, common prudence told us to get it from the first hand. That it was evident teas were now obtained vastly cheaper than before our merchants traded to China. This difference had been stated at fifty per cent. on some teas. It had been alleged against this trade, that it destroyed the lives of seamen. The fact had been represented different to me, by those who had made the voyage. It was the practice of all nations to encourage their own trade; but our permitting the British to supplant us in this trade, was suffering them to encourage their trade at our expense.

It had been said the British would take raw materials from us, and give us teas. I was well informed that the Chinese took many articles from us, and some that no other people would take. A detail of these articles I had no doubt would be more fully entered into by some of the gentlemen who would follow me. To talk of not protecting a trade sought after by all the world, was a new phenomenon in a national council. I, therefore, was clearly for the discrimination.

Mr. Morris followed, and he went most minutely into the India trade. Showed that *ginseng* was a considerable article in that trade, anchors, iron, masts, spars, naval stores of all kinds. He, in fact, made it clear that a dollar, sent to Europe for East India goods, would not import more than half a dollar sent to the East Indies. The debate was amazingly lengthy. Both Few and Ellsworth said the trade had been represented as flourishing. This it had obtained without any protecting duties ; why, then, give any now.

I rose to information, and mentioned that the protecting duty of Pennsylvania was two pence per pound, and the protecting duty of the State of New York two pence ; and that the ill policy of withdrawing these duties now, when the trade to the East was threatened with combination against it, was evident.

We got the *discrimination* carried, by nine votes against eight.

Now for the *duty*. Mr. Morris moved to raise all the tea duties. This was lost. But I wish we had uniformly moved *to raise ;* for by this means we secured it at the rate in the bill.

When we came to the real discrimination, now a great debate arose. Four cents was the difference on *Boheas ;* and so, nearly in proportion, Mr. Lee moved for *eight ;* avowedly on this principle, that the four çents were more than the old protecting duty, under which the trade had flourished. This debate was mostly conducted, on our side, by Mr. Morris. I only showed that though the difference between six and ten cents was more than the old protecting duties, the difference between six and eight was less ; and that the gentlemen, on their own principle, should have moved for more than eight. Bnt in the critical situation of the trade to the East, with combinations in India, and ships fitted out at Ostend, and the increasing endeavors of the English to engross the whole trade of the East, the discrimination of four was not too much. Carried, at four o'clock—nine to eight.

In the first argument, I mentioned that if there had been any exclusive company engrossing the India trade, there might be something in the arguments. This, however, was not the case ; nor could it be.

June 2. After some preliminary business, proceeded on the impost bill, without much opposition, till we came to an enumeration of fifteen or sixteen articles, which all stood at seven and a half per cent. The most of these articles stood, in the old protecting duties of Pennsylvania, at twelve per cent. I feared much the spirit of reduction would get into the opposers of the impost, and that they would be for lowering everything. From this sole motive I would have moved an augmentation, by way of securing the duty where it was. However, here I had better ground. I set out with naming over the greater part of the articles on which the protecting duties of Pennsylvania were twelve and a half per cent.; and thirteen per cent. in New York. I reasoned, from the effect of these duties, on the promoting the manufacture. But by the present duties, the manufacturers would stand on worse ground, by five per cent., than they had done under the States' laws; that, although the United States were not absolutely obliged to make good the engagements of the State to individuals, yet, as individuals had embarked their property in these manufactures, depending on the State laws, I thought it wrong to violate those laws without absolute necessity.

I was, as usual, opposed by the southern people. Before I rose, I spoke to Mr. Morris to rise and move an augmentation. He said, no.

Mr. Few, of Georgia, asserted that the manufacturers of Pennsylvania would be better off under the seven and a half than they had been under the twelve and a half per cent. Mr. Morris got up, and asserted the same thing. I declare, I could not believe either of them. Mr. Morris, however, stated the manufacture of *paper* to be in the most flourishing condition imaginable, in Pennsylvania. Said he was afraid to mention the amount of paper that had been exported last year, lest he might not be believed. That it had been stated to him at not less than £80,000. He went through the business, down to gathering the rags in the street.

After this, it was in vain to say anything more; but the effect was, that it stood at seven and a half.

A number of articles were now raised to ten per cent. But what surprised me was that Mr. Morris was against raising *leather* and leathern manufactures, canes, walking-sticks, whips, ready-made clothing, brushes, gold, silver, and plated ware, jewelry and paste work, wrought tin and pewter ware. He gave no reason for this, which is not usual with him. Some of the articles were, notwithstanding, placed at ten, without him. His weight, in our Senate, is great on commercial subjects.

Mr. Morris moved, at my request, to have cotton exempted for some time, from duty. This carried by a kind of compromise.

We proceeded smoothly till we came to the drawback on *fish*, &c., and New England rum. Long conversations on this subject; but agreed to. We expected a sharp debate on the drawback or, ... in American vessels, but it passed nem. con. The last clause Mr. Morris moved to expunge, but it was carried, and I heard not a no but his own. It was now late, and we adjourned.

I omitted to mention, in its proper place, that Mr. Morris moved for ten per cent. on a long list of scythes, sickles, axes, spades, shovels, locks, hinges, &c., &c., down to plow irons, but none of them were carried, and, of course, stood in the mass of five per cent.

June 3. At eleven, the Senate met. The clerk from the House of Representatives came with a message, and brought up the law about the oaths.

The impost was taken up, the title and preamble debated, and altered a little, and now a lengthy debate took place, on a motion of Mr. Lee to put off the consideration of the bill until Monday next. I spoke first against the motion. I was for proceeding immediately. The bill had been very long under consideration. The public expectation had been tired. A million of dollars had been lost to the treasury, and what was still worse, the people had paid the money; for the merchants had raised their goods, and the impost was in actual collection on all the spring importations. That I wished the new Government might stand fair with the public, and give no just cause of censure at so early a period.

After very considerable debate, Mr. Morris moved that to-morrow be assigned for the second reading in the Senate. This was agreed to.

Now, a very long debate took place about the newpapers. All the printers in the city crowd their papers into the hands of the members. The bulk of the papers consist of advertisements. Useful information ought not to be excluded; but this is over-done. The real mean appeared to me to be the taking of one or two papers by each member. But one part of the House struggled for taking all; the other, for taking none. No vote could be carried for either; and, of course, the printers will continue their old practice of sending, and expect payment.

June 4. Went to the Hall at ten, but found the members occupied by two committees. Sauntered about till eleven; rather disagreeably. Senate was formed. The *minutes* were read. They stood: Mr. Langdon administered the oath to the *Vice President*—the *Vice President* administered, &c. The law is, the oath, &c., shall be administered, by *any* one member of the Senate, to *the President of the Senate*, and by him to all the members. And again: The *President of the Senate*, for the time being.

The minutes are totally under the direction of our President.

The Journal of the Senate stands thus: *Ordered*, That Mr. Langdon administer the oath to the Vice President; which was done accordingly. And the Vice President administered the oath, according to law, to the following members: To Messrs. Langdon,

Wingate, Strong, Dalton, Johnson, Ellsworth, Patterson, Maclay, Morris, Read, Bassett, Carroll, Henry, Lee, Grayson, Izard, Few, Gunn. The same oath was, by the Vice President, administered to the secretary, together with the oath of office. But now a discourse was raised again, whether the members should be styled honorable on the minutes. The President declared, from the chair, that it was a most serious affair, and a vote of the House should be taken on it. He gave us a touch, again, on the subject—was against using the word unless *right* was added to it. He said a good deal to this purpose. Lee was up in a moment for it. The President made us a second speech. He said it was of great importance. If we took the title *honorable*, it was a colonial appellation, and we should disgrace ourselves, forever, by it—that it was applied to the justices of every court.

Up now rose Grayson, of Virginia, and gave us volley after volley against all kinds of titles whatever. Louder and louder did he inveigh against them.

Lee looked like madness. Carroll and myself exchanged looks and laughs of congratulation. Even the President himself seemed struck in a heap. . . . . . Grayson mentioned the *Doge of Venice* in his harangue, as he was mentioning all the great names in the world. Pray, do you know *his title*, said the President, from the chair. No, says Grayson, smartly, I *am not very well acquainted with him.*

We now took up the impost bill, and proceeded smoothly till we come to the article of *molasses.*

It was the wish of a majority of the Senate, to have the question without any debate. But now Mr. Dalton rose ; and we were obliged to hear everything over again, which had been formerly advanced. It was long and tedious. Some observations were just and pertinent, but many quite foreign to the purpose.

Dr. Johnson rose on the same side. Dalton was for lowering to *three* cents ; but Dr. Johnson said he had been convinced that it ought to be but *two*, or rather none at all. The drift of the Doctor's arguments was : Molasses, imported, is either distilled, and then, as a raw material, it ought not to be taxed ; or it is consumed by the poor, as food, and so ought not to be taxed. So it ought not to be taxed at all.

Up rose Strong, and facing himself to the right, where Mr. Morris and myself sat, fell violently on the members from Pennsylvania, with insinuations that seemed to import that we wished to overcharge New England with an undue proportion of the impost. What was the most remarkable, Mr. Morris had whispered to me that he would not get up on the business, but would attend with the utmost attention to all their arguments, fully determined to give them their utmost weight. But when this attack was begun, I could see his nostrils widen, and his nose flatten like the head of a viper. Ellsworth, however, got up before him, and this gave him time to recollect himself. He rose after Ellsworth, and charmingly did he unravel all their windings. It is too long to set down; but he was clear, strong, and conclusive.

I, in the meanwhile, busied myself in examining the abstract of the importations into Philadelphia, given me by Delaney. In this place, I cannot help remarking that there is something of a singularity in my disposition. Although I was equally concerned, I really felt joy on this attack, and the more so when I saw Mr. Morris was moved. The buffetings that I used to get from some of these people, in his absence, and the sentimental insults that I received, seemed now to say, take you, too, a part.

When he had done, I rose, and repeated from their own observation, that the whole of the molasses imported into Massachusetts was three millions of gallons. Two millions they distilled, and had the drawback, if they chose to export it, so that this was totally out of the question. That consumed in the State, in substance, was the remaining million. But *we* imported, last year, so much molasses into Pennsylvania, that, making sufficient allowance for two distilleries that were worked, the remainder for consumption, in substance was half a million. Was this the object to make such a stir about? It was said some of the New England rum was drunk in the State. Be it so. Take any given quantity, be it what it may, it is consumed under a duty of four cents per gallon; for, the gallon of molasses yields, in distillation, rather a larger than a less quantity than gallon for gallon. But we import near one million of gallons of spirits into Pennsylvania, and this is consumed under a duty of from eight to ten cents. We imported, also, five millions of raw sugar; above one million of coffee, which was said to be half of the coffee used in the United States; besides a full proportion of all other goods. I spoke not at random, or without book. Here was the abstract in the handwriting of Sharp Delany, the collector. Were we then the people for imposing unequal burdens? No. We were imposing no burdens of which we were not about to bear a share; a great, perhaps the greatest, share.

Dalton rose, and remarked on the great uncertainty of all calculations. He was, however, modest. A variety of people spoke. Some heat seemed, at one time, to arise between Lee and Langdon. There was a considerable shifting about the question. It was at last settled that the question should be to reduce the duty to *three* cents, expressly on the condition of taking away the drawback. Mr. Morris and myself both voted against it. Izard, Gun, and some others, voted expressly on the condition of the drawback being taken away. The others joined, but with a design of retaining the drawback. So stands this curious affair till to-morrow. Past three, and adjourned.

I must not omit that Carroll got up and spoke well on our side. He stated the inequality of duty on molasses and sugar, as sweets ; that a gallon of molasses was equal, as a sweet, to seven pounds of good brown sugar. Seven cents on one, four on the other.

Friday, June 5. Called, this morning, on Mr. Fitzsimmons, and got from him a list of the imposts into Pennsylvania and into Virginia. Went to the Hall, and waited until the meeting of the Senate. We now fell to the impost, and proceeded to the article of *loaf sugar ;* and here they directly moved a reduction of one cent Lee and Ellsworth spoke against it, as formerly. I rose, and re peated the sum of the old arguments. Dr. Johnson, who was with us before, now fell off. Dalton changed. It was reduced to three.

We swam on, smoothly, to the teas, imported from any other country than China. This clause admitted all foreigners to come directly to America, from China and India.

Dalton moved an amendment, that should confine the direct trade, from India and China to the United States, to our own vessels.

Mr. Morris got up, and said that although he was, in sentiment, with the gentleman, yet, as he believed it would not meet the approbation of gentlemen, he would not second the motion, but leave the matter until experience would fully show the necessity of it.

Mr. Carroll got up, said if the matter was right, it should be tried now, and not wait for experiment, which might be attended with detriment ; and seconded the motion.

And now, strange to tell, both Lee and Ellsworth rose, and supported the motion. I listened, with astonishment, when I recollected the debates, on this very subject, on Monday last. The whole trade to India was then inveighed against, condemned, and almost execrated ; and, now, the very men declared for it, and for securing it exclusively to ourselves. This change I cannot account for. If there was any preconcerted measure, Mr. Morris certainly knew nothing of it. One inference, however, follows clearly, from the conduct of Lee and Ellsworth, that they are governed by conveniency or cabal. Had judgment been the rule of their conduct, their behavior, on Monday, would not have been so inconsistent with that of this day. I was content with the bill as it stood.

The difference of duty, and the discount of ten per cent. in favor of our own vessels, I thought pretty well for protecting our trade, without absolutely excluding all the world. But I had another reason. I doubt much whether the House of Representatives will agree to our amendments. Every new one will, or may be a source of dissension or delay. I have labored with all the diligence in my power, to hasten on the impost; but I am counteracted; for what can one man do. It now seems evident that remarkable influence is exerted to delay the impost until they get in all their summer goods.

Yesterday was the anniversary of his Britannic Majesty's birth. It was a highday, and celebrated with great festivity, on that account. The old leaven of anti-revolutionism has leavened the whole lump; nor can we keep the Congress free from the influence of it.

People may act as they think proper in their elections, and they will still do so. Lawyers and merchants are, generally, their choice. But it seems as difficult to restrain a merchant from striking at gain, as to prevent the keen spaniel from springing at game that he has been trained to pursue. Habit, with them, is become a second nature. Indeed, the strongest propensities of *nature* are often postponed to it. Lawyers have keenness, and a fondness for disputation. Wrangling is their business. But long practice in supporting any cause that offers, has obliterated regard to right or wrong.

About two o'clock, the word *levee*, and adjourn, was repeated from sundry quarters of the House—adjourn to Monday. The President caught hold of the last. Is it the pleasure of the House that the adjournment be to *Monday?* A single no would not be heard among the prevailing ayes. Here are most important bills before us, and yet we shall throw all by for empty ceremony; for attending the levee is little more. Nothing is regarded at such meetings but the qualifications that flow from the tailor, barber, and dancing master. To be clean shaved, shirted, and powdered; to make your bows with grace, and to be master of small chat on the weather, play, or newspaper anecdote of the day, are qualifications necessary. Levees may be extremely useful in old countries, where men of great fortunes are collected, as it may keep the idle from being much worse employed. But here, I think, they are hurtful. They interfere with the business of the public, and instead of employing only the idle, have a tendency to make men idle who should be better employed. Indeed, from these small beginnings, I fear we shall follow on, nor cease till we have reached the summit of court etiquette, and all the frivolities, fopperies, and expense practiced in European Governments.

June 6.   It was half past ten when Mr. B. called on me.   He seemed so earnest that I should go with him that I agreed to meet him in half an hour at the Ferry House, and accompany him home. The wind was high, and direct ahead.   It was five when we reached Elizabethtown Point.   Here was Governor Livingston and a dining party.   They had eat their fish, and were sauntering on a porch. Mr. B. introduced me to the Governor, a man plain and rather rustic in his dress and appearance.   I had often heard of his being a man of uncommon abilities, and was all attention.   But the occasion offered nothing but remarks of a convivial kind.   But we learned that the old gentleman in returning late was overturned in his chair, and much bruised.   Heard, on my coming to my lodging' of the arrival of two India men at Philadelphia, under command of Barry and Truxton, who report all the rest to be on their way ; and, now, perhaps, we shall get the impost and collection bills passed.

On *the Senate Journal,* under date of Monday, June 8, it is stated that Pierce Butler, from South Carolina, appeared, and took his seat.

Tuesday, June 9.   The bill imposing duties *on tonnage* was read a first time, and Tuesday next was assigned for the second reading.

The Senate proceeded in the second reading of the bill for laying a duty on goods, wares, and merchandise imported into the United States, and Wednesday next was assigned for the third reading of the bill.

The journal of Mr. Maclay proceeds :

June 9.   Although I was not present *yesterday,* nevertheless they were busy at the impost.   The affair of confining the East India trade to the citizens of America had been negatived, and a committee had been appointed to report on this business.   The report came in with very high duties, amounting to a prohibition.   But a new phenomenon had made its appearance in the House since Friday.   Pierce Butler, from Carolina, had taken his seat, and flamed like a meteor.   He arraigned the whole impost law, and then charged (indirectly) the whole Congress with a design of oppressing South Carolina.   He cried out for encouraging the Danes and Swedes and foreigners of every kind to come and take away our produce.   In fact, he was for a navigation act reversed.

Ellsworth, Morris, Carroll, Dalton, Langdon for the report ; Few, Izard, Butler, Lee against it.   And until four o'clock was it battled, with less order, less sense, and less decency, too, than any question I have ever yet heard debated in the Senate.

I did not like the report well, but concluded to vote for it, all things considered ; rather than, by rejecting it, to have all set afloat on that subject again. Butler's party had conducted themselves with so little decorum, that any effect their arguments might have had was lost by their manner ; and nobody rose but themselves. This was really the most misspent day that I remember in Congress. I did not rise once, but often called for the question.

To-morrow is assigned for the third reading of the bill, and I hope we will finish it; or at least send it down to the other House. If I had stood in need of any proof of the instability of Lee's political character, this day gave me a fresh instance of it. Now again, he vilified and traduced the India trade.

June 10. Attended at the hall at the usual time, and the impost bill was taken up for a *third* reading. I will not enter into any detail of the speeches and arguments entered into. The lately-arrived Mr. Butler is the most eccentric of creatures. He moved to strike out the article of *indigo*. Carolina was not obliged to us for taking notice of her affairs ; ever and anon crying out against local views and partial proceedings ; and the most local and partial creature I ever heard open a mouth. All the impost bill was calculated to ruin South Carolina. He has words at will ; but scatters them the most at random of any man I ever heard pretend to speak. He seems to have a particular antipathy to Mr. Morris. *Izard* has often manifested something of a similar disposition.

We sat until four o'clock, but did not get quite through it.

June 11. Attended the hall, as usual. Mr. Izard and Mr. Butler opposed the whole of the *drawbacks*, in every shape whatever. Mr. Grayson, of Virginia, warm on this subject. Said we were not ripe for such a thing. We were a new nation, and had no business for any such regulations—a nation *sui generis*. Mr. Lee said drawbacks were right, but would be so much abused he could not think of admitting them.

Mr. Ellsworth said *New England* rum would be exported, instead of *West India*, to obtain the drawback.

I thought it best to say a few words in reply to each. We were a new *nation*, it was true ; but we were not a new *people*. We were composed of individuals of like manners, habits, and customs with the European nations. What, therefore, had been found useful among them, came well recommended, by experience, to us. Drawbacks stand as an example, in this point of view, to us. If the thing was right in itself, there could be no just argument drawn against the use of a thing from the abuse of it. It would be the duty of Government to guard against abuses, by prudent appointments and watchful attention to officers. That as to changing the kind of *rum*, I thought the collection bill would provide for this, by limiting the exportation to the original casks and packages. I said a great deal more, but really did not feel much interested either way. But the debate was very lengthy. Butler flamed away, and threatened a dissolution of the Union, with regard to his State, *as sure as God was in the firmament*. He scattered his remarks over the whole impost bill, calling it partial, oppressive, &c., and solely calculated to oppress South Carolina; and yet, ever and anon declaring how clear of local views, how candid and dispassionate he was. He degenerated into mere declamation. His State would live free, or die glorious, &c., &c. We, however, got through by three o'clock.

I will now memorandum one remark. The Senators from Jersey, Pennsylvania, Delaware, and Maryland, in every act, seemed desirous of making the impost productive, both as to revenue, and effective for the encouragement of manufactures; and seemed to consider the whole of the imposts (salt excepted) much too low. Articles of luxury, many of them would have raised one half. But the members both from the north and, still more particularly, from the south, were ever in a flame when any articles were brought forward that were in any considerable use among them.

Dined this day with Mr. Morris. Mr. Fitzsimmons and Mr. Clymer, all the company, except Mrs. Morris and three children. Mrs. Morris talked a great deal after dinner. She did it gracefully enough. This being a gayer place, and she being here considered as at least the second female character at court. As to taste etiquette, &c., she is certainly the first. I thought she discovered a predilection for New York; but perhaps she was only doing it justice, while my extreme aversion, like a zealous sentinel, is for giving no quarter.

I, however, happened to mention that they were ill supplied with the article of *cream*. Mrs. Morris had much to say on this subject. Declared they had done all they could, and even sent to the country all about, but that they could not be supplied. She told many anecdotes on this subject. Particularly how, two days ago, she dined at the President's. A large and fine looking trifle was brought to table, and appeared exceedingly well, indeed. She was helped by the President, but on taking some of it, she had to pass her handkerchief by her mouth and rid herself of the morsel—on which she whispered the President, the cream of which it is made had been unusually stale and rancid; on which the General changed his plate immediately. But, she added, with a titter, Mrs. Washington ate a whole heap of it.

But where in the world has this trifle led me. I have ever been very attentive to observe, if possible, General Washington's private opinions on the pompous part of government. His address, fellow citizens, to the two Houses of Congress, seems quite republican. Mrs. Morris, however, gave us something on this subject. General Washington, on a visit to her, *had declared himself, in the most pointed manner, for generous salaries ; and added, that without large salaries proper persons never could be got to fill the offices of government with propriety.* He might deliver something of this kind with propriety enough without using the word *large.* However, if he lives with the pompous people of New York, he must be something more than human, if their high toned manners have not some effect on him. On going first among Indians, I have observed decent white people view them with a kind of disgust ; but when the Indians were by far the most numerous, the disgust would, by degrees, wear off—indifference followed, and by degrees attachment, and even fondness. How much more likely are the arts of attention and obsequiousness to make an imitative impression.

It is stated on the *Senate Journal* of the 11th June, (*inter alia*,) that the Senate entered on executive business, and received from the President of the United States a communication in relation to the functions and prerogatives of consuls, vice consuls, &c.

June 12. Mr. Lee, in behalf of the committee thereto appointed, reported a bill to establish the judicial courts of the United States. The Senate entered on *executive* business.

The journal of Mr. Maclay proceeds :

Attended the judicial committee, and had the bill read over. It was long and somewhat confused. I was called out ; they, however, reported it soon after the Senate met, and a number of copies were ordered to be struck off. Monday se-night appointed for it.

The Indian treaties were now taken up and referred to a committee of three to report.

Mr. Butler made a most flaming speech against *the judicial bill.* He was called to order from the chair, and was not a little angry about it.

The French convention was called up and read, respecting the privileges of consuls, vice consuls, &c., but was postponed.

We now adjourned, and I went to the levee. I was rather late. Most of the company were coming, and I felt easier than I used to do, and I believe I had better attend every day until I finish the affair of Davy Harris. I spoke to Col. Humphreys, and desired to know when I should call on him. He said nine o'clock. I believe I will go at that hour to-morrow. In the evening Mr. White, of Virginia, called on me. We walked after tea. Had much discourse on the subject of removing Congress. I have not been mistaken in my opinion of the Virginians. He declared for staying here rather than agree to the Falls of Delaware. As we came home the speaker overtook us on horseback..

My mind revolts in many instances against the Constitution of the United States. Indeed, I am afraid it will turn out the vilest of all traps that ever was set to ensnare the freedom of an unsuspecting people. Treaties formed by the Executive of the United States are to be the laws of the land. To cloak the Executive with legislative authority is setting aside our modern and much boasted distribution of power into legislative, judicial, and executive—discoveries unknown to Locke and Montesquieu, and all the ancient writers. It certainly contradicts all the modern theory of government, and in practice must be tyranny.

Mem. Get if I can the Federalist, without buying it. It is not worth it. But being a lost book, Izard or some one else will give it to me. It certainly was instrumental in procuring the adoption of the Constitution. This is merely a point of curiosity and amusement, to see how wide of his (its) explanations and conjectures the stream of business has taken its course.

June 15. Monday, attended at the Hall, and the tonnage act was taken up. We got about half way through the first clause of it by four o'clock. A clause stood : On all ships or vessels within the United States, and *belonging wholly to a citizen or citizens thereof.* Izard moved to have the latter part of it struck out, the effect of which would have been that no discrimination would have been made between our own citizens and foreigners.

Lee, Butler, Grayson, Izard, and Few argued in the most unceasing manner, and I thought most absurdly on this business.

The first time, I made a short remark that the foreigner and citizen must both build their ships in America ; and then, evidently, for everything that followed, they stood alike. That the superior capital of the foreigners would enable them to build more ships lower than us, and would, in time, give them the whole of our trade. That the bill bore on the face of it a discrimination in favor of our merchants, but the fact would turn out otherwise ; and, therefore, I was for continuing the clause as it stood.

A little before the question was put, I rose a second time. Said no former transaction was so likely to throw light on this subject

Mr. Reed rose, and was on his feet for an hour. He had to talk as a short history of the British navigation act. Cromwell originated it in spleen against the Dutch. But the effects of it were seen before the Restoration, and it was then reënacted. Great murmurs arose. The Scotch thought themselves ruined, and sent their Peers up to remonstrate against it. The tonnage of Great Britain then stood ninety-five thousand two hundred and sixty-six. In fifteen years, it was one hundred and ninety thousand five hundred and thirty-three. In twenty years more, it was two hundred and seventy-three thousand six hundred and ninety-three. The present tonnage of *Massachusetts* alone is now one hundred thousand.

It had been urged that it would be time enough half a century hence to talk of measures for a *navy*. A *single State* was in a better condition now, in point of shipping, than the British nations were at the Restoration. Therefore, delay was the worst of policy. It was generally allowed that the spirit of the navigation act was to give a monopoly of the trade of the British nations to their own shipping and sailors. In view solely mercantile, this was, perhaps, wrong, as by these means our foreign articles would be dearer, and our home produce cheaper. But the object was a national one. Shipping and sailors were the objects, and, though the landed part of the community was not, perhaps, so rich, yet the nation was safe, for national power is of more consequence than individual wealth. The suspension of the navigation act, it was believed, would be productive of a great flow of wealth to the British nation, or, at least, the manufacturing and agricultural part of it; but the purchase would cost them their shipping and sailors. And, finally, the foreigners would have a monopoly of the whole traffic, one of the worst of evils, provided they conducted their navigation on terms of more economy, as was generally believed of the Dutch.

But what were we doing. Were we passing a navigation act? No. A slight discrimination was all that was aimed at, and if the motion was adopted, the discrimination would operate against us.

The question was put, and the clause remained. Near four, and adjourned.

June 16. This day, passed the residue of the tonnage bill, with much debate. Broke up early, and went to hear the debates in the House of Representatives. After dinner, went and walked a considerable time, to gain strength for my knee.

Some observations having called me up this day, I endeavored to comprise all I had to say in as little bounds as possible, by observing that there were two extremes in commercial regulations equally to be avoided. The principle of the navigation act might be carried so far as to exclude all foreigners from our ports. The consequence would be a monopoly in favor of the mercantile interest. The other was an unlimited license in favor of foreigners, the consequence of which would be a monopoly in favor of the cheapest carriers, and, in time, a total dependence on them. Both extremes ought to be avoided, by giving certain indulgences to our own trade and that of our friends, in such degree as will secure them the ascendency without hazarding the expulsion of foreigners from our ports.

On an annexed leaf, under date of June 17, 1789, he remarks: The *balloting* business (see this hereafter referred to) prevented my mentioning in order the more important debate on the tonnage act. The amendments (for which we may thank the influence of this city) for doing away the discrimination between foreigners in and out of treaty with us, have been carried. It was in vain that I gave them every opposition in my power. I laid down a marked difference between impost and tonnage. The former imposition is paid by the consumer of the goods; the latter rests on the owner of the ship, at least in the first instance. That sound policy dictated the principle of encouraging the shipping of our friends; that nations not in treaty would not be considered as the most friendly. I read the fifth article of the commercial treaty with *France*, and denied that we had any power of imposing any tonnage on her shipping, save an equivalent to the one hundred sols on *coasters*. I gave my unequivocal opinion, that a want of discrimination in her favor was contrary to the spirit of the treaty, and expressed fears of her resentment.

Ellsworth answered me; but the most that he said was that *our interest* called for it; and he pledged himself that we would never hear from France about it. But speaking was vain. I never saw the Senate more listless or inattentive, nor more determined.

June 17. Called on Mr. Scott. Told him of the request of the arrangement committee. Met, and made a short report.

The Senate formed, passed the residue of the impost bill, without much debate. In now came Mr. Jay to give information respecting Mr. Short, who was nominated to supply the place of Mr. Jefferson, at the court of France, while Mr. Jefferson returned home.

And now the President rose to give us a discourse on the subject of form—how we should give *our advice and consent*.

I rose, perhaps more early than might have been wished by some, and stated that this business was in the nature of election. That the spirit of the constitution was clearly in favor of *ballot*—that this mode could be applied without difficulty. When the person was

6

put up in nomination, the favorable tickets should have a yea—and the others should be *blanks.*

Few, of Georgia, rose and seconded me. Izard made a long speech against it. Mr. Carroll spoke against it—Mr. Langdon and Mr. Morris; but Lee, Ellsworth, and Butler for it. Mr. Morris' speech principally turned on its being below the dignity of the Senate, who should be open, bold, and unawed by any consideration whatever.

I rose, at last, and spoke perhaps longer than I had done on any former occasion. It had been considered unworthy of a Senator to conceal any vote. The good of the public, however, required secrecy in many things; but the ballot did not take away the right of open conduct. On the contrary, it was the duty of every Senator to disclose the defects of any candidate, where they were great, or might be attended with danger to the public. But, as the nominations came from the President, it was not to be expected that characters notoriously flagitious would ever be put in nomination. Every Senator, when voting openly, would feel inconvenience from two quarters—or, at least, he was subjected to it. I would not say, in European language, that there would be court favor and court resentment, but there would be about the President a kind of sunshine that people, in general, would wish to enjoy the warmth of. Openly voting against the nominations of the President would be the sure mode of losing this sunshine. This was applicable to all Senators, in all cases. But there was more. A Senator, like another man, would have the interest of his friends to promote. The cause of a son or a brother might be lodged in his hands. Will such a one, in such a case, wish openly to oppose the President's judgment.

But there are other inconveniences. The disappointed candidate will retaliate the injury, which he feels, against the Senator. It may be said the Senator's station will protect him. This can extend only to the time of his being in office; and he, too, must return to private-life, where, as a private man, he must answer for the offenses given by the Senator. The ballot left the judgment equally free, and none of the above inconveniences followed. When, then, equal advantages flowed, without any of the disadvantages, the mode least subject to inconvenience was preferable. Many gentlemen had declared how perfectly indifferent it was to them. I believed the same thing of every Senator in the present House. But was this always to continue? No. We must expect men of every class and every description within these walls. The present character of our President was no security that we should always have men equally eminent. That in those places where elections were conducted *viva voce,* the hopes and fears of electors were so wrought on by the wealthy, powerful, and bold, that few votes were given entirely free from influence, unless it was by the happy few who were independent in spirit as well as in fortune; that we need not expect the Senate always to be composed of such desirable characters. It had been clearly stated and admitted, that the mode by *ballot* was equally applicable to the present case as that of *viva voce;* and being free from any inconveniences that the other was subject to, ught, undoubtedly, to be adopted.

June 18. And now the mode of approving or disapproving of the nomination. I did not minute it yesterday. But our President rose in the chair, and delivered his opinion how the business ought to be done. He read the Constitution, argued, and concluded; I would rise in the chair, and put the question, individually, to the Senators: Do you advise and consent that Mr. Short be appointed chargé d'affaires at the Court of France? Do you? Do you?

Mr. Carroll spoke long for the *viva voce* mode. He said ballot was productive of caballing and bargaining for votes. He then wandered so wide of the subject as to need no attention.

Mr. Ellsworth made a most elaborate harrangue. A great part of it was, however, about the duty of our President, and inventing a mode how *he* might also ballot in case of a division. He, however, towards the close of it, made a strange distinction: that voting by ballot suited bashful men best; but was the worst way for bad and unprincipled men.

I wished to repeat nothing of what had been said yesterday, but replied, that so far from balloting being productive of caballing, it was the very bane and antidote against it. That men made bargains for certainties; but it was in vain to purchase or bargain for a vote by ballot, which there was no certainty of the party ever obtaining, as he had no method of securing the performance of a promise or of knowing whether he was deceived or not.

As to the distinction, of balloting being the worst way for bad men, I thought differently. The worst of men were known to respect virtue. The ballot removed all extrinsic force or obligation. It was the only chance of making a bad man act justly—the matter was left to his own conscience; there were no witnesses. If he did wrong, it was because he loved vice more than virtue; which, I believed, even among bad men, was not the fact, in one case out of ten. The question was at last taken and carried by eleven votes—seven voting against it. Z. was so crooked he voted against us, though he had spoken for us, and quoted Harrington to show his reading.

The people who lost this question manifested much uneasiness, particularly the President and Mr. Langdon. Langdon was even fretful. The President threw difficulties in our way. The Senate had decreed their advice and consent *by ballot*. Nothing like this in history, or ever heard of before. But what rank was Mr. Short to hold in the diplomatic corps? What kind of a commission was he to have? This must be settled *by ballot*. He set us afloat by these kind of queries, and an hour and a quarter was lost in the most idle discourse imaginable. He seemed willing to entangle the Senate; or, rather, some of them were entangled about the secretary of the legation and the chargé d' affaires, not knowing a distinction. We, however, got through it by a resolution, declaring our advice and consent in favor of Mr. Short.

In an annexed memorandum, he further remarks as follows:

After having again explained the manner of concurring or rejecting a nomination by ballot, in a manner so plain as did not admit of contradiction, I replied to the observation that no example of anything of the kind could be found in history. That in the old kingdom of Arragon, where, though the executive was monarchical, yet that republican provisions had been attended to with unexampled attention. The court appointed by the Justiza gave their sentence by ballot; and offered to produce history to the point, but was not contradicted.

Took up the impost, and talked idly to past the usual time of adjournment. An adjournment called for, and took place.

I have ever been as attentive as I possibly could be to discover the real disposition of *the President*. He has been very cautious hitherto. The message about Mr. Short touches a matter that may be drawn into precedent. It states the desire of Mr. Jefferson to return for some time, and nominates Mr. Short to supply his place during his absence. The leave for return, &c., is not laid before the Senate. Granting this power to be solely with the President, the power of dismissing ambassadors seems to follow; and some of the courtiers in the Senate fairly admitted it. I chose to give the matter a different turn, and delivered my opinion. That our concurring in the appointment of Mr. Short fully implied the consent of the return of Mr. Jefferson. That, if we chose to prevent the return of Mr. Jefferson, it was only to negative the nomination of Mr. Short or any other one to fill his place. It is the fault of the best governors, when they are placed over a people, to endeavor to enlarge their powers by applying to public stations what would be laudable in private individuals, a desire of bettering their stations. Thus the farmer acts well who, by industry, adds field to field. As so would the governor who would add to the public wealth or happiness ; but adding to the personality, if I may so speak, or to the personal power of the governor, is a faulty industry. A question has been agitated with great warmth in the House of Representatives whether the sole power of displacing officers, or, to speak strictly, the Secretary for Foreign Affairs, shall remain with the President. From the small beginning, in the case of Mr. Short, it is easy to see what the court opinion will be with respect to this point. Indeed, I entertain not a doubt, but many people are aiming, with all their force, to establish a splendid court, with all the pomp of majesty. Alas, poor Washington, if you are taken in this snare. How will the gold become dim ? How will the fine gold be changed ? How will all your glory fade ?

Friday, June 19. And now the impost bill, as sent back from the House of Representatives, with an almost total rejection of our amendments, was taken up. There was but little speaking. Mr. Lee made a distinction, in his parliamentary way, between the word *insist* and *adhere*, and it was carried to use the word *insist*.

After the two first articles were insisted on, Mr. Morris moved that one question should be taken on all the other disagreements. *Saving time* was his object ; but we only lost by it. He did not seem to have been well understood.

I rose and explained his motion, and to his satisfaction, as he said. The result of the whole was that we insisted on nearly all our amendments ; and I suppose they will adhere to the original bill. This really seems like playing at cross purposes, or differing for the sake of sport. I voted on the principles of accommodation through out the whole. Indeed, this was but repeating my former vote. Indeed, there was nothing to differ about—only opinion founded on conjecture. One imagined a thing was too high. Another thought it too low to raise the money which we wanted. Others wished them low, on purpose, that the deficiency might be so great that we would be forced into an excise. I abhorred this principle, though my colleague is fond of it. Adjourned over to eleven o'clock, on Monday.

Mr. Maclay continues :

The Judiciary Bill.

June 22. Attended the Senate. The bill for settling the new *judiciary* was taken up. Much discourse about the mode of doing business. We were *in committee*. The first and second clauses postponed. A question taken whether there should be *district courts*. Much wrangling about words. This was carried.

But now Mr. Lee brought forward a motion nearly in the words of the *Virginia* amendment, viz: that the jurisdiction of the Federal courts should be confined to cases of admiralty and maritime jurisdiction.

Lee and Grayson supported this position. Ellsworth answered them; and the ball was kept up until past three o'clock.

The question was going to be put. I rose and begged to make a remark or two. The effect of the motion was to exclude the Federal jurisdiction from each of the States, except in admiralty and maritime cases. But the *constitution* expressly extended it to all cases, in law and equity, under the constitution and laws of the United States; treaties made or to be made, &c. We already had existing treaties, and were about making many laws. These must be executed by the federal judiciary. The arguments which had been used, would apply well if amendments to the constitution were under consideration; but, certainly, were inapplicable here. I sat down. Some called for the question, and some for an adjournment.

The adjournment carried.

Strong, this day, in conversation, mentioned that *the President would continue no longer in office than he saw matters fairly set going*, and then Mr. Adams will begin his reign.

Mr. Maclay further observed, that Dr. Rush and himself puffed Mr. Adams in the papers, and brought him forward as Vice President, and that this will probably make him President; and that their motive was to make him useful among the New England men, in our scheme of bringing Congress to Pennsylvania, &c.

June 23. Attended at the hall a little after ten. Came into the Senate chamber. There was nobody here but Mr. Adams. He was in the great chair. When I came in, he left it; came and sat near me until he read a newspaper. Shifted to the chair next to me—

NOTE.—The judiciary bill was originated in the Senate. On the 7th of April, the day after a quorum of the Senate was formed, as before observed, Messrs. Ellsworth, Patterson, Maclay, Strong, Lee, Bassett, Few, and Wingate were appointed a committee to bring in a bill for organizing the judiciary of the United States. On the 12th June, *Mr. Lee*, on behalf of the committee, reported a bill to establish the judicial courts of the United States. It is stated in *Flander's Life of Ellsworth*, that the bill reported is *in his hand-writing*, and is still preserved in the archives of the Government. It is there added, that it passed with but little alteration from the original draft; that it is unknown what arguments were employed against it *in the Senate;* but in *the House*, it was decried, as wholly unnecessary; as establishing a government within a government, which would jostle and finally destroy each other. A supreme court, with appellate jurisdiction, together with State courts of admiralty, was the only system, it was said, that the necessities or wishes of the people required. Mr. Livermore, of New Hampshire, declared that he could not conceive the occasion of the new system, "unless to be to plague mankind."—*Flanders Life of Ellsworth, p. 159-60.*

began a discourse on the subject of Pennsylvania. Said they were "the best republicans in the Union. Their adoption was unequiv. ocal. This could not be said of Boston, New York, or Virginia."

I replied, that we had, no doubt, our faults; but certainly the virtues of plainness, industry, and frugality would be allowed to us, in some degree. That Federalism was general, but there was a general abhorrence of the pomp and splendid expense of Government, especially of everything which bordered on royalty. Several members came in and joined us.

Senate formed, and the business of yesterday was taken up just where we left it. The discourses of yesterday were all repeated. Mr. Lee endeavored to give the whole business a new turn, to elude the force of what I had said yesterday. According to his explanation of admiralty and maritime jurisdiction, he would have taken in a vast field.

I rose, and read over from the Constitution a number of the powers of Congress, viz: collecting taxes, duties, imposts; naturalization of foreigners; laws respecting the coinage; punishing the counterfeiting of the coin; treason against the United States, &c.; declared that no force of construction could bring these cases within admiralty or maritime jurisdiction, and yet all these cases were, most expressly, the province of the federal judiciary. So that the question expressly turned on this point, shall we follow the Constitution, or not? I said a good deal more; but this was the substance.

Mr. Lee, after some time, opposed me with a very singular argument. He rose, and urged that the State judges would be all sworn to support the Constitution; that they must obey their oath, and, of course, execute the Federal laws. He varied this idea in sundry shapes.

I rose, and opposed to this, that the oath taken by the State judges would produce quite a contrary effect. That they would swear to support the *Constitution;* that the Constitution placed the judicial power of the Union in one Supreme Court, and such inferior courts as should be appointed; and, of course, the *State judges,* in virtue of their oaths, would abstain from every judicial act under the Federal laws, and would refer all such business to the Federal courts; that if any matter made cognizable in a Federal court should be agitated in a State court, a plea to the jurisdiction would immediately be put in, and proceedings would be stayed. No reply was made, the question was soon taken, and the motion was rejected.

The first clause of the bill was now called for. Grayson made a long harangue. I mentioned that I thought this an improper time to decide absolutely on this part of the bill. If the bill stood in its present form, and the circuit courts were continued, six judges appeared to be too few. If the circuit courts were struck out, they were too many. That it would have pleased me better, but, as we were in committee, I would not consider myself as absolutely bound by anything that happened now; but would reserve myself until the second reading in the Senate.

Mr. Ellsworth rose, and made a most elaborate harangue on the necessity of a numerous bench of judges. He enlarged on the importance of the causes that would come before them; of the dignity it was necessary to support; and the twelve judges of England in the Exchequer Chamber were held up to view during the whole harangue, and he seemed to draw conclusions that twelve were few enough.

I readily admitted that the information respecting the English courts was fairly stated. But in England the whole mass of litigation in the kingdom came before these judges—the whole suits arising from eight or nine millions of people. Here it was totally different. The mass of causes would remain with the State judges. Those only arising from Federal laws would come before the Federal judges, and there would, comparatively, be few, indeed. When they become numerous, it would be time enough to increase the judges.

Mr. Grayson rose again and repeated his opinion, that numbers were necessary to procure respectable decisions.

I replied, that, in my opinion, the way to secure respectable decisions was to choose eminent characters for judges—that numbers rather lessened responsibility; and, unless they were all eminent, tended to obsure the decisions. The clause, however, was passed.

Adjourned at the usual hour.

June 24. The bill for the judiciary was taken up. The first debate that arose was whether there should be circuit courts, or courts of *nisi prius*. This distinction was started by Mr. Johnson, from Connecticut. Was adopted, and spoke long to by Mr. Butler. This kept us most of the day. I did not give a vote either way—indeed, I do not like the bill. The vote was for district courts.

We proceeded to the clause about *Quakers* taking an *affirmation*. I moved an amendment, that *all persons* conscientiously scrupulous of taking an oath, should take the affirmation.

Great opposition to this. The Quakers abused by Izard—Mr. Morris and myself defended them. I read the constitution, by which the affirmation is left open to every one, and called this whole clause unconstitutional. The President himself may qualify by affirmation—the constitution does not narrow the ground of conscience. I was up and down often on this business. A little after three, the House adjourned.

Had a very long walk, this afternoon, with Mr. Contee and Mr. Seney, of Maryland. They seem agreeable and accommodating men. They are very willing to remove Congress from this place. They named Harrisburg, I believe to try me. I said little in favor of it; but assured them that of two hundred acres, which I had adjoining that town, they should have one if they went there.

June 25. Attended at the Hall. First business was to take up the impost bill. Concurred with the lower House about the style of the enacting clause. (See note.)

But a spirit of great obstinacy was manifested with regard to the fourth and fifth clauses. Mr. Morris, most pointedly, against discrimination, &c., between nations in treaty, and others. Lee and Ellsworth same.

The *tonnage* bill was read. The same difference occurred. Managers of conference chosen on both bills. Mr. Morris, Mr. Lee, Mr. Ellsworth.

Read the bill for the Department of Foreign Affairs. Laid on the table.

And now took up the judiciary, and the affair of the affirmations. Ran Ellsworth so hard, and the other anti-affirmants, on the anti-constitutionalism of the clause, that they at last consented to have a question taken, whether the clause should not be expunged; and expunged it was. Labored in the judiciary till three, and adjourned.

26th. Attended the hall at the usual time. The managers were met, and the conference begun. The Senate formed, but the managers were absent at the conference. Some were for proceeding, and others were for waiting. The members strayed to and from the conference chamber. An *adjournment* was often spoken of; at last moved and carried.

Well may it be said that men are but children of a larger growth; for, on this question being carried, there was the same flutter of

Note.—From the proceedings of the House, on the impost bill, it appears (see I Annals, 608-9) that Mr. Thatcher moved to agree to the amendments of the Senate, in the enacting style, with an amendment. The House originally sent the bill up in this form : " Be it enacted by the Congress of the United States." The Senate proposed an amendment : " Be it enacted by the Senate and Representatives." And Mr. Thatcher wished to add the words " House of " before " Representatives " observing that the word *Senate* spoke of the collective body of the Senators; and the word *Representative* alluded to the individual members of this House only, and did not comprehend their legislative function. There ought to be an equality in the enacting style. Therefore the words " House of " were necessary. The motion was agreed to.

joy among the members that I have seen among children in a school, on giving leave ; and away all hurried, except a few that remained a little to see if the conference would finish. Among them, I was one who wished to know the result of the conference.

June 27. The Senate met. The managers of the conference reported an agreement of a number of articles. But the *bill* was not in the Senate. It seems when the conference was agreed to by the Senate, and notice of such concurrence sent down to the House of Representatives, our wise Secretary sent down the bills along with the communication. I was for insisting that, in parliamentary language, the bills were still before the Senate; they had been there when the conference was appointed ; no vote of the Senate had been passed to send them down ; the conference was appointed only on the disagreement. There was a great deal said, the amount of which resolved itself into this, that a mistake had been committed. Mr. Morris said if the bills had been fairly in his possession, he would have brought them back to the Senate. He actually went to try to get them from the managers on the part of the House of Representatives. There seemed to be a jealousy between the two Houses, who should act first, as the one which acted last would reject the bill, or, at least, have the blame of rejection, if the bill was lost. Gentlemen could not reconcile themselves to act without the bills, (for there were two of them, one on impost and the other the tonnage act.) Some moved to act on the report of the managers. After, however, much desultory conversation, it was agreed to take up the bill for the judiciary.

We were proceeding on this, when a message was announced. Sundry communications were brought by the clerk, and the amendments of the Senate were all adopted, on the impost bill, save on the articles of porter and coal. Such was the haste of the President, that he put one question on both these articles at once, and both agreed to. But the tonnage bill was retained, and the principle of discrimination between nations in treaty and those not, was still adhered to by the House of Representatives, on this bill.

Made some further progress in the judiciary, and adjourned about two o'clock.

Monday, 29. Attended at the Hall. Now for the *judiciary*. I made a remark where Ellsworth in his diction had varied from the Constitution. This bill is a child of his, and he defends it with the care of a parent, even with wrath and anger. He kindled, as he always does when it was meddled with. Lee, however, after some time, joined me. Although the President showed himself against us, we carried the amendment.

We got on to the clause where *a defendant was required, on oath, to disclose his or her knowledge in the cause, &c.* I rose, and declared that I wished not to take up the time of the committee, as, perhaps, few would think with me, (this I said in allusion to what had happened in the committee when I had exerted myself in vain against this clause;) but that I would not pass, in silence, a clause which carried such inquisitorial powers with it, and which was so contrary to the sentiments of my constituents. Extorting evidence from any person was a species of torture, and inconsistent with the spirit of freedom. (My reason of acting thus was : I had spoke to Mr. Morris, and found he would not second me in it, as Myers Fisher had not taken notice of this matter in his letter.) Patterson, however, of the Jerseys, sprang up. Declared he disliked the clause, and, having spoke a while, moved to strike it out. I then rose, and declared, since one man was found in the Senate for striking it out, I would second him.

Up now rose Ellsworth, and, in a most elaborate harangue, supported the clause. Now, in chancery—now, in common law, and now common law, with a chancery side. He brought forward Judge Blackstone, and read much out of him.

Patterson rose in reply, and followed him through these thorny paths, as I thought, with good success. He showed, justly enough, that Blackstone cut both ways, and nothing could be inferred from him, but his ridiculing the diversity of practice between chancery practice and that at common law.

Ellsworth heard him, with apparent composure. He rose, with an air of triumph, on Patterson's sitting down. Now, said he, everything is said that can possibly be said to support this motion. The very most is made of it that ingenuity can perform ; and he entered again the thorny thicket of law forms, and seemed to batter down all his antagonist had said by referring all that was advanced to the forms of law, with which everything had been shackled under the British Government. He really displayed ingenuity in his defense. He made repeated use of the term *shackled*, and how we were now free, and he hoped we would continue so.

I determined to have a word or two at the subject. Said I was happy to hear that the world was unshackled from the customs of ancient tyranny. That there was a time when evidence, in criminal cases, was extorted from the carcass of the wretched culprit by torture. Happily, we were unshackled from this ; but here was an attempt to exercise a tyranny of the same kind over the mind. The conscience was to be put on the rack. That forcing oaths or evidence from men, I considered as equally tyrannical as extorting evidence by torture; and, of consequence, had only the difference between excusable lies and willful perjury. I hoped never to see shackles of this kind imposed. Chancery had been quoted—common law had been quoted, as practiced in England; but neither would apply to the present case. The party was to answer in chancery; but it was to the judge; and his questions were in writing. But here, by the clause, he must be examined in open court, before the bench and jury, and cross-examined and tortured by all the address and malice of the bar. I had further to add, that by the bill of rights of the State that I had the honor to represent, no person *could be compelled to give evidence against himself.* That I knew this clause would give offense to my constituents.

Ellsworth rose, and admitted that three new points had been started. He aimed a reply; but, I thought, he missed the mark in every one.

The rage of speaking now seemed to catch the House. Basset was up—Reed—Strong; and at it, we sat till half after three; and an adjournment was called before the question was put.

Ellsworth moved an amendment, that the plaintiff, too, should swear, at the request of the defendant, just before the House adjourned.

June 30. Attended at the Hall at the usual time. The clause, with Ellsworth's amendment, was taken up.

I rose first. Said that instead of the clause being amended, I thought it much worse. That it was alleged with justice against the clause, as it stood before, that great opportunities and temptations to perjury were held out, but this was setting the door fairly open. The contest now would be who would swear most home to the point. If I was against it before, I was much more so now.

Mr. Lee rose, and seemed to mistake the matter. I rose, and endeavored to do the business justice.

Up rose Ellsworth, and threw the common law back all the way to the wager of law, which he asserted was still in force.

Strong rose, and took the other side in a long harangue. He went back to the ancient trial by battle, which, he said, was yet unrepealed; but said repeatedly there was no such case as the present.

Ellsworth's temper forsook him. He contradicted Strong with rudeness. Said what the gentleman asserted was not fact. That defendants were admitted as witnesses. That all might be witnesses against themselves. Got Blackstone; but nothing could be inferred from Blackstone but such a thing *by consent.*

Patterson got up, and back he went to the *feudal system.* He pointedly denied Ellsworth's positions.

Bassett rose. Reed rose, and we had to listen to them all. The question was, however, put first on Ellsworth's *amendment*, and was lost. Next, on striking out, and it was carried.

The tonnage bill was taken up. We concurred in one clause, but adhered in the next.

And now back to the judiciary. Mr. Lee moved that the postponed clause about the ambassadors, consuls, &c., should be taken up. It was so. I saw Mr. Adams begin to fidget, with a kind of eagerness or restlessness. He could not restrain himself long; and up he got to tell us all about ambassadors, other ministers, and consuls; and what he did with his majesty here, and his majesty there; and how he got an answer in this case, and how he never got an answer in that; and how he had, with Mr. Jefferson, appointed Mr. Barclay to the Emperor of Morocco—and how the Parliament of Bourdeaux mistook the matter, and dismissed Mr. Barclay from an arrest, &c., &c. I could not help admiring the happiness of the man. When he had occasion to refer to something said by Ellsworth, he called him *the right honorable gentleman*.

July 1, 1789. Attended at the Hall at the usual time. The clause was taken up, of the judiciary bill, " that suits in equity shall not be sustained in either of the courts of the United States, in any case where a remedy may be had at law.

Dr. Johnson rose first against the clause. Ellsworth answered him, and the following gentlemen, all in turn, Lee, Reed, Bassett, Patterson, and Grayson. Strong spoke in favor of the clause. The lawyers were in a rage for speaking. Many things were said in favor of chancery that I knew to be wrong. Never was there a field more beaten, from the first chancellor down. The lawyers seemed all prepared to show their extensive reading. It was near three, and I determined to say something. A case was often put, of a man, covenanting to convey land, and dying before performance; that there was no relief without chancery.

I, however, rose, said much information had been given on this important subject, but I wished for a great deal more. For instance: I desired to know the number of attorneys and persons employed in the law department in England, and the millions (for it was said to amount to several) extorted by the law department from that nation; particularly, whether the sum so extracted did not exceed the aggregate of the sums in dispute before the courts. Whether any nation in the world, besides the English, would pay their taxes and support such an expensive judiciary. That these points being settled would afford matter of important advice to us, whether it was prudent to imitate the famous English jurisprudence, in all its parts. That the advantages of chancery were, to my certain knowledge, overstated. That the famous case of the bond of performance gave little trouble in Pennsylvania. That the person having paid his bond, brought his suit, and the parties generally consented to a judgment and sale of the lands, and the sheriff made title. That I thought the clause a good one, and wished for it to be more effectual to prevent the flowing of causes into that tedious court.

Up rose George Reed, in angry mood. Said he had a cause of the kind in Pennsylvania; that he had consulted the ablest men there, and received for answer there was no remedy in Pennsylvania; and asserted that the people of Pennsylvania wished for a chancery, and many of them lamented the want of it.

I got up, declared as far as I knew the sentiments of the people of Pennsylvania they disliked a chancery, but that many of them knew not even the name. I never had heard any people speak in favor of it, but some gentlemen of the bar and even among them some doubted whether it would do most harm or good. That in general it was considered, by those who knew anything of the matter, as the field where the gentlemen of the bar would reap the fullest harvest, and it was considered that they enjoyed a plentiful crop as matters now stood. I stated the affair of the bond over again, so plainly that Reed called out, " *in case of consent*, I grant it." I had only to add, in case they do not consent, twelve honest jurors are good chancellors, if not to give the land, at least to give the value of *it*.

The clause stood on the question. The gentlemen of the bar, in the House, seemed to have made a common cause of it, to push the power of Chancery as far as possible. Mr. Morris seemed almost disposed to join them. As we rose, he said, if I had spoke, I believe I should have differed from you about chancery.

This day the discrimination between the ships of nations in treaty and those not, on the tonnage bill, was rejected in the House of Representatives also, and, of course, the tonnage bill now passes. When this doctrine was first treated in the House of Representatives, of no discrimination, it was called *toryism;* and there were but eight votes for it on a division. But mark the influence of the city of New York; or, let me call it British influence. To work, they set in the Senate; and before the impost bill got up, they had secured a majority to reject the discrimination. But some pretext was necessary, even in the Senate. The discriminations in the impost and tonnage bills were said to be arrant trifles—no compensation for the injuries our trade received. That a deeper mode of retaliation should be entered on—such as would effectually cure all disadvantages, and carry the remedy to every particular disease, and retaliate on every nation, exactly in kind ; and where a disadvantage was imposed, a corresponding one should be imposed by us, and not chastise all nations out of treaty with the same punishment. As to *gratitude* or national friendship, they were held not to exist ; and all that was to be done with nations in treaty, was to observe the terms of those treaties. A committee, therefore, of Mr. Morris, Mr. Langdon, and . . . . . . were appointed to examine the state of our commerce, and to bring in a bill for the protection of our commerce. But the discriminations are now struck out of both bills, and I do not expect to hear anything more about the protecting of our commerce, unless it should be taken up in the House of Representatives.

July 2. Went this day to the Hall, at the usual time. The bill for the judiciary was taken up. I really dislike the whole of this bill ; but I endeavored to mend it in several places, and make it as perfect as possible, if it is to be the law of the land. But it was fabricated by a knot of lawyers, who join hue and cry to run down any person who will venture to say one word about it. This I have repeatedly experienced, and when I am certain (for a man may sometimes be certain of being right) of having made obvious and proper amendments, I have been pushed at, from both right and left, by them, and not a man to second me. Be it so, however, this is no reason that I should be silent. I run Ellsworth hard on the uselessness of part of this bill to-day ; and thought I had the advantage in some of the answers I gave. But it was of little avail. Grayson, though a lawyer, told me yesterday, that it was in vain to attempt anything. The people, who were not lawyers, on a supposition that lawyers knew best, but follow the lawyers, and a party, were determined to push it. I needed no information from him on this head.

We, however, came to a clause, the import of which was, that on bonds, articles of agreement, covenants, &c., the jury should find the breach, and the judges assess the damages. I attacked this mixed, half common law, half chancery proceeding—accused the bill of inconsistency ; that a clause had already been adopted, which extended chancery where common law would afford a remedy. Here we had a jury and common law acting with the cause, and we flew from it to chancery powers. This was inconsistency. The jury were the proper chancellors, in such a case, to assess the damages ; and I liked them much better than the judges. They were from the vicinity, and best acquainted with the parties and their circumstances

When the judgment was by default or entered up, a jury of inquiry of damages should ascertain the sum.

Strong made a long speech how this could not be done on the principles of common law and chancery, and seemed willing to show his accurate reading on these points; and concluded by saying either he or the gentleman last up did not understand the principles of these courts, for the gentleman was for doing what he thought could not be done.

I rose quick to reply. Said the clause was before us—the clause was in our power—what I wanted done was clearly expressed. I hoped we were not always to be trammeled with the fetters of English jurisprudence. That we would show we had judgment, and would act for ourselves, independent of any forms, and concluded with a question whether we were always to be considered as empty bottles, that could contain nothing but what was poured into them.

Several gentlemen now rose, and agreed with me in objecting to the clause. But there seemed some difficulty in amending, and it was postponed for amendment.

Attended at the Hall. Business went on at the usual time. It was the judiciary which we were upon. Light and very trifling debates in general. Mr. Reed got up, and kept *hammering* for a long time, (as Mr. Morris termed it,) and really it was difficult to say what he would be at. I did not embark in any debate until we came to the clause empowering the judges, either on their own knowledge, or complaint of others, to apprehend, bail, commit, &c.

I alleged that the judges would be of like passions and resentments as other men. That they should not be both witnesses and judges; accusers and all. That the complaint, also, should be on oath. I moved, therefore, to strike out those words, and insert: Upon oath or affirmation made and reduced to writing, and signed by the party, stating sufficient reason in law.

Lee, of Virginia, seconded me this time. But, according to custom, I had Ellsworth and the gentlemen of the bar up against it. It was insisted that this was agreeable to the laws of England—that the oath of the judge would bind him to all this—that a judge had a right to use his private judgment, just as a juryman had a right to act on his private knowledge. Ellsworth, Strong, Bassett, Grayson, and others, all up; and volumes did they pour out. I could not get speaking for a long time. I, however, made a short reply.

Said we were now framing the law which would be the rule of conduct for the judges. That practice, such as the gentlemen insisted on, had been used by judges; and, from experience, we had learned the danger of it. Cases were known where the resentment of a judge was the accusing spirit, and prejudice pronounced judgment. Every part of English jurisprudence was not unexceptionable, nor would I blindly follow them in everything. That the case adduced, of a juryman using private knowledge, would not apply. A juryman, legally speaking, had no private knowledge; or, at least, none that he ought to keep private. If he knew anything pertinent to the issue, he ought to disclose it, upon oath, to his fellows in court; and this was the law, in daily practice, upon it. If a judge happened to be the only person having knowledge of the commission of a crime, let him apply to some other justice. This I had known done. The case of a forcible entry did not apply to common practice, and yet, in this case, the justices would, generally, bind over witnesses to prosecute.

I hinted at some other points of the clause as imperfect, and said much more before I sat down; particularly as to the dangerous ground on which we trod; considering the interference, or the very possible interference, of the Federal and State Legislatures; and the giving more power over the liberty of the citizen to the former, than was usually practiced by the latter, would not fail to sow the seeds of dissention.

July 4. This, the anniversary of American independence. The day was celebrated with much pomp. The Cincinnati assembled at St Paul's church, where an oration was pronounced by Col. Hamilton, in honor of General Green. The church was crowded. The Cincinnati had seats allotted for themselves—wore their eagles at their button-holes—and were preceded by a flag. The oration was well delivered—the composition appeared good, but I thought he should have given us some account of his virtues as a citizen, as well as a warrior, for I suppose he possessed them, and he lived some time after the war, and, I believe, commenced farmer.

July 6. The judiciary was taken up, and the residue of it passed, without any interesting debate. Our President called for the sense of the House, when it should be read a third time. The members showed plainly that they considered it as not having been touched *in Senate*, on second reading—all that had passed having only been *in committee*. The President insisted that the bill had been *twice* read. So it certainly had—but the second reading was in a committee of the whole Senate. He said former bills had been treated just as he wanted this one treated. We knew, or at least I knew, that this was not the case. He showed a peevish obstinacy, as I thought. He does not like the doctrine of a committee of the Senate; nor has he ever submitted to it, for he ought to leave the chair.

To-morrow, however, was assigned for the third reading, with a kind of saving privilege to make amendments.

Mr. Morris came in a little before we broke up.[e] He put into my hands the letter and remarks of our chief justice, on the judiciary, directed to us jointly. But the Attorney General's remarks, and Judge Hopkinson's, I have not yet had the opportunity of perusing.

Thursday assigned for the bill for foreign affairs; Friday, for the Department of War; and Monday next, for the Treasury Department.

July 7. Attended the Hall at the usual time. The *judiciary* was taken up for a third reading. I can scarce account for my dislike to this bill; but I really fear it will be the gun-powder plot of the constitution. So confused and so obscure, it will not fail to give a general alarm. Ellsworth has led in this business, backed with Strong, Patterson, Reed often, Bassett seldom.

We came to the clause which allowed *the district judges* to sit on the hearing of appeals from themselves. I did not rise to oppose this. Grayson, however, got hold of it, and hammered hard at it. Bassett rose and took, partly, the same side. Now I thought the matter in a hopeful way. Ellsworth immediately drew an amendment, as he said, to cure their objections, though it was nothing like the matter. I drew a clause nearly in these words: Provided that no *district judge* shall sit on the re-hearing of any cause formerly adjudged by him. We got Ellsworth's motion postponed, to put a question on it. It was agreed that the sense of the House should be taken on this. We carried it, and I rose and said, since the sense of the House was declared on this subject, I wished some of the gentlemen of the bar to frame a clause in the spirit of the determination—that the effect of the determination would reach further than the present clause, for it would prevent the *circuit judge* from sitting, in the Supreme Court, on an appeal where he had given original judgment. This was agreed to, and so we killed two birds with one stone.

The most trifling word catching, employed us till after three o'clock.

July 8. Attended, as usual, this day at the Hall. The *judiciary* was taken up. Ellsworth by far more accommodating, this day, than I ever knew him. We sat the usual time, but the debates were very trifling, indeed, and not one worth committing to paper. The chief justice of Pennsylvania, Mr. Wilson, Myers Fisher, the Speaker, Mr. Peters, Tench Coxe, and sundry others, have, in their letters, approved of the general outlines of the bill. Any amend-

ments which they have offered have been of a lesser nature. I own
the approbation of so many men of character for abilities has lessened my dislike of it, yet I cannot think of the expense attending
it, which I now consider as useless, without a kind of sickly qualm
overshadowing me. Bradford's and Judge Hopkinson's remarks I
have not yet seen, nor need I now care about them, as we will probably finish it to-morrow.

July 9. A great part of this day was taken up with light debates,
chiefly conducted by the lawyers, on both sides, and the object
seemed to be the increasing the powers of chancery. Ellsworth
has credit with me. I know not, however, whether it be the effect
of judgment, whim, or caprice, but he is, generally, for limiting the
chancery powers. Mr. Morris and myself differed in every vote
this day. We always have differed on the subject of chancery.

This day I got copies of the three bills for the great Departments.
Besides being calculated on a scale of great expense, two grand
objections offer themselves on these bills : the lessening of the power
of the Senate, taking away from them any vote in the *removal* of
officers, and the power of advising and consenting in one case of
the first consequence ; and the other, the placing the President
above business and beyond the power of responsibility, putting
into the hands of his officers the duties required of him by the
Constitution. Indeed, these appear to me to have been the moving
reasons for bringing forward the bill at all. Nor do I see the necessity of having made this business a subject of legislation. The
point of view in which it presented itself to me was, that the President should signify to the Senate his desire of appointing a minister of foreign affairs, and nominate the man. And so, of the other
necessary departments. If the Senate agreed to the necessity of
the office, and the man, they would concur , if not, they would
negative, &c. The House would get the business before them when
salaries came to be appointed, and could thus give their opinion by
providing for the officer or not. I see this mode might be abused.
But for the House of Representatives, by a side wind, to exalt the
President above the Constitution and depress the Senate below it,
is—but I will leave it without a name. They know the veneration
entertained for General Washington, and believe the people will be
ready to join in the cry against the Senate, in his favor, when they
endeavor to make him a party. They think they have fast hold of
us, and that we dare not refuse our assent to these bills, and so
several of them have not failed to declare.

July 10, 1789. This day the lawyers showed plainly the cloven
foot of their intention in the House. Reed, Bassett, Patterson,

Johnson, Grayson, and others had got a hasty kind of amendment passed late yesterday. The amount of it was, that in the circuit courts, under the name of equity, they should have all the depositions copied and sent up, on an appeal, to the Supreme Court as evidence, on the rehearing of facts, or words to that import. I had some conversation with Ellsworth, in the morning, about it, and offered to him to move for a reconsideration of the matter. He wished to reserve this business for himself, however. He, accordingly, moved the reconsideration, in a lengthy speech, and was seconded by Strong. At it they now went; and until after three, scarce a word could be got in edgewise, for the lawyers. Butler, though lame, bounced up twice. I wished to speak, but could not get leave. The President got up in the chair. I rose, and told him I wished to say a word or two. Sir, I am no professed admirer of the judicial system before you, but the best part of it is the circuit courts. These, sir, the amendments of yesterday, will render abortive. The seeds of appeal and the materials, too, provide for every cause. The system of delay is so firmly established, and the certainty of procrastination such, that justice never can be obtained in it. Let us follow the scheme a moment: The depositions are taken, and carried up six or seven hundred miles, to a Federal court. But, by the law, they cannot be used, if the party is able to attend. The witness is subpœnaed, but does not attend. An attachment issues, but the party will kill the messenger, run to the woods, fly to the Indians, rather than attend. Well, but the court can issue a *dedimus potestatem*, and commissioners may be appointed; and in three or four years the testimony may be collected. Well, and what now? Is the fact to be tried by chancery, powers? I am bold to say that no issue of fact ever was tried or found, for or against, in chancery. Facts often were carried into chancery, as evidence; but, if they were doubted of, issue was joined on them, and directed to be tried by a jury. But now the business unfolds itself. Now we see what gentlemen would be at. It is to try facts on *civil* law principles, without the aid of a jury; and this, I promise you, never will be submitted to.

The question was put, and we carried it.

But the House seemed rather to break up in a storm. Here a leaf from the journal has been destroyed, which was under the date of *Saturday*, July 11. The next entry in the journal is under date July 11, 1789, as follows: Should go to the nearest stack of wheat, rye-straw, hay, or such like material, and draw out two stems; one in the name of each party, and the longest should win the cause. He showed it to me. I gave him a hearty laugh of approbation.

Not, indeed, that I admired either the wit or novelty of it; but I considered it as the index of a sure vote. But I was mistaken. He voted against us, and the clause was lost.

I could see an air of triumph in the visages of gentlemen of the bar, Ellsworth excepted, who has really credit with me on the whole of this business. The part he has acted in it, I consider as candid (bating his caballing with Johnson) and disinterested. Mr. Lee, of Virginia, was for the clause, and spoke well.

As we came down the stairs, Doctor Johnson was by my side. Doctor, (said I,) I wish you would leave off using these side winds, and boldly, at once, bring in a clause for deciding all causes on civil law principles without the aid of a jury. No, no, said he, the *civil* law is a name I am not very fond of. I replied: You need not care about the name, since you have got the thing.

The 12th was Sunday. I was ill last night. My swelled knee gave me great pain, and prevented my rest. Put on flannel, and stayed at home all day. Had no book but Buchan's Family Physician. Read a good deal in it. What a lazar house the world is. Surely the pleasures of life are as chaff in the balance against ponderous lead, compared with the ills and dolors of the human race. Infinite wisdom surely shows us but a small part of His works. There must be a balance somewhere. Or shall we view it in another light? That the only good we enjoy is the effect of prudence. Alas, she does not always command it. It is in vain, however, to attempt to rend the impenetrable veil that conceals the mysterious ways of Providence.

July 13. I forgot to minute yesterday that late in the afternoon Charles Thomson visited me. We had much chat of the political kind. He showed a great disposition to go into the field of the President's power. He was clearly of opinion that the President ought to *remove* all officers, &c. Indeed, he said so much on this subject that I had like to have entertained a suspicion that he came on purpose to sound, or rather prepare, me on the subject. I agreed to sundry of his observations, at the same time dissented, in plain but not pointed terms, from some other things. Perhaps, this is the best way on the whole for an independent man to act. Honesty on the whole is the best policy. I really feel for Mr. Thomson's situation. A man who has been the graphic ___ of the old Congress; the hand and pen of that body from their first organization; and who, I feel a kind of certainty of the fact, wished to die in an eminent office, would not suffer his friends to continue him Secretary of the Senate; and his enemies have taken advantage of it, and declared him out of office, and mean to keep him so. It was certainly bad policy of him to refuse the offer of his friends. The political door is harder to be opened than any other, if once it is thrown in a man's face.

The Senate met, and Mr. Bassett's motion, with respect to the effect of a writ of error as a supersedeas to an execution, was taken up. Mr. Reed spoke long in support of the motion. Mr. Ellsworth equally long against it. I rose, and made sundry remarks; and the amendment was carried. It was not a material one, however, in the bill.

While the minutes were reading, I stepped to Ellsworth, and asked if he would not join me in an attempt to regain the clause we had lost on Saturday. He paused a little, and said he would.

Mr. Ellsworth rose, and spoke long on the subject of a discrimination or some boundary line between the courts of chancery and common law. He concluded with a motion nearly in the words of the clause we had lost. Mr. Lee and myself both rose to second the motion. Mr. Lee, however, sat down, and left me up. I, therefore, determined to avail myself of my situation, and say something. Declared my concurrence of sentiment for limiting chancery strictly. As the bill stood, chancery was open to receive everything. In England, where by the letter of the law, no suit could be brought in chancery if the common law afforded a remedy, yet such was the nature of that court, and so advantageous had it been found to the practitioners, that it had encroached greatly on the common law. Gentlemen would not consider this as an inconvenience. So high were their ideas of *English jurisprudence*, they said all the world admired it, and every member of this House must admire it. (This was Doctor Johnson's language on Saturday.) I was ready to admire it too, but I would first endeavor to describe it.

English Jurisprudence and Chancery.

It (English jurisprudence) consisted of a great number of grades of courts, rising in succession over each other, common pleas, King's bench, exchequer, chancery, &c., so admirably organized and connected that the one was generally ready to begin where the other ended; and so formed, that as long as a client had money he might purchase delay, or in other words get law for it. That in England, at this time, it was rather a trial of the depth of purse than of right, and, accordingly, nothing was more common than for a man who was going to law to calculate and compare his pecuniary resources with his adversary. The cost, however, being fairly counted, and neither party afraid, at it the angry men go. As they are eager, and bleed freely, they mount, perhaps, with tolerable rapidity, until they arrive at the regions of *chancery*. But here their bills are filed and all their facts collected, and in some half dozen of years, it may be, a judgment is given. But mark: the first judgment is seldom or ever final. Here, then, a new number of facts must be adjusted, and some ten or twenty issues, in feigned wagers, must be tried in King's bench. In some three or four years, a new cargo of facts are furnished. The examiner goes to work, and he spends some two or three years. The chancellor, too, perhaps, must have the opinion of the judges of King's bench. Here is a new trial. But at last he gives a judgment. But two of the counsel sign a petition for re-hearing, and the whole business must be gone over again.

But, is the business done? No such thing. Another petition comes in for a *review*, and the whole business must be gone over a third time.

Here I was interrupted by the President, who said there was an instance of a cause being finished, by the present chancellor, in his life time. I answered quick: one swallow does not make a summer, Mr. President; and went on. But are they done yet. No such thing. The House of Lords is before them; and by the time they get out of the far end of it, one, if not both, are completely ruined. This is the progress of your wealthy parties, where plum is matched to plum.

But what of your *unequal* matches—your poor and rich parties. Why, sir, if the relative wealth of one is to that of the other as four to one, the poor man will get about one fourth part of the way; if as two to one, half way; if as three to four, three fourths of the way, before the exhausted party drops off into ruin. (Here, by way of illustration, I repeated the Annesley cause.) For, never was so admirable a machine contrived by the art of man, to use men's passions for the picking of their pockets, and to bring their justice into trade. The present bill has been considered as enjoying perfection, in proportion, as it approaches the British system. Sir, I have given you the opinion which, I know, many sensible Americans entertain of the system of English jurisprudence. With such people, English features will be no recommendation of the bill. Sir, I cannot boast a general knowledge of the sentiments of men in the Union. From what I know of my own State, I am confident a great majority abhor a chancery. Those who I have generally heard advocate the chancery, were professional men. I really believed this was the case, generally, over the Union. I know many people complained of chancery in the Jersey. One hundred and twenty-six pounds had been paid lately for taking the *testimony only* in a chancery suit in that State. Suits had been pending thirty years in their chancery, and had cost thousands. I was clearly of opinion that everything after the verdict of a jury was a mere trap to catch fees, and might be styled the toils of law, added to perplex the truth. The bill, however, before you, sir, as it now stands, is not chancery. It is something much worse. The line between chancery and common law is broken down. All actions may now be tried in the Federal courts by the judges, without the interruption of a jury. The trial by jury is considered the birthright of every American. It is a privilege they are fond of; and, let me add, it is a privilege they will not part with. (See note below.)

This day the committee for considering our commercial injuries reported. I do not like it. The end is answered, perhaps, for which the stir was made when this committee was appointed; and now the business ends in a bubble. I will, however, get a copy of the report before I pronounce on it.

Bill for the Department of Foreign Affairs.

July 14. The Senate met, and one of the bills for organizing one of the public departments, that of foreign affairs, was taken up.

After being read, I begged leave of the Chair to submit some general observations, which, though apparently diffuse, I considered as pertinent to the bill before us. The first clause was there shall be an Executive Department, &c. There are a number of such bills, and may be many more, tending to direct the most minute particle of the President's conduct. If he is to be directed how he shall do everything, it follows he must do nothing without direction. To what purpose then is the executive power lodged in the President, if he can do nothing without a law directing the mode, manner, and, of course, the thing to be done? May not the two Houses of Congress, on this principle, pass a law depriving him of all powers? You may say it will not get his approbation. But two thirds of

---

NOTE.—In the preface to Dicken's Bleak House, it is stated : At the present moment, August, 1853, there is a suit before the court, (meaning of chancery,) which was commenced nearly twenty years ago ; in which from thirty to forty counsel have been known to appear at one time ; in which costs have been incurred to the amount of seventy thousand pounds; which is *a friendly suit ;* and which is (I am assured) no nearer to its termination now than when it was begun. There is another well-known suit in chancery, not yet decided, which was commenced before the close of the last century, and in which more than double the amount of seventy thousand pounds has been swallowed up in costs. If I wanted other authorities for Jarndyce and Jarndyce, I could rain them on these pages.

both Houses will make it a law without him, and the Constitution is undone at once.

Gentlemen may say how is the Government then to proceed on these points. The simplest in the world. The President communicates to the Senate that he finds such and such officers necessary in the execution of the Government, and nominates the man. If the Senate approve, they will concur in the measure; if not, refuse their consent, &c., when the appointments are made. The President, in like manner, communicates to the House of Representatives that such appointments have taken place, and require adequate salaries. Then the House of Representatives might show their concurrence or disapprobation by providing for the officer or not. I thought it my duty to mention these things, though I had not the vanity to think I would make any proselytes in this stage of the business; and, perhaps, the best apology I could make was not to detain them long.

I, likewise, said that if the Senate were generally of my mind, a conference between the Houses should take place. But the sense of the House would appear on taking the question upon the first clause. The first clause was carried.

Now came the second clause. It was for the appointment of a chief clerk by the Secretary, who, in fact, was to be principal, *whenever said principal officer shall be removed from office by the President of the United States.* There was a blank pause at the end of it. I was not in haste, but rose first.

Mr. President, whoever attends strictly to the constitution of the United States, will readily observe that the part assigned to the Senate was an important one; no less than that of being the great check, the regulator and corrector, or, if I may so speak, the balance of this Government. In their legislative capacity, they not only have the concoction of all bills, orders, votes, or resolutions, but may originate any of them, save money bills. In the executive branch, they have, likewise, power to check and regulate the proceedings of the President. Thus—*treaties*, the highest and most important part of the Executive Department, must have a concurrence of two thirds of them. All appointments under the President and Vice President, must be by their advice and consent, unless they concur in passing a law divesting themselves of this power. By the checks, which are intrusted with them, upon both the executive and the other branch of the Legislature, the stability of the Government is evidently placed in their hands.

The approbation of the Senate was certainly meant to guard against the mistakes of the President in his appointments to office.

I do not admit the doctrine of holding commissions, *during pleasure*, as constitutional; and shall speak to that point presently. But supposing, for a moment, that to be the case; is not the same guard equally necessary to prevent improper steps in removals, as in appointments. Certainly common inference or induction can mean nothing short of this. It is a maxim in legislation, as well as reason, and applies well in the present case, that it requires the same power to repeal as to enact. The depriving power should be the same as the appointing power.

But was this a point left at large by the constitution? Certainly otherwise. Five or six times in our short constitution is the trial by impeachment mentioned. In one place, the House of Representatives shall have the sole power of impeachment. In another, the Senate shall have the sole power to try impeachments. In a third, judgment shall not extend further than to removal from office and disqualification to hold or enjoy offices, &c. The President shall not pardon in cases of impeachment. The President, Vice President, and *all civil officers* of the United States, shall be removed from office on impeachment, &c. No part of the constitution is so fully guarded or more clearly expressed than this part of it. And most justly, too; for every good government guards the *reputation* of her citizens, as well as their life and property. Every turning out of office is attended with reproach, and the person so turned out is stigmatized with infamy. By means of impeachment, a fair hearing and trial is secured to the party. Without this, what man of an independent spirit would accept of such an office. Of what service can his abilities be to the community, if afraid of the nod or beck of a superior. He must consult his will in every matter. Abject servility is most apt to mark the line of his conduct, and this, on the one hand, will not fail to be productive of despotism and tyranny on the other; for I consider mankind as composed nearly of the same materials in America as in Asia—in the United States as in the East Indies. The constitution certainly never contemplated any other mode of removing from office. The case is not omitted here; the most ample provision is made. If gentlemen do not like it, let them obtain an alteration of the constitution, but this cannot be done by law.

If the virtues of the present Chief Magistrate are brought forward as a reason for vesting him with extraordinary powers, no nation ever trod more dangerous ground. His virtues will depart with him, but the powers which you give him will remain, and if not properly guarded will be abused by future Presidents, if they are men. This, however, is not the whole of the objection I have to the clause.

A chief clerk is to be appointed, and this without any advice or consent of the Senate. This Chief Clerk, on the removal of the Secretary, will become the principal in the office, and so may remain during the Presidency, for the Senate cannot force the President into a nomination for a new officer. This is a direct stroke at the power of the Senate. Sir, I consider the clause as exceptionable every way, and, therefore, move you *to strike it out.*

Langdon jumped up in haste—hoped the whole would not be struck out, but moved that the clause only of the President removing should be struck out.

Up rose Ellsworth, and a most elaborate speech, indeed, did he make, but it was all drawn from writers on the distribution of government. The President was the executive officer. He was interfered with in the appointment, it is true, but not in the removal. The Constitution had taken one, but not the other, from him. Therefore, removal remained to him entire. He carefully avoided the subject of impeachment. He absolutely used the following expressions, with regard to the President : "*It is sacrilege to touch an hair of his head* and *we may as well lay the President's head on a block and strike it off with one blow.*" The way he came to use these words was, after having asserted that removing from office was his privilege, we might as well do this as deprive him of it. He had sore eyes and a green silk over them. On pronouncing the last of the two sentences, he paused, put his handkerchief to his face, and either shed tears, or affected to do so.

When he sat down, both Butler and Izard sprang up. Butler, however, continued up. He began with a declaration that he came into the House in the most perfect state of indifference, and rather disposed to give the power in question to the President. But the arguments of the honorable gentleman from Connecticut, in endeavoring to support the clause, had convinced him, in the clearest manner, that the clause was highly improper, and he would vote against it. Izard now got at it, and spoke very long against the clause. Strong got up for the clause, and a most confused speech he made indeed. I have notes of it, but think it really not worth answering, unless to show the folly of some things which he said.

Dr. Johnson rose, and told us twice, before he proceeded far, that he would not give an opinion on the power of the President. However, his whole argument went against the clause ; and at last he declared he was against the whole of it.

Mr. Lee rose. He spoke long and pointedly against the clause.

He repeated many of my arguments, but always was polite enough to acknowledge the mention I had made of them. He spoke from a paper, which he held in his hand. He continued until it was past three o'clock; and an adjournment was called for, and took place.

In looking over my notes, I find I omitted to set down sundry arguments which I used. But no matter, I will not do it now.

July 15. Senate met. Mr. Carroll showed impatience to be up first. He got up, and spoke a considerable length of time. The burden of his discourse seemed to be want of power in the President, and a desire of increasing it. Great complaints of what he called the *atrocious assumption of power in the States.* Many allusions to the power of the British kings. *The king can do no wrong.* If anything improper is done, it should be the ministers that should answer.

Collection Bill.

The collection bill was called for, and read for the first time.

The *Senate Journal* states that the Senate resumed the consideration of the bill for establishing an Executive Department, to be denominated the department for foreign affairs.

The journal of Mr. Maclay proceeds :

Now, Ellsworth rose, with a most lengthy debate. The first words that he said were: In this case, the constitution is our only rule, for we are sworn to support it. But neither quoted it, nor ever named it, afterwards, except as follows : He said by allusion : I buy a square acre of land. I buy the trees, waters, and everything belonging to it. The executive power belongs to the President. The removing of officers is a tree on this acre. The power of removing is, therefore, his. It is in him. It is no where else. Thus we are under the necessity of ascertaining by implication where the power is.

He called Dr. Johnson Thomas Aquinas, by implication, too—and said things rather uncivil, of some other of his opponents. Most carefully did he avoid entering on the subject of impeachment. After some time, however, he got fairly on new ground. Lamented the want of power in the President. Asked, did *we ever quarrel* with the power of the Crown of Great Britain ? No ; we contended with the power of the Parliament. No one ever thought the power of the Crown too great. Said he was growing infirm—should die, and should not see it—but the Government would fail, for want of power in the President. He would have power, as far as he would be seen in his coach and six. *We must extend the executive arm.* (Mr. Lee, yesterday, had said something about the Dutch.) If we must have examples, said he, let us draw them from the people whom we used always to imitate—from the nation who have made all others bow before them; and not from *the Dutch*, who are divided, and factions.

He said a vast deal more; but the above was all I minuted down at the time.

Mr. Izard rose, and answered. Mr. Butler rose, and spoke.

It was after three; Mr. Lee rose; said he had much to say, but would now only move an adjournment. As it was late, the House, accordingly, adjourned.

I have seen more caballing and meeting of the members in knots, this day, than I ever observed before. As I came up stairs, Ellsworth, Aimes, and Mr. Morris stood in a knot up stairs. Soon after, Ellsworth, Carroll, and Strong got together. As soon as the House adjourned, Carroll took Patterson aside, and there seemed a general hunt and bustle among the members. I see plainly, public speaking on this subject is now useless; and we may put the question where we please. It seems as if a court party was forming. Indeed, I believe, it was formed long ago.

July 16. Attended pretty early this morning. Many were, however, there before me. It was all huddling away, in small parties. Our President was very busy, indeed; running to every one. He openly attacked Mr. Lee before me, on the subject in debate; and they were loud on the business. I began to suspect that the court party had prevailed. Senate, however, met, and at it they went.

Mr. Lee began; but I really believe the altercation, though not a violent one, which he had with the President, had hurt him; for he was languid, and much shorter than ever I had heard him on almost any subject.

Mr. Patterson got up. For a long time you could not know what he would be at. After, however, he had warmed himself with his own discourse, as the Indians do with their war song, he said he was for the clause continuing. He had no sooner said so, than he assumed a bolder tone of voice—flew over to England—extolled its Government—wished, in the most unequivocal language, that our President had the same powers. Said let us take a second view of England—repeating nearly the same thing. Let us take a third view of it, said he. And he then abused the Parliament for having made themselves first triennial, and lastly septennial. Speaking of the constitution, he said expressly these words, speaking of the removing of officers: *There is not a word of removability in it.* His argument was that the executive held this, as a matter of course.

Mr. Wyngate got up, and said something for striking out.

Mr. Reed rose, and was on his feet for an hour. He had to talk a great deal before he could bring himself to declare against the motion.

But now a most curious scene opened. Dalton rose, and said a number of things, in the most hesitating and embarrassed manner. It was his recantation—had just now altered his mind. From what had been said by the honorable gentleman from Jersey, he was now for the clause.

Mr. Izard was so provoked, that he jumped up—declared nothing had fell from that gentleman that possibly could convince any man; that men might pretend so, but the thing was impossible.

Mr. Morris' face had reddened for some time. He rose hastily. He threw censure on Mr. Izard—declared that the recanting man behaved like a man of honor—that Mr. Patterson's arguments were good, and sufficient to convince any man.

But now recantation was in fashion. Mr. Bassett recanted, too, though he said he had prepared himself on the other side. We now saw how it would go; and I could not help admiring the frugality of the court party, in procuring recantations or votes; which you please.

After all the arguments were ended, and the question taken, the Senate was ten to ten; and the President, with great joy, cried out *it is not a vote*, without giving himself time to declare the division of the House, and give his vote in order.

Every man of our side, in giving their sentiments, spoke with great freedom, and seemed willing to avow their own opinion in the openest manner. Not a man of the others, who made any speech to the merits of the matter, but went about it and about it. I called this singing the war song; and told Mr. Morris I would give him every one who I heard sing the war song—or, in other words, those who could not avow the vote they were fully minded to give, until they had raised spirits enough, by their own talk, to enable them to do it. Grayson made a speech. It was not long, but he had in it this remarkable sentence: The matter predicted by Mr. Henry is now coming to pass—consolidation is the object of the new Government; and the first attempt will be to destroy the Senate, as they are the Representatives of the State Legislatures.

It has long been a maxim with me, that no frame of government, whatever, would secure liberty, or equal administration of justice, to a people, unless virtuous citizens were the legislators and governors. I live not a day without finding new reason to subscribe to this doctrine. What avowed and repeated attempts have I seen to place the President above the powers stipulated for him by the constitution.

For striking out: Butler, Izard, Langdon, Johnson, Wingate, Few, Gunn, Grayson, Lee, Maclay—10.

Against striking out : Reed, Bassett, Ellsworth, Strong, Dalton, Patterson, Elmer, Morris, Henry, Carroll. The President, John Adams—11.

On the *Senate Journal*, under date of Friday, July 17, there is an entry as follows :

Resumed the consideration of the bill for establishing an executive department, to be denominated the department of foreign affairs, and agreed, line first, to expunge the words " Congress of the United States," and insert " Senate and House of Representatives of the United States of America, in Congress assembled," and assigned to-morrow for a third reading.

On motion, that on the final question upon a bill or resolve, any member shall have a right to enter his protest or dissent on the Journal, with reasons in support of such dissent, provided the same be offered within two days after the determination on such final question.

Passed in the negative.

The engrossed bill to establish the *judicial courts of the United States* was read, and upon the question, shall the bill pass ? the yeas and nays being required by one fifth of the Senators present, the determination was as follows : Yeas—Messrs. Bassett, Carroll, Dalton, Ellsworth, Elmer, Few, Gunn, Henry, Johnson, Izard, Morris, Patterson, Read, and Strong. Nays—Messrs. Butler, Grayson, Langdon, Lee, Maclay, and Wingate.

Mr. Maclay's journal proceeds :

July 17. Attended at the Hall, half after nine o'clock. We read and corrected the long judiciary. The Senate met at the usual time. This same judiciary was taken up and went over. And now, Mr. Butler rose against it ; Mr. Grayson spoke against it ; and Mr. Lee was more pointed than any of them. Had Mr. Lee joined us in my objections to it at an early period, perhaps we might have now had it in better form. Mr. Butler offered a motion for leave for any member to enter his dissent on the minutes. This proved a most lengthy debate. It was four o'clock before it was decided. He lost his motion. I thought it right.

And now Mr. Lee, Mr. Grayson, Mr. Butler, Mr. Wingate rose for the yeas and nays on the judiciary bill. They were given. I was in the negative.

I opposed this bill from the beginning. It certainly is a vile law system, calculated for expense, and with a design to draw by degrees all law business into the Federal courts. The constitution is meant to swallow all the State constitutions, by degrees; and this to swallow, by degrees, all the State judiciaries. This, at least, is the design some gentlemen seem driving at.

July 18. We had some debate yesterday about the adjournment. It was agreed to sit this day expressly with a design to take up the *collection bill.* As soon as the minutes were read, Mr. Morris called for it, and I seconded it. But Ellsworth called for the bill on foreign affairs, (as he was sick, and wanted a few days absence, and Bassett, who had stayed over the time he expected, was likewise going out of town.) We had now much curious conversation. Mr. Grayson made some remarks on our mode of doing business. Our doors were shut, and a member was debarred the privilege of a protest. We were shut up in conclave. We, however, have often had this business before us.

The President took occasion to get up, and gave us his history of protests. He said the House of Lords only had that right; they had it in a feudal right. They were, originally, an armed militia for the defense of the country, and were supposed to be possessed of everything honorable. But as to the Scotch peers, that was a piece of patchwork. The Senate were an elective body, and their motives would be to preserve their popularity, in order to secure their elections, and, therefore, they ought not to have any power of protesting.

Ellsworth made a second motion, that the bill for foreign affairs should be postponed till Wednesday fortnight. Langdon seconded this. Sundry gentlemen called, however, for the bill. The President put the question on the bill, and it was taken up. The gentlemen against the bill, Mr. Izard, Langdon, and Johnson, declared all they wished was the yeas and nays, in the same form as they had passed yesterday; the President giving the casting vote. Ellsworth proposed that Bassett should withdraw, and then there would be a tie. Bassett did not like it. Ellsworth proposed to withdraw, and actually did so. All this was occasioned by the absence of Butler.

And now the yeas and nays were taken on the words, *by the President.* Our President gave the casting vote. Mr. Lee moved an amendment, in the forepart of the bill, which did not seem well digested. It was lost, of course. The amount of it was, that the officer should be responsible. I rose, and said I would not consent to it; for, by the third clause of the bill, the officer was made such an abject creature, so dependent on the nod of a superior, I thought it cruel to make him, in any degree, responsible for measures in which he could have no free agency. He had been called servant.

He was more—he was the creature of the President. The President was a responsible officer, by the constitution. It had been said no use would be made of this. I hoped there never would be any occasion ; but *respondeot superior*, was a maxim in law, and I supposed we would have to trust to it.

Mr. Langdon moved to strike out *to be appointed by the said principal officer*. I could not see what he aimed at. Dr. Johnson got up, and complained of the approbation of the President, in the last part of the clause, as reflecting on the Senate, to whom the constitution had given the power of approving. I doubted whether I should rise or no, thinking all opposition vain. I determined, however, to speak.

Mr. President, this clause calls the chief clerk an inferior officer. I think differently of him. This, sir, will be the man who will do the business. In England, sir—that country from which we are so fond of taking examples—the chief clerks do the business ; so much so that on an eminent character being told, by a person who seemed in concern on the occasion, that the ministry were changed, asked, gravely, if the clerks in the office were changed. Being answered, no. Give yourself no further uneasiness, then, the business will meet with no interruption. So will it be here. The calling him an inferior officer, however, paves the way for his appointment by the head of the department. But what is the use of the clause here ? I think freely, and freely will I speak. The Secretary appoints his clerk, of course, and the clerk, of course, will take care of the office records, books, and papers, even if the principal should be removed. They are to be under oath, or affirmation, faithfully to execute the trust committed to them. It is not to be presumed that they will abandon the papers to the winds. What, then, is the use of the clause ? Clearly to put it into the power of a President, if so minded, to exercise this office without the advice or consent of the Senate, as to the affair. The consent of the President, at the end of the clause, points out this clearly. This is a kind of consent, unwarranted by the constitution. The President removes the principal—the clerk pleases him well, being the man of his approbation. The Senate cannot force him to a nomination, and the business may proceed during his presidency. The objects, ostensibly held out by the bill, are nugatory. The design is but illy concealed. It was for these reasons I formerly moved to strike out this clause ; and I am still averse to the whole of it.

Patterson got up, said the latter part of the clause, perhaps, was exceptionable, and he would have no objection to strike it out.

Mr. Morris rose, and said something to the same import ; but as

Dr. Johnson had glanced something at the conduct of the other House, and as what I had said leaned the same way, Mr. Morris said, whatever the particular view might be of the member who brought in this clause, he acquitted the *House*, in general, of any design against the Senate.

Mr. Ellsworth rose, and said much more on the same subject.

I rose, and said I thought nothing on this subject, which I would not avow. The House of Representatives had debated four days on a direct clause for vesting the President with this power; and, after having carried it with an open face, they dropped and threw out the clause; and have produced the same thing, cloaked and modified, in a different manner, by a side wind. I liked, for my part, plain dealing; and there was something that bore a very different aspect in this business.

Monday, 20th July. Asked leave of absence for three weeks, on account of my health. Obtained it without difficulty. I remained some time in my place, after business was over, to give an opportunity to any of the members who chose it to wish me a good journey, or speak to me on business, if they had any. Henry, of Maryland, and a group soon gathered about me. They seemed to think that my going was owing to disaffection to public measures, as much as to indisposition. This I would not own but in qualified sense; that my disappointment with respect to public measures and constant vexation, had, perhaps, aggravated my indisposition. Fun now let loose her frolics upon me, and who, of all the human race, will thank you for that. Not one in a thousand will believe a word of it, and if any do, they will call you fool for your pains. Gratitude no governing principle among the *humanum pecus*. Fear only the parent of obedience among the herd of mankind. Republican theories well enough in times of public commotion, or at elections; but all sensible men, once in power, know that force is the only effectual means to secure obedience. Hence has flowed, and forever will flow, the failure of republican government. Oligarchies and aristocracies follow, till monarchy tops the system, and will continue till some unskillful driver overloads the ass, and then the restive beast throws both itself and the rider in the mire, and the old process begins. A Senator will be in your place before long, said one. Your patriotism will be of great service to you then. A single dinner, given by a speculator, (people who do not like you,) will procure ten votes, where your disinterestedness has not procured you one. And you must intrigue and cabal as deep, and deeper, too, than your adversaries, or we will not see you here again. Is there a single one of the majestic mob who will not belie, defraud, deceive, and cheat you for the smallest interest. Health is too great a sacrifice for such an herd. The whole was delivered with so comic an air, that a serious answer seemed improper, and yet I wished to say something, and, for the sake of harmony, if possible, in the same key. Gentlemen, I have at home good neighbors, good—

[The next leaf has been torn out.]

MEM.—It appears from the Senate Journal, that on the 25th July, *Rufus King*, from New York, appeared, and took his seat; and on the 27th of the same month, *Philip Schuyler*, from New York, took his seat.

The journal of Mr. Maclay proceeds:

Sunday, 16th August. Came to New York at ten o'clock at night, greatly fatigued with my journey. Went after breakfast to Mr. Morris' lodging. He was abroad. Called on Mr. Clymer, at his lodgings, and left his and Mr. Fitzsimmons' letters. Called to see Scott and Elliott; both abroad. Called on *Mr. Izard*. He gave me a short history of the court party, which (as might be expected) is gaining ground. A conference has been held with the President, in which Mr. Izard declares that the President owned he had consulted the members of the House of Representatives, as to his nominations; but likewise said he had not acted so with the Senators, as they could have an opportunity of giving their advice and consent afterwards. Mr. Izard informed me of the attempt of Gorham to get the land commonly called the triangle (now in Erie county) from Pennsylvania, or, at least, to delay the business until he could get a number of New England men settled on it, so as to hold it by force, and make a second Wyoming of it. He said Mr. Morris had got the business put off until Wednesday, expecting my coming to town. By his account, a strong party is forming by Gorham, and they expect to carry it against Pennsylvania.

I immediately left him, Sunday as it was, to call on Scott and Elliott, to prepare for this business. Could find none of them.

My haste and agitation on hearing of Gorham's affair, prevented my noting all Mr. Izard's communications. He said, all your measures are reprobated, and will be rejected. Your voting by ballot,

---

NOTE.—The bill for the government of the Northwestern Territory was first received in the Senate, from the House, on the 21st of July, 1789, when Mr. Maclay was absent, (See Senate Journal, page 52.) He appears to have been absent from about the 20th of July till the 16th of August, 1789.

The bill confirming the ordinance of 1787 for the government of the territory northwest of the Ohio, was approved on the 7th of August.—See Annals of Congress, page 52.

in agreeing to nominations, and so on. We have all been to dine with the great man. It's all disagreeable to him, and will be altered &c. He gave me clear hints of my loss of character at court, and on the direct influence of the President with the members of Congress, &c. For some time past, (as the Indian said,) I could see how the watches went, but I did not know before the way they were wound up.

It was to counteract a growing influence, which I observed to gain ground daily, that I moved the consent to appointments to be given by ballot. The having carried this matter was passing the Rubicon in transgression, as it went to pluck up patronage by the roots.

A thought here on the subject of *influence*. Strip it of its courtly coloring, and it is neither more or less than corruption. When Walpole debauched the British Senate, was it either morally or politically different whether he did it by court favor, loans, jobs, lottery tickets, contracts, offices, or expectancy of them, or with the clinking guinea? The motive and effect was certainly the same.

1789, Monday, 17th August, went out, although I was not very well. It was near nine o'clock before I could see Mr. Scott. I saw Mr. Morris, who had just received, from Mr. Ellicot, all the papers about the triangle. Not one of them had ever thought that Pennsylvania had actually purchased this land from *the Indians*. I called on Gen. St. Clair, who will set this in a clear point of view, if they will not give us time to send to Philadelphia for the deed, &c.

Attended the Senate at the usual hour. The business agitated this day in the Senate, was the bill for regulating the coasting trade. Some progress was made in it, when it was postponed; and the affairs of *Georgia*, with respect to the Indians, was taken up. Some warmth on this business. Sat until after four, and adjourned.

Tuesday, 18th August. Busy preparing for the debate on the triangle, which is to come on to-morrow. Senate met at the usual time. The bill for the Indian treaties was taken up, and considerable debate. I asked for information—for some estimate of the expense; but it seems none had been furnished. A motion was made for reducing the sum appropriated from forty to twenty thousand dollars; but no estimate appeared for either. I lamented my want of information, but declared I hoped the House of Representatives had some just grounds to go on, when they voted the forty—that I would for once trust to them, since I must vote in the dark. But the twenty was carried. We then read over the penal law for the second time, and debated on it until the hour of adjournment.

Wednesday. Senate met, and went on the appointment of an officer to run the line of the triangle. I will not attempt a detail of the arguments, maps, resolves of Congress, contracts, &c., produced by us, which those who voted for us declared carried demonstration with them. We had every man east of the Hudson against us ; and the most of them speakers. Dr. Johnson, in particular, was very uncandid. Ellsworth voted against us, but spoke but little. King and Schuyler managed the debate principally. Langdon was very often up. Every point on the paper annexed was canvassed, and a vast many more. I cannot pretend to say how often I was up ; but my throat was really sore with speaking. So plain a case I never before saw cost so much trouble. At a quarter past three we got the resolve passed.

The following is the annexed paper referred to by Mr. Maclay : Act of cession by the State of New York to the United States, on the 1st March, 1781. Accepted by Congress, on the 29th October, 1782.

Here showed that the cession was made on geographical principles, by the map, and explain how the northwest corner of Pennsylvania came to be placed fifty (say fifty-four and a half) miles further west; and how this company and the State of New York wish to avail themselves of that circumstance.

On the 18th April, 1785, a cession of the same territory was accepted by Congress from the State of Massachusetts, in the same words, only the Pennsylvania line is not mentioned, on a supposition that there was a vacancy of two minutes of a degree between them.

A meridian passing through the westerly bend of Lake Erie, or through a point twenty miles west of the most westerly bend of Niagara river, one or the other must be the western limit of the State of New York, as the boundary is to be a meridian, and must pass through one or other of these points.

On the 6th of June, 1788, Congress ordered the geographer of the United States to run the boundary line, giving notice to the executives of the States of New York and Massachusetts, and to make an accurate survey of the land lying west of the meridian, between Lake Erie and the State of Pennsylvania, that the same might be sold.—(Read the resolution.)

On the 16th of June, 1788, the geographer instructed Andrew Ellicot, Esquire, to perform the service.—(Read the instructions.)

On the 7th of July, 1788, the State of Pennsylvania offered, by William Bingham and James Reed, three fourths of a dollar per acre for this land.—(Read the offer.)

On the 28th August, 1782, the Pennsylvania proposals were accepted, and the bargain closed by the Board of Treasury.—(Read the acceptance.)

On the 4th of September, 1788, Congress vested the right of jurisdiction over the said tract in the State of Pennsylvania.—(Read the resolution.)

Pennsylvania, thus vested with the right both to soil and jurisdiction, pursued her usual system with regard to new lands; and, although it was said that the Congress ought to quiet the claims of the Indians, with respect to lands sold by them, she chose, in conformity to ancient usage, to purchase of the natives. Gen. Butler and Col. Gibson were appointed agents at the treaty at Muskingum; and the purchase of these lands was made. We have not the deeds and other documents to produce. If they are required, we will send for them. But Gen. St. Clair, now in town, was present at making the contract—present at obtaining the deed—and present at the payment of the consideration at Fort Pitt.

The delay of making the survey keeps out of the Treasury of the United States about six hundred and twenty-five thousand dollars, the interest of which is about nine thousand dollars, specie, per annum; and the State of Pennsylvania is retarded in the settlement of the country. If Mr. Gorham or any individual is injured, a Federal court will soon be opened. But the delays are attended with national as well as State disadvantages, and ought not to be protracted.

Mr. Morris will vote with, and support me.

Thursday, 20. This was a dull day in Senate, and might be said to make amends for the bustle of yesterday. The coasting trade bill engaged us all day in a round of dullness. Not one member seemed to understand the whole of it, so much had it been postponed and amended. It really seems rather a system for tolerating and countenancing smuggling, than otherwise. I told them so. I did not choose to embark much in it.

Mr. Lear (one of the secretaries of the President) has for two days past been introduced quite up to the President's table to deliver messages. Mr. Izard rose to know the reason of this. Our President said he had directed it to be so, and alleged that he understood the house so. There was some talk about it a few days ago; but I understood the sense of the Senate to be that the *head of a department*, if he came to deliver a message from the President, should be admitted to the table; but a private secretary received at the bar. It is not one farthing matter; but the clerk of the *Representatives* is received at *the bar*, and I think him a more respectable character than any domestic of the President.

Friday, 21st August. The report of the committee that had conferred with the President was taken up. The most of it was where the President should sit on his being introduced into our chamber, and where our President should sit, &c., &c.

A second resolution was added, declaring that the Senate should give their advice and consent in all cases *viva voce.* This being directly contrary to a former resolution which I had moved for, I rose, and remarked that this matter had been solemnly debated formerly, and decided in favor of a ballot when it came to the single point of consenting to a man's nomination. That I was still of the same opinion, and would vote against the resolution.

Izard rose, and said it was true that the present resolution would repeal the former one, and it was so intended, as he apprehended, there was a change in the sentiments of the Senate on that subject.

Mr. Morris rose, and said there was a change in the sentiments of the Senate, and he hoped his honorable colleague would change his sentiments for *his own sake.*

I rose, and said it was a matter in which I was not in any degree personally concerned, and, if I even were, nothing should make me for *my own sake* change my vote, while my judgment remained unaltered. It could not, so far as I knew, affect me personally; but, even if it did, it should make no odds.

On the question, I gave my no in a voice sufficiently audible. One other faint no only issued from the opposite side of the House. So that now the court party triumphs at large.

The words *for his own sake* were not without a meaning. I have never been at the table of the President or Vice President, or taken the least notice of for a considerable time by the diplomatic corps or the people of ton in the city. But I care not a fig for it. Davy Harris, too, has lost his nomination for an office in Baltimore; but be it so. I have done what is right—I followed my judgment, and rejoice in it.

Notice was given just before we broke up that the President would be in the Senate chamber at half after eleven to-morrow, to take the advice and consent of the Senate on some matters of consequence; but nothing communicated.

From the journal of the Senate, it appears that on the 20th of

---

Note.—David Harris had been a revolutionary officer. He was a son of John Harris, the founder of Harrisburg, and was a brother-in-law of William Maclay. He was subsequently appointed Collector at Baltimore.

August, the President, in written communication to the Senate, nominated General Lincoln as one of three commissioners to negotiate a treaty with the Southern Indians, in pursuance of an act for that purpose. And on the same day General St. Clair was nominated as Governor of the Western Territory.

On the same day Mr. Izard, in behalf of the committee appointed on the 6th August to wait on the President, and confer with him on the mode of communication proper to be pursued between him and the Senate in the formation of treaties, and making appointments to offices, reported; and on the next day it was *Resolved*, That when nominations shall be made in writing by the President of the United States to the Senate, a future day shall be assigned, unless the Senate unanimously direct otherwise, for taking them into consideration; that when the President of the United States shall meet the Senate in the Senate chamber, the President of the Senate shall have a chair on the floor—be considered as at the head of the Senate—and his chair shall be assigned to the President of the United States; that when the Senate shall be convened by the President of the United States at any other place, the President of the Senate and Senators shall attend at the place appointed. The Secretary of the Senate shall also attend to take the minutes of the Senate.

That all questions shall be put by the President of the Senate, either in the presence or absence of the President of the United States; and the Senators shall signify their assent or dissent by answering, *viva voce*, aye or no.

On the same day, the President nominated Cyrus Griffin and David Humphreys as the two other commissioners to negotiate the treaty.

On the same day, the President communicated to the Senate that he would meet the Senate, in the Senate chamber, at half past eleven o'clock to-morrow, to advise with them on the terms of the treaty to be negotiated with the southern Indians.

It is stated on the Journal of the 22d August, that the President of the United States came into the Senate chamber, attended by General Knox, and laid before the Senate the following statement of facts, with the questions thereto annexed, for their advice and consent:

To conciliate the powerful tribes of Indians in the southern district, amounting, probably, to fourteen thousand fighting men, and to attach them firmly to the United States, may be regarded as highly worthy of the serious attention of Government.

Here followed a further statement, for which see Senate Journal of August 22, 1789, Annals of Congress, 68-9.

As it is necessary that certain principles should be fixed, previously to forming instructions to the commissioners, the following questions, arising out of the foregoing communications, are stated by the President of the United States, and the advice of the Senate requested thereon:

1. In the present state of affairs between North Carolina and the United States, will it be proper to take any other measures for redressing the injuries of the Cherokees than the one herein suggested?

2. Shall the commissioners be instructed to pursue any other measures respecting the Chickasaws and Choctaws than those herein suggested?

3. If the commissioners shall adjudge that the Creek nation was fully represented at the three treaties with Georgia, and that the cessions of land were obtained with the full understanding and free consent of the acknowledged proprietors, and that the said treaties ought to be considered as just and equitable: in this case, shall the commissioners be instructed to insist on a formal renewal and confirmation thereof? and in case of a refusal, shall they be instructed to inform the Creeks that the arms of the Union shall be employed to compel them to acknowledge the justice of the said cessions?

4. But if the commissioners shall adjudge that the said treaties were formed with an inadequate or unauthorized representation of the Creek nation, or that the treaties were held under circumstances of constraint or unfairness of any sort, so that the United States could not, with justice and dignity, request or urge a confirmation thereof: in this case, shall the commissioners, considering the importance of the Oconee lands to Georgia, be instructed to use their highest exertions to obtain a cession of said lands? If so, shall the commissioners be instructed, if they cannot obtain the cessions on better terms, to offer for the same, and for the further great object of attaching the Creeks to the Government of the United States, the following conditions: *First*, A compensation in money or goods, to the amount of ———— dollars; the said amount to be stipulated to be paid by Georgia, at the period which shall be fixed; or, in failure thereof, by the United States. *Second*, A secure port on the Altamaha or on St. Mary's river, or at any other place between the same, as may be mutually agreed to by the commissioners and the Creeks. *Third*, Certain considerations to some and honorable military distinctions to other influential chiefs, on their taking oaths of allegiance to the United States. *Fourth*, A solemn guarantee, by the United States, to the Creeks of their remaining ter-

ritory, and to maintain the same, if necessary, by a line of military posts.

5th. But if all offers should fail to induce the Creeks to make the desired cessions to Georgia, shall the commissioners make it an ultimatum?

6th. If the said cessions shall not be made an ultimatum, shall the commissioners proceed and make a treaty, and include the disputed lands within the limits which shall be assigned to the Creeks? If not, shall a temporary boundary be marked, making the Oconee the line, and the other parts of the treaty be concluded? In this case, shall a secure port be stipulated, and the pecuniary and honorary considerations granted? In other general objects, shall the treaties, formed at Hopewell, with the Cherokees, Chickasaws, and Choctaws, be the basis of a treaty with the Creeks?

7th. Shall the sum of twenty thousand dollars, appropriated to Indian expenses and treaties, be wholly applied, if necessary, to a treaty with the Creeks? If not, what proportion?

The President in the Senate Chamber.

Saturday, 22d August. Senate met, and went on the coasting bill. The door-keeper soon told us of the arrival of *the President.*

The President was introduced, and took our President's chair. He rose and told us bluntly that he had called on us for our advice and consent to some propositions respecting the treaty to be held with the southern Indians. Said he had brought General Knox with him, who was well acquainted with the business.

He then turned to General Knox, who was seated on the left of the chair. Gen. Knox handed him a paper, which he handed to the President of the Senate, who was seated on a chair on the floor to his right. Our President hurried over the paper. Carriages were driving past, and such a noise, I could tell it was something about *Indians,* but was not master of one sentence of it. Signs were made to the door-keeper to shut down the sashes. Seven heads, as we since have learned, were stated at the end of the paper, which the Senate were to give their advice and consent to. They were so framed that this could be done by aye or no. The President told us that a paper from an agent of the Cherokees was given to him just as he was coming to the Hall. He motioned to Gen. Knox for it, and handed it to the President of the Senate. It was read. It complained hard of the unjust treatment of the people of North Carolina, &c., their violation of treaties, &c. Our President now read off the first article, to which our advice and consent was requested. It referred back principally to some statements in the body of the writing which had been read.

Mr. Morris rose. Said the noise of carriages had been so great that he really could not say that he had heard the body of the paper which was read, and prayed it might be read again. It was so.

It was no sooner read, than our President immediately read the first head over, and put the question, Do you advise and consent, &c. ?

There was a dead pause. Mr. Morris whispered me, we will see who will venture to break silence first.

Our President was proceeding : *As many as—*

I rose reluctantly, indeed, and from the length of the pause, the hint given by Mr. Morris, and the proceeding of our President, it appeared to me that if I did not, no other one would, and we should have these advices and consents ravished, in a degree, from us.

Mr. President : The paper which you have now read to us appears to have for its basis sundry treaties and public transactions between the Southern Indians and the United States and the States of Georgia, North and South Carolina. The business is new to the Senate. It is of importance. It is our duty to inform ourselves, as well as possible, on the subject. I therefore call for the reading of the treaties and other documents alluded to in the paper before us.

I cast an eye at the President of the United States. I saw he wore an aspect of stern displeasure.

General Knox turned up some of the acts of Congress, and the protests of one Blount, agent for North Carolina.

Mr. Lee rose and named a particular treaty, which he wished read.

The business labored with the Senate. There appeared an evident reluctance to proceed. The first article was about the Cherokees. It was hinted that the person just come from there might have more information. The President of the United States rose—said he had no objection to that article being postponed, and in the meantime he would see the messenger.

The second article, which was about the Chickasaws and Choctaws, was likewise postponed.

The third article more immediately concerned Georgia and the Creeks.

Mr. Gunn, from Georgia, moved that this be postponed till Monday. He was seconded by Few. General Knox was asked when General Lincoln would be here on his way to Georgia. He answered not *until Saturday next*. The whole House seemed against Gunn and Few.

I rose, and said : When I considered the newness and importance of the subject—that one article had already been postponed—that

General Lincoln, the first named of the commissioners, would not be here for a week; the deep interest Georgia had in this affair, I could not think it improper that the Senators from that State should be indulged in a postponement until Monday, and more especially as I had not heard any inconvenience pointed out that could possibly flow from it.

The question was put, and actually carried. But Ellsworth immediately began a long discourse on the merits of the business. He was answered by Lee, who appealed to the constitution with regard to the power of making war.

Butler and Izard answered, and Mr. Morris at last informed the disputants that they were debating on a subject that was actually postponed. Mr. Adams denied, in the face of the House, that it had been postponed. This very trick has been played by him and his New Englandmen more than once. The question was, however, put a second time, and carried.

I had, at an early stage of the business, whispered Mr. Morris that, I thought, the best way to conduct the business was to have all the papers committed. My reasons were that I saw no chance of a fair investigation of subjects while the President of the United States sat there, with his Secretary of War to support his opinions, and overawe the timid and neutral part of the Senate. Mr. Morris hastily rose, and moved that the papers communicated to the Senate by the President of the United States should be referred to a committee of five, to report as soon as might be on them. He was seconded by Mr. Gunn.   •

Several members grumbled some objections. Mr. Butler rose. Made a lengthy speech against commitment. Said we were acting as a council. No council ever committed anything. Committees were an improper mode of doing business. It threw business out of the hands of the many into the hands of the few, &c., &c.

I rose, and supported the mode of doing business by committees. That committees were used in all public deliberative bodies, &c., &c. I thought I did the subject justice, but concluded the commitment cannot be attended with any possible inconvenience. Some articles are already postponed until Monday. Whoever the committee are, if committed, they must make their report on Monday morning.

I spoke through the whole in a low tone of voice. Peevishness itself, I think, could not have taken offense at anything I said.

As I sat down, the President of the United States started up in a violent fret. *This defeats every purpose of my coming here,* were the first words that he said. He then went on that he had brought his Secretary at War with him to give every necessary information. That the Secretary knew all about the business, and yet he was delayed, and could not go on with the matter. He cooled, however, by degrees. Said he had no objection to putting off this matter until Monday, but declared he did not understand the matter of commitment. He might be delayed. He could not tell how long.

He rose a second time, and said he had no objection to postponement until Monday at ten o'clock. By the looks of the Senate, this seemed agreed to. A pause for sometime ensued. We waited for him to withdraw. He did so, with a discontented air. Had it been any other than the man who I wish to regard as the first character in the world, I would have said, with sullen dignity.

The Senate Journal, under date of *Monday, August 24*, is to this effect :

The Senate was to-day wholly engaged in executive business.

The President of the United States being present in the Senate Chamber, attended by Gen. Knox, the Senate resumed the consideration of the state of facts and questions thereto annexed, laid before them by the President of the United States, on Saturday last. And the first question (repeating it) being put, was answered in the negative. The third question (repeating it) was wholly answered in the affirmative—and it proceeds to state the result as to the several propositions before submitted.

The journal of *Mr. Maclay*, under the same date, of Monday, 24th August, is to this effect :

The Senate met. The President of the United States soon took his seat, and the business began. The President wore a different aspect from what he did on Saturday. He was placid and serene, and manifested a spirit of accommodation. Declared his consent that his questions should be amended. A tedious debate took place on the *third* article. I was called on by Mr. Lee, of Virginia, to state something respecting the treaty held by Pennsylvania. This brought me up. I did not speak long, but endeavored to be as pointed as possible. The third article consisted of two questions. The *first* I was for, I disliked the second, but both were carried.

The fourth article consisted of sundry questions. I moved pointedly for a division. Got it. Voted for the first, and opposed the second part. A long debate ensued, which was likely to end only in words. I moved to have the words *in failure thereof by the United States*, struck out, and although Ellsworth, Wyngate, and Dalton had spoke on the same side with me, yet I was not seconded. My colleague had in private declared himself of my opinion, also. It was an engagement that the United States would pay the stipulated purchase money for Georgia, in case Georgia did not. The arguments I used on this subject were so plain, I need not set them down. Yet a shamefacedness, or I know not what, flowing from the presence of the President, kept everybody silent.

The next clause was for a *free* port on the Altamaha or St. Mary's river. This produced some debate, and the President proposed *secure* port in place of *free* port. Agreed to.

Now followed something of giving the Indians commissions, on their taking the oaths to Government. It was a silly affair, but it was carried without any debate.

Now followed a clause, whether the cession of lands should be made an ultimatum with the Creeks. There was an alternative in case this should be negatived; but, strange to tell, the Senate negatived both, when it was plain one only should have been so.

A boundary was named by a following clause which the commissioners were to adhere to. Money and honorary commissions to be given to the Indians. The old treaty with the Creeks, Choctaws, and Chickasaws, made the basis of the future treaty, though none of them were read to us, nor a single principle of them explained, (but it was late.) The twenty thousand dollars applied to this treaty, if necessary. This closed the business. The President of the United States withdrew, and the Senate adjourned.

Just as the Senate had fairly entered on business, I was called out by the door-keeper to speak to Col. Humphreys. It was to invite me to dinner with the President, on Thursday next, at four o'clock. I really was surprised at the invitation. It will be my duty to go; however, I will make no inferences whatever. I am convinced all the dinners he can now give, or ever could, will make no difference in my conduct. Perhaps he knew not of my being in town. Perhaps he has changed his mind of me. I was long enough in town, however, before my going home. It is a thing, of course, and of no consequence; nor shall it have any with me.

Relative to the Permanent Residence of Congress.

The journal proceeds:

Tuesday, 25th August. Attended at the usual hour. On *Saturday* I had proposed to Mr. Morris to bring forward all the places which had been mentioned for the permanent residence of Congress, at one time. He answered, rather roughly: "Let those that are fond of them, bring them forward; *I will bring forward the falls of Delaware.*"

Accordingly, although the President was every moment looked for, he presented the draught of the falls to the Chair.

Yesterday I could do nothing for the attendance of the President. This morning, however, I took the first opportunity and presented the draught with the description of Lancaster. I nominated Wright's Ferry, Yorktown, Carlisle, Harrisburg, Reading, and Germantown, giving a short description of each.

After this the coasting bill was taken up, and read the third time. Then the resolution for adjourning the 22d September. A debate ensued, but was carried.

The amendments to the Constitution sent from the House of Representatives. They were treated contemptuously by Izard, Langdon, and Mr. Morris. Izard moved they should be postponed till next session. Langdon seconded, and Mr. Morris got up and spoke angrily, but not well. They, however, lost their motion, and Monday was assigned for taking them up.

Now came the Compensation bill.

I moved the wages to be five dollars per day. I was seconded by Elmer; but, on the question, only he, Wingate, and myself, rose. Mr. Morris almost raged; and in his reply to me said he cared not for the arts people used to ingratiate themselves with the public.

In reply, I answered that I had avowed all my motives. I knew the public mind to be discontented. I thought it our duty to attend to the voice of the public. I had been informed that the average of the wages of the old members of Congress was a little better than five dollars per diem. I wished to establish this as a principle. I would then have data to fix a price on, as the old wages were never complained of.

Morris, Izard, and Butler were in a violent chaff. Mr. Morris moved that the pay of the Senators should be eight dollars per day.

Up now rose Izard—said that members of the Senate went to boarding-houses, lodged in holes and corners, associated with improper company, and conversed improperly, so as to lower their dignity and character ; that the delegates from South Carolina used to have £600 sterling per year, and could live like gentlemen, &c.

Butler rose—said a great deal of stuff of the same kind ; that a member of the Senate should not only have a handsome income, but should spend it all. He was happy enough to look down on these things—he could despise them; but it was scandalous for a member of Congress to take any of his wages home—he should rather give it to the poor, &c., &c.

Mr. Morris likewise paid himself some compliments on his manner and conduct in life, his disregard of money, and the little respect he paid to the common opinions of people.

Mr. King got up. Said the matter seemed of a delicate nature, and moved a committee to whom the bill might be referred. This obtained, and a committee of five were appointed. By the complexion of the committee, it would seem the Senate want to have their wages enlarged.

August 26. Attended the Senate. The minutes were lengthy, but I was surprised to find no notice taken of my presenting the draft of Lancaster, the letter, and my nomination of the other places in Pennsylvania, although I had put in writing the whole matter, and given it to the Secretary. When he had read about half way of his minutes, I rose, and called on him to know why he had not inserted them. He said he was not come to them, but seemed much confused. He, however, got the letter, and handed it to the President to read it, and it was read. After this, the nomination was read, and Butler opposed their being put on the minutes. I, however, had a vote for their going on.

The penal law was taken up. Ellsworth had a string of amendments. For a while he was listened to, but he wrought himself so deep in his niceties and distinctions as to be absolutely incomprehensible. He fairly tired the Senate, and was laughed at.

I forgot to minute yesterday that the Treasury bill was taken up.

A number of the Senate had recanted again on this bill, and were against the power of the President's removing, and had answered accordingly. The House of Representatives sent us up an adherence, and now Mr. Morris proposed to me to leave the House. I would neither do this, nor change my mind, and he was angry. This was before we had the difference on the compensation bill.

The Permanent Residence.

Last night there was a meeting of the Pennsylvania delegation on the subject of fixing the permanent residence. There was little of consequence said. They mentioned their former agreement to vote for every place that should be nominated in Pennsylvania. Clymer said some things that savored more of independence than any of them. Scott declared he would put himself entirely in their hands, and move anything that should be agreed on. Mr. Clymer declared for the Potomac rather than stay here. I understood him that he thought this politically right. Fitzsimmons and the Speaker seemed to second everything that Mr. Morris said. Hartley was for Susquehanna and Yorktown. But, indeed, I think the whole measure likely to be abortive. They have brought the matter forward, but have no system. I saw this, but did not hazard a single sentiment on the subject. Indeed, I could not, without implying some kind of censure.

I called this morning, and endeavored to put Mr. Scott on tenable ground on the affair of removal, and left him in a proper way of thinking. At least, if he should be defeated, to advance nothing but what is defensible.

Thursday, 27th August. The business in the Senate was the third reading of the penal bill. We had but little debate until we came to a clause making it highly criminal to defame a foreign minister. Here Izard, King, and Johnson made a great noise for the paragraph. Mr. Adams could not sit still in his chair. It was a subject of etiquette and ceremony. Two or three times did his impatience raise him to talk in a most trifling manner. However, it did not avail. The paragraph was lost.

Mr. Morris could not sit one moment with us—the subject of the permanent residence was in agitation in the other House. To tell the truth, Mr. Morris' whole attention seems bent to one object, to get the Federal residence to Trenton. Mr. Scott (agreeable to what had been settled this morning) brought in a motion to the following effect: That a place ought to be fixed for the permanent residence of the general Government as near the center of population, wealth, and extent of territory, as is consistent with the convenience of the Atlantic navigation, *having, also, a due regard to the Western Territory;* and concluded that Thursday next be assigned for taking it up. This was carried.

Senate adjourned early. At a little after four, I called on Mr. Bassett, of the Delaware State. We went to the President's, to dinner.

Dinner with the President.

The company were: President and Mrs. Washington, Vice President and Mrs. Adams, the Governor and his wife, Mr. Jay and wife, Mr. Langdon and wife, Mr. Dalton and a lady, perhaps his wife, and Mr. Smith, Bassett, myself, Lear and Lewis, the President's two secretaries. The President and Mrs. Washington sat opposite each other, in the middle of the table. The two secretaries, one at each end. It was a great dinner, and the best of the kind ever I was at. The room, however, was disagreeably warm. *First,* was soup; fish, roasted and boiled; meats—gammon, fowls, &c. This was the dinner. The middle of the table was garnished in the usual tasty way, with small images, flowers, (artificial,) &c.

The desert was *first* apple pies, puddings, &c.; then iced creams, jellies, &c.; then water-melons musk-melons, apples, peaches, nuts.

It was the most solemn dinner ever I sat at. Not an health drank—scarce a word said, until the cloth was taken away. Then the President, taking a glass of wine, with great formality, drank to the health of every individual, by name, round the table. Everybody imitated him—charged glasses; and such a buzz of health, sir, and health, madam, and thank you, sir, and thank you madam, never had I heard before. Indeed, I had like to have been thrown out in the hurry; but I got a little wine in my glass, and passed the ceremony.

The ladies sat a good while, and the bottles passed about—but there was a dead silence almost. Mrs. Washington at last withdrew with the ladies. I expected the men would now begin, but the same stillness remained. The President told of a New England clergyman, who had lost a hat and wig in passing a river called the Brunks. He *smiled*, and everybody else laughed. He now and then said a sentence or two on some common subject, and what he said was not amiss. . . . . There was a Mr. Smith, who mentioned how *Homer* described Æneas leaving *his wife* and carrying *his father* out of flaming Troy. He had heard somebody (I suppose) witty on the occasion; but if he had ever *read* it he would have said *Virgil*. The President kept a fork in his hand, when the cloth was taken away, I thought for the purpose of picking nuts. He eat no nuts, but played with the fork, striking on the edge of the table with it. We did not sit long after the ladies retired. The President rose, went up stairs to drink coffee—the company followed. I took my hat, and came home.

August 28. There was a meeting of the Pennsylvania delegation, at the lodgings of Clymer and Fitzsimmons. I did not hear of it until I came to the Hall; but I hastened there. The Chief Justice of Pennsylvania and Mr. Pettit attended, with a memorial from the public creditors. Their business was soon done, as we promised to present it in both Houses.

But it seems there was a further design in this meeting. Mr. Morris attended to deliver proposals from Mr. Hamilton, on the part of the New England men, &c., &c. Now, after the eastern members have deserted the Pennsylvanians, they would come forward with proposals through Mr. Hamilton. This same Mr. Morris is as easily duped as another.

I spoke early, and declared that now the New England men find their deceitfulness has not availed them; and yet they wish to try their arts a second time—that their only view was to get a negotiation on foot between them and the Pennsylvanians, that they might break the connection that is begun between the Pennsylvanians and the Southern people.

I was extremely happy to find this sentiment pervade the Pennsylvanians. Mr. Morris labored in vain, and his chagrin was visible.

We came from the hall. In coming up Broad street, Mr. Morris declared he would oppose the Susquehanna as the permanent residence, for it was unfavorable to commerce. He observed me, and added, as far as he could consistent with the engagements he had come under to the delegation. I need no such declaration of his to fix my opinion of his conduct; he has had no other object in view, but the Falls of Delaware, since he has been a Senator—at least this has been his governing object.

Attended at the Hall; and now the report of the committee on the compensation bill was taken up.

As I knew there was a dead majority against everything I could propose, I had determined not to say a word ; but flesh and blood could not bear them. The doctrine seemed to be that all worth was wealth; and all dignity of character consisted in expensive living. Izard, Butler, King, Morris, led boldly. They were followed by the bulk of the Senate, at least in the way of voting. Mr. Carroll, of Maryland, though the richest man in the Union, was not with them.

I did not speak long; and enraged as I was at such doctrines, I am sure I did not speak well. I endeavored to show what the true dignity of character of individuals consisted in, as well as of the assembled Senate. And then, turning, showed that extravagant expense, haughty and distant carriage, with contemptuous behavior to the mass of mankind, had a direct contrary effect; that, in short, mankind were not esteemed in the ratio of their wealth, and that it was in vain for the Senate to attempt acquiring dignity or consequence in that way; that I was totally against all discrimination, (meaning between the Senators and Representatives as to pay;) that we were all equally servants of the public; that if there really was any difference in dignity, as some had contended, it could not be increased by any act or assumption of ours—it must be derived from the Constitution, which afforded, in my opinion, no authority for such distinction.

Ellsworth seemed to aim at a kind of middle course—said he agreed there was a difference in dignity, &c.; but at present was against any difference in pay.

Mr. Adams was too impatient to keep his seat. Dignities, distinctions, titles, &c., are his hobby horses. Three times did he interrupt Ellsworth. He asked him if the dignity of Senate was to be settled by the people? If the old Congress had not degenerated for want of sufficient pay? When Ellsworth said the House of Lords in Britain had no pay, he hastily rose and said a seat in the House of Lords was worth £60,000 sterling per annum. Ellsworth laid a trap for himself.

Up rose Izard, Lee, and others, and called for the sense of the House, on the principle whether there should be a discrimination

or not. It was in vain to urge that this was out of order. Lee
said it was a division of the clause. I mentioned that if they must
have such a question, they should move a postponement. It was
in vain—either way they would have this question, which was a
leading one. Ellsworth and sundry others, who had, occasionally,
hinted something of the superior standing of the Senate, voted with
it. The yeas and nays were called. Mr. Ellsworth now took the
back scent. He had voted for a discrimination, but had repeatedly
in his former arguments mentioned six dollars as enough for the
Senate. To be consistent, he moved the pay of the Representatives
should be five dollars, and mentioned my principle of the average
of the pay, which, he said, applied well to the Representatives.

I rose and mentioned that this was the sum I aimed at for both
Houses. But if this was carried, and the Senate stood at six, we
who had voted against a discrimination, if there was no division of
the House, might stand in an odd light on the minutes.

There really was nothing of consequence in the last observation,
and it was not very well founded; but when the question on the
five dollars was taken and lost, King and sundry others called for
the yeas and nays, with an avidity that I had never observed before.
I voted against the clause, as I did against every other clause of
the bill.

When the pay of the Senators came forward, in the next clause,
at six dollars, I rose and declared I did not wish to detain the Senate; but I had voted against a discrimination when the yeas and
nays were taken. I had voted a pay of five dollars per day to the
Representatives. This, in my opinion, was sufficient pay for the
members of either House. The yeas and nays were, likewise, taken
on this question. Therefore moved that six dollars should be struck
out and five inserted, and concluded that then there would be consistency in my votes. I had voted no discrimination—I had voted
for five dollars to the Representatives; I now wished to have my
vote for five dollars to the Senators on the minutes.

Such a storm of abuse, never, perhaps, fell on any member. It
was nonsense, stupidity—it was a misfortune to have men void of
understanding in the House. Izard, King, and Mr. Morris said
every rude thing they could. I did not retort their abuse; but still
explained the consistency of my motion. I stood the rage and insult of the bulk of the House for what appeared to me an hour and
an half—but it was not half so much, perhaps. Izard was most ve-
hement that no such motion should be admitted. It was foolish—
it was nonsense—it was against all rule, &c.; and all this although
there never was a fairer or plainer motion before the House.

It was in vain that I declared I did not begin the business of the yeas and nays. It was in vain that I offered to withdraw the present motion, if all the yeas and nays were taken off. Izard moved for the previous question. He was replied to that this would not smother the motion. When abuse and insult would not do, then followed entreaty. We adhered to the motion, and had the yeas and nays. General Schuyler joined us; so that we had *four*.

August 29, 1789. The House having adjourned over till Monday, I had nothing to do. I wished to see the Pennsylvania Representatives, and went to the Hall. I saw Hartley, and exhorted him against entering into any cabal with regard to the residence. That the line now marked out, and the principles laid down for fixing the Federal residence, were broad, open, and honorable, and such as any man might avow; and, above all, cautioned him to beware of the arts and devices of the New England men. He took it kindly, but did not seem to stand in need of any such caution. A moment after, I met Mr. Smith, of Maryland. He had a terrible story, and from *the most undoubted authority*. A contract was entered into by the Virginians and Pennsylvanians to fix the permanent residence on the Potomac, right or wrong, and the temporary residence was to be in Philadelphia; and Clymer and Fitzsimmons were gone to Philadelphia to reconcile the citizens of that place to it. I answered I knew nothing of all this. I doubt it. I really do not believe it. So far as respects myself, if I am considered as included, I know it to be false. He adhered to it with a firmness that surprised me. I called on almost all the Pennsylvanians during the course of the day, and informed them of the tale. They all disowned every communication whatever in the way of contract with the representation of any State. I called on Mr. Smith in the evening. Told him he must be misinformed. He declared he had it through one person only—from one of the Pennsylvanians themselves. He, however, would give no names. I told him be that as it might, I believed the matter to be groundless. I left him, having paid more attention to this business than, perhaps, it merited.

Had a card to dine with the Vice President on Friday. Excused myself on account of my health.

September 1. The *salary* bill was taken up. There seemed a disposition, in a number of the Senators, to give princely incomes to all the Federal officers. I really was astonished. Can it be that they wish to surround the President with a set of lordly and pompous officers, and thus having provided the furniture of a court, nothing but the name of majesty, highness, or some such title will be wanted to step into all the forms of royalty. My honorable col-

league seemed particularly attached to all the officers of the Treasury. He either moved or seconded motions for augmenting the
salaries of every one of them. I cannot, however, blame him, in
particular. He was more decent than many of them. The avowed
object of these proposed augmentations was to enable the officers
to live in style, to keep public tables, &c. I was not able to rise
against this principle; but Ellsworth and others did the subject
justice. I found the parties so nearly balanced that my vote generally decided in favor of the lowest sum. This made me sit in extreme pain until we got over the bill. I then withdrew, and it was
really with difficulty that I got to my lodging. Almost every motion for increasing the salaries was accompanied with a declaration
how vastly the salary was below the dignity of the office; and that
they moved such small additions, despairing of obtaining greater
from the House. The citizens of New York, where it is expected
their salaries will be spent, and I really believe the candidates themselves are busy, and perhaps others, too, who expect favors from
the officers.

September 2. I cannot attend the Hall. Mr. Morris called late
in the evening. By him I find advantage was taken of my absence,
and a reconsideration was moved, and an addition carried to some
of the salaries, (Adams giving the casting vote.)

The moderate part of the House exclaimed violently against the
taking this advantage of my absence, and obtained a poseponement
of the bill until to-morrow. But, alas, I cannot attend, if the whole
Union were at stake. . . . . . To give me any information on this
subject was not, however, Mr. Morris' object. There has been a
violent schism between him and the Pennsylvania delegation, or, at
least, a part of them. He begged leave to give me the whole detail of it. It was long, containing the first engagements at the City
Tavern, viz: That whatever place in Pennsylvania the New England men should name, the Pennsylvanians should vote for it. That
every place named in Pennsylvania should be voted for by the whole
delegation. These things I knew not, they having been transacted
while I was absent. But what I well knew was that, when Scott's
motion came forward, the New England men, instead of naming the
Falls of Delaware, as Mr. Morris expected, this being the point to
which all his negotiations with Say, Hamilton, &c., tended, were
prepared to expose the Pennsylvanians, and ridicule the whole. In
this critical moment, the Virginians stepped into the support of
Scott's motion; rescued the Pennsylvanians from ridicule; and gave
the whole a serious face. In this state were matters on the 28th
ultimo, and I thought then that all negotiation with the New Eng-

land men was at an end. Indeed, I was not for entering into any private engagements with any of them. My constant language to the delegation was: You are on tenable ground. Now, keep yourselves there. Something was, however, said, as we parted on the 28th, if the New England men have anything to say, it must come from them. Mr. Morris catched this, and opened a negotiation with them, and carried matters so far that a meeting was appointed by Mr. Morris of the Pennsylvania delegation at Clymer's and Fitzsimmon's lodgings, at five o'clock yesterday evening. Mr. Morris whispered me in Senate the whole business is settled, and you must come to Clymer's and Fitzsimmon's lodgings, at five o'clock.

On quitting the Senate chamber, I called Scott out of the Representative chamber, to tell him to apologize to the meeting for my absence, as I found myself scarcely able to move one step. All this was new to him. He said if any agreement was made, it must be with the Virginians. I saw a cloud of mystery in the business, wished to attend, and parted with Scott, telling him if I cannot attend, I will send an apology by Mr. Wynkoop. I could not attend; but so nobly was the matter managed, that while Mr. Morris was introducing Mr. Goodhue and Mr. King, on the part of the Eastern States, Mr. Madison was introduced on the part of Virginia, or introduced himself. There, however, he was; and occupied a room down stairs, while Goodhue and King sat with Mr. Morris up stairs. Messages were exchanged. The result was, that Clymer, Fitzsimmons, Hiester, Scott, and the Speaker, declared totally against any treaty with the New England men. Hartley and Wynkoop declared themselves disengaged; and all parties departed. What Mr. Morris complains most bitterly of, is that Fitzsimmons should permit him to bring the New England men to his lodging on the terms of treaty, when he was determined against treating with them; and that there should be any terms of communication with Madison to which he was a stranger.

Mr. Morris, however, has not quitted the game. He told me that all the New England men and York delegation were now met, and they would, on the terms of the original proposals, name a place *in Pennsylvania,* for they had actually agreed on one, which he had no doubt was *the Falls of Delaware,* (by the by, I doubt it,) and then we would see how the delegation would answer it to their constituents to negative a place in Pennsylvania. He then said something to me as to our conduct in the Senate. I said I thought we had better come under no engagements to any of them, but regulate our conduct on the principles of the interest of our State, subordinate to the great good of the Union. He agreed to this, and took his leave. And now we shall see what a day will bring forth. The Virginia terms seem to be : give us the permanent residence, and we will give Philadelphia the *temporary* residence. Mr. Morris declared a vote could not be obtained in the Senate for an adjournment to Philadelphia.

September 3. Mr. Wynkoop went early to a meeting of the Pennsylvania delegation. They were staggered at the thoughts of voting, in the first instance, for a place out of the State.

The business came on in the House of Representatives. Goodhue took the lead. And here I could give an advantageous lecture on scheming.

The mariner's compass has thirty-two points ; the political one, perhaps as many hundreds, and the schemers an indefinite number. And yet there is but one of them that will answer. It is true there were not so many points in the present case, but the wind came from an unexpected quarter. All Mr. Morris' expectations were blasted in a moment, for Goodhue moved a resolution for the *Susquehanna*, as the sense of the Eastern States, exclusive of New York.

The debate was long and tedious, and the business of this day ended with carrying Scott's motion. Goodhues' stands until to-morrow.

September 3. Ellsworth popped in this morning, to see if I could not possibly attend on the *salary* bill ; but I could not.

Mr. Elmer called in the evening. I know not in the Senate a man, if I were to choose a friend, on whom I would cast the eye of confidence, as soon as on this little doctor. He does not always vote right, and so I think of every man who differs from me ; but I never yet saw him give a vote, but I thought I could observe disinterestedness in his countenance. If such a one errs, it is the sin of ignorance, and I think Heaven has pardons ready sealed for every one of them. Behold, O God ! can such an one say, the machine which thou hast given me to work with, faithfully have I played its powers ? If the result has been error, intentional criminality was not with me.

He was very urgent for my attendance on the salary bill ; but seeing the state of my knee, readily admitted there could be no expectation of it.

He told me Mr. Morris was exerting his utmost address in engaging votes against the Susquehanna—he had influence with the Jersey members. The argument was, that they had been treated with disrespect in not having been consulted when the York and eastern members fixed on the Susquehanna.

If Mr. Morris really expects to obtain a vote for the Delaware, after what has happened, it is a proof how far interest will blind a man. But I do not believe he has any such expectation. His design must be to ruin the Susquehanna scheme, and, in fact, keep Congress in New York. I have heard him declare it ought never to be any where but in Philadelphia or New York. Those places suit his plans of commerce. Nor do I believe he ever will consent to its being any where else, unless it be on his own grounds at the Falls of the Delaware.

Sept. 4. Goodhue's motion was carried.

Mr. Morris called in the evening. He sat a long time. I never saw chagrin more visible on the human countenance. "Well," said he, "I suppose you are gratified." I really was vexed to see him so deeply affected. I said, cooly, "I could not be dissatisfied." He repeatedly declared he would vote for the Susquehanna, because he had said so; but he would do everything in his power against it. This he called *candor;* but I think he cannot call it consistency. It has long been alleged in this place that Mr. Morris governed the Pennsylvania delegation, and I believe this idea has procured Mr. Morris uncommon attention. The delusion must now vanish. He made a long visit. Mr. Wynkoop and myself said everything in our power to soften him, and we seemed to gain upon him. He mentioned, with apparent regret, some rich lands in the Conestoga manor, which he had exchanged with John Musser for lands on the Delaware.

5th. Worse—confined mostly to bed. Visited by sundry gentlemen. Scott, Hiester, Fitzsimmons called in th evening. The Susquehanna, Potomac, and Delaware in every mouth. I find Mr. Wynkoop has revived his hopes of the Delaware. He said, "If we lose the Susquehanna, then it will be fixed at the Delaware." I looked hard at him—asked if he had seen Mr. Morris. He answered "no," hesitatingly. I can find by several hints this day that there is some new scheme on foot.

September 6. Very ill, and close confined. Izard called to see me. The moment I saw him I understood that he came on a scrutinizing errand. I made no mystery of anything I knew—told him that the certain effect of any new scheme in the Yorkers or New England men would most infallibly place us at the Potomac. He repeatedly mentioned a new scheme being on foot; but I could not learn what it was. Mr. Morris is in close connection with the Yorkers, and communicates everything to them.

Mr. Clymer called on me. He spoke highly in favor of the Susquehanna, as being the most favorable position in the State for the benefit of Pennsylvania. Blamed Mr. Morris much—said *he would yet ruin all.* In the evening, the Speaker called. He speaks more confidently of the Susquehanna than any of them. I told him I did not like the adjournment, when the question was ready to be put, yesterday. He endeavored to account for this; but I think it bodes ill.

Monday. I am still very ill. This day was the trial of shift, evasion, and subterfuge, in the House of Representatives; but the *Susquehanna* vote was carried, by a majority of seven; and Ames, Lawrence, and Clymer appointed a committee to bring in a bill. Close confined, and very ill. Unable to get information, or to minute it down if I had it.

Tuesday 8. Still close confined, &c. The Speaker called, and gave us an anecdote of Mr. Madison, which seems to discover some traits of the less amiable in his character. While the salary of the Governor of the Western Territory was before the House, in the first stage of the business, Madison had supported it at $2,500. But during the Susquehanna debate, Mr. Clymer, seeing Gov. St. Clair in the gallery, addressed a note to him, for information. The Governor sent back an answer in writing, which contradicted the position of the friends of the Potomac. This day Madison moved a reduction of five hundred dollars from his salary.

This week has been one of hard jockeying between the Senate and House of Representatives. The Senate insisted, and hard, too, for a mark of superiority in their pay. It was a trial who should hold out longest. The House of Representatives gave way, more especially after the Senators told them, that if you want your pay, send us a bill·for yourselves only, and we will pass it. I really wonder, in the temper the House is in, that they had not done it; but they were aware that the majority of the Senate would fly from this proposal, as I believe many of them need money as much as any of the Representatives can do. It was a trial of skill, in the way of starvation; and the dignity or precedence, or call it what you will, which could not be gained from the understanding of the House of Representatives, was extorted from their pockets.

I have been visited this week by . . . . Pennsylvanians, and by Doctor Elmer and Wingate, of the Senate.

I will venture but one remark on the . . . . of the permanent residence. It will, however be rather a series of remarks.

Neither New England men nor Yorkers are sincere about moving from this place. They firmly believe the whole will end in vapor. Mr. Morris is to destroy the Susquehanna scheme in the Senate, if not sooner, in order to bring forward the Delaware. This he will do, with small assistance from the Yorkers, by engaging the Senators of Jersey and Delaware; and, this being done, the Delaware destroys itself, for the New England men fall to pieces, their engagement having only been for the Susquehanna. These arts are likely enough to succeed.

Sunday, 13. In the evening, Mr. Morris, Mr. Clymer, and Mr. Fitzsimmons called on me. I thought that the Susquehanna had not got justice done in the arguments. Spoke long on this subject to possess them of my ideas of it. All the talk and speculation about the Western Territory is visionary. Nothing will come on to the Atlantic rivers from the western waters. If it should, the Susquehanna has the advantage in the double connection by Juniata and the West Branch. I was listened to throughout with apathy.

Monday, 14th. About twelve Mr. Clymer called in—said he had a letter from Reading Howell, with important explanation. He read part of it, and desired I would draw up the thoughts I had expressed last night, that a publication might be prepared against the time of taking up the bill. Dr. Johnson and Mr. Carroll called while he was in, and interrupted us a little. He stayed a moment after them, and said he would call early to-morrow morning, that we might settle on something for publication. I confessed plainly to him the same thoughts which I minuted on Saturday; but he said Mr. Morris was now contented. I was so unwell that I had to go to bed; and here, leaning on my elbow, I arranged something, but was greatly at a loss for maps, and for the distances on the Susquehanna and Potomac, beginning at tide water, to Fort Pitt, so that what I composed was with blanks.

Tuesday, 15th. Between ten and eleven Mr. Clymer, Mr. Fitzsimmons, and Governor St. Clair called. I read what I had prepared, and it seemed to give satisfaction; but I took notes of sundry matters from them to be inserted. The blanks were, however, still open. They promised to furnish these distances from Mr. Ames. This was done after I had finished the composition, and the putting them in could not be done but clumsily. I hastened to get over the business, expecting they would call soon; but night came without my hearing from them. I cannot go out, and there is a listlessness in all our Pennsylvanians on this subject. I can think of many things which I would have done, could I go about, which must now remain undone.

Wednesday, 16th. To-morrow the bill for the permanent residence is to be taken up, and yet all is quiet on our part. Mr. Wynkoop told me he had walked a long time opposite Trinity church, with Mr. C. and Mr. F., and that they had spoke of me, and nothing more. He offered to do anything. I thought of Hartley. He is active, and will be in earnest. Mr. Wynkoop went for him. He came, and I put the paper in his hands. Mr. Wynkoop returned before the House met, told me Child was to print it, and they would send the proof-sheet to me for correction.

About two o'clock, Mr. Morris, Mr. King, and Mr. Butler called on me. The talk was only about the judiciary. Mr. Morris said he had followed Ellsworth in everything; if it was wrong he would blame Ellsworth. King said he had never had an opportunity of judging of it. I censured it as freely as ever.

There was a meeting of the Pennsylvania delegation this evening, to regulate their conduct respecting the part they would act about the opening of the Susquehanna. They agreed to wait on Smith and Jeney in the morning. I had begged Mr. Wynkoop that they should get the proof-sheet and correct it; but it is likely they would not send for it. The printer's boy, however, called on me, and I corrected it. I can find that *Germantown* is the place that is to be played against the Susquehanna. I had hopes that this opposition was dropped. I believe they are not as active as some days ago, but lie by, fully bent to take all advantages. We will see what they will do. But I have laid it down as the only sure ground, to adhere to the Susquehanna.

Thursday, 17th. Some people are so hardy, as to deny that the Susquehanna affords any navigation at all. Boudinot is one of them. I wrote to Mr. Burrell to furnish an extract of the stores forwarded on the Susquehanna in the year 1779, and the usual load of a river boat. My Wynkoop went to him with the letter. He said he would do what he could, but rather excused himself. I sent some information to Mr. Ames, by Mr. Wynkoop; and now we must see what they will do.

The day is rainy, and nobody has called. About dark Parson Lynn came in. Joy was in his countenance. He told me the Maryland condition was carried, and of course there would be schism among the Pennsylvanians—that Gerry had moved for the Falls of Delaware, instead of the Susquehanna. The whole of what he said convinced me that I was not in the least mistaken as to the measures they are carrying on. The Pennsylvanians will divide; the New England men and Yorkers both will come off with apparent honor, and Congress remain where it is. Late at night, in comes Mr. Wynkoop in higher spirits than ever I saw him. It is all over with the Susquehanna. We must vote against it now. I have just come from Clymer and Fitzsimmons' lodgings; they are of the same opinion; and now for the *Falls of Delaware*. The Marylanders have carried a clause, that Pennsylvania and Maryland shall consent, to the satisfaction of the President, that the navigation of the Susquehanna shall be cleared, but not at their expense. We never will consent to lay our State under any restrictions. The only reply I made was : So then, rather than consent that the navigation of the Susquehanna should be opened, you will drive Congress away from its banks. This is the point of view in which it will be considered, and in which you must expect to answer for it.

18th. I wished to see some of our Pennsylvanians. Clymer and Fitzsimmons had called a meeting last night, in order to make them change their ground and vote for the Falls of Delaware. This was the intention of the meeting, from what Wynkoop clearly enough expressed. I wrote a note to Hartley, but he came in just as I was sealing it. He was in a high rage at the Philadelphians, and declared they had been insincere from the beginning. He seemed to want my opinion. I gave it freely—to adhere firmly to the ground that had been taken, and support the bill at all events. I had written a note to the Speaker, but he came in immediately after I had sent it away. He seemed clearly in sentiment with Hartley, and gave substantial reasons for it. He said an absolute agreement had been made between the Pennsylvanians on one part, and Smith and Seney, of Maryland, on the other, that the Maryland condition should be that " Pennsylvania would throw no impediment in the way of clearing the Susquehanna." This gave entire satisfaction to Smith and Seney—was to have been brought forward by the friends of the Susquehanna, and Smith and Seney, by voting for it, would have carried this and rejected the other Maryland condition. But Mr. Fitzsimmons broke the agreement and flew off yesterday morning. This, of course, fixed Smith and Seney to the exceptionable condition which was carried by means of their votes. So that it seems as if Mr. Fitzsimmons wished some vote to be carried that would furnish him and others with a pretext for breaking off from the Susquehanna ; for they could have prevented this Maryland condition, if they had chosen so to do.

Further, that his partner in Philadelphia mixes with all classes of people ; that the common people were well satisfied with Congress being on the Susquehanna ; but of late he could hear among the leading men about the bank, &c., many opinions and predictions that it never would be on the Susquehanna, &c.

I think it no unfair conclusion to say that Philadelphia spite hath done this, although it be the act of but a few individuals in that place. I can now clearly account for the listlessness and apathy of some persons respecting the Susquehanna. Indeed, it is questionable whether the late application to me was anything more than a blind to cover their intended defection.

By this and yesterday's papers, France seems travailing in the birth of freedom. Her throes and pangs of labor are violent. God gave her an happy delivery. Royalty, nobility, and the vile pageantry by which a few of the human race lorded it over, and trod on, the necks of their fellow mortals seem likely to be demolished with their kindred Bastile, which is said to be laid in ashes. With what indignation do I review the late attempt of some among us to revive the vile machinery.

This evening the Speaker called. He repeated the whole of what he had told me in the morning, in the presence of Mr. Wynkoop. Said he did not know what to make of men who agreed to a thing over night, and denied it in the morning. Fitzsimmons and Clymer were tired of the Susquehanna, &c., &c.

September 19. This morning, Colonel Hartley's son called on me with a note, and showed me the copy of a letter which the Colonel had written to Clymer and Fitzsimmons. He called on them for an adherence to their former tenor of conduct respecting the Susquehanna, and plainly declared that their defection now would be considered as a proof of their insincerity from the beginning. I am unwilling there should be any schism among the Pennsylvania representatives. Perhaps, this letter may lay the foundation of it. Perhaps, it may have the contrary effect. It is, however, done without the advice of any person, and we are left to attend to the event.

I have wished much to have seen Clymer and Fitzsimmons, for some days past. I dropped distant hints of this often to Mr. Wynkoop. This had no effect—I could not justify myself in sending for them. However, I know not if I could have any influence with them, and I know that Wynkoop carries, faithfully, every word which I say, to them. Dr. Franklin says *the world will do its own business.* I must let it do so on this occasion, for my lame knees will not let me help it.

Had a note from Col. Hartley. The permanent (residence) business is put off until Wednesday next, on account of the indisposition of some members. The House, by joint resolution with the Senate, are to break up on Tuesday. Appointing Wednesday seems like the oblivion committee in the British Parliament, on the American petitions, before the Revolution. But we will see what will come of it.

(In a marginal note, it is simply observed that Mr. Hartley was mistaken when he wrote this note.)

The journal proceeds: In the evening, Mr. Dalton called to see me. Soon after, Mr. Morris and Mr. Fitzsimmons came in. Soon after, Mr. Scott—Mr. Dalton went away. Mr. Scott said, what shall we do with the residence? I believe we must vote for it. I don't know, said Fitzsimmons, if the condition had only been *that we should not prevent the clearing of the Susquehanna,* I should not have cared. Scott said, in fact it amounts to no more now. I don't know, said Fitzsimmons. Mr. Morris said, abruptly, the contract is broke—we were to have this thing free of any condition. I have, however, a letter from Peters, on this subject. He got out the letter, but did not read it. Mr. Scott was on his feet, and went away. The others soon followed.

When Mr. Morris talked of the contract being broke, I asked: Have any of the eastern people given way? Have any of them voted against the Susquehanna? Mr. Fitzsimmons said, none.

I can readily guess what Mr. Morris means by saying the contract is broke. Need his vote be expected?

September 20. Col. Hartley called in this morning; says the business of the permanent residence will come on to-morrow. I could clearly gather from what he said, that the effort would be to throw off the whole business for this session; for, from what I can learn, they are not able to engage the New England men for *the Delaware;* therefore postpone, and wait for the chapter of chances.

Monday, 21. Dressed myself. Weak and languid, but went to the Hall. Thought I would not be able' to stay long; but when the business began I seemed amused, and grew better. I stayed it out until after three o'clock.

The judges' salaries were taken up. That of the chief justice had been settled before, at $4,000; that of the *puisne* judges was put at $3,000. Mr. Morris moved for $500 more, seconded by Izard—a division, nine and nine; the President had to give the casting vote, and had the yeas and nays called on him. He, however, made a speech: Somebody had said judges could be had for less. That people must be abandoned and forsaken by God, who could speak of buying a judge as you would a horse. Judges should portion their children, bring them up, provide for them, &c., &c. Many families in New England had suffered by the head of it being a judge.

Motions were made for increasing everything almost. None, however, carried until they came to the Attorney General. Mr. Morris moved it should be $2,000. King seconded. A division, nine and nine; and the President voted for it. Wyngate called for the yeas and nays. Adams looked pitiful. Said he would be made the scape-goat for everything, A member got up to have the yeas and nays retracted. Grayson, who had been with us before, spoke against having them now. So they were not called. The House of Representatives threw out this amendment, and it was reduced to $1,500.

Hartley called me out to tell me that *the Susquehanna bill* was carried. (This meant in the House of Representatives.) Mr. Morris was all day calling out members. Grayson, Gunn, King, Reed, and Butler were some of them that I saw him take aside. The citizens and Wynkoop dared not vote against it. It would have had no effect if they had. Mr. Morris, being a six years' man, considers himself as independent, and he is to destroy it in the Senate. The others think to escape censure by this shift. When I consider how agreeable it will be to the eastern members, and to the Yorkers, to destroy all this business, I really fear Mr. Morris. It is so easy persuading men to do what they wish for. We must, however, wait the event.

22. Dressed, and went to the Hall. Resolution came up from the other House rescinding the resolution of adjournment on this day, and for adjourning on Saturday. Concurred.

The Permanent Residence.

Bill for the permanent residence read the first time. Butler moved to postpone *till next session*. Seconded by Grayson. Lee, Butler, and Grayson spent about an hour. They had only Izard and Gunn to join them on this business—five in all. From hence, I think, we may prognosticate that the bill will pass in some shape or other. Mr. Morris in the deepest chagrin. Did not speak to me in the morning. Left his usual seat to avoid me. Never spoke until we were coming out of the Senate Chamber. He then asked if I continued to grow better. I answered in the affirmative, but he could not talk to me.

I met General St. Clair at the Hall. If I had no other clue, I could tell how the Philadelphians stood, by him. He was all full of doubts—the bill would never do—the President would never act on it—the river might not admit of navigation, &c., &c. The bill, however, passed, 31 to 17, in the House of Representatives.

Wynkoop cannot sit with me this evening; he is caballing down stairs. Mr. Linn called; told me the design of the Virginians and the Carolina gentlemen was to talk away the time, so that we could not get the bill passed.

23d. Went to the Hall early. Mr. Carroll came in; told me Mr. Morris was against the bill, and wanted to bring forward *Germantown* and the *Falls of Delaware*.

The Senate met, and every endeavor was used to waste time. Lee, Butler, Grayson, refused to go on with the business, as Gunn was absent. Gunn came, and then they wanted to go and see the balloon let off. But at last the bill was read over. I was called out. There was Mr. Morris, Mr. Fitzsimmons, and Col. Hartley. Fitzsimmons, began telling me what the Pennsylvanians had agreed to do—first, strike out the proviso clause. If this could be done, then agree to the bill; but if this could not be done, then abandon the Susquehanna, and try for the Falls of the Delaware and Germantown. As he stated it to me, I understood that all the Pennsylvanians but myself had agreed to this. I told him it was a late moment to call on me when the bill had actually been read over, and the first clause taken up; that the *proviso* had nothing so terrible in it as to make me abandon the bill, rather than consent to it; that I saw no safety in anything but adhering to the bill, and if we lost the bill, we must go to the Potomac.

Mr. Morris raged out something against the proviso, or to the advantage the State would lose by such a proviso being adopted; and concluded: "I never will vote for the bill unless the proviso is thrown out." I said, slowly, he would act as he pleased.

He knows as well as I do, that the Senate never will reject the proviso. Fitzsimmons and Morris, however, said, "let us call King out." King came. Fitzsimmons said, "The Pennsylvania delegates were against the proviso; and in case the proviso was continued, five were for trying the Falls of Delaware and Germantown." Col. Hartley corrected him and told him "only *four*." As I had nothing to do with their bargain, I turned on my heel and left them.

I thought it strange conduct of our delegates, after they had all voted for the bill, to be making such offers. If the proviso is struck out, the two Marylanders will vote against us. If in, Mr. Morris will vote against it. I have expected nothing else of him for some time.

Mr. Morris moved that the first and second clauses should be postponed, so as to come at the proviso. This brought on a lengthy debate. Butler was severe on Mr. Morris. Said his views were totally local. Let us keep the Federal town on the Susquehanna, and let there be no navigation out of it, and then you must come to Philadelphia. But rather than have the Susquehanna opened, which will take some of our trade away, we will not let you put the Federal town there.

Morris replied with apparent heat, The other retorted. Grayson and Lee were both up. Izard was up; and long speeches were made. The question was, however, put and carried.

And now, Mr. Morris moved to strike out the proviso. I forget who seconded him. The reason he gave was that the State of Pennsylvania had a bargain on hand with Maryland, about this matter, and commissioners were appointed to negotiate it. Pennsylvania would suffer the Susquehanna to be opened, if Maryland would suffer a canal to be dug between the bays of Chesapeake and Delaware. That he would be betraying the interest of the State in so imminent a degree, that he dared not go home to Pennsylvania if such a clause was in the bill.

I had hinted to Mr. Morris that the last law for clearing the Susquehanna had no condition; but he answered, the Marylanders thought it had.

It was now that the most unbounded abuse was thrown on the State of Pennsylvania. Lee, Grayson, Butler, and Izard struggled who should be up to rail at the Government.

Mr. Carroll got up and answered Mr. Morris mildly. I whipped out, and sent for Col. Hartley, and got from him the late law for clearing the Susquehanna. So great was the rage for speaking, that I could scarce get a word said. I endeavored to be up first on the sitting down of Butler, but Lee was up with me. I begged for indulgence, as I had information to give which I thought very material. I stated the importance of the question, and declared it my duty to give all the information in my power. That the State of Pennsylvania deserved none of the illiberal abuse that had been bestowed on it. That no such design as shutting up the Susquehanna could be charged on Government. I then read several clauses of the act, declaring the Susquehanna and its branches highways, to the Maryland line. I declared I did not think there was a single Pennsylvanian of character that could be so base as to wish the shutting up the mouth of that river. That for my part, I considered the proviso as harmless, and if it tended to give satisfaction to the public at large or any individuals, I had no objection to it. That I thought the business, on the part of Pennsylvania, done already; but if any more was wanted, I had no doubt of their doing it. I could, for my part, apprehend no danger from the proviso. Much, it was said, was put by it in the President's power. But he had his honor to support. I was convinced he would neither traffic with his own character, nor the public expectation; and I was convinced no defect would be experienced on the part of the State of Pennsylvania.

The rage for speaking did not subside; but it took a different

NOTE.—Such a canal is now in agitation.

turn. Mr. Morris said he did not know of that law. The question, however, was put, and five only rose for rejecting the proviso: Morris, Knox, Schuyler, Johnson, and Dalton. There was now a cry for adjournment, to see the balloon, and the Senate rose.

September 23. *Mr. Clymer* called about eight o'clock. Began to speak against the Susquehanna. Said there was an old interest, and a new interest starting up to destroy it in Pennsylvania, by sending the trade into the new interest. That he would not for a thousand guineas the law would pass. That the old commercial interest had nourished Philadelphia—it was an ornament to the State. He seemed willing to persuade me that I should vote against the bill. I asked him how he thought it would look for me to vote against it, when they had all voted for it on Monday last? He said he was induced to do so, expecting a change in the Senate. That he would not for half his estate he had done so. That he was duped into it. I told him that was not my case, for I had followed my judgment hitherto, and would continue to do so. That if we changed our ground in the Senate, and could insert any other place than the Susquehanna, we lost our hold of the eastern people, and the whole fell to the ground, agreeable to what I had told him on Monday week, and that at the next session Virginia would come forward with five members from North Carolina, and be joined by two or three from Pennsylvania, and we should infallibly go to the Potomac; and for my part I would rather stay on the Susquehanna. He declared, for his part, he would not.

Mr. Clymer used to extol the advantages of the Susquehanna; and declared, as he sat on my bedside about a fortnight ago, that no position in Pennsylvania was equal to Susquehanna. All this change has taken place since Gen. Irwin came to town, and declared there was a contract on foot for clearing the Conewago falls for four thousand pounds.

Now what am I to think of the citizens of Philadelphia, and some others of the Pennsylvania delegation. Can I help concluding, on the most undeniable data, as well from what I have heard as from circumstances and their own declarations, that they ever have been opposed to the Susquehanna, and voted for it purely to save their popularity in the State; and trusted to Morris, who is a six-year man, to destroy the bill in the Senate. Have I a name for such conduct? Thus to drive away Congress from the State, rather than a few barrels of flour should pass by the Philadelphia market, in descending the Susquehanna; and rather than the inhabitants of this river should enjoy the natural advantages of opening the navigation of it. I think it probable these arts will prevail.

September 24.　This day Morris voted against the Susquehanna. King, Schuyler, and all the New England men, except Doctor John- son, voted against it.　Mr. Morris' vote alone would have fixed us on the Susquehanna forever.　The affair has taken the very turn I predicted.　Our ruin is plotted, contrived, and carried on, in con- junction with the Yorkers.

I gave an account of the center of population being in Pennsyl- vania ; the center of wealth ; and the geographical center.　Went at large into all the detail of the Potomac and the Susquehanna. When the Potomac was voted for, I was long on my legs, or I shall say my knees, and they grew weary.　We easily threw out the Po- tomac ; but I well knew all this was in vain.

This whole morning, and for an hour after the Senate met, the York Senators and representatives were in the committee-room, and Mr. Morris running backwards and forwards, taking out one Senator after another to them, and Adams delaying business for them.　No business was ever treated with more barefaced partial- ity.　Mr. Morris moved that the words at some convenient place on the banks of the Susquehanna, &c., should be struck out, and that it might remain a blank for any gentleman that pleased to name a place.

I objected to this as unfair, for, by this means, the banks of the Susquehanna would be thrown out, when, in fact, that place might have more friends than any other individual place, for all those who wished a different place would unite on this vote, however different their views might otherwise be ; and thus the place rejected in the first instance would be laid under an unfavorable impression.　That I saw no reason to deviate from the common mode, which had al- ways been to move to strike out certain words in order to insert certain other words, and thus men would plainly see their way clear, and the intention of the mover.

Mr. Adams answered me from the chair.　Said it was all fair.

It was in vain to argue.　The question was put, and seven only rose.

Up got Mr. Morris.　Said the question was not understood, and begun his explanations.　He said he had often wished to explain himself on the subject of the residence, but was always prevented. That Pennsylvania was averse to the Susquehanna, and would give $100,000 to place it at Germantown.

I rose to the point of order.　Declared that no motion or appli- cation for reconsideration could be received from a member *in the minority*.　Quoted parliamentary practice, and appealed to the Chair.

Mr. Adams now made one of his speeches. Unfortunately, it seems none of our rules reached the point. New matter had been alleged in argument, &c.

It was in vain that I alleged that no business ever could have a decision, if minority members were permitted to move reconsiderations under every pretense of new argument. Adams gave it against me.

Mr. Morris now assumed a bolder tone. Flamed away in favor of Germantown. Repeated his offers in the name of the State, &c.

I declared I considered myself to enjoy the confidence of Pennsylvania in as unlimited a manner as my honorable colleague. That I firmly believed the general sense of the State was more in favor of the Susquehanna than Germantown; and that, if money was to be given, the Susquehanna was most likely to obtain it. I, however, denied that any State money was appropriated to any such purpose, and called on my colleague to produce the authority on which he made the offer.

He now came forward the great man and the merchant. Pledged himself that, if the State would not, he would find the money.

A vacant stare on this seemed to occupy the faces of the Senate. But the New England men helped him out. It was proposed that the validity of the law should depend on the payment of the money, and that a clause for this purpose should be now inserted in the bill. And to work some of them went in fabricating such a clause. Mr. Morris had not yet been regularly seconded; but I began to see, when it was too late, that I had committed a mistake in not appealing to the House from the decision of the Chair.

Bassett got up and recanted—said he had not understood the question. It was in vain that we urged that the question was fairly put. A reconsideration was called for. There is really such a thing as worrying weak or indifferent men into a vote. Urging that the matter had not been sufficiently explained and understood—how fair and inoffensive the measure, &c.—all these arts were played off with the utmost address on this occasion; and with the weight of John Adams, succeeded. It was reconsidered, and eleven voted for this fair and inoffensive measure.

In a moment, by way of fixing them against the Susquehanna, although it was still called out, we will take a vote on the Susquehanna, the yeas and nays were called. And now Grayson and Lee moved for the Potomac.

They had moved for striking out the word Pennsylvania, so as to leave the whole banks of the Susquehanna open, and lost it.

Now was a lengthy debate, in which I supported the Susquehanna; but it is too much to insert what I said. The Potomac lost it, and the *blank* now remained.

Mr. Butler now rose and moved to fill the blank with the words, "banks of Susquehanna, &c.,"—the same words which had been struck out. I seconded the motion.

Up got Mr. Morris, and opposed this with warmth. He allowed that there might be a question taken on the Susquehanna; but he would have a vote taken on his place first.

Butler insisted that as his motion was fairly before the House, and seconded, it must be disposed of.

Morris replied without any reason on his side, indeed; but he had no need of *reason*, when he had votes enough at hand.

King got up and said he had no objection to a vote being taken on the Susquehanna; but it ought to be the last place.

However, for the sake of order, they had to move a postponement of the motion on the Susquehanna. The postponement was carried.

Mr. Morris then came forward with an amendment for locating, ten miles square, adjoining the city of Philadelphia, in the counties of Philadelphia, Chester, and Bucks, including Germantown, with a proviso that the act should not be in force until the one hundred thousand dollars should be secured to the United States by Pennsylvania, &c.

I could not abandon the Susquehanna, at any rate in the present stage of the business; but for me to enter into a proviso which would operate as an engagement on the State, without the least authority for so doing, appeared to me highly improper. I therefore, under every view of the matter, concluded, in a moment, to vote against his motion.

The Susquehanna bill placed the Federal town in the heart of Pennsylvania, provided for purchasing the land, erecting the buildings, &c , without one farthing expense to the State, to say nothing of the most important subject of clearing the Susquehanna, which would be done by Federal and Maryland money, in case of Congress being placed on its banks. I therefore reserved my vote for the Susquehanna.

The House divided on Mr. Morris' motion—nine and nine. The President rose to give the casting vote. He spoke well of the Potomac, (to gratify the Virginians;) slightly of the Susquehanna, (which had but few friends;) highly of Philadelphia and New York, in each of which places he said the Congress ought to stay alternately, four years at a time; said if the question were to reject the whole business, he could have no doubt, but as Pennsylvania had offered the money, he would vote for *Germantown*.

Thus fell our hopes. This unwarranted offer of the money knocked down the Susquehanna. It was now near four o'clock, and an adjournment was called for and took place.

25th September. A good deal unwell, but attended the Hall. The Secretary had omitted the first question on the striking out of the Susquehanna, and the reconsideration. He, however, corrected it himself, afterwards, with the leave of the House.

Carroll now moved to strike out the residence being in New York until the Federal buildings should be erected. I determined to leave myself free from any obligation to stay in New York, and voted with him, more especially as I was free from all obligation whatever.

Mr. Morris now began to dress the bill, but seemed slack about the one hundred thousand dollars. He was called on from the chair, however, and sundry parts of the House to bring it forward. I was very unwell, and left him to dress his own child as he pleased, and came home.

This evening Mr. Scott called to see me. He said Mr. Morris, Mr. Clymer, and Mr. Fitzsimmons, assured him that the Yorkers and New England men would pass the bill, and that they, the Pennsylvanians, Mr. C. and F., had promised that Congress should stay three years in New York. Mr. Wynkoop then said that they had made such a bargain. I told them that was the first account I had heard of the matter. I expressed my doubts of their sincerity. Wynkoop was sure of them, and that he could depend on them, &c.

26th. Very unwell this day, but dressed, and went to the Hall. Sat some time. The appropriation bill was taken up. And now Col. Schuyler brought forward an account of $8,000, expended by Mr. Osgood, in repairing and furnishing at the house which the President lives in.

When I first went into the Senate Chamber this morning, the Vice President, Ellsworth, and Ames stood together, railing against the vote of adherence in the House of Representatives on throwing out the words *the President*, in the beginning of the Federal writs. I really thought them wrong, but as they seemed very opinionated, I did not contradict them. This is only a part of their old system of giving the President, as far as possible, every appendage of royalty. The original reason of the English writs running in the king's name, was his being personally in court, and English jurisprudence still supposes him to be so. But with us, it seems rather confounding the executive and judicial branches. Ames left them, and they

seemed rather to advance afterwards. Said the President, personally, was not subject to any process whatever; could have no action, whatever, brought against him; was above the power of all
judges, justices, &c. For, what, said they, would you put it in
the power of a common justice to exercise any authority over him,
and stop the whole machine of government.

I said, that although President, he was not above the laws.

Both of them declared you could only impeach him, and no other
process whatever lay against him.

I put the case: Suppose the President committed murder in the
street. Impeach him? But you can only remove him from office
on impeachment. Why, when he is no longer President you can
indict him. But, in the meanwhile he runs away.

But I will put another case. Suppose he continues his murders
daily, and neither House is sitting to impeach him?

Oh! the people would rise and restrain him. Very well; you
will allow *the mob* to do what the loyal justice must abstain from.

Mr. Adams said I was arguing from cases nearly impossible.
There had been some hundreds of crowned heads within these two
centuries in Europe, and there was no instance of any of them
having committed murder.

Very true, in the retail way, Charles the IX, of France, excepted.
They generally do these things on the great scale. I am, however,
certainly within the bounds of possibility, though it may be very
improbable.

General Schuyler joined us. What think you, General, said I,
by way of giving the matter a different turn, I am not a good civ-
ilian, but I think the President a kind of sacred person.

Bravo, my *jure divino* man.

Not a word of the above is worth minuting, but it shows clearly
how amazingly fond of the old leaven many people are. I needed
no index, however, of this kind, with respect to John Adams.

September 28. Went to the Hall. Sat a little while, but had to
get up and walk in the machinery-room. Viewed the pendulum
mill, a model of which stands here. It really seems adapted to do
business. Returned and sat awhile with the Senate, but retired and
came home to my lodgings. Sincerely hope an adjournment will
take place to-morrow. The pay list is making out, which seems
likely to finish the business.

Mr. Wynkoop came in the highest joy. All was well. Germantown, happy Germantown, has got the Congress. He ravished up
his dinner, got his trunk and boots, and away with him to tell the
glorious news.

I have just been thinking how impossible it is for the Yorkers to be so blind as to let Congress go away in the manner Wynkoop says they have done. If the lower House have really passed the bill, the Yorkers have no resource but in the President. I am greatly surprised at this day's work.

I have opened the book, and taken up my pen to wipe away the surprise above mentioned. Parson Linn has just told me that some trifling amendment was tacked to the bill, just sufficient to send it up to the Senate, and the Senate have thrown it out; and with the consent of the Philadelphians, too, I suppose.

Just as I was leaving the Hall, Izard took me aside. Asked me to stay. Said a trifling amendment will be made in the lower House, just enough to bring it up here, and we will throw it out. I told him I wished nothing so much as to see an end of the business. I was not able to attend, but if I was, could not be with him on this question. Well, then, you must not tell Morris of this. I was just going away, and said I will not.

In relation to the amendment to the residence bill, it appears from the debates in the House of Representatives, that when the amendments proposed by the Senate to the residence bill were before the House, on Monday, the 28th of September, *Mr. Madison* contended that the amendment proposed by the Senate, was a departure from every principle adopted by the House, but he would not trouble them with a recapitulation of arguments. He wished, however, that the House would provide against one inconvenience, which was, to prevent the district in Pennsylvania, chosen by Congress, from being deprived for a time of the benefit of the laws. This, he apprehended, would be the case, unless Congress made provision for the operation of the laws of Pennsylvania, in the act by which they accepted of the cession of that State, for the State relinquished the right of legislation from the moment that Congress accepted of the district. The propriety of this proposition, he observed, was so apparent, that he had not a doubt but the House would consent to it. He then moved the following proviso: "And provided, that nothing herein contained shall be construed to affect the operation or the laws of Pennsylvania, within the district ceded and accepted, until Congress shall otherwise provide by law."

Mr. Livermore objected to this motion, because he supposed there was no necessity for it.

The question was then taken: Does the House agree to the amendment? And was decided in the affirmative. The yeas and nays being demanded, and were as follows:

YEAS—Messrs. Ames, Cadwalader, *Clymer*, *Fitzsimmons*, Floyd,

Foster, Gerry, Gilman, Goodhue, Grout, Hartley, Hathorn, Heister, Huntington, Lawrence, Leonard, Livermore, Muhlenberg, Partridge, Van Rensselaer, Schureman, Scott, Sherman, Sylvester, Sinnickson, Thatcher, Trumbull, Vining, Wadsworth, and Wynkoop—31.

NAYS—Messrs. Baldwin, Bland, Boudinot, Brown, Burke, Carroll, Coles, Contee, Gale, Griffin, Jackson, Lee, Madison, Matthews, Moore, Page, Parker, Seney, Smith, (of Maryland,) Smith, (of South Carolina,) Stone, Sumter, Tucker, and White—24.

From the *Senate* Journal it appears that, on the 28th September, a message from the House of Representatives brought up the bill for establishing a permanent seat of Government ; and informed the Senate that the House had concurred in the amendments thereto, with the following amendment : "And provided that nothing herein contained shall be construed to affect the operation of the laws of Pennsylvania within the district ceded and accepted, until Congress shall otherwise provide by law."

After some other business was attended to, a motion was made that the further consideration of the above bill be postponed *to the next session of Congress ;* and it passed in the affirmative.

29th. Came to the Hall. Saw Mr. Morris. I did not envy him his feelings. I determined not to say a word to him, save the salutation of good morning ; which passed mutually between us. To praise his management was impossible. I could not sit in the Senate. Came out, and reclined, as well a I could, in the little committee-room. Ellsworth came out in a little time. I asked him if the business was got through in Senate. He said yes. I then went to the Treasury, drew my pay, discharged my lodgings, took a place in the stage, and set off for Philadelphia.

The Senate was adjourned on the 26th September, until the first Monday in January, 1790, then to meet at the City Hall, in New York.

SECOND SESSION OF THE FIRST SENATE.

January, 1790. Arrived at New York late on the 5th, and went to lodge at the same house with the Speaker of the House of Representatives, Frederick A. Muhlenberg, and Peter A. Muhlenberg, his brother.

6th. Attended at the Hall, and my presence completed a quorum. A letter from the President of the United States was received, desiring to be informed of the time a quorum would be formed, &c. Was committed to Izard and Strong. Nothing else of any consequence. Adjourned.

7th. Attended as usual. When the minutes were read, Mr. King rose and made a motion to amend the journals of yesterday with respect to the President's letter, by striking out a part, and inserting a clause which he held in his hand.

Strong and Dalton moved to have the word *honorable* struck out from before the names of the members. Lost. Motion for leave to protest, by Butler, not seconded.

Strong and Izard reported that the President would attend in the Senate chamber at eleven o'clock to-morrow.

A resolution of the Representatives for appointment of a chaplain was concurred in, and the bishop appointed on the part of the Senate.

This day, at and after dinner, I thought uncommon pains were taken to draw from me some information as to the part I would act respecting the Federal residence. The whole world is a shell, and we tread on hollow ground every step. I repeatedly said, I have marked out no ground for myself. My object shall be the interest of Pennsylvania, subordinate to the good of the Union.

Mr. Wynkoop called in the evening. He was directly on the subject of the permanent residence. Susquehanna must never be thought of. He repeated this sentiment more than once. To have been silent would have implied consent to it. I said for my part I should think of Susquehanna, and I considered Mr. Morris' conduct in destroying the bill for that place as the greatest political misfortune that ever befel that State.

January, 8. All this morning nothing but bustle about the Senate in hauling chairs and removing tables. The President (Washington) was dressed in a second mourning, and read his speech well. The Senate, headed by their President, were on his right. The House of Representatives, with their Speaker, were on his left. His family, with the heads of departments, attended. The business was soon over, and the Senate were left alone. The speech was committed rather too hastily, as Mr. Butler thought, who made some remarks on it, and was called to order by the Chair. He resented the call, and some altercation ensued. Adjourned until Monday.

January 11. The Senate received from General Knox the proceedings of the commissioners on the embassy to the Southern Indians. A considerable part of the day spent in reading them. 'Tis a spoiled piece of business; and by way of justification of their conduct in not having made peace, they seem disposed to precipitate the United States into war, the not uncommon fruits of employing military men. This, however, is but my idea of the business. Wish I may have occasion to alter it.

Mr. Lear brought in a ratification from the State of North Carolina, or rather a copy of it, from the President.

And now the committee reported an answer to the President's speech. The most servile echo I ever heard. There was, however, no mending it. One part of it seemed like pledging the Senate to pay the whole amount of the public debt. This was, however, altered. Many of the clauses were passed, without either aye or no, in silent disapprobation. I told both King and Patterson that I had never heard so good an echo, for it repeated all the words entire. They both denied that they had anything to do with it, and said it was Izard's work.

January 12. In now came General Knox, with a bundle of communications. I thought the act a mad one when a Secretary of War was appointed in time of peace. I cannot blame him. He wants to labor in his vocation. Here is a fine scheme on paper: To raise five thousand and forty officers, non-commissioned officers, and privates, at the charge of $1,152,000, for a year, to go to war with the Creeks, because the commissioners, being ignorant of Indian affairs, failed of making a treaty after having spent $15,000 to no manner of purpose. But we will see what will come of it.

January 12. I made an unsuccessful motion when it was proposed that the whole Senate should wait on the President, with the

NOTE.—The Speaker told me this day what I have been no stranger to, that a certain set in Philadelphia were determined to have me out of the Senate.

answer to the speech.   First, I wished for delay, that we might see the conduct adopted by the House of Representatives.   I thought it likely they would do the business by a *committee*.   In that case, I wished to imitate them ; and as a committee with us had done all the business so far, I wished it to continue in their hands, that they might have exclusively all the *honors attendant on the perform- ance*.   That I, as a republican, was, however, opposed to the whole business of echoing speeches.   It was a stale ministerial trick in Britain, to get the Houses of Parliament to chime in with the speech, and then consider them as pledged to support any measure which could be grafted on the speech.   It was the Socratic mode of argument introduced into politics, to entrap men into measures they were not aware of.   I wished to treat the speech in quite a different manner.   I would commit it, for the purpose of examining whether the subjects recommended in it were proper for the Senate to act upon.   If they were found to be so, I would have committees appointed, to bring forward the necessary bills.   But we seem to neglect the useful, and content ourselves with compliments only, and dangerous ones, too.   But for my part, I would not consider myself as committed by anything contained in the answer.

January 13. This was a day of small importance in the Senate. Mr. Hawkins, a Senator from North Carolina, took his seat. Adjourned.

January 14.   This was the day devoted to ceremony, by both Houses of Congress.   At eleven o'clock the Senate attended at the President's to deliver their answer.   At twelve the House of Rep- resentatives attended.   It is not worth while minuting a word about it.   We went in coaches.   Got our answer, which was short.   Re- turned in coaches.   Sauntered an hour in the Senate Chamber, and adjourned.   Every error in government will work its own remedy, among a free people.   I think both Senators and Representatives are tired of making themselves the gazing stock of the crowd, and the subject of remark by the sycophantic circle that surround the President in stringing to his quarters ; and I trust the next session will either do without this business altogether, or do it by a small committee, that need not interrupt the business of either House. I have aimed at this point all along.

It is evident, from the President's speech, that he wishes every- thing to fall into the British mode of business.   *I have directed the proper officers to lay* before you, &c. Compliments for him, and business for them.   He is but a man, but really a good one ; and we can have nothing to fear from him ; but much from the prece- dent he may establish.

Dined this day with the President.   It was a great dinner—all in the taste of high life. I considered it as part of my duty as a Senator to submit to it, and am glad it is over. The President is a cold formal man, but I must declare he treated me with great attention. I was the first person with whom he drank a glass of wine. I was often spoken to by him. Yet he knows well how rigid a republican I am. I cannot think that he considers it worth while to soften me. It is not worth his while. I am not an object, if he should gain me, and I trust he cannot do it by any improper means.

January 14. This day the *budget*, as it was called, was opened in the House of Representatives. An extraordinary rise of certificates has been remarked for some time past. This could not be accounted for neither in Philadelphia nor elsewhere. But the report from the Treasury explained all. He recommends indiscriminate funding, and, in the style of a British minister, has sent down his bill. 'Tis said a committee of speculators in certificates would not have formed it more for their advantage. It has occasioned many serious faces. I feel so struck of an heap, I can make no remark on the matter.

January 15. Attended at the Hall. A committee was appointed to bring in a bill for extending the judiciary of the United States to North Carolina. Senate adjourned.

It appears that a system of speculation for the engrossing certificates has been carrying on for some time.

January 17. I have attended, in the minutest manner, to the motions of Hamilton and the Yorkers. Sincerity is not with them. They never will consent to part with Congress. Advances to them are vain. One session or two more here will fix us irremovably. We can move from here only by means of the Virginians. The fact is indubitable.

January 18. Senate met, and adjourned.

Hawkins, of North Carolina, said as he came up he passed two expresses with very large sums of money on their way for North Carolina, for the purpose of speculation in certificates. Wadsworth has sent off two small vessels for the Southern States, on the errand of buying up certificates. I really fear the members of Congress are deeper in this business than any others.

As to whether Former Bills be taken up de novo.

January 19, 1790. Senate met at the usual hour. I had observed *Ellsworth* busy for some time with Izard. There had been some intercourse between him and Izard. He rose with a motion in his hand, which he read in his place. The amount of it was that a committee should be appointed to bring in a bill defining crimes and punishments under the Federal judiciary. He did not affect to conceal that a bill of this nature had been left pending before the Representatives at the end of the last session, but declared he wished to settle an important point in practice : *whether all business should not originate de novo with every new session.* He then labored long to show that this was a new session, and concluded, as the session was new, everything else should be new. Mr. Izard seconded him in a speech which I thought contained nothing new.

Bassett got up, and declared that he had but just taken his seat; that everything was new to him; that he could not determine in such haste, and moved a postponement.

I rose, seconded Bassett, and gave as additional reasons: that the matter had been acknowledged to be of great importance; that I, therefore, trusted it would not be gone into with so thin a representation of the Southern States; that the most respectable State was not represented at all; that I thought it improper to attempt deciding on a matter which would go to regulate the future proceedings of Congress, in both Houses, as it would be fixing a precedent, without some communication with the House of Representatives; that they had appointed a committee to bring forward the unfinished business, which had a very different appearance from beginning *de novo.* Gentlemen had argued much to show this was a new session. But granting this, I could not see that the inference they wished to draw from it would follow. They need not fear a deficiency of business. There would be enough to do without rejecting the progress we had made in the former session, &c., &c., for I was up a good while.

King got up. He labored to support Ellsworth, and to show from parliamentary proceedings that new sessions originated new business after every prorogation of Parliament. He was long.

I rose, however, and took him on his own ground with regard to the prorogation of Parliaments. Showed that it was a prerogative of the Crown to prorogue the Parliament. That the British Crown generally exercised this power when the Parliament went on what was considered as forbidden ground. That the Parliaments were forced into this mode of procedure, for, when any Parliament had been prorogued for handling disagreeable subjects, to attempt to take them up in the same stage would inevitably be followed by the same fate. They were, therefore, obliged to begin *de novo*, at least, with every subject the least disagreeable to the Court; and, indeed, it was the best policy to begin all *de novo*, thus affecting to conceal their knowledge of the offensive subjects. But these were reasons of conduct which had no existence here. The President had no proroguing power. He could not check our deliberations. I had no objection to adopt rules similar to those of the Parliament of Great Britain when they would apply. Not because they were in use there, but on the principle of their utility. But when a direct inconvenience attended them, as in the present case, where the deliberations of the former session on the subject before us would be lost, they ought to be rejected.

Ellsworth found it would go against him. He then moved the postponement should be until to-morrow. It was lost.

Moved it should be to Monday. It was lost. General postponement took place.

Wyngate now rose, and made a singular motion. It was that the bills formerly before the Senate for regulating the process in the Federal courts should be taken up.

A pause ensued, as this was certainly unfinished business of the former session, the bill in question having been postponed on the bringing forward a temporary law.

Langdon said he would have seconded the gentleman, but he considered this bill as involved in the matter which had just been postponed.

Ellsworth, who sometimes contradicts Langdon for the sake of contradiction, said it was not involved in it, and seconded Wyngate for bringing it on, and on it was brought. The Secretary served the members of Senate with copies of it. Wyngate put it into the hands of the President, and he read it all over, and was returning to the first paragraph, when Ellsworth, finding where he was, got up. Said his intention was to second the gentleman to have a committee appointed to bring in a bill for regulating processes, &c.

Adams attended to him, and without any question how to get rid of the bill, Adams put a question for a committee, and a committee was accordingly appointed.

And now we will see what for a figure Otis will make of the minutes in the morning. I do not want to be captious, but I must not let them draw this into precedent.

January 20. I came early to the Senate Chamber, but found our President and Ellsworth there before me. Izard, Few, and Schuyler were all in conference with Ellsworth. The minutes were no sooner finished, than Ellsworth rose and called for the motion of yesterday, and made a speech in support of his motion. It could not be said to be very long, though he said a great deal. To do business, to prevent idleness, to satisfy our constituents, to prevent loss of time, &c., &c., was the subjects of it.

I began, with declaring that the gentleman's ardor to do business was highly laudable, but there was such a thing as making more haste than good speed. That if economy, and to prevent loss of time were his object, I thought he missed the mark, by attempting to take up everything *de novo:* for thus all the time spent on the unfinished business in the former session would be lost; that I thought the present motion scarce in order. It had been moved, yesterday, that the motion should be taken up this day, and negatived; Monday, next, had also been negatived. But there was a reason of much more consequence, which, though it had occurred to me yesterday, I had forborne to mention; but had since inquired of sundry members of the House of Representatives, and was assured that the very bill in question was reported by the committee for unfinished business, and the report remained on the Speaker's table unacted upon. That for us to decide on a business actually before the Representatives, I considered as highly improper, and would not fail of giving offense.

After I had done speaking I left the Senate Chamber, came down stairs, called out General Muhlenburg, gave notice, by him, to the Speaker, how much I wanted the report of the committee.

Mr. Buckley was good enough to send up, by the door-keeper, the original report. I got it—found the bill reported as I had mentioned. Returned, and read in my place the part I had alluded to.

The affair took now a new turn, and a motion was made to appoint a committee to confer on the subject, with a committee of the other House.

I rose, and enforced this with all the energy I was master of. It was carried, and the committee were Langdon, Henry, and myself. The Yorkers lost countenance when they saw the committee, but now they brought forward a curious motion. It was to take the sense of the Senate, in order that it might stand, as a rule of conduct, for the committee.

I rose against this with all my might. I have not time to set down my arguments; they are obvious. Several followed me. I had, however, concluded with a motion for postponement, which was seconded. They saw how it would go, and withdrew their motion.

The members of the committee on the part of the Representatives, are Sherman, Thatcher, Hartley, Jackson, and White—to meet to-morrow, at ten o'clock.

January 22. I met the committee a few minutes after ten. Ellsworth began a long discourse, and concluded for all business which had passed between the Houses to begin *de novo.* He, Jackson, and White, had much parliamentary stuff; but Hartley had some books, and the precedents were undoubtedly against them. Ellsworth made room for Henry to speak, by desiring him to do so, from which it was plain enough that they had communicated. He seemed willing I should not speak. I, however, made way for myself, and reprobated every idea of precedent drawn from England, though I declared if notice were to be taken of them, I thought they were made for us. I read from the Journals the postponement of the bill, which I told them plainly had given rise to the present contest. On motion, that the further consideration of the bill be postponed to the next session of Congress, it passed in the affirmative.

By the minutes on the journals, the bill must be taken up in the present session. Any proceeding of a contrary nature must depend on an *ex post facto* principle. We may enter into rules for the future government of our conduct, but the past is out of our power, constitutionally speaking. The general practice of all the Legislatures is in favor of taking up the unfinished business in the state they were left. So far is this from being considered as improper, that the constitutions of some of the States enjoin it as a principle, that no bill, unless in case of necessity, shall be enacted into a law in the same session in which it originated. It is the common practice, in all the arrangements of life. It stands highly recommended by economy, which is certainly a republican virtue. I considered it undeniably certain, that a particular fact had given rise to this whole business. Here then, to control a single incident, we are attempting to establish a general rule. This is inverting the order of business with a witness; and to get rid of a particular bill must involve ourselves in perpetual inconvenience.

Mr. White alleged the opinion was not new. I appealed to the minutes of both Houses, where bills had been postponed to this session. In the Senate, the bill for the permanent residence; in Chamber of Representatives, the bill on crimes and punishments. It was in vain to argue. The vote went against us; and a report agreed to, that the bills which had been in passage between the two Houses should be regarded as if nothing had passed in either, respecting them; or words to that amount.

After the report was made in the Senate, our President wanted us to proceed immediately on it. I moved some delay, and it was postponed to Monday.

Saturday, 23. This was a most delightful day.

January 25. The Senate met, and the President informed the House of the order of the day, to take up the report of the joint committee.

I rose and observed, that I saw many empty seats ; the Senate was thin. I, therefore, wished for a little delay until the members were collected. After the House filled, the business was entered on. Mr. Morris showed a disinclination to rise. Mr. Bassett was up, and, after he sat down, I hinted to Mr. Morris a point that I thought might be proper in support of Bassett. Said he had better rise ; if he did not, I would. He said he thought I *had better not.*

I rose, however, and one word brought on another. All the arguments of the committee were had over again, much enlarged and amplified. I was four times up in all ; for the two last times I asked leave. I really thought I had the advantage over both Ellsworth and Henry; but when is it that I do not think well of my own arguments ? I found that I had made some impression on Izard. He was up, and concluded with saying something that seemed like a wish for further time to deliberate. I rose, said I considered what the honorable gentleman had said as amounting to a motion for postponement, and I begged leave to second him. He said he wished it postponed.

But now, Patterson rose on our side; but he displeased Izard, and the question on the postponement was put ; but we lost it after I had been twice up. But it was all in vain. Cicero, with all the powers of Apollo, could not have turned the vote in our favor. I had a small scheme in protracting the time until the other House would break up, that the example of our House might not add any weight to their scale of deliberation ; and I hoped that in the meantime they might, perhaps, pass on the business.

Mr. Morris stuck fast to his seat, nor did he rise or say a word during the whole time. Eight voted for us, and ten against us. The yeas and nays were called. The vote was hurried down into the chamber of the Representatives, and they adopted it almost without a division.

January 26. A committee was moved for, to bring in a bill for ascertaining crimes and punishments under the Federal Legislature. The committee were appointed, withdrew for a few moments into the Secretary's office—returned with the *old bill,* which had been before us last session, and reported it. This was really ridiculous ; but the vote of yesterday seemed to call for it.

Butler moved that a letter from some foreigner should be sent to the chamber of Representatives. The letter had been read formerly, but in so low a voice that I could not tell a word of it. It was not read now. Mr. Morris left his seat and went and looked at it ; came back and said nothing about it. I was silent on Butler's motion. But when I came home, the Speaker immediately attacked me for the absurdity of our conduct in sending them a letter of much importance, touching proposals of a treaty with the Republic of Genoa. I really knew nothing of the letter, but it was my own fault; and it really ought to be a lesson to me and every Senator to attend well to what is done at our chamber.

January 27. The bill of yesterday was read by paragraphs. It was curious to see the whole Senate sitting silent and smiling at each other, and not a word of remark made or making on the bill.

Ellsworth rose to inform the Senate that it was the same bill which had been gone through all the forms in the last session.

Strong moved an amendment, however, that the judges should issue the warrants for execution of criminals.

I rose and showed, from the Constitution, that the President of the United States had the power of granting pardon in all cases except those of impeachment; that by the judges taking on them to issue the warrants, the opportunity of his granting pardon was taken away.

Ellsworth, according to custom, supported his bill through thick and thin. There was a great deal said, and I was up three or four times. I moved a postponement of the clause, and it was carried.

Hawkins, the new member from North Carolina, rose and objected to the clause respecting the benefit of clergy. He was not very clear.

I, however, rose, really from motives of friendship, I will not say compassion, for a stranger. I stated that as far as I could collect the sentiments of the honorable gentleman, he was opposed to our copying the law language of Great Britain. That for my part, I wished to see a code of criminal law for the Continent, and I wished to see a tone of originality running through the whole of it. I was tired of the servility of imitating English forms. I could not say whether the bill would not be materially injured by leaving out the clause. I wished it should be left out, but I thought, at any rate, it had better be postponed. It was postponed.

Received sundry letters this day from Philadelphia. I told Mr. Morris that the chancery was rejected. [This probably refers to action in the convention in Pennsylvania for the formation of a new Constitution.] He said he was sorry for it. I said frankly, that is not my case. He asked, is there anything further? I told him a sharp debate had taken place, whether persons holding Federal appointments could act under *State* commissions, which had been determined in the negative. He replied, this is leveled at me and Wilson. My friends have named me for Governor, and Wilson for Chief Justice; but I will save them the trouble by declaring off.

January 28. Attended at the Senate Chamber. The bill for crimes and punishments was taken up. Strong's amendment was rejected, and I offered one, which was also rejected, and the bill passed. Bassett moved something like an amendment. He went to Ellsworth, and it, between them, was really altered for the better.

The Carolina bill was now taken up, and specially committed to Hawkins, Ellsworth, and Butler.

Mr. Lear, from the President, communicated the act of Rhode Island appointing a convention.

There was a request also from some public characters of the State requesting a suspension of the effects of the funding law respecting that State.

Ellsworth moved that the same committee might bring in a clause for the Rhode Islanders.

I voted against this, and gave as a reason : That as it respected the revenue, although not raising it, yet it should be left to the other House.

Mr. Morris this day, as he sat beside me in our places in the Senate, whispered to me that he would not be as regular in his attendance as he used to be. That he was engaged in settling his public accounts, which would engage him for a great part of his time.

I remarked that cannot be helped. The business is a necessary one. Indeed, I think it highly so to him, if he regards his reputation ; and, in my opinion, he has left it too long at stake already.

Friday, January 29. Samuel Jackson, one of the Senators from North Carolina, attended ; was sworn ; and he and his colleague were classed.

A letter was received from the Treasurer of the United States, with his accounts. They were read by the Secretary, and attended to with great listlessness by the Senate. The amount was $350,207 24, and may, generally speaking, be called civil list disbursements, and said to be expended in New York.

1790, February 1. This was an unimportant day in the Senate. The North Carolina members produced an act of session, which was committed. But Mr. Ellicott sent in for me, and I chatted with him in the committee-room until the Senate was about to adjourn, which was early.

Mr. Hamilton is very uneasy, as far as I can learn, about his funding system. He was here early to wait on the Speaker, and, I believe, spent most of his time in running from place to place among the members.

Mr. Ellicott's accounts of the Falls of Niagara are amazing, indeed. I communicated to him my scheme of an attempt to account for the age of the world, or, at least, to fix the period when the waters began to cut the ledge of rock over which it falls. The distance from the present pitch to where the fall originally was is now seven miles. For this space a tremendous channel is cut in a solid limestone rock, in all parts one hundred and fifty feet deep, but near two hundred and fifty at the mouth or part where the attrition began. People who have known the place since Sir William Johnson took possession of it, about thirty years ago, give out that there is an attrition of twenty feet in that time. Now, if twenty feet = thirty years = seven miles, or thirty-six thousand nine hundred and sixty feet, ÷ answer fifty-five thousand four hundred and forty years.

February 3. The Speaker and Gen. Muhlenburg made a point of my going with them to dine with Mr. Fitzsimmons and Clymer. I would not go until they declared that they had authority to invite me. I went.

The company were Pennsylvanians. No discourse happened until after the bottle had circulated pretty freely. Mr. Scott joined us. He declared it was in vain to think of any place but the *Potowmack*. Mr. Wynkoop declared the utmost readiness to go to the Potowmack. Mr. Fitzsimmons seemed to bark in for some time. Clymer declared, over and over, he was ready to go to the Potowmack.

After some time, I spoke most decidedly and plainly. I will not go to the Potowmack. If we once vote for the Potowmack the die is cast, Pennsylvania has lost it, and we never can return. I will bear with the inconveniences of New York much longer rather than do it. At one time, when they were regretting the influence of New York in keeping us here, I said, gentlemen, we once had it in our power to fix ourselves elsewhere. As the Scotchman said, in his prayers, we were left to the freedom of our own will, and a pretty hand we have made of it.

February 4. This an unimportant day in the Senate. The bill for extending the impost to North Carolina was brought in to be signed. The President got up, and had a good deal to say—that a question was put in the House of Representatives; and if gentlemen wished any other method they should say so.

Ellsworth was immediately up. Said all was perfectly right. The House had passed the bill, they had nothing more to do with it.

Strong got up. Had some sleeveless things to say about the practice of Parliament, but concluded all was right.

I got up and declared, since gentlemen were speaking their minds, I would declare that I thought the business wrong. That after both Houses had elaborately argued and passed a bill, it was referred to a committee of one from the Senate and two from the House of Representatives. That it was then in their power to alter the bill. If they were bad men, there was no check on them. If even a member knew of a bill to be vitiated, he could not correct it. An if or an and might most materially affect a bill. The change of the tense of a verb might alter a whole sentence. I was clearly of opinion every bill ought to be compared at the table; and as the President, when he signed a bill, did it for and in the name of the Senate, the question should be put: Shall it be signed or no?

It was, however, of no avail, nor, indeed, did I conclude with any motion; but meant my observations to open the way for taking up the business some other time.

Hints were thrown out about uniting the delegation, and much could be done by their effort. I wonder if they are silly enough to think that their arts cannot be seen through. The government of Pennsylvania is the object.

The Speaker mentioned Charles Thompson as having been spoken of. Clymer said, in such a tone of voice as he did not expect me to hear, "*He will make a good Senator.*" Perhaps, if I were to consult my own feelings and general interest, I would wish Charles Thompson, or any other person in my room.

Mr. Morris threw a paper on the table before the Speaker. The Speaker took it up. Clymer muttered something. Fitzsimmons looked confused, and went away. I will know what this paper was. Mr. Morris said I am quite off with the Yorkers. I will have nothing more to do with them. I cannot penetrate the scheme of the Philadelphia junto as to the person they contemplate for Governor. A man who will be their tool is the design; but they have not yet fixed on the particular object.

5. This morning at breakfast the Speaker told me what the paper was. The Yorkers had stipulated, under their hands, to go to the Susquehanna, and the Pennsylvania delegation, myself excepted, (who, by the by, was the moving spring of the business,) had agreed, under their hands, to stay two years in New York. This engagement of the Pennsylvanians had been in the hands of the Yorkers until now; that Mr, Morris had possessed himself of it— had crossed the names, and now showed it at the same time that he made the declaration against having anything to do with the York ers. Well might I say "a pretty hand we made of it."

Under date of February 6, Mr. Maclay observes that the charges against Mr. Morris are not as financier, but as chairman of the secret committee of Congress, and for money received as a merchant in the beginning of the business.

February 8. Attended Senate. The first business that presented itself, was a letter from R. Morris to the President, inclosing a long memorial praying commissioners to be appointed to inquire into his conduct while financier, and mentioning his unsettled accounts as a partner in the house of Willing & Morris, which were in train of settlement. He requested the memorial might stand on our minutes. Some little objection was made. No particular vote was taken, and it went on, of course.

February 9. Mr. Morris' memorial was committed this day to Izard, Henry, and Ellsworth.   *   *   *

10. Attended the Senate. The committee reported yesterday, while I was out, on Mr. Morris' memorial, that the prayer of it should be granted.

There was no order of the day. I wished to hear the debates of the House of Representatives, and went down and found Madison up. He had got through the introductory part of his speech, which was said to be elegant. The ground I found him on, was the equity power of Government in regulating of property, which he admitted in the fullest manner, with this exception, when the State was no party. The United States owe justly and fairly the whole amount of the federal debt. The question then is, to whom do they owe it ? In this question they are not interested, as the amount is the same, let who will receive it. The case of the original holder admits of no doubt. But what of the speculator, who paid only a trifle for the evidences of the debt. The end, however, of his speech produced a revolution, to the following effect : That the whole should be funded ; but that in the hands of speculators at the highest market price only, and the surplus to the original holder, who performed the service.

The debate lasted to the hour of adjournment, and they rose without deciding.

Dined this day with General Knox. The company large and splendid, consisting of the diplomatic corps, members of Congress, &c.

February 12. Attended the Hall. The order of the day was, to take up the enumeration bill. I objected to the whole of a lengthy schedule, and moved a commitment. I was seconded, but some gentlemen wishing to proceed on the bill till they came to the clause, I withdrew my motion.

Ellsworth came forward with a motion to strike out the clause about the marshal, and insert one to do it by a commissioner. I opposed him—was joined by Patterson.

I got a hard hit at Ellsworth. He felt it, and did not reply. The bill was immediately after committed, and the Senate adjourned.

Ellsworth came laughing to me, said he could have distinguished with respect to the point I brought forward. I said: Ellsworth, a man must knit his net close that can catch you; but you trip sometimes; so we had a laugh, and parted. Went immediately into the Representative Chamber, but the whole day was spent on the Quaker memorial for the abolition of slavery.

February 13. I called on Mr. Scott, and endeavored to give him every argument in my power against Hamilton's report. I shall not minute them here. I wish, however, to arm him and every friend to discrimination, with every possible argument; as I fear, if the business is lost with them, there will be small chance with us.

February 15. Attended in Senate. Our President produced the petitions and memorials of the *Abolition* Society. He did it rather with a sneer, saying he had been honored with a visit from a society, a self constituted one, he supposed. He proceeded to read the petitions and memorials. Izard and Butler had prepared themselves with long speeches on the occasion. Izard, in particular, railed at the society—called them fanatics, &c. Butler made a personal attack on Dr. Franklin, and charged the whole proceeding to anti-Federal motives; that the doctor, when member of convention, had consented to the Federal compact. Here was he acting in direct violation of it. The whole business was designed to overturn the constitution.

I was twice up. The first time, I spoke generally as to the benevolent intentions of the society, &c., &c. Upon Butler's attack, I requested Mr Morris to rise and defend him. King was up speaking in favor of the Carolina gentlemen. I remarked, King is courting them. Yes, said he, and I will be silent, from the same motive that makes him speak. He then bade me rise. I did so. Showed that the doctor was the head of a society which was not of yesterday. That he could not strictly have the acts of the society charged to his personal account. That the society had persevered in the same line of conduct long before the constitution was formed; that there was nothing strictly novel in their conduct, &c., &c.

Nothing was done or moved to be done, as the matter is in commitment with the Representatives, where the measure has many friends.

Adjourned, and went to hear the debates in the lower House. Sedgwick, Lawrence, Smith, and Ames took the whole day. They seemed to aim all at one point, to make Madison ridiculous. Ames delivered a long string of studied sentences, but he did not use a single argument that seemed to leave an impression. He had public faith, public credit, honor, and, above all, justice, as often over as an Indian would the Great Spirit, and, if possible, with less meaning, and to as little purpose. Hamilton, at the head of the speculators, with all the courtiers, are on one side. These I call the party who are actuated by interest. The opposition are governed by principle. But I fear in this case interest will outweigh principle.

The enumeration bill was before us. The point at which I aimed at was to begin the enumeration in *April*, that so the census might be taken before our election; and the universal belief is that Pennsylvania would be a gainer.

Butler moved to have the time extended one year from the 1st of August next.

Here I threw in the most pointed opposition, and laid down the principles of the amendment which I proposed.

Ellsworth said he would be for extending the time to nine months, and Mr. Morris, to my astonishment, rose, and supported Ellsworth for the nine months. So Butler's motion was carried.

The arguments I used were that every measure tending to give the people confidence in our government should be adopted without delay. The present representation was on a suppositious enumeration, and was believed to be erroneous. A second election, therefore, ought not to proceed on such uncertain ground, &c.

February 17. The business done this morning was receiving the report of the committee to whom was committed the sixth clause of the enumeration bill. It had been recommitted at the instant and urgent motion of Mr. Butler, and the committee, as if to insult him reported the clause, without alteration. The bill was passed; and ordered for a third reading to-morrow. Adjourned, and went to hear the debates in the Chamber of Representatives.

18. We had a message this day from the President of the United States respecting the boundary between Nova Scotia and the State of Massachusetts. A committee was appointed some time ago, to whom the business was referred.

The report of the committee on the cession from North Carolina was called up. Some time spent on it, and it was postponed to Monday next.

The Senate now adjourned, and we went into the lower House to hear the debates on Mr. Madison's motion. Madison had been up most of the morning, and was said to have spoken most ably, indeed. He seemed rather jaded when I came in. He had early in this business been called on to show a single instance where anything like the present had been done. He produced an act of Parliament in point in the reign of Queen Anne. But now the gentleman quitted this ground, and cried out for rigid right on law principles. Madison modestly put them in mind that they had challenged him on this ground, and he had met them agreeably to their wishes. Adjourned, without the question.

February 19. Went to hear the debates in the House of Representatives, but they were dull and uninteresting, and yet the question was not put. All parties seemed tired, yet unwilling to give out. I am vexed with them. The real good and care of the country seems not to enter into all their thoughts. The very system of the Secretary's report seems to be to lay as much on the people as they can bear. Madison's yields no relief as to the burden, but affords some alleviation as to the design the tax will be laid for; and is, perhaps, on that account more dangerous, as it will be readier submitted to. There is an obstinacy, a perverse peevishness, a selfishness, which shuts him up from all free communication. He will see Congress in no other light than as one party. He seems to prescribe to them to follow laws already made, as if they were an executive body. Whereas, the fact is that the majority of the people, say three millions, (the payers,) and the holders of certificates, a few thousands, (the receivers,) are the parties, and the business of Congress is to legislate on the principles of justice between them. A funding system will be the consequence—that political gout of every government which has adopted it—with all our western lands for sale, and purchasers every day attending at the Hall begging for contracts. What villainy to cast the debt on posterity. But pay the debt, or even put it in a train of payment, and you no longer furnish food for speculation. The great object is by funding, &c., to raise the certificates to par; thus the speculators, who now have them nearly all engrossed, will clear above three hundred per cent.

Saturday, 20th February. The Speaker mentioned at dinner how accommodating Fitzsimmons had been—that he had declared Mifflin must not be Governor; if he was, they would be worse off than if no new Constitution had been made. They then naturally agreed that Mr. Morris's memorial should be pushed in Congress as the grand preparatory for his appointment to the Government.

I have observed a kind of spirit of uncertainty hover over the Representative body—a want of confidence either in the Secretary's scheme, or in Madison's proposal. Like a flight of land fowl at sea, they seem bewildered, and wish for a resting place, but distrust every object that offers. I think now would be the time to fix them on some moderate measure. I drew the following resolutions:

Resolved, That funds be immediately provided sufficient to pay three per cent. on the domestic debt of the United States, which has been liquidated before the 4th of March last, and that the same be paid annually to the persons holding the evidences of such debts upon their application for the same.

Resolved, That a land office be opened for the sale of the western territory, in which certificates of the domestic debt only shall be receivable, to operate as a sinking fund for the extinguishment of the said debt, and the arrears of interest due on the same.

I went with these resolutions to Mr. Scott's lodgings. (He was not in, but Mr. Maclay afterwards saw him,) and he observed: "I gave him my sentiments on the trim of his house, and read the resolutions, explaining as a kind of *interim* or *passo tempo*, on something that would perhaps take, as nothing was committed or decided finally on. The child, however, was not his own, but he declared that if Madison would join, they could be carried. I wished him to communicate with Madison. He was afraid of Madison's pride. I agreed to do it, and to communicate the result to him. Called, but Madison was out."

Monday, 22. Called on Madison. He made me wait long. He came down stairs and returned with me to his room. I enlarged on the business before the House as much as I thought my time would allow. Told him plainly there was no chance of his succeeding. It hurt his *Littleness*. I do not think he believed me. I read the resolutions. I do not think he attended to one word of them, so much did he seem absorbed in his own ideas. I put them into his hand. He offered them back without reading them. I did not readily hold out my hand to take them. He tendered them a second time. I took them, and then, by degrees, wound up my discourse so as to draw to the point of wishing him a good morning. His pride seems of that kind which repels all communication. He appears as if he could not bear the condescension of it.

Went to the Senate. A motion was made to adjourn. Izard objected—expected some resolutions would be sent in from the House of Representatives, to wait on the President, with compliments on his birth-day, &c. I took my hat and came down stairs. Those who stayed were disappointed. Madison's matter was over before I came down, and a poor show his party made. The obstinacy of this man has ruined the opposition. The Secretary's report will now pass through, perhaps unaltered. I could not help observing that now both Fitzsimmons and Clymer spoke, and they were Secretary all over. Fitzsimmons gave me notice of a meeting of the Pennsylvania delegation at his lodgings at six o'clock. I went. The ostensible reason was to consult on the adoption of the State debts; but the fact to tell us that they were pre-determined to do it.

Clymer, strange to tell, expatiated on the growing grandeur of Pennsylvania if it was done. Our roads would be all made, and our communications all opened by land and water, &c., &c.

Fitzsimmons was much more argumentative; but they were all pre-determined, and only called on our complaisance to assent to their better judgment.

I chose to mention publicly, that I thought we scarce did justice to the State we represented, that we did not meet oftener, and consult on her interest. This met with an echo of applause. Fitzsimmons proposed his lodgings as a rendezvous weekly. Mr. Morris spoke of wine and oysters, and it was ageed to meet every Monday evening at Simons'. I took, however, care to bear my unequivocal testimony against the adoption now proposed, and, in fact, made the above proposition, to obviate any suspicion of obstinacy or unsociability.

22. The Senate sat more than an hour, doing nothing at all but looking at each other. Ellsworth and Strong got together at a time when we had all got in chatting parties about the fires or stoves. We were suddenly called to order, and Ellsworth was up. It was a most formal motion, indeed, which he made, and then read a resolution, stating that a mistake had been made yesterday in a communication which had been sent to the House of Representatives, and desiring them to return the paper. It was about the North Carolina session, and I suspected all was not very right. But, indeed, as much through pastime as otherwise, I opposed him. He grew serious and solemn, and I grew rather sportive, with a grave face on, and we made a noble debate of it. It would be idle to blot an inch of paper with it. The question was at length put, and Ellsworth lost it. Greatly was he mortified, indeed, and sat down in a visible chagrin.

Doctor Johnson, who had not spoke before, got up and said angry things. He did not move absolutely for a reconsideration, but Ellsworth followed him, and urged a reconsideration. It was seconded by Strong. I got up, and opposed the reconsideration as out of order, and another most important debate ensued. The Chair was called on, and he declared the question out of order, *marabile dictu*. I turned to Mr. Morris. Had he decided so in the case of the Susquehanna bill, said I, we should have had Congress on the banks of that river. Mr. Morris said yes.

Mr. Morris got on the subject of the difficulties he labored under in the settlement of his account. Told me that he had to send again to Philadelphia for a receipt book, in which were some trifling accounts for money paid to expresses of 40/, and such small sums;

but concluded, I will *have* everything settled, and the most ample receipt and certificate of the accounts being closed.

24. Attended this day in Senate. No business of any conse- quence done. This was a day of company at our house. Madison was in the invitation, and came early and asked for me, but I could not come down stairs. * * * I was sorry for this, but as the saying is, there is no help for sickness. Drank tea, and felt better after it, but kept my bed.

February 27. No Senate this day. Went with the Speaker to buy books. I bought Peter Pindar, whose sarcastic and satirical vein will write monarchy into disrepute in Britain. His shafts are aimed personally at his present Majesty, but many of them hit the throne, and will contribute to demolish the absurdity of royal gov- ernment. Thus even Peter, who I guess to be a servile creature paying court to the heir apparent and the rising royal family, may be a useful instrument in opening the eyes of mankind to the ab- surdity of human worship, and the adulation, nay almost adora- tion, paid to work of their own hands. Kings and governors origi- nally were meant for the use and advantage of the governed, but the folly of mankind has puffed them out of their places and made them not only useless but burdensome.

1790, March 1. Returned to the Hall; sat for some time; nothing done. Received a note to dine with the President of the United States. Went into the Chamber of the Representatives and heard the debates till three o'clock, which I thought unimportant. Ames, however, read in his place a string of resolutions touching the man- ner in which the States were to bring forward their claims, which I thought alarming.

March 2. Just nothing done this day in Senate save receiving Bailey's bill for certain inventions from the Representatives. Some spiteful remarks made on it. To-morrow assigned for a second reading.

A resolve passed the Representatives this day that seems to show that they begin to think. It is a call on the Secretary to ascertain the resources that may be applied to the payment of the State debts, if they should be adopted.

The Spreaker was at the levee to-day. When he came home, he said *the State debts must be adopted.* This, I suppose, is the lan- guage of the court.

March 3. This day Bailey's bill taken up for second reading. Five members rose to oppose it. I was up three times, and I am convinced we should have carried it. Mr. Morris rose, however, and proposed that it should be committed to the very men who opposed it. Langdon made a formal motion to this purpose, and was seconded by Bassett. Such a committee was accordingly appointed. It is a new way to commit a bill to its enemies. We will see what will come of it.

March 4. . . . . My bodings of yesterday were not ill founded, with respect to Bailey's bill. A man ought not to put his hand in a dog's mouth, and trust to his generosity not to bite it. Commit the bill to its declared enemies, and trust to their generosity to report in favor of it. My conjectures were right, and they have reported dead against it.

Dined with the President of the United States. It was a dinner of dignity. All the Senators present, and the Vice President. I looked often around the company to find the happiest faces. Wisdom forgive me, if I wrong thee; but I thought folly and happiness were the most nearly allied. The President seemed to bear in his countenance a settled aspect of melancholy. No cheering ray of convivial sunshine broke through the cloudy gloom of settled seriousness. At every interval of eating or drinking, he played on the table with a fork or knife, like a drum-stick.

March 5. This the important week, and perhaps the important day, when the question will be put on the assumption of the State debts. I suspect this from the rendezvousing of the crew of the Hamilton galley. It seems all hands are pressed to quarters.

Four o'clock. I was rather deceived, as the adoption party do not yet consider themselves strong enough to risk the putting of the question, for it seems the day has passed and nothing is done.

The naturalization bill was taken up. The debates were exceedingly lengthy, and a great number of amendments moved. Mr. Morris stood by me in one, that was to enable aliens to hold lands in the United States. 'Tis said, he has an agent in Europe now for selling lands. I am wrong to minute this circumstance; he is, however, very seldom with me. I know not how it came, but I was engaged, on one side or the other, warmly on every question. The truth of the matter is, it is a vile bill, illiberal and void of philanthropy, and needed mending much. We complained, to the Representatives from Pennsylvania, that such an ungenerous bill should be sent us. At least, I did. They answered, you have little to do, and they sent us employment.

This night the Pennsylvanians supped together at Simmons'. 'Twas freely talked of that the question was to have been taken this day on the assumption of the State debts, but Vining, from the Delaware State, is come in, and it was put off until he would be prepared, (by the Secretary, I suppose,) so that my morning creed was a well founded belief. The language of the Philadelphia gentlemen is still for adoption. The great reason formerly urged for it was, that Pennsylvania would draw a great revenue from the Union. I brought forward the case of Amsterdam, to which the United Provinces owed great balances which were not paid a century after their revolution.

Mr. Fitzsimmons said they were not paid yet, nor never would be ; but then, with one voice, all the three citizens said little if anything would be due to Pennsylvania, and declared that settling old accounts was misspent time. Burn all old accounts, said Mr. Morris, and pay only the people who now hold certificates. I wished for harmony and declined argument, but said the citizens of Pennsylvania would not abandon the State securities. This was admitted, but Mr. Morris said the State might subscribe the amount of them. This would be sinking two per cent. to the State, as they would subscribe in at four per cent. and pay six to their own citizens. But I forbore entering into argument. Colonel Hartley kept still repeating, all depends on the adoption of the State debts. If this is not done, New England and Carolina will fly off, and the Secretary's scheme is ruined. We must adopt.

9th March. In the Senate Chamber, this morning, Butler said he heard a man say he would give Vining one thousand guineas for his vote, but added, I question whether he would do so in fact. I do not know that pecuniary influence has actually been used, but I am certain that every other kind of management has been practiced and every tool at work that could be thought of. Officers of Government, clergy, Cincinnati, and every person under the influence of the Treasury ; Bland and Huger carried to the Chamber of Representatives—the one lame, the other sick ; Clymer stopped from going away, though he had leave ; and at length they risked the question, and carried it, thirty-one votes to twenty-six ; and all this after having tampered with the members since the twenty-second of last month, and this only *in committee*, with many doubts that some will fly off, and great fears that the North Carolina members will be in before a bill can be matured or the report gone through. Mr. Morris received a note signed S. C., communicating the news. He only said, I am sorry it is by so small a majority. General Muhlenburg and G. Hiester, of the Pennsylvania delegation, only, were in the negative.

I had to wrangle with the New England men alone on the naturalization bill till near one o'clock. Johnson, of North Carolinia, took, in some degree, part with me. I held my own, or at least I thought so, with tolerable success; but I certainly, however, gained greatly. Twice yesterday did we attempt, without success, to throw out the two years' residence. The amendments which I had offered went to cure this defect, with respect to the power of holding lands. Numbers of gentlemen now declared their dislike of the two years, and wished the bill committed, for the purpose of having this part rejected. I agreed, but we were very unlucky in our committee. We Pennsylvanians act as if we believed that God made of one blood all families of the earth; but the eastern people seem to think that He made none but New England folks. It is strange that men born and educated under republican forms of government should be so contracted on the subject of general philanthropy. In Pennsylvania, used as we are to the reception and adoption of strangers, we receive no class of men with such diffidence as the eastern people. Yet these are the men who affect the greatest fear of being contaminated with foreign manners, customs, or vices.

10. Was the first at the Hall this morning. However, it was not long before some of the Secretary's gladiators came in. What an abject thing a man becomes when he makes himself a tool to any one. I ventured to predict to one of them that the Secretary's system would fail. Why, but the assumption of the State debts is carried already. I ventured to tell how. From me, distant as the room would let him, did he fly off. Bassett has this day declared in the most unequivocal manner against the adoption of the State debts. Says, if they are adopted, he will move for two per cent. I asked him how Mr. Reed would be on this question. He said against assumption. We had company this day. The greater part were New England men, who soon went away. Burke and Tucker both voted for the assumption of the State debts. Tucker declared his views in the most unequivocal manner; after the States were discharged by the Federal assumption, to spunge the whole. Burke reprobated the whole of the Secretary's report, and declared it would blow up. He was not so explicit, but seemed in unison with Tucker. What must come of the report, if these men are sincere.

March 11. Attended at the Hall. Two bills came up from the Representatives. The bill for inventions, and one to give additional salaries to clerks. Read the first time. A bill for the mitigation of fines and forfeitures was taken up for a second reading. Opposed by Bassett and Few. A commitment was early moved, and seemed generally agreed to; but the members popped up and down talking about it for above an hour.

March 12. Attended this day at the Hall. No business of consequence done. The committee on the naturalization bill reported, but far short of the points which I wished established in it. There really seems a spirit of malevolence against Pennsylvania in this business. We have been very liberal on the subject of admitting strangers to citizenship, we have been benefited by it, and still do benefit. Some characters seem disposed to deprive us of it. I moved a postponement of a day, that we might consider of the amendment. It was easily carried; but Izard said no, alone.

Mr. Morris turned towards me this day and seemed to invite a *tete-a-tete*. We spoke of who would be Governor. He declared in favor of St. Clair—spoke against Mifflin and Bingham. I said I had heard Miles spoken of. He objected to Miles as wanting knowledge. I never made any mention of any of the Muhlenbergs. He objected to Mifflin—said " See what sort of people he has put in office." S. G. was mentioned. He said " you should have had that office." I went into some detail of the duties of that office—showed that it was one in which a drone might slumber; but if filled well, was a most laborious office, and pointed out how.

March 15. The only debate of any consequence this day in Senate was on the naturalization bill. The same illiberality as was apparent on other occasions possessed the New England men. Immigration is a source of population to us, and they wish to deprive us of it. I was up several times, but always endeavored to be concise and to the point as much as I possibly could. Mr. Morris was up once; I thought he lost himself, and by way of getting out, said he was of the same opinion as the member from New York—Mr. King. Mr. King is as much against us as any of them, but he does it in an indirect manner.

March 16. Mr. Morris, after sitting serious a good while, turned to me, and began a familiar chat. At last asked me to walk on one side from our seats, and asked me if back lands could still be taken up. I told him yes. He immediately proposed to me to join him in a speculation in lands, which he said he thought that he, from his connections in Europe, could sell at a dollar an acre. I paused a moment, said as our waste lands were totally unproductive, such a thing might be beneficial to the public as well as ourselves; that in this point of view I saw no objection. I stated some affairs of our land office briefly, and he concluded we would make up our estimates the first leisure moment. If he is in earnest in this matter, he will be favorable to the lowering of the terms of the land office.

March 16. The principal debates this day were on the naturalization bill, and were characterized with the same illiberality as those before mentioned.

We had company this day, mostly Virginians. Colonel Bland was of the number. He is an assumer on the subject of the State debts. He avowed his design to be a demonstration to the world that our present constitution aimed directly at consolidation, and the sooner everybody knew it, the better. So that, in fact, he supported the Secretary on anti-Federal principles. This, I believe, is the design of Gerry and many more. The New England men, however, want to get their State debts shook off before they declare themselves completely. In their former attempt to sink them, they raised Shay's rebellion.

The appropriation bill was just read, and the President passed to, and took up, the mitigation bill, (of fines, forfeitures.)

It was on the third reading, and Ellsworth offered an amendment, and the bill was committed.

The Naturalization Bill.

Now, the naturalization bill was taken up, and all our old arguments went over and over again. The fact is the adoption of strangers has set Pennsylvania far ahead of her sister States. They are spiteful and envious, and wish to deprieve her of this source of population ; but it will scarcely do to avow openly such ungenerous conduct. It, therefore, must be done under various pretenses and legal distinctions. Two years residence was insisted on in the bill. We cared not for this, but let the stranger hold land the moment he comes, &c., &c.

March 17. Two law opinions were supported in the debates of this day. One, that the power of holding lands was a feature of naturalization—that lands, &c., could not be held without it. This doctrine was pushed so far by Ellsworth as to declare that the rights of electors, being elected, &c., should attend and be described in the act of naturalization. All that could be said would not support this doctrine. Ellsworth was even so absurd as to suppose if a man acquired the right of suffrage in one State, he had it in all, &c. This doctrine it was seen would not carry, and now one more conformable to the common law was set up.

It was alleged that the disability of an alien to hold lands arose from the common law, and was separable from the rights of natu-. alization, as in the case of denization in England, where the Crown could confer the right of giving, receiving, and holding, real property. When an alien, therefore, was enabled to hold real estate, it was, in reality, by repealing part of the common law, with respect to him. Not by giving a power, but taking away a disability. It, therefore, strictly speaking, rested with the respective States whether they would repeal the common law, with respect to aliens, touching the point of holding property, and, being a pure State concern, had no occasion to be made any mention of in the naturalization act, but must remain to be settled by the different States by law, as well as the rights of election, &c. We, of Pennsylvania, contended hard to have a clause for empowering aliens to hold, &c., but the above reasoning prevailed, and we lost it.

Before Senate was formed, this morning, Mr. Carroll, of Carrollton, happened to be sitting next to me. We were chatting on some common subject. The President was in the chair, which he had taken on the performance of prayer. He hastily descended, came and took the chair next to Mr. Carroll's. He began abruptly : How have you arranged your empire on your departure ? Your revenues must suffer in your absence. What kind of administration have you established for the regulation of your finances ? Is your Government entrusted to a viceroy, nuncio, legate, plenipotentiary, or chargé d'affaires, &c., &c. ? Carroll endeavored to get him down from his imperial language by telling him he had a son-in law who paid attention to his affairs, &c. 'Twas in vain. He wou d not dismount his hobby. At it again ; nor was there an officer in the household, civil, or military departments of royal or imperial government that he had not an allusion to. I pared my nails, and thought he would soon have done, but it is no such easy thing to go through the detail of an empire. Guardian goddess of America, canst thou not order it so, than when thy sons cross the Atlantic they may return with something else beside European forms and follies ! But I found this prayer ruffled me a little, so I left them before Adams had half settled the empire.

Mr. Morris had some further chat on the proposal of yesterday. I told him if I thought it possible that disadvantage could flow either to the public or individuals, I never would hear of it. He said advantage would probably flow to the public from it. It would be the means of bringing us both money and people. I now touched him on the subject of lowering back lands of Pennsylvania. It was a cold scent. I find he is for what the speculators call dodging— selling the land in Europe before he buys it here. He repeated that a dollar an acre could be got for it.

March 18. The burden of this day's debate was the naturalization bill over again. From the most accurate observation I have been able to make, the conduct of the members has been influenced by the following motives : As Pennsylvania is supposed likely to derive most benefit by migrations, the eastern members are disposed to check it as much as they can. Jersey, nearly indifferent ; Delaware, absolutely so ; Maryland, as Jersey ; Virginia, unrepresented ; North Carolina, favorable. South Carolina and Georgia want people much, but they fear migrations, and will check them rather than run the chance of importing people who may be averse to slavery. Hence the bill passed the House nearly as it came up from the Representatives.

The governing ideas seemed to be the following : That the holding property was separable from and not absolutely connected with naturalization; that laws and regulations relating to property, not being among the powers granted to Congress, remained with the different States. Therefore Congress would be guilty of an assumption of power if they touched it; that the holding of property was a common law right; and the disability of aliens to hold property from that quarter. Patterson, Bassett, Henry, and Johnson, all finally settled in this way. Ellsworth dead against this; the holding property, (real,) a feature inseparable from naturalization, &c. Strong rather inclined to Ellsworth. Dr. Johnson said about as much on one side as the other. Few, too, is said to be a lawyer; but though he spoke a great deal, he did not seem to enter into the distinctions. For our parts, we wished the naturalization bill to be in as exact conformity as possible to the existing laws relating to aliens in Pennsylvania; and this I am convinced would have been the case, had it not been for that low spirit which contaminates public characters as well as private life.

March 19. The naturalization bill taken again. Now, Butler, too proud to have lent his aid to any motion that was not his own, came forward with two motions. They were, in fact, nearly the same which had been negatived three or four times before. It was alleged they were all out of order; but he was indulged, and lost them both.

Now, Few must bring forward his motion, too. It was equally out of order, but he was indulged in the loss of it.

It appears that all over Europe where the *civil* law prevails, aliens hold property. It is the common law of England that deprives them of holding real estate. The common law has been received by us, and with it, this consequence.

However, since we cannot get the rights of property fully acknowledged, it is best that the naturalization bill say nothing about it.

Mr. Morris got warmly at me this day about the affair of land. Repeated he thought even more than a dollar per acre could be got, and requested me to write him an account of the kind of land, distance to market, &c., &c. I wrote to him as follows :

NEW YORK, *20th March, 1790.*

SIR: The lands, concerning which you have made inquiry, are situated in the county of Northumberland, on the heads of Lycoming, Pine Creek, and Tioga, branches of the river Susquehanna. Their distance from Philadelphia, as the roads now go, is from one hundred and eighty to two hundred miles, but it may be shortened by opening a more direct communication. The county of Northumberland, in which the first settlements were made about the year 1770, was totally desolated by the incursions of the Indians during the Revolution, a misfortune it never can experience a second time, as the late settlements of the State of New York (being extended north of it) and Luzerne county form a complete barrier, and the savages have greatly diminished, must soon be totally excluded by the increasing settlements from the Atlantic side of the great lakes Ontario and Erie. Northumberland county now contains between two and three thousand families. Provisions of all kinds can be had in abundance. The average price of wheat, rye, Indian corn, barley, buckwheat, and speltz, when compounded, has seldom been equal to half a Spanish dollar per bushel. The present year it is higher, not owing to any failure of crops, but the uncommon demand for exportation. The country in which these lands are situated is mountainous, but the high ridges are never included in the surveys. It is covered with an immense forest of timber. Maple; sugar tree; buck; beech; oak of all kinds; pine, mostly of the white and spruce kinds; white walnut; wild cherry; hickory; ash, &c. These forests sometime ago seemed to set husbandry at defiance, but we now know that, independent of the advantage of clearing the ground, they can be converted to useful purposes in the manufacture of potash. The different streams of the Susquehanna offer the means of conveying any produce whatever to market. This country has been observed to be particularly favorable to grass, and, perhaps, the raising of cattle may be the most profitable object of husbandry, as stock carries itself to market. These parts enjoy, in an eminent degree, the advantage and security of double crops.

The snows, which fall regularly at their proper season in winter, insure a plentiful harvest of the fall grain; wheat, and rye with tolerable husbandry, seldom yielding less than twenty bushels per acre. The length of the summer is well adapted to Indian corn, flax, oats, spring barley, summer wheat, tobacco, and vegetables of all kinds. Buckwheat is often sowed with success in the same summer on the ground from whence wheat, rye, or winter barley had been reaped. Perhaps, so far as respects seasons, the interests of husbandry are no where better secured than in Pennsylvania. The abundant exports of flour, grain, &c., from the port of Philadelphia afford full proof of this. It is certain that as you advance southward, and diminish the rigors of winter, you lessen the certainty of the winter crops; while ascending to the north, the contracted and chilly season seldom brings to maturity the summer produce, which is often blasted or perished by early frosts. Yet such is the rage of migration, that lands, with all the advantages of soil and climate, in the bosom of society are neglected for fancied elysiums in Yazoo or Kentucky. I cannot state with precision the quantity of these lands, having no actual surveys before me, but I know they are not less than fifty thousand acres. If I can render you any further information, I shall be happy in doing so.

I am, sir, yours most, &c.,

W. M.

Honorable R. Morris, Esquire.

Writing the foregoing letter was all I did this forenoon. The Speaker took me in his carriage, and we rode in the afternoon.

Sunday, 21st. Wrote letters to my family this forenoon.

After dinner, walked alone, up and down, back and forward, on the island. The Speaker told me the report was not to be taken up until Fitzsimmons came back, which was to be on Thursday. He knows all the motions of the janizaries and gladiators.

March 22. Visited Mr. Wilson's lodgings with the Speaker. I then went with Mr. Wynkoop to visit Mr. Carroll, of Carrollton. We got on the subject of the State of Carolina having *instructed* their representation.

Could any hints have gone from here, said he, to set them on this measure? He is a Roman Catholic, and the intimate friend of Mr. Fitzsimmons. This question raised the following train of ideas in my mind: Fitzsimmons is gone to prevent a similar measure in Pennsylvania, and I am suspected of having given hints to set such a measure going. Perhaps something of this kind may be alleged against me with justice. The doctrine of instruction may certainly be carried so far as to be in effect the tribunitial veto of the Romans, and reduce us to the state of a Polish diet. But it is introduced. Perhaps the best way is for all the States to use it, and the general evil, if it really should be one, will call for a remedy. But here is a subject worthy of inquiry. Is it to be expected that a Federal law passed directly against the sense of a whole State will ever be executed in that State? If the answer is in the negative, it is clearly better to give the State an early legislative negative than finally let her use a practical one which would go to the dissolution of the Union.

A memorial of one Tracy was read, praying a bankrupt law to be passed under the authority of the United States. A motion for the appointment of a committee to bring in a bill for such purpose. There was a great deal of speaking on this subject, and really I thought had not justice done to it. I got up, and was listened to with attention while I explained the difference between the common laws for the discharge of insolvent debtors and the laws respecting commission of bankruptcy, and confined the latter to its proper field, the trading part of the community; and this part only belonged to the Congress to take up, and I doubted whether they had done most harm or good, &c. I was led into a detail of the laws of England on this head. Much was said on all hands, but we negatived the motion.

The moment it was through, General Schuyler and Mr. Morris called for it on the third and last reading, for they said the Secretary wanted to make remittances to Europe. They got what they wanted, and thus we had done with it.

This mode of business cannot last long. All evils, it is said, cure themselves. Here is a general appropriation of above half a million of dollars—the particulars are not mentioned—the estimate on which it is founded may be mislaid or changed; in fact, it is giving the Secretary the money for him to account for as he pleases. This is certainly all wrong. The estimate should have formed part of the bill, or should have been recited in it.

Mr. Morris this day asked me if I had prepared anything on the subject we had been conversing about. I put the letter into his hands. He read it with apparent satisfaction—put it into his pocket. He asked me if some kind of houses could not be raised and covered with bark at a small expense on these lands. I told him they might, if honest men were employed who would not make a job of it.

The Senate adjourned about two o'clock. I was told there was warmth in the House of Representatives on the Quaker memorial, and went in. The House have certainly greatly debased their dignity, using base, invective, indecorous language; three or four up at a time, manifesting signs of passion, the most disorderly wanderings in their speeches, telling stories, private anecdotes, &c. I know not what may come of it, but there seems a general discontent among the members, and many of them do not hesitate to declare that the Union must fall to pieces at the rate we go on   Indeed, many seem to wish it.

March 23. Went with a party to wait on Mr. Jefferson. He was out. We left our names.

Mr Morris chatted with great freedom with me this day on his private affairs. Explained some of the difficulties he had met with in the settlement of his accounts. Says the balance will be in his favor. Declares he will soon have done and put to silence his adversaries. Justice says plainly this ought to be the case, if he has been injured. He is very full of the affair between him and me. His countenance speaks the appearance of sincerity and candor. Interest, however, the grand anchor to secure any man, lies at the bottom.

24. This day little of consequence done in the Senate.

I was called out of the Senate. When I came in the report of the committee on the difference of boundary between the United States and Nova Scotia was under consideration. I said a few words, which appeared to be well received, on the subject. Izard and Butler both manifested a most insulting spirit this day, when there was not the least occasion for it, nor the smallest offense offered. These men have a most settled antipathy to Pennsylvania, owing to the doctrines patronized in that State on the subject of slavery.

March 25. The Speaker told me last night that Mr. Clymer wished to see us this morning at his lodgings. As I always embrace the smallest hint to meet the delegation, I was early ready, but the *Friends*, who had been in town on the abolition business, called, in two parties, to take leave of us. I, however, hastened to Mr. Clymer's lodgings. Found Scott, Hiester, and Wynkoop at the door. I asked what had happened. Scott, with a great laugh, said Clymer had read them a letter to the Speaker, and was dreadfully afraid all the people would fly to the western world. I replied, Scott, I told you some time ago that all this would happen if you taxed the Atlantic States too high, and you gave me a great Monongahela laugh in answer. Aye, says he, and I will give you many more. I went up stairs, and had a letter of Clymer's composing put into my hands; the amount of it was that every man was worth £200 sterling; that every man that went to the western country was lost to the United States, and therefore every tract of land we sold to a settler would be attended with the loss of a man, or his equivalent, £200, deducting the trifle the United States would get for the land.

All this fine reason falls dead to the ground should it appear that the man is not lost to the United States. It is, however, fact that by an impolitic oppression of taxes we may detach the whole country from us, and connect them with New Orleans; and in that case, we will get nothing for the lands. Clymer came in, and said, on the principle of that letter, he would vote against paying any of the public debts with back lands. What a deal of pains he has been at to fish up some kind of reason to accommodate his vote to the wish of the *public creditors, alias* speculators. They are a powerful body in Philadelphia, and, therefore, not to be neglected. I asked what our friends in Philadelphia thought, particularly on the assumption of the State debt. He said they were divided, but there were more *against it* than *for it.* He now said some fine things on the improvement of the State, &c. I walked with him and Colonel Hartley. All the way to the Hall did his tongue run on the subject of going to the Potomac. I bore my testimony in the plainest language against all this ; regretted our not having tried an adjournment to Philadelphia a year ago. Said if we would go to Philadelphia, with the promise of the permanent residence on the Potomac, we could without it. He was peevish and fretful.

No business of consequence done in the Senate. Two bills came up to be signed. Our President used these words from the chair, before he signed them : Is there any objection, gentlemen, to the signing of these bills ? He seems a tone lower than he used to be. The amendment on the mitigation bill was non-concurred in, and managers for a conference appointed.

26. The bill for augmenting the military to sixteen hundred men came up. Read, and Monday appointed for a second reading.

A petition read from Captain Barry and others for commutation. Nothing else done in Senate. Spent some time on the bill for the encouragement of inventions, &c.

The Speaker had company this day. All Pennsylvanians. Mr. Morris took pains to make himself agreeable. The Speaker told him they had determined to risk the revenue business, as they now found Williamson and Ash would be for the assumption, as they had changed their minds. How true is the observation made by Henry, of Maryland : All great governments resolve themselves into cabal. Ours is a mere system of jockeying opinions. Vote this way for me, and I will vote that way for you.

March 27. Received a few lines from Doctor Rush, in which he tells me I am complained of for corresponding with the Controller General. This I well know comes from Fitzsimmons. He would wish that no man but himself should know anything of the finances of Pennsylvania. I have made advances to the Philadelphians repeatedly, but they shake us off; and, when meetings had been settled for the communication of knowledge, they have broken them up. But I am found to possess knowledge of the finances of Pennsylvania. The presumption is that I correspond with Nicholson. Am become independent of them, and, therefore, criminal.

Mr. Morris has made no agreement with me about lands. He said he would draw up something on this subject in writing. Nothing of this has happened, and, perhaps, never will. I thought such a thing might happen, and was careful in my letter.

I wish I was honorably off with this same business of Senate. If Congress continues to sit in New York, I cannot pretend to continue a member of it. Circumstances may direct me to what is best. God has, however, given to every man his talent for the express purpose of making use of it; or, in other words, that he may conduct himself on the principles of right reason. May he enable me to keep my lamp trimmed always.

29th March. Committee on the bill for the progress of writs, &c., reported. Three other bills came up to us—one for treaty with Indians—for extending the effect of the State inspection laws, and the North Carolina cession. The last, amended by striking out the word "Honorable" from before the names of the Senators. Butler bounced, and Izard made frightful faces at it. They were opposed by King, Ellsworth, and Patterson. I was pleased to see the Yorkers and Southern people at it. The business was got rid of by a new clause altogether in the beginning of the bill, from which a clear inference in practice follows, viz: That the whole of the bill is in the power of the Senate, notwithstanding their former agreement, and the concurrence of the other House to any part or parts of it; and then deliberations are not confined to the parts only respecting which the disagreement subsists. I have spoken to Otis to copy all the papers, that I may plead this precedent, if necessary; for this doctrine was pointedly denied in the disputes respecting the permanent bill.

This day the House of Representatives took up the report of the Committee of the Whole House on the Secretary's report; and after adopting the three first clauses, re-committed the one on the assumption of the State debts—29 to 27; so that I hope this will be rejected at last.

The Speaker has declared that he will vote against it, if there should be a tie in the House. This was my opinion, which he early adopted, and which he has so often subscribed to, that it will be impossible for him to recede from it, upon this principle—that a matter of moment, not absolutely necessary, had better be omitted than carried by so small a majority as one vote. This opinion has met with much approbation from many members of Senate; and I have taken care to let the Speaker know it.

March 30. Third reading of the bill for the progress of useful arts produced a debate by the New England members in favor of a man from their country; but by being joined by the southern men we defeated them.

Read the law for giving effect to the inspection laws of the States. Message from the Representatives, with cession bill agreed to. Message from the President, with nominations to vacant offices. The bill for the military establishment took up the rest of the day in desultory debate, and was finally committed to seven members. This bill seems laying the foundation of a standing army.

The justifiable reasons for using force seem to be the enforcing of laws, quelling insurrections, and repelling invasions. The Constitution directs all these to be done by the militia. Should the United States unfortunately be involved in war, an army for the annoyance of an enemy in their own country, (as the most effective mode of keeping the calamity at a distance, and forcing an adversary to terms,) will be necessary. This seems the meaning of the Constitution, and that no troops should be kept up in peace. This bill certainly aims at different objects. The first error seems to have been the appointing a Secretary at War when we were at peace: and now we must find troops, lest his office should run out of employment.

Dressed, and attended the levee. I generally used to leave this part of duty to Mr. Morris; but now he is gone, and, lest there should be any complaints, I will discharge this piece of etiquette. The day was fine, and the levee large.

March 31. A call of the gladiators this morning. Therefore, expect it will be a day of some importance in the House of Representatives.

In Senate, the bill for enforcing the inspection laws of the State had a third reading. The appointments of Rufus Putnam, a judge of the Western Territory; James Brown, attorney for Kentucky; and Henry Bogart, surveyor for Albany, were consented to. Senate adjourned.

Early went to hear the event of this day's debates in the House of Representatives. Nothing remarkable, save a violent personal attack on Hamilton by Judge Burk, of South Carolina, which the men of the blade say must produce a duel. The question was not taken on the assumption.

Mr. Wynkoop spoke to me in the Representative Chamber to have a meeting of the delegation. I supported this idea, and we agreed to meet at the Speaker's. But I first went, and drank tea with Mr. Wynkoop and Mrs. Wynkoop.

There was a great deal of desultory discourse at the meeting. Mr. Clymer took on him to assert that the State of Pennsylvania was in debt to the Union, and disbelieved all Mr. Nicholson's statements, and declared unequivocally for burning all old accounts.

I metioned Nicholson's statements as being made from authority, and that they neither ought nor could be invalidated on supposition. That the old confederation had proceeded every step on the grounds of a final settlement. That to annihilate the old accounts was contrary to the new constitution, which had sanctified every act of the old Congress; nor could I see how any State could call on the Union to assume any debt of theirs until she showed, by a settlement, that she had exceeded her requisitions.

April 1, 1790. This day, in Senate, two bills were signed: The Carolina cession act and the bill for giving effect to the State inspection laws. A committee was also appointed to settle the pay of the Senators up to this time.

The Senate adjourned, and I went into the Chamber of Representatives to hear the debates. It was a dull scene. Gerry took up the time of the committee to the hour of adjournment. He is a tedious and most disagreeable speaker. The committee rose, and no question was taken.

Soon after I came in, I took an opportunity of speaking to Mr. Wynkoop. I was pointing out some inconveniences of the assumption. I found he seemed much embarrassed. Lawrence and Benson had got him away from his usual seat to near where they commonly sat. He paused a little. Got up rather hastily. Said: God bless you. Went out of the Chamber, and actually took his wife, and proceeded home to Pennsylvania.

April 2. The House of Representatives met, but adjourned on account of the holiday.

I conversed this day at the Hall with George Gray. He declares the people of Pennsylvania are universally opposed to the assumption, now the matter seems understood. This is the effect of the publications, which I have labored hard indeed to get into the prints. The Speaker is now firm against the assumption, and so is Scott. Clymer is so, too, but I am not quite certain whether his wish of popularity has yet been able to subdue his pride. I have put my political life in my hand in starting this opposition in the teeth of the Philadelphians. If I fail, my seat in Congress and disgrace in the public eye will follow. But I am conscious of rectitude of intention, and *hic murus aheneus esto, nil conscire sibi, nulla pallescere culpa.*

April 3. Called in the morning at Mr. Hamilton's office to make an apology for not dining with him. Could not see him. He was closeted with the Secretary at War. Was desired to stay until he was disengaged. The importance of my business would not justify this. Gave my name and compliments to Colonel Hamilton, and information that the badness of the weather prevented my dining with him yesterday, as I happened to be so unfortunate as not to be able to procure a carriage.

And now, this momentous affair being settled, went to the Hall. The minutes were read. A message from the President of the United States. A report handed to the Chair. The report was the pay due to each member. Doctor Elmer and Mr. Bassett whispered me, after the report was handed in, that King and Schuyler were allowed full pay, notwithstanding they had not been much with us, and that Dr. Johnson was allowed full pay and mileage to Connecticut, though he lives here; while the time Dr. Elmer was absent was deducted.

I went into the Representative Chamber expecting the assumption would be taken up. A listless apathy seemed to pervade the whole. Two motions were negatived touching some appointment of a foreign nature, that did not seem to have been well digested. Somebody said adjourn, and they adjourned accordingly. This really seems like the mockery of business. The New England men despair of being able to saddle us with their debts, and now they care not whether they do any business or not.

April 4. When I was called down to dinner, the Speaker and General were closeted with Clymer and Jackson. All was profound mystery. We had half finished our dinner before they joined us. I saw they were filled with thoughts of importance, but I scorned to be inquisitive. I retired to my chamber. The Speaker soon came to me, and unfolded the mystery. Clymer had a proposal to barter away the Pennsylvania votes, for an assumption, for the Carolina and Massachusetts votes, for an adjournment to Philadelphia. The Speaker, however, avowed to me the reason of the vote for assumption, viz : consolidation, and uniting in one government.

I told him plainly Hamilton had no abilities for such a work, and the thing would miscarry in his or any other hands. I determined to go and call on Clymer about this business. I did so, but he had Jackson (of the President's family) with him. I sat till I was tired and rose with the first of the company to come away. Clymer asked me to walk on the Battery, and we roamed almost the whole length of the town, up the East river and back again, without his giving me an opportunity of speaking with him. I felt hurt at his distant treatment. I went with him home. He called Jackson in. Jackson made a florid harangue on the golden opportunity of bartering the votes of Pennsylvania with South Carolina and Massachusetts, to give the assumption and get the residence of Congress.   Whatever I might have done in other company, I would not commit myself to Jackson.   I spoke my sentiments sincerely on the villainy of bartering votes ; declared my opinion that Pennsylvania need make no sacrifice to obtain Congress ; that matters were working as favorably as could be wished ; that I entertained no doubt of adjourning to Philadelphia ; that assuming the State debts, in the manner proposed, was so radically wrong that nothing could justify the act, and that the postponement of it ought to take place at any rate.

Clymer said it would not be postponed—it would be carried.

I said the Pennsylvanians might see each other before that time. He said they could not.   I told him if the Pennsylvanians were able to postpone it after a contract was made, they were able to do it without any contract ; and if they really meant to sell their votes, it was idle to talk of giving them without and before a contract was made.   Make a present of a thing, and you need not demand a price afterwards.   I concluded with saying I would have time enough to make up my mind before the business appeared before the Senate, but had no objection to deliver my sentiments at any time, and had given them now with freedom.

Hence appears plainly how much the assumption of the State debts made a point of by the court party.   In fact the reduction of the State governments was the object in theory in framing both the Constitution and Judiciary, and in as many laws of the United States as were capable of taking a tincture of that kind.   But it won't do.

Monday, 5th April.   The bill for the progress of the useful arts was concurred with after considerable debate.   The report of the Senators from the joint committee on the mitigation bill was, that the disagreement continued.

A communication of the President of the United States of three acts of the Legislature of New York.   The whole papers were read. The act of transmission from the government of New York was pomposity itself.   They, however, often reiterated the words, *Free and Independent*, which I thought done designedly.

I had some discourse with Col. Hartley, and he has promised to withhold his vote for the assumption for some time at least.

I went this afternoon to hear a negro preach.   I can only say it would be in favor of religion in general if preachers manifested the same fervor and sincerity that was apparent in his manner.   He declared himself untutored, but he seemed to have the Bible by heart, *Tempora mutantur, et nos mutamur in illis.*

April 6.   The Senate seemed likely to have no business before them this day ; but all at once up rose Few, and offered a report of the bill for the military establishment.   Some trifling amendments were made in the compensation to the officers, but the bill was materially the same.   It was generally agreed to, as the sense of the Senate, that no report should be offered until the bill for regulating the intercourse with the Indians and the treaty bill should be put into the hands of the same committee ; but whatever is, is best.   It is out of the hands of that committee, and postponed.   I spoke against the whole bill as the egg from which a standing army would be hatched, as it is a standing army in fact, for the smallness of the number does not diminish the principle.   But I foresee I will have much to say under this head at a future day.

Carroll, of Carrollton, edged near me in the Senate Chamber, and asked me if I had seen the King of France's speech and the acts of the *Tiers Etats*, by which the distinctions of nobility were broken down.   I told him I had, and I considered it by no means dishonorable to us that our efforts against titles and distinctions were now seconded by the representative voice of twenty-four millions.   A flash of joy lightened from his countenance.   How fatal to our fame as lovers of liberty would it have been had we adopted the shackles of servility which enlightened nations are now rejecting with detestation.

April 7.   A committee was appointed in the Senate to bring in a bill for the territory of the United States south of the Ohio.   I did not oppose the appointment of a committee, but told some of them that they must make it stand alone, as I wished to avoid all expense.   I had no notion of salaries to the Governor, judge, &c.   I considered the motion brought forward by way of making some entry on the journals as much as anything else·   A short bill, however, came up, and had a first reading.

The Speaker had company this day.   I was wanting in spirits, and did not seem to enjoy it.   The table was, however, filled well, and there was a good flow of conviviality.   After dinner, the Speaker told me that Fitzsimmons and Clymer wanted to see the delegation at their quarters.   I was not well.   It was late ; and a tempest of wind, and very cold.   But I went.   I told Fitzsimmons that everything, in a pecuniary point of view, must remain in doubt until the accounts were settled.   That the only man who had it in his power to give an opinion on the subject (the Comptroller General) had taught us to think differently.   I said that the State, navy, and defense of the river Delaware, had cost vast sums.   I could not see that the defense of the Delaware, &c., was any more a charge against

Pennsylvania than the expense of the American arms before Boston was a demand against Massachusetts, or the charges at York-town against Virginia. If Pennsylvania advanced the money, it was in the general defense as well as her own, and the charge lay well against the Union.

The business of the meeting was to consult about an adjournment to Philadelphia, and as the votes of Pennsylvania would determine for or against assumption, whether they could not be so managed as to effect that measure. I will only set down what I said on the matter as opinion, that to barter votes was unjustifiable; that the risk of losing votes was as great as the chance of gaining by making a bargain with the other side, for Philadelphia had friends on both sides; that the best way was to postpone the assumption and push the adjournment to Philadelphia, while both parties feared and both courted the Pennsylvania vote.

April 8. A bill which came up yesterday for suspending part of the revenue law, with respect to the port of Yeomus, in Virginia, was read a second time. Now Ellsworth moved some alteration of the law with regard to some ports in Connecticut. Langdon wanted an alteration in New Hampshire, and Dalton one for Massachusetts. It was committed to these three members.

April 9. The committee of yesterday reported the bill with Ellsworth's amendment only. Said Mr. Hamilton was of opinion when the new impost law was enacted the other amendments could be introduced. This is art in him to make friends to his new bill, and shows that he either is still confident of success or affects it. There was no objection, and the bill had all its readings.

Ellsworth reported a bill for the government *south* of the Ohio. It was to be the same as the government of the Western Territory, *mutatis mutandis*. I had some previous discourse with Ellsworth on this subject.

In Senate this day the gladiators seemed more than commonly busy. As I came out from the Hall, all the President's family were there—Humphreys, Jackson, Nelson, &c., &c. They had Vining with them; and as I took it, were a standing committee to catch the members as they went in or came out. The crisis is at hand. At dinner the Speaker told me there had been a call of the Secretary's party last night. Fitzsimmons, he said, had been sent for, and they had determined to risk an action to-morrow.

April 10. Dressed and attended to see the event of the day; but it was put off by consent. The Treasurer told me the reason of it afterwards. Sherman, who is against the assumption, is expected to go away, and thus the other party will be less stronger, or at least more so, by one vote. The Secretary's people scarce disguise their design, which is to create a mass of debt which will justify them in seizing all the sources of government, thus annihilating the State Legislatures, and creating an empire on the basis of consolidation.

Monday, April 12. The business done in Senate this day was trifling. A bill for establishing the government of the North Carolina cession was taken up. I had occasion to speak to it, and moved a postponement until the bill be printed and put into the members' hands. It was carried. Ellsworth was fretted, and I cared not.

Two amended bills came up from the other House and were postponed. We adjourned.

I went into the House of Representatives to hear the question of assumption taken. Clymer got up, said the assumption was two millions and a quarter against his State—more than it ought to pay; but for confirming the Government and for national purposes, he would vote for it. I could not hear all he said, but the above was the amount of it.

Fitzsimmons hoped to have a great many conditions obtained, such as that the interest of the State debt should be paid in the respective States; that no improper charges should be brought forward. But he would vote for it now in expectation that these conditions would be obtained afterwards.

Certainly this could not be called the conduct of a wise man; he voted, as well as Clymer, for it formerly, and took all the Pennsylvania delegation with him except Hiester and General Muhlenberg, without any condition whatever. The question was, however, taken and lost—thirty-one against it, twenty-nine for it. Fitzsimmons, Clymer, and Hartley voted for it. Sedgwick, from Boston, pronounced a funeral oration over it. He was called to order. Some confusion ensued.

Fitzsimmons first recovered recollection and endeavored to rally the discomfited and disheartened heroes. He hoped the good sense of the House would still predominate, and lead them to reconsider the vote which had been now taken; and he doubted not but it would yet be adopted, under proper modifications. The Secretary's group pricked up their ears, and speculation wiped the tear from either eye. Goddess of description, paint the gallery. Here's the paper—find fancy, quills, or crayons yourself.

Tuesday, 13. Nothing of moment done this day in the Senate. The bill for the territory south of the Ohio passed a second reading. Some trifling debate on the amendments of the bill defining crimes and punishments.

Thursday, April 15. The bill for regulating the military establishment was called up. The friends of this bill seem to be chiefly Butler, King, and Schuyler. I have opposed this bill hitherto, as often as it has been before the House, as the foundation, the cornerstone of a standing army. The troops are augmented one half. The reasons hitherto given have been the distressed state of Georgia. Butler has blazed away on this subject at a great rate. Declared over and over that Georgia would seek protection elsewhere if troops were not sent to support her, and said fifty Indians had penetrated into the State, of which he had authentic information, &c. Carroll joined him. King and Schuyler, Ellsworth and Lee opposed them. Lee made a set speech against standing armies. He really spoke well. King at last got up, and rather upbraided the Georgia members for their silence on this question. This brought up Colonel Gunn. He declared he knew nothing of fifty Indians making any inroad into Georgia. He was just from there, and had the latest accounts. Georgia was in peace, and never had a better prospect of continuing so. There existed no cause in Georgia for augmenting the troops; and since that was the reason assigned for it, he should vote against it.

April 16. And now again for the augmentation of the troops. I took a minute view of all the papers forwarded by General Knox. They were copies of letters which he had received from different places, and carried, evidently, management on the face of them. Thus, for instance, General Knox writes to General Wayne, in Georgia, to inform him whether the Spaniards had not lately supplied the Indians with arms and ammunition. General Wayne answers that his inquiries on this head resolved themselves into the affirmative, and adds his opinion that it is highly probable hostile uses may be made of those supplies by the savages. In this manner, leading letters procure favorable answers from men who expect to be employed in case troops are raised. Before Colonel Gunn came, the dangers and distress of Georgia were magnified as far as fancy could from frightful pictures. Colonel Gunn contradicts all this. New phantoms for the day must be created. Now a dreadful and dangerous conspiracy is discovered to be carrying on between the people of Kentucky and the Spaniards. King unfolded this mysterious business, adding he conceived his fears were well founded. He firmly believed there was a conspiracy. That it was dangerous to put arms into the hands of the frontier people for their defense, lest they should use them against the United States.

I really could scarce keep my seat and hear such base subterfuges made use of, one after another. I rose, demanded what right gen-

tlemen had to monopolize information. If they had it, let them
come forward with it and give other people an opportunity of judging of the authenticity of the information, as well as the persons in
possession of it. Declared I could not tamely sit and hear the
characters of the people on the western waters traduced in the
lump. This day was the first ever I heard of the word conspiracy
being applied to the inhabitants of the western waters. I had a
right to doubt it until authentic proof was brought forward of the
fact. I felt myself disposed to wipe King hard, and certainly did
so. It was moved and seconded very fairly to reduce the number
to one thousand, and carried, eleven to nine. Ellsworth, though
he spoke for the reduction, voted against us. Mr. Morris desired
to be excused from voting, as he had come but lately. Ellsworth
said he voted against one thousand because he wanted twelve hundred ; and, though it was certainly out of all order, got a question
put on this number, and carried it by one vote. No man ever had
a more complete knack of putting his foot in a business than this
same Ellsworth. At one thousand we should have had but one
regiment. Now the committee to whom it is re-committed will try
to continue them in two. And yet, economy is all his cry.

I gave notice that, when the title of the bill came to be considered,
I would move to strike out for regulating· the military establishment of the United States, and mention particularly what I took
the intention of the troops to be agreeable to the old acts of Congress, viz : Protection of the frontiers of the United States ; facil-
itating the surveying and selling the public lands, and preventing
unwarrantable encroachments on the same. The man must be blind
who does not see a most unwarrantable management respecting our
military affairs. The constitution certainly never contemplated a
standing army in time of peace. A well regulated militia to execute the laws of the Union, quell insurrection, and repel invasions,
is the very language of the constitution. General Knox offers a
most exceptionable bill for a general militia law, which excites a
general opposition. Thus the business of the militia stand still,
and the military establishment bill, which increases the standing
troops one half, is pushed with all the art and address of ministerial
management.

Tuesday, 20. We sat a long time in the Senate without doing anything. At last, the committee on the *military bill* reported. The
report was a mere matter of detail, only the clause limiting the bill
to two years was struck out. I had given notice that I would move
to alter the title of the bill so as to express the use and intention
of raising the troops, but our President was for putting the question

on the bill without saying anything about the title at all. Ellsworth, who cannot bear that anybody should move anything but himself, and to whom I showed the title I had proposed to offer, pushed himself before me with a title different and much shorter. He was not seconded. I offered mine, and was seconded by Lee. A long debate ensued. Ellsworth now gave all the opposition in his power. It was really painful to hear the servile sentiments that were advanced. The spirit of the whole was that we had nothing to do with the troops ; had no right to know what the President did with them, or applied them to—it was interfering with his command, &c. I thought they were well answered. But what of that, we lost it. Ellsworth now showed plainly that he cared little about his motion, and that he had only started his to draw off the Senate from mine. Butler had declared he would second him during the debate on mine. I, therefore, called for it. He now moved it different, viz : An act *to raise troops for the service of the United States.* His first motion was for the defense of the frontiers, and for other purposes. All we could do was to get a question on it, such as it was. The Senate divided—ten to ten. The President made a remarkable speech. He said to raise troops for the service of the United States was as much a standing army as a military establishment, and voted for the old title. I thought I confirmed every argument I advanced, either from the old or new constitution of Pennsylvania, or from the constitution of the United States.

The limiting clause at the end of the bill, confining it to two years, being lost, I moved that the three years in the first clause should be struck out, and two inserted. I brought forward the *appropriation* clause in the constitution to support me in this motion, but, as it was known where the majority was, I could not obtain a second.

We (had) a meeting last night of our delegation on the subject of removing Congress. The language of the Philadelphians (was) to make a Potomac contract. I insisted we should lose as much on one hand as we could gain on the other, and infamy was certain. That the business could be better done without it, &c.

April 21. The bill for regulating the military establishment was taken up for a third reading. Being in Senate, and, of course, in order, I moved to restore the seventeenth section, which had been struck out yesterday, in the following words : And be it further enacted that this act shall continue and be in force until the 26th day of March, 1792.

Note.—Article one, section eight, pl. twelve, of Constitution United States : That Congress shall have power " to raise and support armies, but no appropriation of money to that use shall be for a longer term than *two* years."

I went over the constitutions of Pennsylvania—old and new. That they were abhorent of a standing army in time of peace. Inferred, as I thought, clearly the same doctrine from the constitution of the United States. I then showed that this bill established a standing army. It was for regulating the military establishment of the United States. It carried a permanent establishment on the face of it, as it was unlimited in point of time. It clearly carried with it a permanent standing army. I compared it to the mutiny bill of Great Britain. All the world knew Great Britain had a standing army, and her soldiers were enlisted generally for life ; and yet the jealousy of the nation was such that the boldest minister dared not propose the extending the mutiny bill to more than one year. In legislative theory, the English had no standing army. It was but an annual one. But, if the bill passed in its present form, we should not have even theory to oppose to a standing army, &c. Ellsworth got up, and said the reason the clause was struck out was that it contradicted the terms of enlistment, and he made a distinction between enlisting men for three years and appropriating pay for them for three years. We could do the one. We could not do the other without breaking the constitution. He wished they were enlisted for seven or ten years, &c. I answered that it seemed as if men strained their ingenuity to try how near they could approach an infraction of the constitution without breaking it. There could be no doubt but the clause limiting the appropriation to two years was meant as a bar against a standing army, and yet gentlemen seemed to strain their faculties to accomplish the very end prohibited without being chargeable with a direct breach of commandments, &c.

Ellsworth declared, both yesterday and this day, that military establishment meant and could mean nothing short of a standing army.

Carroll used the same language, and expressly said that though the Constitution of Pennsylvania might forbid it, we were not to be governed by any State constitution. But of all the flamers, none blazed like Izard. He wished for a standing army of ten thousand men. He feared nothing from them. No nation ever lost their liberty by a standing army, &c., &c. The Romans lost their liberty, but it was not by the army under Julius Cæsar.

He was well answered by Lee, but it was in vain. A standing army was the avowed doctrine, and on the question, Lee, Wyngate, and myself rose. I openly declared my regret that there were not enough of us to call the yeas and nays. Mr. Morris was not in at taking the question.

April 22. The morning looked so tempting I could not resist the impulse I felt for walking out. The Speaker joined me at the door. We called on Mr. Wynkoop, who is confined, &c. We got on the assumption of the State debts. I find the Speaker rather wavers of late. Wynkoop seemed all Secretary. I embarked as I generally do, and I endeavored to speak so plain that I scarce think it possible I could be misunderstood ; and I could not help thinking that to understand and obtain consent were inseparable.

Attended at the Hall. A bill was committed, a message received, and Senate adjourned. Wrote short piece. against the assumption of the State debts ; sent a copy to Bailey for publication.

This day there were accounts published of the death of Dr. Franklin, and the House of Representatives voted to drape their arms for a month. When I consider how much the Doctor has been celebrated, and when I compare his public fame with his private character, I am tempted to doubt whether any man was perfect. Yet perhaps it is for the good of society that patterns of perfection should be held up for men to copy after. I will, therefore, give him my vote of praise, and if any Senator moves crape for his memory, I shall have no objection to it, though we suffered Grayson to die without any attention to his memory, though he belonged to our body, and perhaps had some claim to a mark of sorrow.

April 23. A bill had been committed yesterday *for the relief of a certain description of officers*. I believe it came from the Secretary at War. It was absolutely unintelligible, and it really struck me it was meant as the stock to engraft some mischief on with respect to the commutation pensions and half pay of the old army, everything relating to which we had generally considered as settled. I spoke freely of it yesterday and this day, though I was not of the committee. The committee, however, reported against the whole of it, and it was rejected.

Carroll rose and made a motion that the Senate should wear crape a month for the loss of Dr. Franklin. Before he was seconded, Ellsworth got up and opposed it—said as it would not be carried in the Senate, he trusted it would not be seconded. I rose and seconded Carroll. Izard and Butler hated Dr. Franklin, and I well knew that this opposition of Ellsworth aimed at their gratification. Perhaps my supporting Carroll had something of a tincture of the same kind. King and Dr. Johnson joined Ellsworth. Ellsworth addressed Carroll and told him (through the Chair) that he might as well withdraw his motion, as it would be lost. This was really insulting. But as the matter, strictly speaking, was not *senatorial*, or such as belonged to us in our capacity as a public body, and as it was opposed, Carroll looked at me and I nodded assent, and it was withdrawn.

Monday, 26th April. Attended at the Hall. Mr. Walker, from Virginia, the member elected in the room of Mr. Grayson, took his seat. The progress bill, which, in fact, consisted only of one clause continuing the old one to another session, had a second reading. We did not continue in our seats for more than three quarters of an hour till King moved an adjournment. Modesty by degrees begins to leave. We used to stay in the Senate Chamber till about two o'clock, whether we did anything or not, by way of keeping up the appearance of business. But even this we seem to be got over.

Doctor Elmer asked me to walk with him. I saw cards handed round the Senate, but this happens so often that I took no notice of it. When we were in the street, the Doctor asked me if I had not a card to dine with the President. I told him, with all the indifference I could put on, no, and immediately took up some other subject, which I entered on with eagerness, as if I had hardly noticed his question. This is the second time the Doctor has asked me the same question, so that the President's neglect of me can be no secret. How unworthy of a great character is such littleness? He is not aware, however, that he is paying me a compliment that none of his guests can claim. He places me above the influence of a dinner, even in his own opinion. Perhaps he means it as a punishment for my opposition to court measures. Either way, I care not a fig for it. I certainly feel a pride arising from a consciousness that the greatest man in the world has not credit enough with me to influence my conduct in the least. This pride, however, or perhaps I should call it self-approbation, is the result of my conduct, and by no means the motive of it. This I am clear in.

I am so very intent on getting Congress away from this place, that I went to see the Philadelphians, and concert what further was to be done. I wished to communicate to them the result of my inquiries and receive their stock of information on the subject of removal. I had some time ago determined never to call on them any more, but my anxiety on this point made me break through this rule. But the result has made me reënact my former resolution. I think it is best to respect myself. Let this resolution be as a ring on my finger, or the shirt on my back—let me never be without it.

This day Mr. Clymer made his famous speech for throwing away the western world. A noble sacrifice, truly, to gratify the public creditors of Philadelphia. Reject territory the extent of an empire, so that it may be out of the power of Congress to oblige the public creditors to take any part of it. This added to the confiscation of the 17/6 in every pound of the alienated certificates, which virtually belonged to the person who performed the original service, and bestowing it on base speculation, completes the counterpart of villiany to the meritorious soldier, on the one hand, and the defrauded and betrayed country on the other, whose resources are rejected that the debt may become irredeemable and permanent.

27th April. This a day of no business in Senate. Before the House formed, Mr. Adams, our President, came to where I was sitting, and told how many late pamphlets he had received from England. How the subject of the French revolution agitated the English politics. That, for his part, he despised them all, but the production of Mr. Burke, and this same Mr. Burke despised the French revolution. In the evening, I called at the post office on a business of the Zantzingers. Langdon, who lodges nearly opposite, called to me from a window. I went over, and had a long discourse with him on the subject of removing Congress. He wants to make the assumption of the State debts the condition of it. I was guarded as to any concessions on this subject. He avowed in the most unequivocal manner that *consolidation* of the different governments was his object in the matter. That, perhaps, it was against the interest of his State in particular, &c.

No business was done in Senate, but consenting to some nominations sent down yesterday, and the Senators from Virginia laid a resolution on the table for *opening the doors of the Senate* on the *discussion of legislative subjects.*

April 30, 1790. A flood of business came up to-day from the Representatives, but none of it was acted upon, save the first reading of bills and appointing a committee to confer with them on some point of order or etiquette. Mr. Morris spoke to me as to repealing the law, or that part of the judiciary about holding a district and circuit court at Yorktown. I gave it as my opinion that it was best to let the other House do it, as they had introduced Yorktown; and I find Boudinot has this day carried in a bill for this purpose. I hate the whole of the judiciary, and, indeed, made no place at first but Philadelphia for holding the courts. I shall not, therefore, give them my opposition. If a place is hereafter appointed for holding any circuit court, it perhaps should be Harrisburg. Senate adjourned over to Monday.

May 1, 1790. This is a day of general moving in New York, being the day on which their leases chiefly expire. It was a fine day, and I could not forbear the impulse of walking out. . . . . Fell in with Walker and Parker, of Virginia. They were coming

to visit our house. They pressed us so hard for dinner that we
consented.   .   I had not walked enough, and went to see Mr.
Wynkoop. We got again on the subject of the State debt. I never
saw a man take so much pains *not* to see a subject. It is, however,
now disposed of, at least for this session.

I have a letter from Dr. Rush. He praises the piece I sent him.
Calls it sensible ; owns himself convinced. His words : " *I have
erred, through ignorance, on this subject* "—-speaking of the State
debts.

With less prudence than integrity, I attacked the Secretary's report the moment it appeared. When that leading feature in it, the
assumption of the State debts, was carried by a majority of five in
the Committee of the Whole Representatives, I redoubled my efforts
against it ; and I really believe that by my endeavors it was finally
rejected. I am fully sensible that I staked every particle of credit
I had in the world on this business, and have been successful. But
let me lay my account, never to be thought of for it. Be it so. I
have made enemies of all the Secretaries, and perhaps of the President of the United States.

Williamson coming in, and one of his colleagues, had a considerable effect. When the whole of the North Carolina delegation
appeared, it settled the business. The assumption would have
completed the pretext for seizing every resource of government,
and subject of taxation in the Union ; so that even the civil list of
the respective governments would have depended on the Federal
treasury.

Mount Vernon.

No Virginian can talk on any subject, but the perfections of General Washington interweaves itself into every conversation. Walker
had called at his farm as he came through Virginia. It consists of
three divisions. The whole contains some ten or fifteen thousand
acres. It is under different overseers, who may be styled generals,
under whom are grades of subordinate appointments descending
down through whites, mulattoes, negroes, horses, cows, sheep, hogs,
&c.; it was hinted at, all were named. The crops to be put into the
different fields, &c., and the hands, horn cattle, &c., to be used in
tillage, pasturings, &c., are arranged in a roster calculated for ten
years. The Friday of every week is appointed for the overseers, or
we will say, the brigadier generals, to make up their returns. Not
a day's work but is noted—what and by whom and where done.
Deaths, &c., whether accidental or by the hands of the butcher, all

minuted. Thus the etiquette and arrangement of an army is preserved on his farm. When once the human mind is penetrated by any system, no matter what, it never can disengage itself. Quere, did not the Roman poet understand nature to perfection, who makes his heroes marshal their armies of ghosts in the Elysian Fields; and spirits imitate in shadows the copies of their former occupations.

Monday, 3d May. There really was a considerable deal of business done this day in Senate, and would have been much more had it not been for an appeal that was made to the Chair for information respecting the salary necessary for an ambassador. Full one half of our time was taken up in two speeches on the subject of etiquette, and expense attending and necessary to constitute the very essence of an ambassador. The lowest farthing should be £3,000 sterling per annum, besides a year's salary at setting out. A commitment of the bill was called for, and I was, contrary to my expectation, put on it.

For some time past, the Philadelphians had been proposing a weekly dinner. Our former meetings sunk into disuse, but they now are very urgent, and this day we began the business. Judge Wilson, being a Pennsylvanian, was, of course, invited. We soon relaxed into conviviality, and, indeed, something more. We expected something political would be proposed by Fitzsimmons, and out it came. Gentlemen, it is expected of us that we should fix the Governor of Pennsylvania. I introduced some trivial remarks of the weather, &c., and the thing was checked for a time. Scott, General Hiester, and General Muhlenburg went away. It was now broached seriously by Fitzsimmons. Morris made a public declaration that he was fully sensible of the honor done him in the present appointment; but, if the chair of Governor fell on him, he would discharge it with impartiality, &c. Mr. Morris, by way of finishing the business, addressing himself to the Speaker, may you or I be Governor.

We got on the subject of the finances of Pennsylvania. Fitzsimmons asserted that our State had drawn between two and three millions of dollars from the continental treasury, and that we had not more than four millions substantiated against the Union. I hinted to him that from anything I had seen, we had not drawn more than about a million from the Continental treasury. That Nicholson had rendered accounts to the amount of ten millions, and had stated an unliquidated charge at five millions. But, I added, let the account be settled fairly, and, if we really are in debt, let us pay it. We sat too long, and drank too much; but we seemed happy, and parted in great good humor.

Tuesday, 4th May. I felt in some degree the effects of the bad wine we had drank, for I had a headache. Dressed, however, for the levee. I had a card yesterday to dine with the President on Thursday. The pet, if he had any on him, has gone off.

A great deal of business was done this day in the Senate in the way of passing and reading bills, but no debate of any consequence. Went to the levee, made my bows, walked about, turned about, and came out.

Wednesday, 5th May. A considerable deal of business was done in Senate, but no debate was entered on. The Rhode Island committee reported. The amount of it was to put that State in a kind of commercial coventry—to prevent all intercourse with them in the way of trade. I think the whole business premature. We adjourned early. The Secretaries have had a clear majority in the House of Representatives on every question, save the adoption of the State debts. They carried this at first, but some publications reminded gentlemen that there was an election approaching.

May 6. Little was done this day in Senate. Two bills came up agreed to from the House of Representatives. The Rhode Island committee requested that they might have back their report to amend it. This was complied with.

An adjournment was called, and I joined the committee on the bill for the salaries of ministers plenipotentiary, chargé d'affaires, &c. I bore my most pointed testimony against all this kind of gentry. Declared I wished no political connection whatever with any other country whatever. Our commercial intercourse could be well regulated by consuls, who would cost us nothing. All my discourse availed nothing. The whole committee agreed with me that they were unnecessary. Why then appoint any or make provision for the appointment of any, for so sure as we make a nest for one, the President will be plagued till he fills it. We agreed to the bill as it stood, but I proposed twice to strike out all about ministers plenipotentiary.

Went to dine with the President, agreeable to invitation. He seemed more in good humor than ever I saw him, though he was so deaf that I believe he heard little of the conversation. We had ladies: Mrs. Smith, Mrs. Page, and Mrs. White. Their husbands all with them.

Friday, May 7. The ailment called the influenza rages to a great degree all over the city.

On my return into the Senate Chamber, one member of it only remained, sitting in a state of *ennui*. I have remarked him for some weeks past, and he really affords a striking proof of the inconveniency of being a fashionable.   He set up a coach about a month ago, and, of course, must have it come for him to the Hall.   But behold how he gets hobbled : The stated hour for Senate to break up is three, but it often happens that Senate adjourns a little after twelve, and here a healthy man must sit two or three hours for his coach to take him three or four hundred yards.   This is highly embarrassing, and some excuse must be found for his staying for the carriage, and he is now lame and stays alone till the carriage comes for him.   Thus folly often fixes her friends.

Tench Coxe came this day to town, in order (as is said) to enter on the assistancy of the Treasury.   He is deeply affected with the literary itch, the *cacoethes scribendi*.   He has persevering industry in an eminent degree.   These are the qualities that have recommended him to this appointment.   Hamilton sees that the campaign will open against him in the field of publication, and he is providing himself with gladiators of the quill, not only for defense but attack.

May 8.   The Senate was engaged in business.   When we came in, we found them on the Rhode Island resolves.   The committee had been called on to give reasons on which they founded their resolutions.   Ellsworth spoke with great deliberation often and long, and yet I was not convinced by him.   I saw I must, if I followed my judgment, vote against both resolutions.   It was, therefore, incumbent on me to give some reasons for my vote.

I observed that the business was under deliberation in Rhode Island.   That the resolves carried on the face of them a punishment for rejection on supposition that they would ruin our revenue.   Let us first establish the fact against them that an intercourse with them has injured our revenue, before we punish them with a prohibition of all intercourse.   This resolution I considered premature.

The other, for the demand of $27,000, I considered as equally so.   Let the accounts be settled, and Rhode Island has a right to be charged with, and has a right to pay, her proportion of the price of independence.   By the present resolutions, the attack comes visibly from us.   She is furnished with an apology, and will stand justified to all the world, if she should enter into any foreign engagements.

The Rhode Island resolutions were taken up.   I was twice up against these resolutions.   They admitted, on all hands, that Rhode Island was independent, and did not deny that the measures now taken were meant to force her into an adoption of the constitution of the United States ; and founded their arguments in our strength and her weakness.   I could not help telling them plainly that this was playing the tyrant to all intents and purposes.   I was twice up.   Said a good deal, but it answered no purpose whatever.

May 12. This day exhibited a grotesque scene in the streets of New York. Being the old 1st of May, the sons of *Tammany* had a grand parade through the town in Indian dresses. Delivered a talk at one of the meeting-houses, and went away to a dinner. There seems to be some kind of scheme laid of erecting some kind of order or society under this denomination, but it does not seem well digested as yet. The expense of the dresses must have been considerable, and the money laid out in clothing might have dressed a number of their ragged beggars. But the weather is now warm.

Fell in with Fitzsimmons. He talked familiarly with me. I must note part of his discourse. Those southern people have a matter much at heart, and it is in my power to oblige them. They fear a settlement. They cannot bear it. They have been negligent of their accounts, and the eastern people have kept exact accounts of everything. (An interruption.) We were approaching the Hall, where I knew we would part. I began. They will want you to support them on the discrimination of tonnage, too, against the New England men ; but as they are the people who keep us here by joining the New England and York votes, I have no objection to see them whipped with their own rod. He seemed to enjoy this thought, and laughed heartily ; but the Hall was at hand, and the old subject lost.

May 14. The business of most importance agitated this day was the Rhode Island bill, which must have had a first reading yesterday when I was out. . . . . . I contented myself with giving my negative to every particle of it. I knew I could gain no proselytes, and that as the bill could not be justified on the principles of freedom, law, the Constitution, or any other mode whatever, argument could only end in anger. Mr. Morris was one of the warmest men for it, although he knows well that the only views of the Yorkers are to get two Senators more into the House, on whose votes they reckon on the question of residence. But he must think the getting Rhode Island in superior to all other considerations. The yeas and nays were called, and now, after the question was taken, there seemed a disposition for argument, and some very remarkable expressions were used. Izard said, "*If gentlemen will show us how we can accomplish our end by any means less arbitrary and tyrannical, I will agree to them.*"

When we came on the clause for demanding $25,000, Mr. Morris said, "this is the most arbitrary of the whole of it." The nays were Butler, Elmer, Gunn, Henry, Maclay, Walker, Wyngate—seven. Yeas—Bassett, Carroll, Dalton, Ellsworth, Johnston, Izard, King, Langdon, Morris, Strong, Schuyler, Reed—twelve.

This day, to my great joy, a statement of the Pennsylvania accounts came forward—$10,642 43$\frac{4}{90}$ specie, and $47,010,138 Continental money, liquidated and charged against the United States by our State, and delivered to Mr. White, the general agent, and his receipt taken for it in due time. Besides an unliquidated claim of five millions specie.

I understood this to be the state of our accounts at the beginning of the session; and so it seemed to be considered by all of us; for Mr. Morris, Mr. Clymer, and Fitzsimmons used to harangue on this subject, and cry up that so large an annual interest would be due to Pennsylvania that she would draw money enough from the Continent to pay her whole civil list, make her roads, build her bridges, open her canal. I know that Hamilton thought that he could make the State governments dependent on the General Government for every shilling. I used to oppose all this dream of folly, but all at once the State debts must be assumed. It was demonstrable that this measure would defeat all settlement.

Now the very gentlemen who had promised us such revenues from the Union cried out, burn the books; no settlement; Pennsylvania is in debt—she has drawn from the Continent between two and three million of good dollars, and has not substantiated but between four and five millions against the Union. A mutilated account of but about this sum was actually exhibited and handed about by Clymer and Fitzsimmons, and an attack begun on the Comptroller about the same time, as if to annihilate his reputation and turn him out of all employment, as if it had been foreseen that he was the only one who could detect this management, or obtain justice for the State.

15th, Saturday. Devoted this day, although I was sick, to the matter of removing to Philadelphia. Mr. Morris entertained me with a long detail of the difficulties he met with in the settlement of his accounts. I believe the clamors against him make the officers inspect everything with a jealous eye.

Called to see the President. Every eye full of tears. His life despaired of. Doctor MacNight told me he would trifle neither with his own character or the public expectation—his danger was imminent; and every reason to expect that the event of his disorder would be unfortunate.

May 18. No debate of any consequence arose this day until the Rhode Island bill, which had been recommitted, was reported. Mr Lee opposed it in a long and sensible speech. Butler, in a loose and desultory manner. King, Ellsworth, Strong, Izard, spouted out for it. It was long before there was a slack. As this was to be

ι he last reading, and as the yeas and nays would, in my opinion, be
called, I took what I thought was new ground.   The bill had been
assigned to various motives—self-defense, self-preservation, self-in-
terest, &c.   I began by observing that the convention in Rhode
Island met in a week ; that the design of this bill evidently was to
impress the people of Rhode Island with terror.   It was an application to their fears, hoping to obtain from them an adoption of
the Constitution, a thing despaired of from their free will or their
judgment.   It was meant to be used the same way that a robber
does a dagger or a highwayman a pistol, and to obtain the end desired by putting the party in fear.   That where independence was
the property of both sides, no end whatever could justify the use
of such means in the aggressors.   I, therefore, was against the bill,
in every point of view, &c.   The debate was long.   I was up a second time, but to no avail.   The question was put, about three o'clock,
and carried.   The yeas and nays were called, and stood nearly as
before, with the addition of Mr. Lee to the negative.

1 labored hard to arrange our affairs for bringing on our question
of removing to Philadelphia, and cannot help remarking that the
Philadelphians seemed the slackest of any people concerned in the
business.   I appointed—warned, or I know not well what to call it—
a meeting of the delegation at Clymer and Fitzsimmons' lodgings.
Mr. Morris and the Speaker were all that met.   The Philadelphians
really threw cold water on the business.   Mr. Morris twice proposed that it should be the new Congress that was to meet in March
next that should assemble in Philadelphia.   Once he got on the subject of *Trenton.*   Here he and I rather clipped.   I proposed that
we should all be busy in the morning among the members.   I engaged to call on Gunn, Langdon, and Bassett, and set them to work
on others.   The form of the resolution was agreed to, but it all
seemed up hill, or like a cold drag, with the Philadelphians.   I hope
one day to be independent of them, but this is a matter I must consult them in now.

May 19.   I run this morning like a foot boy from post to pillar.
Now, to Gunn ; then, Langdon, Bassett, &c.   Langdon refused to
bring forward our motion, and I then called on Bassett.   He excused himself.   With much ado, I got them to keep the motion
which I put into their hand.   Neither of them would make the motion.   Mr. Morris did not come near the Senate Chamber until after
twelve o'clock.   I called him out.   He said it must be omitted this
day.   I found I need not oppose him, and we came into the Senate
Chamber.   Langdon soon after came, and told us that *Dalton* objected to going to Philadelphia until March next, and that we must

alter the resolution. Mr. Morris and Dalton went together, and Mr. Morris returned, and told me he had agreed with Dalton that it should be the 1st of March next. Thus it is that all our measures are broken in upon, and, after all the pains I have taken, this business will end in smoke.

General Hiester and Mr. Buckley called on us this evening. We talked over the affairs of the day. Mr. Wynkoop came in, and a kind of agreement was made that the Pennsylvanians should meet to-morrow at Clymer's.

May 20. I could not attend at Clymer's this morning. I, however, saw the Speaker at the Hall. Some strange maneuvers have taken place. Jackson, of the President's family, has been with both Morris and Langdon. Morris is set right, and Dalton will agree with us; but new mischief has happened. Dr. Elmer has crossed to the Jerseys; Patterson is not yet come; Few and Gunn are both absent; so that two States are this day unrepresented. I offered to make the motion. Mr. Morris, however, now makes a point of doing it; but the thinness of the Senate seems a good reason for putting it off for this day. I cannot account for Jackson having meddled in this business, or his knowing anything of it, by any other means than through Buckley. However, we have got the errors of yesterday corrected. Mr. Morris was called out and came in with a most joyous countenance. " I was called out by Boudinot," said he, " to make proposals to me from the New England men, in favor of *Trenton*." I immediately told him you cannot possibly make any bargain by which you will not lose as much as you can gain. A bargain with the eastern people is to lose Maryland, Virginia, and all southward. A southern bargain will, on the contrary, lose all the eastern interest. We must be able to declare, upon honor, that we have no bargain.

He was a little hurt, and said " leave all that to me." No, sir; I will make no bargain; if it is but suspected that we have a bargain, we are ruined.

I was called out, and took that opportunity of calling out Mr. Fitzsimmons, and told him of Boudinot being in treaty with Mr. Morris, and begged him to counteract everything of this kind. He promised that he would.

The Senate got into a long debate on the resolves relating to arrears of pay due to the Virginia and North Carolina lines of the army, in 1782–3, which have been made the subject of an abandoned speculation. The report has an addition of Ellsworth's, calculated as much as possible to favor the speculation. It was debated to three o'clock, and adjourned.

May 21. And now again Elmer is absent, and Patterson is not returned, and Mr. Morris thinks the motion had not best be made until they return; so one day more is lost.

I spent a good deal of time on the affair of the Baron Steuben— got the report agreed to. And now the debate of the day came on, respecting the *resolutions*, (relative to the troops of Virginia, North and South Carolina, who were entitled to arrears of pay,) or rather the amendment offered to the last one. The amendment was supported by King, Ellsworth, Dr. Johnson, Izard, and others. Lee answered them. Towards the end of the debate, I rose and explained the reasons of the resolves—that they regarded the sums due—the places in which the payments were to be made, and what kind of transfers were to be considered as valid. All this was directory to our own officer, and had nothing to do with the proceedings of courts. Soldiers had entered into contracts, the resolves before the chair neither defaced writings nor tore the seals from obligations, and the law was open. The directions were, moreover, in conformity to the laws of North Carolina, one of the States whose citizens were concerned. That the present amendment was a modification of the resolution to protect the interest of the late speculation. The reason offered for it was, that probably some innocent person might suffer. I did not believe this was possible. I would cheerfully agree that it was better ten guilty should escape, than one innocent suffer; but no innocent man was privy to this business. The soldiers knew nothing of the matter. The speculators know, and they only know, in whose hands the lists were lodged, for the soldiers having received their final settlements since the service was performed, concluded that nothing more could remain due, &c., &c. The question was put on the amendment, and lost—ten for, twelve against.

The question was now put on the third resolution, and carried, thirteen and nine. King, however, and a number of gentlemen, called for the yeas and nays. Yeas—Bassett, Butler, Carroll, Few, Gunn, Hawkins, Johnston, Henry, Lee, Maclay, *Reed*, Walker, Wyngate. Nays—Dalton, Ellsworth, Johnson, Izard, King, Langdon, Morris, Strong, Schuyler.

Now a new whim came into their heads, and they would have the yeas and nays on the former question. They were told it was out of order. However, they had them, and now Mr. Butler voted for the amendment, least he should lose his interest at the Treasury, and, of course, we were tied, eleven and eleven. But for once, in my opinion, our President voted right, and gave it against the amendment.

22d May. In the evening a large number of gentlemen called at our house. My barber had disappointed me in the morning. I was rather in *dishabille*, but came down stairs. Although I am not in the least given to dress, yet I found that I was, on this occasion, below par ; and to know that any point about one is deranged, or improperly adjusted, imparts an awkward air to one. It is on this account, more than any other, that a propriety of dress should be attended to. To suspect that your company believe anything wrong about you, distresses a modest man. Of the company was Mr. Fitzsimmons. He took me by the hand, and said, to-morrow at nine I wish to meet with you and the Speaker.

May 23. It was near ten when I was called down, on the coming of Fitzsimmons. He had been some time with the Speaker. We had considerable loose talk on the subject of the removal of Congress. But Fitzsimmons, after some time, declared that was not the business on which he came. It was to settle something as to the government of Pennsylvania. Who should be run for the chair of it at the next election. He spoke of the dignity of the Speaker's present place, and the certainty of his continuance in it. It was evident that he wished the Speaker to decline. The Speaker said, very well ; I will give you an answer to-morrow morning.

May 24. I dressed, and went early to work. Called on R. H. Lee, of Virginia ; on Walker ; and Doctor Elmer. After Senate met, I reported the amendments on the Baron Steuben bill. It was the opinion of the committee that he should have an annuity of $1,000. It lay, however, over for to-morrow. Some business came up from the Representatives.

And, now, Mr. Morris rose, and made the long expected motion in the following words : *Resolved*, That Congress shall meet, and hold their next session, in the city of Philadelphia.

Langdon seconded the motion. A dead pause ensued.

Our President asked if we were ready for the question. General Schuyler got up, and hoped not, as it was a matter of great importance to move the seat of Government. He moved a postponement.

Mr. Morris said : If the gentleman will name to-morrow, he had no objection ; and to-morrow was accordingly named for it. The House soon after adjourned, and now Izard, Butler, Doctor Johnson, Schuyler, and King flew about. The people they mostly attacked were Governor Johnston, Hawkins, and Gunn. I soon left them, and came home.

But this was mess day, and I went at half past three, and found the company already seated, and the dinner almost eat up. I could not stay long, as we had an appointment with Jefferson, the Secretary of State, at six o'clock. When I came to the Hall, Jefferson and the rest of the committee were there.

Jefferson is a slender man. Has rather the air of stiffness in his manner. His clothes seem too small for him. He sits in a lounging manner on one hip commonly, and with one of his shoulders elevated much above the other. His face has a sunny aspect. His whole figure has a loose shackling air. He had a rambling vacant look, and nothing of that firm collected deportment which I expected would dignify the presence of a secretary or minister. I looked for gravity, but a laxity of manner seemed shed about him. He spoke almost without ceasing. But even his discourse partook of his personal demeanor. It was loose and rambling, and yet he scattered information wherever he went, and some even brilliant sentiments sparkled from him. The information which he gave us respecting foreign ministers, &c., was all high spiced. He has been long enough abroad to catch the tone of European folly. He gave us a sentiment which seemed to savor rather of quaintness : " It is better to take the highest of the lowest than the lowest of the highest." Translation : It is better to appoint a chargé d'affaires, with a handsome salary, than a minister plenipotentiary, with a small one. He took his leave, and the committee agreed to strike out the specific sum to be given to any foreign appointment, leaving it to the President to account, and appropriated $30,000 generally for the purpose.

25th May. This day again I was engaged in the main business. Called on sundry of the members. The Yorkers are now busy in the scheme of bargaining with the Virginians, offering the *permanent* seat on the Potomac for the *temporary* one in New York. Butler is the chief agent in the business. Walker, a weak man, seemed taken off by it. Patterson, however, is not yet come.

Baron Steuben's business was taken up. The committee were called on to give the reasons of their report. As I was chairman, I had to take the lead. I knew there was blame ready to fall on us. I, however, did not decline the business, but laid down the outlines in as strong colors as I thought consistent with the truth—that those who came after me might not be bashful, and thus taking scope enough for them to act in. I thought I took many of the Senate with me—some I know it was impossible. In fine, I thought demonstration was on our side—that the Baron could demand nothing. Izard drew conclusions that were obviously wrong, indeed, to his own party. Even Butler disowned his reasons ; but he was for doing the same thing without a reason. Ellsworth got up and spoke exceeding well for more than an hour. He was severe in some of his strictures, but I was pleased to hear him. The debates lasted until past three o'clock, and an adjournment took place without any question. One object of the delay was to put off our question on the residence.

The baron's bill, as it was called, was taken up. The cabals of the Secretary were successful, and the baron's bill was triumphant.

. . .

But after this was done Mr. Morris called for his motion. If he really intended to lose it, he could not possibly have taken a more certain method. He (Mr. Morris) rose, laughing heartily every time he got up. King laughed at him, and he laughed back at King, and a number more joined in the laugh. This was truly ridiculous. Few, King, and Butler rose, and the amount of all they said was, that a removal was inconvenient—that Philadelphia was not central; if we once got into it we would be accommodated in such manner that we never could leave it, &c.

I replied that a removal was not called for immediately by the resolution—that the next session of Congress was to meet in Philadelphia—that although it was not central, it was more so than the place where we now were. The universal consent of the Provinces before we were States, and of the States since, was in favor of Philadelphia. This was verified by every public assembly which had been called, from the meeting of the first Congress down to the late meeting of the Cincinnati. The arguments drawn from the conveniences of Philadelphia, and the insinuations that if we were once there nobody would ever think of going away from it, I thought were reasons which should induce us to embrace this place, which would come so completely up to our wishes. I begged gentlemen, however, to be easy on that subject. Philadelphia was a place they never could get as a permanent residence. The government neither would nor could part with it. It was nearly equal to one third of the State in wealth and population. It was the only port belonging to the State. It was excepted by the government in her offers to the Congress.

In such a place, the deliberations of Congress on the subject of the permanent residence, could be carried on to the greatest advantage, &c., &c. I was up a second time, but to no purpose. A postponement was moved by Butler, and seconded by Gunn. For the question of postponement, Strong, Dalton, Johnson, Ellsworth, King, Schuyler, *Patterson*, Hawkins, Johnston, Butler, Izard, Few, Gunn—thirteen. Our side, Langdon, Wyngate, Elmer, Morris, Maclay, Reed, Bassett, Carroll, Henry, Lee, Walker—*eleven.*

27. Mr. Morris went off yesterday, in company with King, and I really thought there was too much levity in his conduct all through. I really suspected that he did not treat the matter with sufficient seriousness. This day he showed a violent disposition of anger; he would go anywhere; but insisted on withdrawing the motion. I could not readily agree with him as to the propriety of withdrawing the motion. . . . . Butler rose, and said he gave notice that he would bring in a bill on Monday next, to establish the permanent residence. Mr. Morris jumped up in haste, and moved for leave to withdraw his motion. Langdon agreed. There was some demur, but the question was carried.

Now the baron's bill, as we have called it, was taken up. If the fate of the Union had depended on it, it could not have been more pertinaceously adhered to. Ellsworth persevered, and cut King in argument more severely than ever I heard any member of the Senate heretofore. King felt it, and I confess I enjoyed it. Butler, by one of those eccentric motions for which he is remarkable, flew his party, and voted on our side. . . . . What a consternation! I observed him rising, and said aloud it is carried. As the arguments were nearly the same on every question, it is in vain to repeat them.

I voted uniformly against allowing him one farthing, as I was convinced nothing was due to him.

I cannot help noting Mr. Adams' speech. In extolling the baron, he told us that he (the baron) had imparted to us the arts and principles of war, learned by him in the only school in the world, where they were taught by the great King of Prussia, who had copied them from the ancient Greek and Roman lessons; and in fine, to these arts and principles we owed our independence. Childish man to tell us this, when many of our sharpest conflicts and most bloody engagements had terminated fortunately, before ever we heard of the baron.

May 28. This day we had expectations that the House of Representatives would have brought on the vote for adjournment to Phil-

NOTE.—The Baron Steuben arrived in this country in December, 1777. The battle of Trenton was fought in December, 1776, and that at Princeton in January following. The baron joined the army at Valley Forge, in February, 1778. He took part in the battle of Monmouth, in 1778, and also took part in the siege of Yorktown. Congress granted him an annuity of $2,500 for life; and the State of New York granted him sixteen thousand acres of land near to Utica, portions of which he gave to his aids, and the balance he leased.— *Appleton's Cyclopedia—Steuben.*

adelphia, but the day passed without anything being done.   No debate of any consequence in Senate.   I feel exceedingly indisposed.

Last night Fitzsimmons and Clymer called on me.   They agreed to call on Goodhue, Gilman, Huntingdon, and some other of the New England men, and tell them calmly that the Pennsylvanians would not stay in New York.   That if they, of New England, would persist in voting for New York, the Pennsylvanians would agree to any other place whatever, and from here they would go.   Fitzsimmons and Clymer were appointed for this service.   I readily agreed to join Mr. Morris in a similar service, with respect to the Senate.

Monday, May 31, 1790.   Went early out to call on sundry members, and try to prepare them for the grand question.   Came to the Hall at the usual time.   The bill for intercourse with foreign nations came up from the Representatives, with an insistance.   Both Houses having insisted, it remained for us to recede or call for a conference.   It ended in a conference.   A considerable debate, however, or rather delivery of sentiments, took place.   Ellsworth, in a slow, languid manner, said it was easy to see that the Representatives had in view some old regulations, by their insisting on the $9,000.   That formerly the business had been done by some gentlemen for about $6,000 per annum.

Mr. Adams jumped up ; said that could not be ; that he had kept the accounts with his own hand at Paris, and they amounted to about three thousand guineas yearly.   He had now a vast deal to say.   When he had done, Ellsworth took a small paper out of his pocket ; said he was very willing to show the documents from which he had spoken.   Here was an abstract of the accounts of the honorable President while he was in Paris, and all the particulars for twenty months, amounting to $9,800, which was not more than at the rate of $6,000 per annum.

Now Butler rose, and had a good deal to say on the merits of the permanent residence, and concluded with asking leave to bring in a bill for a permanent and temporary residence.

Lee made a long speech.   I felt so much interested that I could not help rising.   I observed that fixing the permanent residence to a future period would work no relief of present inconveniences ; that the complaints were felt and well-founded as to the place in which we now were ; that the gentleman had given notice, some days ago, that he would offer a bill for the permanent residence. He now added the temporary residence, &c., &c.   The end of the matter was, that he delivered in his bill.   (Mr. Morris was absent at this time.)

June 1. I called early this morning on Fitzsimmons and Clymer.

I told them that, all things considered, I thought it best in me to endeavor to postpone Butler's bill. They both approved of it.

I went to the Hall to observe the members as they came in. Langdon was there. He certainly manifested something which I thought singular in his manner. If I had not such strong proofs of him heretofore, I would have suspected him. He desired me to assure the two members of Massachusetts that there was no bargain with Virginians. I told him I would do anything he requested, and I·did so.

The Senate met. The President was hasty enough to take up Butler's bill. Butler absolutely spoke ,against taking it up at all as he said he was a fraid of a difference arising between the two Houses.

The word agreed, agreed, was heard from different parts of the House. I really felt happy.

A message was read from the President, and some other trifling business done. There was some small talk and communications which I did not mind. But all at once the President began to read the bill. I wished much for somebody else to begin an opposition, and was determined to throw myself along with them, let them mould the attack as they would. Mr. Reed spoke against proceeding on the bill, but made no motion. Butler got up, and moved that the bill should be committed. Gunn seconded. Mr. Carroll said there could be no use in committing it.

I said the honorable gentleman had set out with declaring that he wished to avoid any difference with the other House. None of us could affect ignorance of what had passed in the House of Representatives yesterday. A vote had passed for the meeting of the next session at Philadelphia. That we might every moment expect our door to be opened for the receipt of such a communication. For us, therefore, to adopt a different mode of treating the same subject would have the appearance of courting a difference, &c., &c.

Butler got up in reply, and said every insulting thing in his power. I had concluded that I thought it best that the bill should lie on the table until the resolution came up, and that they should be considered at the same time. This took place, after a good deal of talk. It was remarkable that the resolution came up just as Butler began to rail at me. The Senate adjourned early, and soon after in came Mr. Morris covered with sweat and dust.

June 2. I went early this morning to meet our delegation, and to inculcate this doctrine on our representatives : That in all cases we should be prepared for the worst, and that we should now think of the next step to be taken in case of the worst happening in our House. That a conduct of this kind would keep the matter alive— keep (the) party collected and in spirits. They admitted the principle, but seemed at a loss for the means. I hinted the propriety of bringing forward a resolution naming the day of adjournment and the time of meeting. Fitzsimmons and Morris (all that were present) seemed to carp at it. However, I told them I only urge you to think of and provide your next step. A hint was dropped that I had better be at the Hall. I readily agreed, and went there. I could see, as the members came in, that we had nothing to expect from North Carolina, South Carolina, Georgia, nor Massachusetts.

The Senate met, and waited and waited for Mr. Morris. I never wished for him more in my life. I saw now that Butler's bill would be committed, and I wished to arrange something of a ticket for the committee. Several of the Senate asked why I did not send for him. I went out, and desired the doorkeeper to go for him. Mather answered : I have sent for him long ago. It was past twelve before he came, and now we went at the business.

I could remark something of a partiality in Adams at the setting out. The first question for commitment of Mr. Butler's bill. It was moved to postpone this, and take up the resolution for holding the next session in Philadelphia. Senate divided, twelve and twelve. J. Adams gave it against postponement. Now on the commitment, twelve and twelve. J. Adams gave it for it. This division was by States, on both these questions, or at least they divided so. We had New Hampshire, Jersey, Pennsylvania, Delaware, Maryland, Virginia. The others against us. Now it was that I regretted Mr. Morris' absence. Had he been here in time I could have settled with him who should have been the committee. Now we could communicate only with our friends on one side of the House. The committee rather unfavorable—Butler, Dalton, Lee, Johnston, Henry.

Now it was moved to refer the resolution (from the House) to the same committee. The Senate divided equally, but Dalton was against it and Patterson for it. As they sat next each other, I believe this was settled between them, and shows that Patterson is not to be depended on.

June 3. Attended at the usual time at the Hall. I determined to behave, in personal deportment, as nearly as I possibly could to my former habits, and I believe I effected it. Of this, however, I could not judge as well as perhaps others. Mr. Morris came the last of any of the members this day, but nothing remarkably so—

much earlier than yesterday. I got into chat with him, and, after some time, remarked how unfortunate we had been yesterday in not pre-arranging a ticket for the committee. I said his absence had been unlucky, but could not now be helped. He said *his accounts had engaged him so closely he could not come.* I thought this stranger than ever, that he should stay away on no other excuse than his daily business. Wyngate, Elmer, almost the whole Senate, have taken notice of it. How can I avoid observing it, for I have smarted under it.

No business of consequence took place this day. The nominations for the officers of the army had come in yesterday and were taken up this day.

I had made some objections a few days ago to giving my advice and consent to the appointment of men of whom I knew nothing. Izard now got on the same subject, and bounced a good deal. However, the thing was got over by the members rising and giving an account of the officers appointed from the different States, and all were agreed to.

The funding bill, which has engaged the Representatives almost the whole session, came up yesterday—was taken up this day, and Monday assigned for it.

June 4. This is a day of small consequences in the Senate. . . We called on the committee to report. Butler excused himself, and the burden of the excuse was that Governor Johnson, one of the committee, had fallen sick. Mr. Morris moved, and was seconded by Lee, to add another member in his room. This occasioned considerable debate. Reed, however, declared against us, and we lost the question. Izard manifested the most illiberal spirit—asserted, in opposition to Lee, things that even his own party were ashamed of. I left the Senate chamber this day, completely sickened at the uncandid and ungentlemanly conduct of the South Carolina men. Few, of Georgia, said some improper things; but I this day was almost altogether an hearer. There really was no serious debate. It was nothing but snip-snap and contradiction.

June 5. Called on sundry people. Went and sat a long time with Mr. Morris and repeated to him all the arguments I had made use of on Monday and Tuesday last, when he was absent. One in particular he seemed pleased with, drawn from the difference of mileage, which would arise to the treasury of about $1,100 in favor of a residence in Philadelphia. I desired him to get from the treasury an account of the expense of removing Congress from Princeton to New York. He said he would do it. There seemed really to be more of cordiality in this *tete-a-tete* which I had with him than any ever I had.

I then called on Mr. Wynkoop. I chatted a good while with him, and had again occasion to observe the blind obedience which he pays to the opinions of his Philadelphia colleagues.

June 6. . . . I received yesterday a letter from Geo. Logan. He is greatly displeased about the grant to Baron Steuben. This is really a worthy man. I think he holds the first place in point of integrity. He has invited me strongly to call and see him. I believe I must do so.

This old man, the Baron, it seems, talks in the most insulting manner of the grant which has been made to him, and tells that he must and will have more when a new Congress meets, &c. Being at the head of the Cincinnati, makes him assume those arrogant airs

The funding bill, the basis on which speculation has built all her castles, is now to come before us; and woe to him who says a word in favor of the country. Load the ass—make the beast of burden bear to the utmost of his abilities. I am really convinced that many a man has gone into the martial field and acquitted himself with gallantry and honor, with less courage and firmness than is necessary to attack this disposition in our Senate.

Monday, 7th June. The funding law underwent some debate this day. We adopted, by a kind of common consent, a mode somewhat different from former practice respecting it. Supposing ourselves in Committee of the Whole, a paragraph is read, and the members generally express their sentiments on it. After every one has given his sentiments, it is passed by postponement, with a design to commit it to a special committee. We proceeded about half way with the bill in this way.

The committee on the bill for the *permanent residence*, and the resolution sent up from the Representatives, were called on to report, and Butler, their chairman, did so. He read the report, which was a sleeveless thing, for the Potomac to be the permanent residence; but alleged the ground was too narrow to fix the *temporary* residence. Many desultory things were said, and all went off until to-morrow.

This was Pennsylvania mess day. . . . We agreed to send for all the Senators who were friends of moving to Philadelphia. Eleven attended—Virginia, Maryland, Delaware, Pennsylvania; Dr. Elmer, from New Jersey, and New Hampshire. Much desultory discourse was held. Virginia and Maryland manifested a predilection for the Potomac; but the final resolutions, in which Virginia led the way, were as follows: That as the business of a permanent residence was brought forward by our enemies evidently with a design of dividing us, we would uniformly vote against every plan named for the permanent residence.

The Virginians and Marylanders declared they would vote against the Potomac. Mr. Morris declared he would vote against Germantown, and the Falls of Delaware. The Susquehanna was not publicly named, but of course implied ; for Mr. Morris, in enumerating the places to be voted against, named Potomac, Germantown, Falls of Trenton. The line of proceeding for to-morrow was agreed to. Mr. Lee to move, and Langdon to second, the postponement of the permanent seat, in order to take up the resolution for the next session being held in Philadelphia. If all was lost, let it go down to the House of Representatives, for them to originate new measures on it.

Tuesday, June 8. How shall I describe this day of confusion in the Senate.

Mr. Lee laid on the table a report of some additional rules, relative to the intercourse between the two Houses. After this, he moved that the bill for the permanent residence of Congress shall be postponed, to take up the resolution of the representatives for adjoining to Philadelphia.

Now it was that Izard flamed, and Butler bounced, and both seemed to rage with madness. Mr. Lee's motion was in writing, and they moved a postponement of it. The division was eleven and eleven, and the President gave it against postponement. Now all was hurry and confusion. Izard and Butler actually went and brought Governor Johnson, with his night-cap on, out of bed, and a bed with him. The bed was deposited in the committee-room. Johnson was brought in a sedan. Few was well enough to come without being carried, and we waited half an hour. The vote was taken. We had our eleven, and they had thirteen against the resolution. I thought all was over now ; but no such thing, they must carry their conquest further.

In the meanwhile, a mob and noise was about the Hall as if it had been a fish market. The postponed bill, and the report of the committee on it, was called for. The report was read. The first clause of the report was a resolution that the permanent residence should be now fixed. The question was taken on it, and it was negatived. This threw them all in the dumps. The report was, however, lost.

But now they would have the bill. They accordingly had it, for they had the most votes ; and, although the Senate had decided by a most unequivocal vote that the permanent residence should not be taken into consideration, yet they moved to fill the blank with the Potomac. This was lost—fifteen and nine.

Much desultory discourse was now engaged in, and many motions were made of postponement of the bill. Some of them actually carried, and yet they still made new motions for the blank to be filled. Baltimore was named. This was lost—seventeen to seven. Wilmington was named. It had only three or four. A motion was made to adjourn. The first was lost. A motion was even made to pass the first clause of the bill with a blank, notwithstanding the absurdity of it, even in the face of a vote that this was an improper time to fix the permanent residence. All, in fact, was confusion and irregularity. A second vote of adjournment was called for, and carried. So ended the uproar of the day. John Adams has neither judgment, firmness of mind, nor respectability of deportment, to fill the chair of such an assembly. Gunn had scolded out a good deal of stuff—were (we) forever to be plagued with a removal, &c. This I thought deserved some answer.

I went over all the disadvantages of New York contrasted with Philadelphia, and concluded that such inconveniences would always produce such complaints and uneasiness, and could not be removed but by taking away the cause. I was listened to, but made no converts. I was a good while up, as I went largely into the business, but I took the same ground which I had before traveled over, the notes of which I sent to Doctor Rush.

Just before I rose, I asked Mr. Morris for the estimate of removing Congress from Trenton, which he had promised to procure. Had nothing of it. I really communicated this matter to him to enable him to make some figure in the debate, and, if possible, to bind him to me by this kind of confidential communication. But I have another proof that all advances on my part are in vain. I walked this evening with Mr. Wynkoop. Fell in company with several of the representatives. Exhorted them all, as much as I possibly could, to unanimity and firmness, and did not fail to recommend to steady perseverance under the assurance that we would be successful.

June 9. Attended the Hall at the usual time. The Rhode Island bill had a third reading.

And now the funding bill was taken up. We had passed the clause funding the old continental money, and left a blank, on Monday. I then called it the resurrection of a dead demand against the public. Mr. Morris seemed in sentiment with me. King spoke against the clause altogether. But now the Secretary's report was the text-book, and it must be funded at forty for one. I called the attention of the Senate to the characters who now had this money. Many meritorious persons received it as gold and silver, and still kept it as the monuments of the sacrifices which they made in the cause of America. Would seventy-five for one—forty for one, or a hundred for one—indemnify such characters? Would it not be a mockery of their demands? A time might come—a manner might be thought of—for their relief, but this was not, perhaps, the time, nor was it the manner.

The other class of individuals who were possessed of it, had collected it from holes and corners after it had ceased to be an object of speculation, when it was really worth nothing; and who neither gave value for it, nor had any merit in the act of collection. For these humble speculators, infinitely too much was done. They had no claims in justice. The whole of the Continental money was sunk by depreciation, a most unequal mode of taxation truly, but an effectual one. He that touched it, was taxed by it. This was creating a claim. A defunct demand was conjured up against the Union, as if they feared the mass of debt would be too small, though I feared they would find it much larger than we could discharge, &c., &c. The clause was passed, and we went to the fourth.

Mr. Morris moved, in a moment, to strike out the two first alternatives, and blazed away for six per cent. on the nominal amount of all public securities. Ellsworth answered, want of ability. Mr. Morris made nothing of the whole of it. The broadside of America was able enough for it all. We had property enough, and he was for a land tax; and if a land tax were laid, there would be money enough. He said many weak things, and was handled closely for them by Ellsworth. The debates, loose, indeed, and desultory, continued until three o'clock. Adjourned.

June 10. Attended at nine o'clock at the Hall, on the bill for making compensation to one John McCord. It was a painful business. His claims do not seem overly well founded in point of law, or any act of Congress. He is seventy-nine years old, and appears to have suffered deeply in the American cause. We spent a considerable time on his business.

The funding bill was under consideration. It was passed over without much debate, in our cursory way.

But now rose Ellsworth, and in a long, elaborate discourse, recommended the assumption of the State debts. He concluded that he would read his motion, which he said had the approbation of the Secretary of the Treasury. It was verbatim one of Gerry's papers, which had been moved, and laid on the Speaker's table in the House of Representatives about a week ago.

We had speakers enough now. Dr. Johnson was somewhat singular in his operations. He denied there was any such thing as a State debt—they were all equally the debts of the United States.

The day was mostly spent in this business.

I rose, and took the field which I had several times labored in with my pen. The old acts of Congress settle and assume the balances, &c. A short publication which I wrote, and which, by one means or other, got into almost all the newspapers, was the basis of it.

The Boston men and King talked much of their fears of the consequence, &c. I objected Hancock's speech to one, and the divided votes of their Representatives to the other.

One of the Massachusetts men now produced instructions from their government, authorizing their voting for the measure.

I alleged that if one State instructed, all should instruct, and perhaps this should be considered as a good reason of postponement until all had instructed on the subject, &c. The consideration was postponed until to-morrow.

June 11. Attended the Hall on Mr. McCord's bill early. Mr. Morris joined us. Went in and attended the funding bill—the clause for the assumption of the State debts.

Mr. Gerry's amendment was negatived. Nine only rose for it. The bill was now committed. The only debate of any consequence was between Ellsworth and myself. He set forth, in a curious argument, that the debts contracted near the seat of Congress were made Federal; that those at a distance were made State debts, supposing that the authority of Congress was less efficacious.

There really was not a shadow of truth in this. He only adapted his argument to an accidental fact, South Carolina and Massachusetts having the largest State debts.

I rose, and showed that there really was nothing at all in this matter. That the origin of some of the State debts was their adopting the debts due to individuals, which they did by way of paying their requisitions, and got credit for them accordingly. This was the origin of the large State debt of one of them at least.

King was obliging enough to get up and tell the House I meant South Carolina, &c.

This brought up Butler and Izard with some degree of warmth.

It was a good while before I could get saying anything. I, however, avowed and supported all I had said—that the fact was indubitably so—that no censure was implied in anything I had said—that South Carolina had assumed debts due to her citizens to the amount of $186,799, and had credit in full of her quota of the requisitions of 10th September, 1782. On that account Pennsylvania had paid at the same time $346,632, and Massachusetts a large sum of the said requisition. That Pennsylvania might have brought forward her State debt, and had credit for it in the requisitions, but she did not do so, but remained burdened with both her State debt and requisitions, and had done much towards payment of both, while South Carolina had paid nothing to either. The committee were Mr. Lee, Ellsworth, Maclay, King, and Patterson. Some little council business was done, and we adjourned.

Just as we adjourned, Butler wished Carroll joy of a vote being carried in the Representative Chamber for the temporary residence to be in Baltimore.

There was some kind of entertainment, to which I heard Fitzsimmons, a few days ago, inviting the Speaker. I thought he took him to the door to do it. The Speaker asked me to go with him. I declined it, as well I might. After the Speaker came home, I asked him what he had heard Mr. Morris say of the Baltimore vote. He had not made up his mind. I can find he is now scheming, and will not vote for Baltimore.

I have had a spell of fishing, of which I was the subject, to know whether I would not oppose the Baltimore vote. I saw, clearly, the person was set on to do it, and will report to his employers, L. L. I, in all probability, am come to the point that will be seized, to turn the whole city of Philadelphia against me, but I trust no taint of dishonor will ever stain my conduct. As to consequences, I care not.

June 12. A day of storm and rain. I attended at the Hall at eleven, on the funding bill. The alternatives, as they were called, were the chief subjects of discussion until near three o'clock Candor sit by me, while I describe the committee:

R. H. Lee, the man who gave independence (in one sense) to America. A man of a clear head and great experience in public business; certainly ambitious, and vain-glorious, but his passions seek gratification in serving the public.

Ellsworth, a man of great faculties, and eloquent in debate, but he has taken too much on himself; he wishes to reconcile the Secretary's system to the public opinion and welfare; but it is too much—he cannot retain the confidence of the people, and remain in the good graces of the Secretary. He may lose both.

Patterson, more taciturn and lurking in his manner, and yet when he speaks, commits himself hastily. A *summum jus* man. Both lawyers, and both equally retained by the Secretary.

And now, Billy, what say you of yourself. Not over-burdened either with knowledge or experience, but disposed to make the best of your tools.

I objected, in general, to the bill; disliked funding at all; was willing to pay as an interim three per cent., and place it on the footing of disability to do more. I objected to funding the interest; proposed to establish a land office, to sink the interest now due, and that indents should be given to all persons entitled to them, receivable in that office; declared that even prodigals abhorred compound interest; that the bill went on this principle, though not in an annual ratio. It was, however, in vain, although I could perceive that I made an impression.

There were three alternatives in the Secretary's report. The last was by much the most favorable to the public. This, however, really meant only to try the disposition of Congress, and Fitzsimmons, when he took in his resolutions, contrived to have this rejected, and one substituted vastly more favorable to the subscribers.

I found I could not effect anything on my own plan. I therefore watched, and promoted every favorable sentence that fell from Lee and Ellsworth. The result of all was, that we struck out all the alternatives, and voted a general fund of four per cent.

In the evening came Wynkoop, hey-day, all wrong to go to Baltimore, &c., &c., full charged with the permanent seat, &c., &c. I know he had not this of himself. I, however, delivered myself with firmness on the subject; recapitulated the conduct of the Yorkers, &c.; showed him (as I thought) that to concur with the Baltimore vote was politically right. He found he could make no impression. It was nearly dark as he went away. I followed to the door. He took the way of Queen street, and the Speaker, who was with me, said he is going to Fitzsimmons.

Monday, 14. I left home early and called on the assistant of the Treasury, on McCord's affair. He would not let me tell my business, so keen was he on the subject of proposing a bargain to me. Pennsylvania to have the permanent residence on the Susquehanna, and her delegation to vote for the assumption.

I constrained my indignation at this proposal with much difficulty within the bounds of decency, and the more so as I knew that however it might be with him, Hamilton, the principal in this business, was not sincere. I gave him such looks and answers as put an end to this business. I then got my errand settled. Went to Mr. Jefferson's office, on Mr. Bailey's affair. Arranged his affair, and went down Broad street. Here I met Mr. Lee. Spoke a few words with him, and passed on to the lodgings of Mr. Carroll. My only business with him was to forewarn him that an objection would be made to Baltimore that there were no public buildings, and that he should be prepared on this subject.

From here I went to Mr. Morris' lodgings. I found him somewhat engaged, but the moment he disposed of a small matter of business he dismissed his clerk—told me he was just going to look for me,·and was fortunate in my coming in. Said he had much to say, but some part of it must be on the most entire confidence. That on Friday, Jackson, of the President's family, in whom he said he could not have confidence, had been at Clymer and Fitzsimmons' lodgings; that Coxe, of the Treasury, had been there; that their business was to negotiate a bargain—the permanent residence in Pennsylvania for her votes for the assumption, or, at least, as many votes as would do the needful. The burden of their business seemed to be to open the conference with Mr. Hamilton on this subject. Mr. Morris continued : I did not choose to trust them, but wrote a note to Colonel Hamilton, that I would be walking early in the morning on the battery, and if Colonel Hamilton had anything to propose to him he might meet him there as if by accident. I went in the morning there, and found him on the *sod before me*. Mr. Hamilton said he wanted one vote in the Senate and five votes in the House of Representatives. That he was willing and would agree to place the permanent residence of Congress at Germantown or Falls of Delaware, if he would procure him these votes.

Mr. Morris owned that he complied on his part so far as that he agreed to consult some of the Pennsylvania delegation, (I abruptly said, you need not consult me,) but proposed that the temporary residence of Congress in Philadelphia should be the price. They parted upon this, but were to communicate on the subject again.

Mr. Morris and Fitzsimmons made a party out of town, and took Mr. Reed with them, yesterday, as the man whose vote they would engage. (Let me here recollect the application made to me on Saturday night by Mr. Wynkoop. I now know that he was trying me on that subject, and the Speaker was not much out when he said Wynkoop was gone to Fitzsimmons. He should have added, and Morris'.)

Mr. Reed's answer was what Mr. Morris called polite : *Gentlemen, I am disposed to facilitate your wishes.*

But now, this morning, says Mr. Morris, I have received a note from Colonel Hamilton that he cannot think of negotiating about the temporary residence. That his friends will not hear of it. Mr. Morris added : I know he has been able to manage the destination of the Baltimore vote without me, but I cannot yet tell how. I sent for Mr. Reed.   He says they have accounts that the Senators from Rhode Island are appointed, and expected every moment. But Mr. Morris added : I think he has some other assurances.   I now parted with Mr. Morris, and joined the committee on the funding bill.

The Senate were formed some time before we joined them, and, after some of the routine business of the day was done, and the Baltimore resolution handed in, it was called for.   Schuyler moved it should be postponed a fortnight.   Governor Johnson, of North Carolina, seconded him.

Ellsworth got up.   Said this matter mixed itself with all our affairs.   There was a secret understanding—a bargaining—that run through all our proceedings, and, therefore, it ought to be postponed.

I retorted his *secret understanding, bargaining,* &c., on himself. As he knew there were such things, he knew where they arose, and, if they mixed with and polluted our proceedings, it was time to put an end to them, which could only be done by deciding the matter, &c.   The question was put, and it was the old eleven and thirteen.

This was mess day.   I did not join the company until about five o'clock, and stayed until after eight.   But, oh, such noise and nonsense.   Fitzsimmons railed out at one time against Pennsylvania interferences about the assumption of the State debts.   Had it not been for these, the funding system would have been completed months ago.   He had received letters that stones would be thrown at him in the streets of Philadelphia if he were there, &c.

June 15.   We finished our observations on the funding bill, and reported.   The whole day was spent in debate on it.   I have so often expressed my sentiments respecting the subject of this bill, that I need not set any of them down here.   I was not often up.   I took, at one time, some pains to explain the nature of   and indents, but no question was taken on any point.   All was postponed.

Doctor Elmer told me, as I left the hall, that he had something to impart to me.   Mr. Morris, however, called me aside, and told me that he had a communication from Mr. Jefferson of a disposition of having the temporary residence fifteen years in Philadelphia, and the permanent residence at Georgetown, on the Potomac, and that he, Mr. Morris, had called a meeting of the delegation at six o'clock, this evening, at our lodging, on the business.   I was really unwell, and had to lie down the most of the afternoon.   The delegation met at six.   I was called out.   However, when I came in, what passed was repeated to me.   Hamilton proposed to give the permanent residence to Pennsylvania, at Germantown or the Falls of Delaware, on condition of their voting for the assumption. In fact, it was the confidential story of yesterday all over again. Mr. Morris also repeated Mr. Jefferson's story, but I certainly had misunderstood Mr. Morris at the Hall, for Jefferson vouched for nothing.

I have seen no prospect of fixing the permanent residence of Congress in the proper place at the present session ; and whenever it is gone into, will be involved in much difficulty. I have, therefore, declared uniformly against everything of the kind ; but to continue the temporary residence here under the promise of the permanent residence being in any part of Pennsylvania, I considered as madness. It was giving them time to fortify and entrench themselves with such systematic arrangements that we never should get away while the law acted as a tie on us, and bound us hand and foot, but gave them all the power and all the opportunity of fixing us permanently in this place. I would rather be under no obligation, and keep up an unremitted effort to get away, which I had no doubt would be crowned with success.

I know not whether what I said was the reason of it, but these sentiments seemed to be adopted. As to the bargain proposed by Hamilton, I spoke of it with detestation. Mr. Morris now proposed that a paper should be drawn up, with reasons of our conduct, that they might not be able to brand us with any neglect of the interests of Pennsylvania ; and a committee for this purpose was appointed— Mr. Morris, Mr. Fitzsimmons, Mr. Hartley.

June 16. I called early this morning at Col. Hartley's lodgings, in order to give him a sketch of what I thought might be well enough for us to sign. He was gone, but I fell in with him at the Hall, and delivered it to him.

I sauntered about till Congress formed ; and now we got at *the funding bill.* Here we had all the stuff over again of public credit, &c. The great question was, whether the report of the committee for *four* per cent. should be adopted. I soon committed myself in such sort that I must expect all the public creditors to be my enemies. The great ground that I took was, that I did not believe we could impose any direct taxes on our constituents for a purpose which they knew, as well as I did—that the holders of certificates in Pennsylvania had them funded when they were but 2/6 on the £ ; that 100 : 0 : 0 purchased 800 ; that they had drawn interest on the nominal amount for four years=£192. Justice and law allowed them but 124 ; hence they had £68 clear already, and the certificates into the bargain, &c.

I was up a long time. Mr. Morris rose against the report. His choler fairly choked him. He apologized to the House that his agitation had deprived him of his recollection on the subject, and he sat down. He rose again some little time before the Senate adjourned; mentioned his late confusion, but declared it did not arise from the personal interest he had in public securities; that although he was possessed of some, he was no speculator, &c., &c.

We spent until past three o'clock, but took no question; and, indeed, it seemed almost agreed that we would not proceed without the other bill.

June 17. The Senate met, and until near two o'clock we were engaged on the subject of consuls and vice consuls. The grand question was, whether foreigners were eligible to those offices. It was admitted that they were, and a number accordingly appointed. When I came home at dinner, the Speaker told me that a bill was proposed in the House of Representatives for giving them salaries. Thus it is that we are led on, little by little, to increase the civil list—to increase the mass of public debt, and, of course, the taxes of the public. This, however, is all of a piece with former management from the offices.

The funding bill was now called for. Butler repeated the same things he had said yesterday. But now up rose Patterson, with a load of notes before him. To follow him would be to write a pamphlet, for he was up near an hour.

Near the beginning he put a question: What principle shall we adopt to settle the business. If we follow justice, *she says three per cent.; or even two is as much as the holders of certificates can demand.* But what says law—six per cent., and he was a *summum jus* man to the end of the chapter. It was near three when he had done.

I felt an impatience to attack him, and up I got. At first exploded a doctrine which he had stated, of Congress being a party and the claimants another. I stated the people at large as being the debtors, and the holders the creditors, and Congress the umpire—the legislator between them. I then stated his two principles of justice and law—declared myself an adherent of the former. Law was the rule for courts and magistrates, in the execution of their offices. But justice was our guide, and had been the guide of all just legislation, from the Jewish jubilee to the present day. That even in law it was a maxim, that rigid law was rigid injustice—hence the necessity of courts of chancery, expressly for mitigating the severity of unjust contracts. I repeated his own words, of *three per cent.—perhaps two per cent.*, being the voice of justice. If then the point of justice stands at three per cent., or if at **two**

per cent., all beyond that point is injustice, and injustice to whom ?
To that very people whose interest it is our bounden duty to support and protect. I reprobated his positions even with acrimony,
as the Shylock doctrine of my bond, my bond.

June 18. We went early to the Hall, as I was on two committees
this morning—the one, the case of one Twining, the other, McCord's.
We spent a considerable space of time on Twining's affair, which
to me did not seem a just subject of legislation. I then joined the
committee on McCord's case.

This was truly one in which compassion mingled herself with justice. The Generals, Thomson, Irvine, and others had received effects
from him in Canada, in the year 1776. They gave him a bill, which
was never paid. The Auditor and Comptroller settled the sum
due on this bill, $809 71. He had suffered greatly in Canada—had
his house burned, took our Continental money to a considerable
amount as specie, which he produced to us to the amount of twelve
or thirteen hundred dollars ; advanced money and goods to many
people who now refuse to pay him, and many of them he cannot
find. All these things are indubitable. I had no difficulty in allowing him the $809 71, in ready money, in lieu of a certificate, but
anything more I seemed to feel a difficulty in. Lands had been set
apart by the old Congress, to make compensation for Canadian suf-
ferers. We reported the bill, with the $809 71, and left a blank for
the value of his lands. The Senate filled the blank with five hundred
dollars. My heart would not let me rise against the motion. Though
it is a trifle to his sufferings, yet how many hundreds of our own
people suffer equal distress.

Up now came the funding bill. Butler railed at Ellsworth. Ellsworth talked back. There really was no entertainment. No man
ever rambled, or talked more at random, than Butler. He is ever
quoting authors on trade, finance, &c. Ever repeating what he has
seen in Europe. This day he asserted that the circulating coin of
Great Britain was three hundred millions. Authors (if I remember
right) place it about sixteen. There really was nothing new. Some
were pressing for the question, but it was postponed generally.

This evening, Mr. Morris and Fitzsimmons called on us. Hamilton has been with them again. Never had a man a greater propensity for bargaining than Mr. Morris. Hamilton knows this, and is
laboring to make a tool of him. He affects to tell Mr. Morris that
the New England men will bargain to fix the permanent seat at the
Potomac or at Baltimore. Mr. Fitzsimmons counted all the members who it was likely would vote for such a measure, and the conclusion was that no such measure could be carried by them.

June 19. We then walked to view the demolitions of Fort George —the leaden coffins and remains of Lady and George Bellamont, now exposed to the sun, after an interment of about ninety years. They and many more had been deposited in vaults in a chapel which once stood in the fort. The chapel was burned down about fifty years ago, and never re-built. The leveling of the fort, and digging away the foundations, have uncovered the vaults.

June 21. Attended at the Hall early on the bill for remitting certain penalties to one N. Twining.

The Senate met. I observed a strangeness of disposition in the House the moment, or rather a few moments, after the minutes were read. Patterson moved to adjourn. Schuyler seconded. This was lost. It was now moved to take up the vote of the House of Representatives for fixing the time of adjournment. This was agreed to, and King, Bassett, and Walker appointed on our part to confer.

Izard now rose, said there was something to put on the minutes, and renewed the motion for adjournment. Seconded by Patterson. This was lost. The funding bill was taken up.

We had a great deal of the old ground gone over again. King received a note. Rose and moved that the funding bill should be postponed, as the House of Representatives had negatived the bill for the ways and means. He was seconded by Schuyler. We had now a long, desultory kind of debate, whether the bill should be postponed. It was not postponed.

Now the debates on the merits of the bill. The question was whether all the alternatives should be struck out, and a fund of four per cent adopted. Adopted—thirteen for, ten against. Now the question on the striking out of the indents. Ellsworth and the New England men knew that Pennsylvania has a number of indents, and the invention of all of them is at work to turn it to her disadvantage. The vote was, however, carried to keep in the indents, since the other back interest was to be funded. I bore my testimony, in the strongest terms, against funding any interest, and proposed to open a land office, as a sinking fund for the whole of the back interest, including the indents, but I found no second. The interest of the whole was placed on one footing, almost without a division.

Now a long debate ensued about the Jersey payments, and a proviso which had been inserted to favor them. No other question was, however, taken, and the House adjourned a quarter after three.

This was mess or club day. I went and stayed till the fumigation began, *alias* smoking of cigars, a thing I never could bear.

Ellsworth made a long speech, amounting to this : that since a general system of funding could not be obtained, gentlemen would be against all funding whatever.

I placed his speech in as strong colors as I could. That since a party in Congress could not build as they pleased, they would turn and pull it down. There was a majority against the assumption of the State debts, and the minority, indignant at being controlled, since they could not rule, would join the discontented part of Congress, and stop all business. Adams affects to treat me with all the neglect he can, while I am speaking, by turning his head a different way, looking sideways, &c. But I care not. I will endeavor to bear it.

June 22. I called this morning on General Irwin, who is one of the commissioners for settling the accounts between the United States and the individual States, for the amount of the Jersey claims for interest paid by that State on the Continental certificates. Found it to be about a half million.

Now attended the committee on Twining's case. Mr. Morris called me aside. (I had yesterday expressed my indignation of the New England attempt upon Pennsylvania, in excluding or trying to exclude those indents, which would pass into her hands in consequence of the late funding law, from being funded ; had endeavored to possess him of the facts to obtain his assistance, and, indeed, expressed, perhaps, ungarded solicitude on that subject.)

(*He*) told me this is an important affair respecting the indents to Pennsylvania. I would have you to think well of it. The New England men are determined to carry it against us. The assumption is the only way we can rid ourselves of this thing. I would have you think of it—think of it.

I had to say, I will think of it. I felt a little disturbed ; not, if I knew my own mind, with regard to the part I should act, but to think that everything should be set to sale, and that even just measures could not be pursued but by contract, and that men should be hunted into measures. I have often thought myself deficient in readiness of judgment, or quickness of determination. Perhaps any man can think more and better too, at twice than at once. I, however, in a few minutes, took my seat beside Mr. Morris. Told him that I considered the assumption so politically wrong and productive of so much injustice, that no offer could be made which would induce me to change my mind. I had, however, means of another nature. I could depend nothing on the promises of the New England men ; but, further, I had calculated that the State of New York was circumstanced nearly in the same way as Pennsylvania, with respect to indents; and I considered this as the sure pledge that we should not be pushed to extremities on that ground.

The result showed that I was right, for after a great deal of debate in the House, affairs settled nearly as I would have them.

The bill for establishing the post office was read the first time. We adjourned early.

Mr. Fitzsimmons called this afternoon. We had much loose conversation on the subject of adjournment. I expressed a wish, the sooner the better. Fitzsimmons said it never would do to go away without funding the debts. Pennsylvania was too deeply interested. She would draw three millions of dollars annually from the funds. I stared, as well I might; for at four per cent. she must possess more than the whole of the Continental debt to do it, viz: seventy-five millions. He corrected himself, and said above fifteen millions would belong to her and her citizens. I said this might be.

The Speaker walked away with Mr. Fitzsimmons. When he returned, I asked him to repeat what Mr. Fitzsimmons had said. He said Mr. Fitzsimmons had explained himself in their walk. That the State of Pennsylvania possessed three millions on which she would draw interest, and that the citizens of the State possessed fifteen millions on which they would draw interest.

Wednesday, June 23. This day could not be considered as very important in the Senate. The funding bill was called for, and postponed.

The intercourse bill, or that for appointing ambassadors, had been referred to a committee of conference so long ago that I had forgot it, but the thing was neither dead nor sleeping. It was only dressing and friends making. The report increased the salaries, and added $10,000 to the appropriations. I concluded they had secured friends enough to support it before they committed it to the House. This turned out to be the case. The whole appropriation was $40,000, and they were voted with an air of perfect indifference by the affirmants, although I consider the money as worse than thrown away. For I know not of a single thing that we have for a single minister to do at a single court in Europe. Indeed, the less we have to do with them, the better. Our business is to pay them what we owe, and the less political connection the better with any European power. It was well spoken against. I voted against every part of it.

We received also a bill for the Indian trade. Read for the first time.

Mr. Morris was called often out. He at last came in, and whispered me: The business is settled at last. Hamilton gives up the temporary residence. I wrote on a slip of paper, (as we could not converse freely :) *If Hamilton has his hand in the residence now, he will have his foot in it before the end of the session.*

I afterwards told Mr. Morris that this seeming willingness of Hamilton proceeded from his knowledge that the North Carolina Senators and Colonel Gunn could not be restrained from voting for Baltimore, and that the present proposal and bill (for a bill was showed to me by Mr. Morris) were meant to divert the southern members from Baltimore, and they would finally destroy the bill.

I got Henry, of Maryland, into the audience-room, and gave him a detail of what was going on, and made the same reflections on it to him. I saw he believed the North Carolina men would vote for Baltimore. I find there is a ferment among them, and good may come of it.

There is a jockeying and bargaining going on, respecting which I am not consulted, and which I hear of only by the by. The temporary residence in Philadelphia for fifteen years, and the permanent residence on the Potomac. A solemn engagement has been entered into by eleven Senators to push the temporary residence only. On this ground, we of Pennsylvania are perfectly safe, and our interest is to keep this contract alive. If we go from this, the temporary residence may remain in New York and the permanent residence to the Potomac. It is a species of robbery to deprive Pennsylvania of the residence. How can a delegate reconcile himself to such a vote unless he confide in future contingency to repair his errors, which is neither safe nor honorable.

June 24. This was a day of small business in the Senate. The report on a bill for remitting fines to one Twining was rejected, and the bill confirmed.

Though little business was done in the Senate, yet I ought never to forget this day.

In the Senate Chamber, Mr. Walker told me that the Pennsylvania delegation had, in a general meeting, agreed to place the permanent residence on the Potomac and the temporary residence to remain ten years in Philadelphia. I answered, I know nothing of any such agreement. No truth was ever better founded. He said Scott had come from the meeting to him. He seemed willing I should take a lead in the business. I heard nothing further on the business.

Dr. Elmer and I called on Mr. Morris, and here, for the first time, I heard him declare he was satisfied with ten years. He did not say much to me, but the moment I came home the Speaker attacked me.   Here, you have been doing fine things—you have broke the bargain, &c.

I denied that I had broke any bargain—that I never knew of any bargain for ten years being made.   Did not General Muhlenburg speak to you?   Yes; on Monday last he bid me tell Mr. Morris that he thought Mathews could not make them agree to more than ten years.   I forgot to mention it to him then, but mentioned it to him afterwards.   He said if we agree to ten, they would propose seven, &c., and declared himself against listening to any such proposals.   We, however, met in the evening.   Bassett and Reed, of the Delaware State, came with Mr. Morris.   Doctor Elmer came some time after.   I now did the most foolish thing I ever did in my life.   I declared that I considered the permanent residence as a matter that ought to belong to Pennsylvania, in whatever point of view it was considered, geographically or politically.   That to deprive her of it was, in my opinion, a species of robbery ; but *since we came there to consult the public good, I was willing to be governed by republican principles, and would stand by the vote of the majority on this point, as a house divided against itself could not stand.*

Mr. Morris now said that my arguments were too late.   I should have made these objections when the contract was made for fifteen years' residence at Philadelphia.   I very freely declared I never entered into any such contract.   Morris, Fitzsimmons, and the Speaker declared that I did, and the Speaker reminded me that a committee was appointed.   I agreed that a committee was appointed, but it was to draw up our reasons for rejecting Hamilton's proposals ; and that I understood them so would be evident from my sentiments which I had committed to paper at the time, and which were now in the hands of Col. Hartley.   They all three persisted in the charge.   Hartley, however, had spirit enough to say there was no such contract.   This seemed to cool them a little.   But, after some time, Scott came in.   The matter was repeated to him. He declared there was no number of years mentioned at all as any bargain, and, of course, no contract.   This made them look a little blue.

I must note that I read the sketch which I gave to Hartley to the Speaker, and that he approved of it; and I expressly mentioned, both to him and Col. Hartley, that all we did respected only what was past.

But now the Speaker put the question, Shall we vote for a bill giving the temporary residence ten years to Philadelphia and the permanent residence to the Potomac?   They all said yes but myself. I said no; but unluckily am bound by my foolish declaration. Good God, deliver me this once. Fate, familiar as her garter, ended the difficulty. But the tale is long, and I had better begin the business of the day on the next page.

Friday, 25, 1790. A day of excessive rain. I went to the Hall, in the Speaker's carriage, at an early hour to attend the committee on the post office business. I found Mr. Carroll there. We had much loose talk. He told me his plan, which was to take Butler's bill—amended so that the residence should be ten years in Philadelphia, at the end of which the permanent residence should be on the Potomac.

The first business was the report on what was called Stephen Moore's bill. This man is the owner of the land on which the old fort of West Point stands. He is got in debt in town to the amount of two thousand or some such sum. He has nothing but the rocks of West Point. The Secretaries of War and Treasury, &c., and other influential characters, have interested themselves in getting this bill passed to buy the land from him to pay his debts, under the notion that the ground is necessary for a fortress. It was carried in the Senate by a great majority. Am I mistaken, or is the spirit of prodigality broke loose since Rhode Island came in?

This day Moore's case, and a bill for claim for one Gould came up. The ayes and noes are on the journals, and, strange to tell, for once Mr. Morris was with me.

Mr. Carroll now rose, and was seconded by Lee. Izard, Few, King. on one side; Carroll and Lee, on the other. Butler bounced between both, but declared for the bill, and he would be for it. The motion was to take up the bill.

The President, from the chair, said: *There has been a motion for postponement. I do not know whether it has been seconded.* No such thing had happened, but the hint was soon after taken.

All now was consternation and commotion. Out ran King, Schuyler, Izard, and sundry of the eastern gentry, and in were ushered the Senators from Rhode Island.

And now the hinted-for postponement was called for of the bill, which, in fact, had not been taken up. But the new members, just sworn and seated, did not get up. Signs and motions were ineffectual; they kept their seats; and the bill, of course, was taken up, or, in parliamentary style, not postponed.

Izard begged leave to explain; or in other words, to tell the new come gentlemen that they ought to have voted for the postponement.

Mr. Adams, without any ceremony, put the same question over again. King got on one side, and Ellsworth on the other, of the new members, and up they got them. Butler, too, after all his declarations, voted for the postponement. It was thirteen and thirteen, and Mr. Adams voted the postponement; and thus the business of the day was got over without much difficulty so far, or at least the knotty parts of it, and thus my neck got out of the noose. Adjourned until Monday.

I must note here that a number of our own people were duped in pushing the Rhode Island bill. They are now paid for it. I told them at the time what was intended. They must take what follows.

Saturday, June 26. Attended this day on the committee on the *post office bill.* The bill came up from the Representatives, with every post-road described—both main and cross-roads.

Carroll and Strong were for blotting out every word of description, and leaving all to the Postmaster General and the President of the United States.

I proposed a different plan. That one great post-road should be described by law, from Portland, in New Hampshire, to Augusta, in Georgia, passing through the seats of the different goverments; and that two cross-roads only should be described, from New York to Canada, and from Philadelphia, or some other proper place, to Fort Pitt, for the accommodation of the western country. The other or block system prevailed; but we are to meet again on Monday, at ten o'clock.

Monday, June 28. Met at ten on the post office committee, but such running and caballing of the Senators, nothing could be done.

Now the Baltimore vote was read. Carroll and Lee moved to postpone it. It was postponed.

Carroll now moved to read some representations from Baltimore and Georgetown. This was complied with. Carroll surprised me by taking me out and requesting me to move the insertion of Baltimore for the permanent residence. Said he wished it to be put and negatived. This had a crooked aspect. I declined it. Izard, however, moved this very thing, and Walker told me it was expected that he would do it.

I called for the amendment that had been proposed on Friday, but Carroll got up and wished the vote on Baltimore. It was negatived.

Carroll now got up with the amendments. He surprised me with his slowness. We wrangled on till near three o'clock, calling yeas and nays on almost every question—but for these, *vide* the minutes.

When we came to the blank for the place of the temporary residence—and, by the by, there was no blank in the amendment which Carroll read on Friday, but he now suffered Adams to proceed on the original bill. He evidently waited, and paused until Izard moved to fill the blank with New York.

Now we had the warmest debates of the day. Mr. Morris took no part whatever. Langdon and myself were the warmest. The question was put at three o'clock, and carried for New York—thirteen to twelve. Col. Gunn has been absent all this day—designedly, it is supposed.

This day the delegation had invited the Vice President and the other officers of the General Government. The Chief Justice and Vice President did not attend. The three Secretaries were with us. The discourse, before dinner, turned on the manner of doing business in the Senate. It was remarked, that as every question of moment was carried only by a majority of one, or, for the most part, by the casting vote of the President, it might be as well to vest the whole senatorial power in the President of the Senate.

I could not help making some remarks on our three Secretaries. Hamilton has a very boyish, giddy manner. Jefferson transgresses on the extreme of stiff gentility, or lofty gravity. Knox is the easiest man, and the most dignity of presence. They retired at a decent time, one after another. Knox stayed longest.

June 29. The tonnage bill was taken up, and committed. This bill uses the same rates of tonnage as the old bill, and why it was brought forward is more than I can say, unless it was solely to employ time.

And now the residence bill was taken up.

The joy of the Yorkers made them cry out for an adjournment when they had filled one of the blanks. Now the other one was to be filled, with the time of the temporary residence. It was carried for ten years, and Carroll voted for it—thirteen to twelve. But now the question was taken on the clause, and the whole was negatived—sixteen to nine.

Now Izard and the adherents of New York showed visible perturbation, and bounced at a strange rate. I looked at Carroll, and got him now to rise with his clause, ten years for Philadelphia. Why he kept it back so long explains itself.

Schuyler and King offered to amend it by dividing the time—five years to each place. Long debates here. The question was lost, thirteen to thirteen, Vice President against.

They now moved Baltimore. Lost it, ten to sixteen.

Butler now moved to stay two years in New York. Thirteen to thirteen. President against.

The question put on the clause. Thirteen to thirteen. President against it. So the clause was lost.

The question was now put, Shall the bill pass to a third reading? The noes certainly had it, but the House did not divide, and an adjournment obtained before anything more was finished.

June 30. When I came to the Hall, Doctor Elmer told me that Carroll & Co. were using every endeavor to pass the bill to a third reading without anything of the temporary residence. Here we certainly had every right to leave them; yet Walker said they would drop Philadelphia if we would not go with them. I am fully satisfied that they have had an under plot on hand all this time with the Yorkers.

Carroll, finding the bill could not be carried to a third reading, moved a reconsideration of the Philadelphia clause. But he was out of order, not having been of the majority.

I passed the word to get Butler to move, as he had been of that side. He did so, after talking almost half an hour. It was reconsidered and adopted, fourteen to twelve, Butler changing his ground.

Before we could get a question on the paragraph, they moved the question of five years in New York, and five in Philadelphia. Lost, twelve and fourteen. Then to stay two years in New York This Butler joined them in, and the House stood thirteen and thirteen. The President gave us a long speech on the orderly, decent behavior of the citizens of New York, especially in the gallery of the other House. Said no people in the world could behave better. I really thought he meant this lavish praise as an indirect censure on the city of Philadelphia, for the papers have teemed with censorious charges of their rudeness to the members of public bodies. Be that, however, as it may, he declared he would go to Philadelphia without staying a single hour, and gave us his vote. I think it was well he did not know all; for had he given this vote the other way, the whole was lost. The question on the passage was carried, fourteen to twelve. (See postea 250 as to the residence.)

Mr. Langdon now moved a reconsideration to strike out the loan of the $100,000. A long debate ensued. It was evident his vote would turn it. This I mentioned to Walker. We told them, however, that we were with them. But they did what good policy directed. They gave the matter up, and the appropriation was struck out. The question on the bill passing to a third reading was now taken. Carried—fourteen to twelve.

I am fully convinced Pennsylvania could do no better. The

matter could not be longer delayed. It is, in fact, the interest of the President of the United States that pushes the Potomac. He, by means of Jefferson, Madison, Carroll, and others, urges the business, and, if we had not closed with these terms, a bargain would have been made for the temporary residence in New York. They have offered to support the Potomac for three years' temporary residence, (in New York, I presume,) and I am very apprehensive they would have succeeded, if it had not been for the Pennsylvania threats that were thrown out of stopping all business, if an attempt was made to rob them of both temporary and permanent residence.

July 1, 1790. Knowing nothing of immediate consequence, I attended the Hall early. Took a seat in the committee-room. Began an examination of the journals of the old Congress touching some matters before us in committee.

When the minutes were read, King observed that the yeas and nays were not inserted on the motion for staying two years in New York. The President and Secretary both denied that they were taken, but I believe they erred. This, however, I did not consider as much for them. We read the Rhode Island enumeration bill. Committed the settlement bill, and the one for the regulation of seamen.

And now came the residence. Ellsworth moved that the extent on the Potomac should be thirty miles above, and thirty below, Hancocktown. Lost. Second motion: To insert the first Monday in May instead of first Monday in December for removal. The yeas and nays equal, and now John Adams gave us one of his pretty speeches. He mentioned many of the arguments for removal, and concluded that justice, policy, and even necessity, called for it.

Now, King took up his lamentations. He sobbed, wiped his eyes, and scolded and railed and accused, first, everybody, and then nobody, of bargaining—contracting—arrangements and engagements that would dissolve the Union.

He was called on sharply. He begged pardon, &c., and railed again.

Butler replied in a long unmeaning talk. Repeated that he was sure the honorable gentleman did not mean him, and yet, if there really was any person there to whom King's mysterious hints would apply, Butler's strange conduct marked him as the most proper object for them. Talk followed talk. It was evident they meant to spend the day. Doctor Johnson cried adjourn. Question, question, re-echoed from different quarters of the House. Few begged leave to move an amendment. It was to restore the appropriation clause. It was lost, and, at last, we got the question on transmitting the bill to the Representatives. Yeas, fourteen; nays, twelve.

As I came from the Chamber, King gave me a look. I replied, "*King's lamentations.*" "That won't do," said he. When we were down stairs he turned to me, said, "Let us now go and receive the congratulations of the city for what we have done." I had heard so much and so many allusions to the hospitality, &c., I thought it no bad time to give both him and them a wipe: "King, for a session of near six months I have passed the threshhold of no citizen of New York; I have no wish to commence acquaintance now." He uttered some ejaculation and went off. In truth, I never was in so inhospitable a place. The above declaration I thought it not amiss to make, that they may know that I am not insensible of their rudeness; and further, that I am quite clear of any obligations to them.

July 2. Attended the committee on the affair of Gould's bill. There did not appear much animation in the House. That keenness of look and eagerness which marked all our former looks, had departed with the residence.

Ellsworth moved a commitment of the resolution with regard to the State debts. I saw we were taken unawares on this subject. They carried the commitment and the committee both against us. Carroll joined them.

Wyngate told me this day of a violent breach having happened between King and the Massachusetts men. They would not vote for the Potomac, as King wished them to do. Had they joined the Connecticut and York votes, we would have obtained the temporary residence on much worse terms. This is a still further proof of what I knew before—that there was an under plot and a negotiation still open between the Potomac and New York.

The Speaker told me this day that the assumption would pass. I heard him with grief, and trust I may yet disbelieve him. He dined with the President yesterday.

July 3. General Irwin called early on me this morning. It was to tell me that King and Lawrence had been asserting, with great confidence, that we had bargained to give the assumption for the residence, &c.; that I was to go away, and Carroll to vote direct for it, &c.; that a very great hubbub was raised among the southern gentlemen, &c.

I could only tell him that it was false; and much, indeed, as I wished to see my family, that now home I would not go; that I would stay, and he was at liberty to say so. I called on Williamson as I went to the Hall, and on Hawkins, and told them so.

When I came in the Speaker told me that the York malevolence was showing itself in curious caricatures, in ridicule of the Pennsylvanians, &c.

July 4. Being Sunday, was celebrated only by the firing of cannon about noon. I walked to Scott's lodging. He came home with me. He showed a disposition to go over all the arguments which I had used in the Senate on that subject. I did so with much cheerfulness. I called this evening on Mr. Lee, and showed him plainly, as I thought, how we could, by a side wind in the bill for the settlement of accounts, give the assumption a decided stroke. I promised I would see him again to-morrow.

July 5. I was detained long before I could get to see Lee. He had consulted Madison, as he said, and had altered the amendment in point of form. But it certainly was much more obscure. Said he would second the motion, if I made it.

The post office bill was taken up, and a long debate whether the Postmaster should appoint the post roads or the Congress declare them so by law. It was carried in favor of the Postmaster's doing it.

A motion was made that Congress should adjourn, to wait on the President with the compliments of the day. Negatived.

A second motion to adjourn one hour, for the above purpose. Lost. Some business was done, and a second motion for adjournment was called. All the town was in arms—grenadiers, light infantry, and artillery passed the Hall, and the firing of cannon and small arms, with beating of drums, kept all in uproar. This motion carried, and now all of us repaired to the President's. We got some wine, punch, and cakes. From hence we went to St. Paul's, and heard the anniversary of independence pronounced by a Mr. B. Livingston. The church was crowded. I could not hear him well. Some said it was fine. I could not contradict them. I was in the next pew to General Washington. Part of his family, and Senators filled the seats with us.

Some say that the Yorkers will make desperate resistance to-morrow. Others say that they will die soft. Jackson gave me the President's compliments, and an invitation to dinner on Thursday.

July 6. Was called on, early this morning, by Mr. Hanna, of Harrisburg. Attended at the Hall, after having paid some visits. The post office bill passed, after some debate. Now came the settlement bill. Mr. Lee had spoiled my amendment, or at least greatly obscured it , but if I stirred at all, must use his motion, and, great man as he is. there really was mis-spelling in it.

The ground I took was, that the fifth section of the bill laid down a ratio, in consequence of which there must, in the nature of things, be creditor and debtor States. The sixth section told us how the creditor States were to be paid, but not one word was said as to the debtor States. Paying one was as necessary as the other. Justice demanded it. *Vide* my amendment:

"And those States against whom balances shall be found, shall have a portion of their State debt, which shall have accrued as aforesaid, left charged upon them, equal to such deficient balance; and if it should so happen that the whole State debt of any particular State shall fall short of such balance, such deficiency shall remain charged against such State, on the books of the Treasury."

I attacked the Secretary's system of supposititious balances, as not only unjust, radically, and a total departure from acts and requisitions of Congress, but as going to lay great taxes, and increase the volume of our debt.

Ellsworth and Strong answered. King admitted every principle which I laid down, but wavered. Lee seconded, and forsook me. The child was none of his. I really thought I had the best of the arguments, which grew bulky, and by degrees spread over all our fields of finance. But on the question, I had a small division in favor of the motion.

July 6. The true history of the bill is, that it has been fabricated by the Secretary's people, particularly Fitzsimmons, and is meant as a mere delusion, or to amuse the public, for they seriously never wish the accounts to be settled. But a show must be kept up of giving satisfaction on this point.

As to myself, I may draw a lesson from Lee's conduct, to bring forward my own motions only. I spoiled the amendment to obtain his support, and he saw it perish, with the indifference of a stranger.

July 7. Attended at the Hall. Every face bore the marks of anxious expectation. Schuyler came to me, and owned the bill for the settlements of accounts was to the full as important as I had stated it yesterday, and showed me a long amendment. Said the bill should be committed. Wished me to second him. I readily agreed to it, and now we went on the subject of debate. I was not alone, as yesterday. I supported my old system of ascertaining the expenses of the war; agreeing to the ratios and fixing the quotas; giving certificates to the creditor States and leaving the State debts on the debtors, respectively, so far as to equalize the accounts.

Ellsworth certainly confused himself. He wished to equalize the accounts by credits only, taking the lowest Ex as the basis, and setting off to each State in proportion to it and funding all over it, as the Ex of some of the States stood nearly at 0. This, in fact, would be funding nearly the whole expense of the war.

Butler had a third system, viz : Take no notice of anything bygone, but divide the existing debt among the States. I thought it strange to hear my colleague declare for the last opinion. After a very long debate, the bill was committed.

Sundry questions were taken in the House of Representatives on the residence bill. The decisions have hitherto been favorable, but the question on the bill not yet taken.

July 8. This day was slack in the Senate until the report came in on the bill for the settlement of the accounts. As might be expected, then amendments followed the Secretary's report, or nearly so. It amounted to this : That the net advances of the States should be made an aggregate of, and this aggregate divided by the ratio of population, which would fix the quotas. Then the quotas, compared with their respective advances, would determine the balances of debt or credit, or turn out just equal. And here it was agreed to leave the matter for the present, as the bill respected the ascertaining the balances only, and left the payment to the creditor States and the payment from the debtor States to the future operation of the Legislature. All this was far short of what I wanted, and, indeed, the bill will turn out, as I fear, a mere delusion ; but, under its present form, the State debts must be embraced in the accounts, if the commissioners do their duty ; and if so, this will operate as a reason why they should not be assumed.

I wrote a hasty line . . . to Charles Biddle, that the votes stood this day twenty-eight and thirty-three on the residence.

Stayed at the Hall until four o'clock, and went to dine with the President. It was a great dinner, in the usual style, without any remarkable occurrence. Mrs. Washington was the only woman present.

I walked from the President's with Mr. Fitzsimmons part of the way to his lodgings. He really seemed good humored, and as if he wished to be on good terms with me. Clymer called at our lodgings in the evening, and seemed condescending and good humored in a remarkable degree. But all in the dumps again about the residence; only thirty real friends to the bill in the House, &c., &c.

It is time, indeed, that this business should be settled, for all our affairs are poisoned by it.

Nothing can be plainer than the simple mode of Dr. and Cr. for the settlement of the public accounts of the Union. But the State of South Carolina is most miserably in arrear, and wishes to avoid all settlement, or to have such a partial one as will screen her defects. She has been devoted to New York on the subject of the residence. Therefore, New York (or I should rather write Hamilton) labors incessantly to confuse, embarrass, and confound all settlement. The thing cannot be openly denied, but they will involve it in so many difficulties as will either prevent it altogether, or render it useless, if it should take place.

July 9. Attended the Hall at the usual hour. There was much whispering of the members, Ellsworth, Strong, and Izard. We had a bill for regulating the intercourse with the Indians, which was passed. A thing which may be made the basis of much expense. Superintendents are to be appointed, although the superintendence of the Indians in the Government northwest of the Ohio is already vested in the Governor; and so south of the Ohio. By and by we shall have a call for their salaries. It really seems as if we were to go on making offices until all the Cincinnati are provided for.

The settlement bill engaged us warmly for the most of this day. The object was to find the balances due to the creditor States, and how. Ingenuity itself is tortured to find ways and means of increasing the public demands, and passing by and rendering the State governments insignificant. I declared what I thought plainly on the subject: that the bill was one for the settlement, but not the payment, of the respective balances. That the old confederation clearly contemplated the payment of the balances from the delinquent States to the creditor States; that every act of the old Government carried this on the face of it; that although we could not lay unequal taxes, yet the adoption of the new constitution did not go to the discharge of just debts due from the States which might be hereafter found debtors; and that Congress certainly had the power of liquidating the balances and making the demands from the debtor States. The bill, after a long debate, passed on the principle of a settlement bill only.

I find by letters which I have received, that the public creditors are to be the body who are to rise in judgment against me, and try to expel me from the Senate. This is only what I expected. Nor are they the only ones. The adoption of the new constitution raised a singular ferment in the minds of men. Every one ill at ease in his finances; every one out at elbows in his circumstances; every ambitious man, every one desirous of a short cut to wealth and honors, cast their eyes on the new constitution as the machine which could be wrought to their purposes, either in the funds of speculation it would afford, the offices it would create, or the jobs to be obtained under it. Not one of these has found a patron in me. In fact I have generally set my face against such pretensions. As such men are generally wanting in virtue, their displeasure—nay, their resentment—may be expected. "*Why you want nothing neither for yourself nor friends,*" said a Senator one day to me, in some surprise. It was somewhat selfish, but I could not help uttering a wish *that he could say so with truth of every one.*

July 10. Being Saturday, the Senate did not meet, but I went to the Hall by a kind of instinct created by custom; something like a stage coach, which always performs it tour, whether full or empty. I met King and Langdon here. We spent an hour or two in very familiar chat. Nothing worth noting, unless it was the declaration of King, that a bargain was certainly made on the subject of the residence, to obtain at least one vote in the room of his, as it was mostly likely he would vote against the assumption, if the residence went to Philadelphia. I was astonished at King's owning this, which, in fact, amounted to this : that he had engaged his vote for the assumption, if the residence stayed in New York.

Sunday, the 11th, was, with me, a very dull day. I read at home, wrote the usual letters to my family, and other correspondents. After dinner, walked alone out on the commons beyond the Bowery, wherever I could find any green grass, or get out of the dust, which was very troublesome on the roads.

Monday, July 12. Attended at the Hall at the usual time. We received two messages from the Representatives; one of them contained the residence bill. We had considerable debate on the post office bill. Insisted on our amendments, and appointed a committee to confer.

Insisted on our amendment to the Indian intercourse bill, and passed the tonnage. This bill deserves a remark.

The bill is, in every respect, the same as the old one, bating the remission of some unintentional severities, which had fallen on some fishermen and coasters, which were remitted. The taking all the time, and passing all the forms of a new bill, would perhaps bear an interpretation as if we feared running out of work.

A motion was made for taking up the funding bill, but withdrawn. No other serious business was gone on. The House adjourned.

A number of us gathered in a knot, and got on the subject of the assumption, the report on which had been just handed in by Mr. Carroll. It is in favor of it. And now, from every appearance, Hamilton has got his number made up. He wanted but one vote long ago.

The sums they have reported to be assumed, is twenty-one millions of dollars. This is most indubitably to cover the speculations that have been made in the State debts. This assumption will immediately raise the value of the State securities, and enable those people who have plunged themselves over head and ears in those speculations, to emerge from impending ruin, and secure them the wages of speculation. The report is ordered to be printed.

After dismissing this subject, we got on the prospect of an approaching war between Spain and England. Here was a large field for conjecture, and we indulged our fancies on the subject, until near three o'clock.

I will here note down an observation, which I wonder never made an impression on the Pennsylvanians. Every State is charged with having local views, designs, &c. Could any motive of this kind be justly chargeable on our State in adopting the constitution? By our impost, we laid many of the neighboring States under contribution —part of Jersey, Delaware, part of Virginia, and almost the whole of the western country. It appears one fourth of the whole impost is received at Philadelphia. This was a great sacrifice. Quere— Did our politicians ever think of this advantage?

July 13. I attended this day at the Hall, at the usual time, or rather sooner. General Schuyler only was before me. Our President came next. They sat opposite to me, and we had a long chat on various subjects, but nothing very interesting. Mr. Morris came at last.

The resolution for the assumption of twenty-one millions of the State debts, was taken up. This was perhaps the most disorderly day ever we had in Senate. Butler was irregular, beyond all bearing. Mr. Morris said openly, before Senate was formed, *I am for a six per cent. fund on the whole; and if gentlemen will not vote for that, I will vote against the assumption.* I thought him only in sport then. But he three times, in Senate, openly avowed the same thing, declaring he was, in judgment, for the assumption; but if gentlemen would not vote for six per cent., he would vote against the assumption, and the whole funding bill. His adding the funding bill along with it, in the last instance, operated as some kind of palliation. Izard got up, and attacked him with asperity. Mr. Morris rose in opposition. Then Izard declared he did not mean Mr. Morris, so much did he fear the loss of his vote. But his invective was inapplicable to anybody else. I was twice up, and bore my most pointed testimony against the assumption. It was incurring a certain debt, on uncertain principles. The certain effect was, the incurring and increasing our debt by twenty-one millions, by mere conjecture. This debt was already funded by the States, and was in a train of payment. Why not settle, and let us see how the accounts stand, before the States are discharged of their State debts. I alleged the funds, on which these debts were charged by the States, were those which the States could pay with the greatest facility, as every State had facilities of this kind. The transferring the debt to any general fund, would lose these local advantages. It was dealing in the dark—we had no authentic evidence of these debts. If it was meant as an experiment how far people would bear taxation, it was a dangerous one. I had no notion of drilling people to a service of this kind, &c., &c. But I cannot pretend to write all I said. Mr. Morris has twice this day told me what great disturbances there would be in Pennsylvania, if six per cent. was not carried. I considered these things as threats thrown out against my reappointment. But be it so ; so help me God, I mean not to alter one tittle. I am firmly determined to act without any regard to consequences of this kind. Every legislator ought to regard himself as immortal.

July 14. This day the resolutions on the assumption were taken up. I am so sick and so vexed with this angry subject that I hate to commit anything to writing respecting it. I will, however, seal one of the copies of it in this book as a monument of political absurdity. It had friends enough—fourteen to twelve—so far, but I am not without hopes of destroying it to-morrow. I am now convinced that there must have been something in the way of bargain, as King alleged on Saturday. Ellsworth, at one time this day, used the following words : *No man contemplated a final liquidation of the accounts between the U. S. and the I. S. as practicable or probable.* I took them down, and showed them to Mr. Morris and Mr. Walker. He observed me, and, after some time, got up, and in the course of speaking, said : *A settlement was practicable, and we must have it.*

Mr. Morris, Langdon, and others moved to strike out the third section. We, of the opposition, joined Ellsworth, and kept it in. The State of Pennsylvania has not but about one million of existing State debt. This clause, if the vile bill must pass, may be considered as in her favor ; more especially if they prevail, and prevent a settlement of the accounts.

For some time after the war, certificates were sold as low as nine pence on the £. John Ray, my old servant, told me that he sold one of £80 for £3, and could get no more. But it appears, by a remonstrance of the Executive Council to the Legislature of Pennsylvania entered on their minutes, that the market price was 2/6 on on the £ at the time of passing the funding law. Yet by the instrumentality on a weak, and in some cases interested, Legislature, six per cent. was given on the certificates, or forty-eight per cent. on the real specie value. This Pennsylvania paid for four years. As the certificates were generally below 2/6, it is no exaggeration to say every speculator *doubled* his money in four years, and still has the certificates, on which he expects forty-eight per cent. with respect to the original cost. Thus £100 specie bought £800 in certificates, (perhaps, much more.) These certificates brought £48 per annum for four years=£192, and the holders of certificates remain as clamorous as ever.

July 15. The business of the Senate was soon done this day. The President took up the funding bill without any call for it.

Mr. Morris appeared in high good humor—asked me if anybody had taken me aside to communicate anything to me. I told him no. But it was easy to observe that something was going on. He said there was, but did not tell me what it was, nor did he affect to know. I saw Carroll writing a ticket with a number of names on it, sand, and put it by. In the meanwhile, up rose Ellsworth, and moved that both the funding bill and the resolutions for the assumption should be referred to a committee. He was seconded soon. Lee rose—said, we know no good could come from a commitment. Mr. Morris rose—said he was for the commitment; that they might be made in one law, and the rate of interest fixed at six per cent. I rose—said I knew of but two ends generally proposed by commitment. The one was to gain information; the other to arrange principles agreed on. The first was out of the question; the second only could be the object; but what was the materials to be arranged? A bill originated in the other House, and resolves on the assumption, which had originated in this. I knew the opinion of many of the Representatives was opposed to our power of originating anything relating to the subjects of the public debts. Taking two so dissimilar objects together, more especially if our powers were called in question, was the way to lose both. Gentlemen hoped much good from this measure. I wished they might not be disappointed; but I was not certain of anything but delay, which, in our present circumstances, I considered as an evil, &c.

The President, who was, to appearance, in the secret, seemed impatient until I had done; and putting the question, it was carried. The . . . . were all the six per cent. men, and all the assumption men. They carried the committee, all of their own number. This done, the Senate adjourned.

Henry came and sat beside me a good while. He told me that

Carroll wrote his ticket with the seven names, (that being the number of the committee,) before any business whatever was done. This I had observed, in part, myself. We did not need this demonstration to prove that the whole business was prearranged; nor can any person be now at a loss to discover that all the three subjects—residence, assumption, and funds equivalent to six per cent.—were all bargained and contracted for on the principles of mutual accommodation for private interest. The President of the U. S. has (in my opinion) had great influence in this business.

Mr. Maclay intimates that the plan acted on was to give to either New York or Philadelphia the *temporary* residence for the *permanent* residence on the Potomac; and that he found, by demonstration, that this was the case; and that York (New York) would have accepted of the temporary residence if we had not. "But," he adds, "I did not then see so clearly that the abominations of the funding system and the assumption were so intimately connected with it."

July 16, 1790. Senate had not been formed but a few minutes when a message from the President of the U. S. was announced. It was Lear; and the signature of the President to the residence bill was the communication.

Statement of Mr. Jefferson.

In the first volume of Randall's Life of Jefferson, pages 608–11, is a statement of Mr. Jefferson relative to the assumption bill. He observes, that this great and trying question was lost in the House of Representatives, and that Hamilton was in despair. As I was going to the President's one day, I met him in the street. He walked me backwards and forwards before the President's door for half an hour. He painted pathetically the temper into which the Legislature had been wrought; the disgust of those who were called the creditor States; the danger of the secession of their members and the separation of the States. He observed that the members of the administration ought to act in concert; that though this question was not of my department, yet a common duty should make it a common concern; that the President was the center on which all administrative questions ultimately rested, and that all of us should rally around him and support with joint efforts measures approved by him; and that the question having been lost by a small majority only, it was probable that an appeal from me to the judgment and discretion of some of my friends might effect a change in the vote, and the machine of government, now suspended, might be again set in motion.

I told him that I was a stranger to the whole subject; that not having yet informed myself of the system of finance adopted, I knew not how far this was a necessary sequence; that undoubtedly, if its rejection endangered a dissolution of our Union at this incipient stage, I should deem that the most unfortunate of all consequences, to avert which all partial and temporary evils should be yielded. I proposed to him, however, to dine with me the next day, and I would invite another friend or two—bring them into conference together, and I thought it impossible that reasonable men, consulting together coolly, could fail, by some mutual sacrifices of opinion, to form a compromise which was to save the Union.

The discussion took place. I could take no part in it but an exhortatory one, because I was a stranger to the circumstances which should govern. But it was finally agreed that whatever importance had been attached to the rejection of the proposition, the preservation of the Union and of concord among the States was more important, and that, therefore, it would be better that the vote of rejection should be rescinded, to effect which some members should change their votes. But it was observed that this pill would be peculiarly bitter to the southern States, and that some concomitant measure should be adopted to sweeten it a little to them. There had before been propositions to fix the seat of Government either at Philadelphia or at Georgetown on the Potomac, and it was thought that by giving it to Philadelphia for ten years, and to Georgetown permanently afterwards, this might, as an anodyne, calm, in some degree, the ferment which might be excited by the other measure alone. So two of the two Potomac members, White and Lee—but White with a revulsion of stomach almost convulsive—agreed to change their votes, and Hamilton undertook to carry the other point. In doing this, the influence he had established over the eastern members, with the agency of Robert Morris with those of the middle States, effected his side of the engagement, and so the assumption was passed, and twenty million of stock divided among favored States, and thrown in as a pabulum to the stock jobbing herd. This added to the number of votaries to the Treasury, and made its chief master of every vote in the Legislature which might give to the Government the direction suited to his political views.

I know well, and so must be understood, that nothing like a majority in Congress had yielded to this corruption. Far from it. But a division not very unequal had already taken place, in the honest part of that body, between the parties styled Republican and Federal.

Mr. Randall observes that the whole amount of State debt and interest included in " the assumption " ultimately proved about two and a half millions of dollars more than named by Mr. Jefferson. Mr. Gallatin, a few years afterwards, observed, that had the United States waited to assume the State debt till the accounts had been finally settled, instead of assuming at random before a final settlement had taken place, the very same result which now exists might have been effected; and the amounts of the Union with the individual States might have been placed in the same relative situation in which they now stand, by assuming eleven millions, instead of twenty-two. The additional and unnecessary debt created by that fatal measure amounts, therefore, to $10,883,628 58. (The State debts were assumed to the amount of about twenty-one millions and a half.)

Mr. Maclay Proceeds.

The pension bill came up from the House of Representatives. The committee on the Indian bill reported that twenty thousand dollars, in addition to seven thousand in the hands of the Secretary at War, and six thousand in Georgia, in goods, should be granted for the holding treaties with the Indians, and all this, when there does not appear a shadow of reason for holding a treaty at all with any Indians whatever. Opposition was vain. It was carried.

Now Mr. Morris came raging angry—said he would vote against everything. The committee had agreed to the Secretaries third alternative for the principal, and three per cent. on the interest due, and he had left them. The report came in after some time, and it was proceeded on. I whispered to Mr. Morris, now we had got the residence, it was our province to guard the Union, and promote the strength of the Union by every means in our power, otherwise our prize would be *a blank*. I told him I would move a postponement of the business, and I would wish a meeting of the delegation this evening. He assented. A vast deal was said on the subject of the contract, and breach of obligation. When I rose,

---

NOTE.—The Elder Walcott writes, April 23, 1790, "Your observations respecting the public debts as essential to the existence of the National government, are undoubtedly just. There certainly cannot, at present, exist any other cement. The assumption of the State debts is as necessary, and, indeed, more so, for the existence of the National government than those of any other description. If the State governments are to provide for their payment, these creditors will forever oppose all National provisions, as being inconsistent with their interest; which circumstances, together with the habits and pride of local jurisdiction, will render the States very refractory. A refusal to provide for the State debts, which, it seems, has been done by a committee of Congress, if persisted in, I consider as an overthrow of the National government."—*Gibbs' Memoirs of Wolcott, I, page 45. See also Von Holst's Constitutional History of the United States, page 84.*

and stated that I had no difficulty on that head.   That we stood here as legislators.   Judges, and executive officers, were bound to observe laws and contracts.   But justice was the great rule which we should govern our conduct by.   The holder of the certificate called: Do me justice.   But the original performer of the service, who sold it for one eighth part of the nominal value, and on whom the tax to make it good is about to fall, cries : Do me justice also. Both sides of this picture ought to be viewed, and their relative numbers to each other.   No guess could be made in this matter, but by comparing the number of speculators with the number of those who had sold, and perhaps the ratio would not be one to one hundred.   It was also true, there were a class of men, the original holders, who were not embraced in the above description ; but if we cast our eye over the calamities of the late war, they would appear to be the fortunate characters.   All the others who touched Continental money, were taxed by it, and it finally sunk in their hands.   The original holders have, if not the whole value, at least something to show, &c., &c.   I hoped for the progress of the public business, and that a short postponement would perhaps bring us nearer together, and moved for to-morrow, but it was not carried.   The report was pushed with violence, and all carried, twenty members rising for it, four only sat—two going out.   The President said twenty for, four against.

When they came to the part for engrafting the assumption resolves on the bill, Mr. Lee, with what assistance I gave him, retarded the business a little.   When I spoke I endeavored to narrow the ground a little, and spoke solely to the question of combining the assumption with the funding bill.   The funding bill was to provide for the domestic debt which floated at large, and was at this time in no train of payment.   The propriety of paying the foreign and domestic was admitted by every person.   It was really the business which brought us together.   But here we must not pass it unless we tack it to another, which we consider as a political absurdity.   This was contradicting the spirit of free legislation.   Every subject ought to hang on its own merits.   It was offering violence to our understandings.   I said a good deal on the subject, and could not restrain myself from going into the merits of the assumption.   But I might as well have poured out speech to senseless stalks or stones.   It was carried against us, fifteen to eleven.   A committee was immediately appointed to make the arrangements.   We adjourned.

I came down stairs, and all the speculators, both of the Representatives and city, were about the iron rails.   Ames and Sedgwick were conspicuous among them.   The Secretary and his group of speculators are at last, in a degree, triumphant. His gladiators, with the influence that has arisen from six dollars per day, have wasted us many months in this place. But I cannot see that I can do any further good here, and I think I had better go home. Everything, even to the naming of a committee, is prearranged by Hamilton and his group of speculators. I cannot even find a single member to condole in sincerity with me over the political calamities of my country.

July 17. Attended the Hall. Little was done, and we sat waiting an hour for the committee to report the bill, with amendments. It was done. An attempt was made to pass it immediately by a third reading down to the House of Representatives. It was moved that it should be printed. This was opposed. The President gave the history of both the bill and resolutions. With respect to order, he made this out to be third reading ; and of course the question would be the sending it to the Representatives.

It was now proposed, as an expedient, that the Secretary should read the bill from his desk, for information of the members. This obtained, and now, behold, to a great many innovations and amendments, a whole new clause was added. There was something of unfairness in this. It was, however, ordered to be printed for Monday.

When I came down stairs, Mr. Clymer came to where I stood, with General Irwin. We talked over the general belief that the assumption was forced on us to favor the views of speculation.. Mr. Clymer mentioned one contract on which about 8/ in the pound had been cleared on £80,000. General Irwin seemed to scruple—8/ in the pound. Mr. Clymer said he was not so sure of the rate cleared, but the sum speculated on was £80,000. Much of this business was done in the 'Change alley way. Constable, however, is known, in the beginning of the session, to have cleared thirty-five thousand dollars on a contract for seventy thousand. The whole town almost has been busy at it ; and of course all engaged in influencing the measures of Congress. Nor have the members of Congress themselves kept their hands clean from this work. The unexampled success has obliterated every mark of reproach, and from henceforth we may consider speculation as a congressional employment. Nay, all the abominations of the South sea bubble are outdone in this vile business. In wrath, I wish the same fate may attend the projectors of both.

18th July. This day the delegation dined at Brandon's. Mr. Morris stated to the representatives the train the business was in with the Senate. Mentioned the importance of completing the funding law, particularly to us who now had the residence of Congress before us. That the rising of Congress without funding might go to shake and injure the Government itself, &c. We had much talk, but nothing was concluded, or any agreement entered into. Mr. Fitzsimmons averred, in the most unequivocal manner, the grand object of the assumption to be *the collecting all the resources of the United States into one treasury.* Speaking of the State of Pennsylvania, he avowed she would be a debtor State to a large amount on the settlement of the accounts, and the next moment said she would draw interest on $3,000,000 annually. It is not easy to reconcile his assertions on this subject. A great deal of loose talk passed among us. As I had the delegation together, I mentioned my intention of going home, and desired to know if any of them had any objection; but no objection was made, and I believe I will set off to-morrow afternoon.

July 19. I attended the Hall at the usual time. And now the material business of the day, the consolidated funding bill and assumption, were taken up. Mr. Morris showed a vindictive and ireful disposition from the very start, and declared he would have the yeas and nays on every question. This, in fact, is declaring war against me only, as it is me only who they can affect in Pennsylvania. I know they mean to slay me with the sword of the public creditors. He was as good as his word, and moved every point to increase the demand against the public, and uniformly called yeas and nays. All the motions were made for augmentations by him, Schuyler, and King. *Vide* the minutes for the yeas and nays.

When he moved that six per cent. should be paid on the back interest, as there were but four of them for it, and enough did not rise for the yeas and nays, I told him I was sorry to see him in distress, and jumped up. If I can turn these yeas and nays against him, the act will be a righteous one.

In the language and calculations of the Treasury, the third alternative is actually six per cent., without taking in the advantage of quarterly over annual payments, grounded on the irredeemable quality of the debt. But I really question if we shall ever see that 'Change alley doctrine established here, which makes debt valuable in proportion to that qualification. It never can happen without a gradual fall of interest, which, in this country, may be rather considered as impracticable.

Before Congress met, I walked awhile across the Chamber with Mr. Lee. He lamented, equally with me, the baneful effects of the funding disease. No nation ever has adopted it, without having either actually suffered shipwreck, or being on a voyage that must inevitably end in it.   The separation from Great Britain seemed to assign us a long run of political existence ; but the management of the Secretary will soon overwhelm us with political ruin.   Schuyler assigned a new kind of reason this day for taxation.   Three million and a half of dollars raised annually, would be only one dollar per head on an average.   It was nothing, &c.   It is true, it is not an heavy tax, but it ought not to be imposed without necessity.

July 20. We went this day at the funding system, and pursued it with nearly the same temper that we did yesterday.   Mr. Morris had often declared himself, that he would be for an assumption equal to the representation, and had calculated a schedule for the purpose ; but all I could say to him, he would not gratify me in moving it.   I knew there was no chance of carrying it.   But he levelled his whole force against the nineteenth section, which, in fact, is the only one favorable to our State, for our existing State debt cannot be much more than one million.   I will refer to the minutes for the proceedings of the day.   Mr. Morris having often threatened that he would vote against the bill, at last made this remarkable speech : *Half a loaf is better than no bread.   I will consent to the bill on behalf of the public creditors, for whom I am interested,* (I looked up at him, and he added,) *as well as for the rest of the Union.*   This last shed some palliation over his expressions.

I contended that the speculators, generally, had dealt on the face of the certificates ; or, if they dealt on the amount, it was always at an abated rate.   Clear proof they never expected the back interest to be funded.   By the bill, every hundred of principle draws four annually ; and as the back interest is about on an average equal to half the principal, (at least it is so by the Secretary's report,) this, at three per cent., adds one and a half more—equal five and one half per cent. per annum for ten years ; and then the other third, (or what is equal to it in 'Change alley circulation,) comes in at six per cent., which added, gives about seven and a half per cent. on the face of the original certificate.

I have turned the leaf, to note that I may consider myself as now having passed the Rubicon with the Philadelphians.

Mr. Morris told me this day, I must allow myself to get the lands of which he had spoken to me.   I told him all on my part was ready, only put the warrants into my hands.   I, however, added : We have ruined our land office by the assumption.   The State certificates were the materials to buy lands with.   The offices will now be shut, for neither State money nor specie can be got or spared for it. He was silent, and I really thought he looked as if he feared that his conduct would be turned against him in the public eye.

July 21, 1790. King's motion of yesterday for postponement, and sundry other matters which I had observed, made me fearful that some storm was gathering. I called on Mr. Morris and expressed my apprehension, and proposed to him that if any unexpected maneuver should display itself, we should, with the utmost apparent coolness, call for a concurrence of the resolution for the adjournment on the 27th.

Attended at the Hall. The first business in the Senate was the new bill of ways and means. Committed.

A message, with a bill, respecting consuls and vice consuls.

The bill for the military grants of lands to the Virginia officers. Committed.

The Senate was now full, and the funding bill was taken up for the last time. I made a despairing effort.

Having almost uniformly opposed the measures of Congress during the present session, some general declarations of my principles or motives may be necessary, to prevent any suspicion of a disposition inimical to the Government itself.

First, then, I am totally opposed to the practice of funding, upon republican as well as economical principles. I deny the power, as well as justice, of the present generation charging debts, more especially irredeemable ones, upon posterity; and I am convinced that they will one day negative the legacy. I will suppose (suppositions are common in this House) that not one member of Congress has been influenced by any personal motive whatever in arranging the American funding system, which now spins on the doubtful point of pass or not pass; and as it falls may turn up happiness or misery for centuries to come. No; I will take gentlemen at their word, and believe that it is the glare of British grandeur, supposed to follow from her funds, that has influenced their conduct, and that their intentions are pure, wishing to render America great and happy by a similar system. This will lead to an inquiry into the actual state of Britain, and here, I trust, we shall find all is not gold that glitters.

It is (if I mistake not) about a century since the commencement of the English funds, or, in other words, since that nation began to mortgage the industry of posterity to gratify the ambition and avarice of the then Government. Since that period, wars have been almost continual. The pretexts have been ridiculous—balance of power, balance of trade, honor of the flag, sovereignty at sea, &c.; but the real object was to fill the treasury to furnish opportunity for royal peculation, jobs, and contracts for needy courtiers ; to increase the power of the Crown by the multiplication of revenue and military appointments, and the servility of the funds, for every stockholder is, of course, a courtier. The effect of these wars has been the commotion of almost the whole world ; the loss of millions of lives ; and the English nation stands at this day charged with a debt of about two hundred and fifty millions sterling, the annual interest of which, and charges of collecting in that country, is above eleven millions annually, and would be above fifteen in this.

It has been said that this is nothing in a national point of view, as the nation owes it to individuals among themselves. This is true only in part, as foreigners draw great sums. Yet it is believed that near half a million of the inhabitants of Great Britain, including army, navy, revenue, and stockholders, are supported from the treasury. The whole of them, be the number what it may, must be considered as unproductive drones, who are ever ready to support administration, be it ever so oppressive to their fellow-citizens.

There is another calculation said to be much more exact, viz : That near a million of paupers, reduced by exorbitant taxes below the power of housekeeping, are dependent on national charity and poor rates. Great cry has been made about Mr. Pitt as the political savior of his country. That he has paid part, and will, finally, discharge the whole of the national debt. This is a vile deception. By some management between him and the stockholders, as he buys, they raise the price of the remaining stock, the aggregate value of which is now greater, at market price, than when he began to purchase, so that the nation, instead of gaining, is a loser to the amount of the new duties imposed. It is not likely that the trading of government in stock or certificates ever will have a different effect.

There is another part of his conduct for which I am ready to give him proper credit.

It is in vain to expect the payment of the British debt in any other way than by a national bankruptcy and revolution. Is this, then, the precipice to which we would reduce the rising nation of North America. It may be said none of us will live to see it. Let us, at least, guard our memories from the reproach of such misconduct.

It may be here asked : What then is to be done ?

Just what the public expectation called for. The western lands have been considered from the beginning of the late contest as the fund for discharging the expenses of the war. The old Congress made laudable advances in this way. The present session has not passed without applications on that subject, as well from companies among ourselves as persons from Europe. We have now a revenue far exceeding the limited five per cent., which was the desideratum of the old Congress, and the want of which occasioned the formation of our present constitution, and fully sufficient to discharge a reasonable interest, proportionate to the market price of the public debt, until the whole is extinguished by the western sales. Thus no one will sustain loss. Substantial justice will be done, and the public expectation will be fully satisfied. But to bind down the public by an irredeemable debt, with such sources of payment in our power, is equally absurd as shackling the hands and feet with fetters rather than walking at liberty.

The friends of the bill paid no attention whatever to me, and were but too successful in engaging the attention of others by nods, whispers, engaging in conversation, &c. Morris, Dalton, and some others went out, and stayed for an hour. They carried the bill against us—fourteen to twelve. It is in vain to dissemble the chagrin which I have felt on this occasion.

We had a resolution relating to Howell's committee. I am of the committee.

Report of joint committee on settlement bill read for information, but could not be acted on, as the bill is in the power of the lower House.

I find I need be under no uneasiness about the residence bill.

July 22, 1790. Attended the Hall this day, as much to take the wrinkles out of my face which my yesterday's disappointment had placed in it, as for anything else. It is in vain to think of changing a vote any way. I can be of no further use, and will absolutely leave them. It is certainly a defect in my political character that I cannot help embarking my passions, and considering the interest of the public as my own. It was so while I was at the bar, in respect of my clients, when I thought their cause just. Well, be it so. It has its inconveniences, and hurts my health; but I declare I never will endeavor to mend it.

Attended all the committees on which I was, and gave my opinion as to the reports, &c.

In Senate the collection bill was reported. Almost an entire new system, or the old one so renovated as to make a volume of new work for Congress. I listened an hour to the reading of it. Rose, bade a silent and lasting farewell to the Hall, and went to my lodgings for the purpose of packing.

The following is written with a different ink, and may have been written on a subsequent day.

And now at last we have taken leave of New York. It is natural to look at the prospect before us.

The citizens of Philadelphia (such is the strange infatuation of self love) believe that ten years is eternity to them with respect to the residence, and that Congress will, in that time, be so enamored of them, as never to leave them; and all this with the recent example of New York before their eyes, whose allurements are more than ten to two, compared with Philadelphia. To tell the truth, I know no so unsocial a city as Philadelphia. The gloomy severity of the Quakers has proscribed all fashionable dress and amusement. Denying themselves these enjoyments, they, as much as in them lies, endeavor to deprive others of them also; while at the same time there are not in the world more scornful or insolent characters than the wealthy among them. . . . No; these feeble expectations will fail. Go they must.

Nay, taking it in another point of view. Political necessity urges them, and a disruption of the Union would be the consequence of a refusal.

There is, however, a further and more latent danger which attends their going. Fixed, as Congress will be, among men of other minds, on the Potomac, a new influence will, in all probability, take place, and the men of New England, who have hitherto been held in check by the patronage and loaves and fishes of the President, combined with a firm expectation that his resignation (which is expected) will throw all power into their hands, may become refractory, and endeavor to unhinge the Government. For my knowledge of the eastern characters warrants me in drawing this conclusion, that they will cabal against and endeavor to subvert any government which they have not the management of.

The effect must be sensibly felt in Philadelphia, should a great commercial town arise on the Potomac. She now supplies all the over hills country, and even the frontiers of Virginia and other Southern States, with importations. This must cease; nor need she expect a single article of country produce in return from the west side of Susquehanna.

It is true that the genius of Virginia and Maryland is rather averse to exclusive commerce. The Southern planter, situated on his extensive domain, surrounded with his slaves and dependents, feels diminution, and loses his consequence by being jumbled among brokers and factors. And yet we have seen what Baltimore has become, in a few years, from the small beginnings of a few Pennsylvanians at first, and afterwards by the accession of other strangers, for, wherever the carcass of commerce is, thither will the eagles of traffic be gathered. For my own part, I would rather wish that the residence of Congress should not be subject to commercial influence.

Too much has that influence, conducted by the interest of New England, whose naval connections throws them into that scale, governed—nay, tyrannized—in the councils of the Union. My consolation for going to the Potomac is: That it may give a preponderance to the agricultural interest. Dire, indeed, will be the contest, but I hope it will prevail. I cannot, however, help concluding that all these things would have been better on the Susquehanna. But, quere, is not this selfish, too? Aye; but it may, nevertheless, be just.

End of journal of the second session, and the last at New York.

Mr. Maclay has intimated that President Washington, during the second session of Congress, exercised an influence in favor of locating the permanent seat of government on the Potomac. Washington probably felt a strong desire in favor of such a location, but there is no reasonable probability that he used or encouraged any means deemed by him improper in order to effect or promote it. But Mr. Maclay has not furnished any evidence that the President interfered during the *first* session in favor of the Potomac.

But from the journal it appears that the *permanent* seat might then have been fixed on the Susquehanna, with the aid of Mr. Morris; and at Germantown, with the assistance of Mr. Maclay. So it appears that the permanent seat was lost to Pennsylvania by a want of concert, or by reason of disagreement, between its own Senators.

The speculations of Mr. Maclay as to the effect upon *Philadelphia* of the location upon the Potomac, have been futile. Washington has not become " *a great commercial town ;*" it has little or no foreign commerce, but derives most of its mercantile supplies from Baltimore and other more northern cities, and the commercial interests of Philadelphia have not been materially impaired by the southern location of the seat of government. The railroads and coal fields, the vast agricultural and manufacturing operations, and other industrial pursuits, of the people of Pennsylvania, have made Philadelphia a great and prosperous city, worthy of the great State in which it is situate.

Congress continued to sit after the termination of Mr. Maclay's journal relative to proceedings during the second session, and adjourned till the first Monday of December, 1790, then to meet at Philadelphia.

THIRD SESSION OF THE FIRST SENATE.

On Monday, the 6th of December, 1790, the two Houses assembled at the city of Philadelphia.

The Senate having assembled, it was ascertained that the Vice President and thirteen Senators were present, (*Mr. Maclay* included.) The Senate then received the credentials of Philemon Dickinson, of New Jersey, in the place of Governor *Patterson*, *resigned*, and of *James Monroe*, in the place of William Grayson, *deceased*.

The President, (Washington,) in his address, states that the district of *Kentucky*, now a part of Virginia, has concurred in certain propositions contained in a law of that State, in consequence of which the district is to become a distinct member of the Union, in case the requisite consent of Congress be added. For this same, the application is now made.

Mr. Maclay, in his journal, proceeds :

December 1, 1790. Late in the afternoon I arrived in Philadelphia, in order to attend Congress, which is to meet on Monday next. Saw nobody this afternoon nor evening.

2. Dressed, and called first on General Mifflin. He was abroad. Then on Mr. Morris, who received me with frankness. Called on the President, Clymer, and at Fitzsimmons'.

Met with Mr. Langdon, and went a visiting, in which we spent the forenoon. Called in the evening at McConnell's, the broker. He told me the public creditors were very busy, under their chairman, preparing petitions, memorials, &c., for Congress. He readily joined me, said it was carried on to answer electioneering purposes.

Saturday, 4. I have deliberated much on the subject, whether I will call to see Bingham, Powell, and others. I have called on Morris, Clymer, and Fitzsimmons. Why not on them? By the rules of etiquette, perhaps, they should call on me. I have resolved all over in my mind, *Jacta est alea*, and I will go. But as I went, I fell in with Mr. Clymer, and away we went a visiting. Clymer certainly means to be on good terms with me. We had two long visits. I called at Bingham's. Found him at home, and had a long

(263)

chat. Took leave, and left a card at Mr. Powell's. Called at Mr. Chew's, who urged me to stay for dinner. I accepted his invitation for two o'clock, and the rest of the day was accordingly disposed of, for it was past three before we sat down.

I called twice this day at Dr. Rush's, but saw him not. Saw the Speaker. The Speaker said, on the authority of Dr. Rush, that we would all be reëlected. Believe it not.

Sunday, 5. Was sent for early by Mr. Morris on the subject of taking up frontier lands. I agreed to procure him a draft of such parts of the State as had vacant lands in them. No contract with him. I mean to have such a draft made for the use of the members of the Assembly, or, at least, for their information. Pressed me to dine with him. Did so.

Mr. Powel returned my visit. Visited Langdon in the evening.

Monday, 6. My brother informed me this morning that Charles Thompson had applied to one Collins, a member from Berks, for his interest to obtain my place as Senator.

Attended at the Hall at eleven. A Senate was formed, but no business done, save the sending a message by our Secretary to the Representatives that the Senate was ready to proceed to business. Spent the rest of the day in visiting.

December 7. Attended, at eleven, at the Hall. A House was formed by the representatives. On the 7th of January last, King had introduced a new record altogether on the minutes, the intention of which was to secure the delivery of the President's speech in the Senate Chamber. A resolution verbatim with the entry of last January was moved, carried, and sent down for concurrence. While this was done with us, a resolution passed the Representatives for a joint committee waiting on the President, with information that quorums were formed in both Houses. Our Secretary and the clerk passed each other on the stairs with their respective resolutions. Each House appointed committees under their own resolutions, and the committees met. The representatives urged that it was idle to name any place to do business in until it was known whether any business would be done. The President was in our favor. This silly thing kept us talking an hour and a half. The clerk of the Representatives announced the non-concurrence of our resolution. This had like to have raised a flame, but a motion was at length made and carried for the concurrence of the resolution which came up. The joint committee now waited on the President, who charged them with information that he would to-morrow, at twelve o'clock, deliver his speech to both Houses in the *Senate Chamber*, and so ended this arduous affair. The Senate adjourned.

The first levee was held this day, at which I attended.

8. This was the day assigned for the President to deliver his speech, and was attended with all the bustle and hurry usual on such occasions. The President was dressed in black, and read his speech well enough, or at least tolerably. After he was gone, and the Senate only remained, our President seemed to take great pains to read it better. If he had such a view, he succeeded; but the difference between them amounted to this : one might be considered as at home, and the other in a strange company. The speech was committed. Let me return to the President. Does he really look like a man who enters into the spirit of his employment ? Does he show that he receives it in trust for the happiness of the people, and not as a fee simple for his own emolument ? Time and practice will, perhaps, best elucidate this point.

December 9. This day in the Senate afforded neither motion nor debate. The communications hinted at in the President's speech were delivered to us and continued to be read till past two o'clock, when the Senate adjourned.

A war has been actually undertaken against the Wabash Indians, without any authority of Congress ; and what is worse, so far as intelligence has come to hand, we have reason to believe it has been unsuccessful. Mind what comes of it.

The Vice President, Mr. Wyngate, and some more of us, stood by the fire. When the affairs of France were talked, I said the National Assembly had attacked royalty, nobility, hierarchy, and the bastile altogether, and seemed likely to demolish the whole. The Vice President said it was impossible to destroy nobility—it was founded in nature. . . . . The Vice President's arguments were drawn from the respect shown to the sons of eminent men, although vicious and undeserving.

When the parties had nearly exhausted themselves, I asked whether our Indians might not be considered as having devised an excellent method of getting rid of this prejudice by ranking all the children after *the mother*. This sent off the whole matter in a smile. Adams, however, either never was cured, or is relapsed into his nobilimania.

December 10. This day was unimportant in the Senate. The committees reported an answer to the President's speech. The echo was a good one, and was adopted without material amendment.

A packet had arrived from France some time ago, directed to the President and members of Congress. The President, from motives of delicacy, would not open it. It came to the Senate and was sent back to the President, and now returned opened. It contained a number of copies of the eulogiums delivered on Doctor Franklin, by order of the National Assembly. Our President looked over the letter some time, and then began reading the additions that followed the President's name. He was a Doctor of the Sorbonne, &c., &c., to the number of fifteen, (as our President said.) These appellations of office he chose to call *titles;* and then said some sarcastic things against the National Assembly, for abolishing titles. I could not help remarking that this whole matter was received and transacted with a coldness and apathy that astonished me ; and the letter and all the pamphlets were *sent* down to the Representatives, as if unworthy the attention of our body. I deliberated with myself whether I should not rise and claim one of the copies in right of my being a member. I would only have got into a wrangle by so doing, without working any change on my fellow members. There might be others who indulged the same sentiments, but 'twas silence all.

13th. The Senate having adjourned over from Friday to this day, (Monday,) nothing of public nature has taken place. I was engaged Saturday and this morning in negotiating the sale of some certificates, which I completed, and placed the money in the bank.

The minutes were read about half after eleven, and the committee on the business reported that the President had appointed twelve to receive our address. Twelve soon came, and we went on this piece of formality, which finished the senatorial business of the day.

This day completed the sale of Mr. Harris' certificates* at the most I could make of them.

General Harmer's Expedition.

Official information was communicated to the Senate of General Harmar's expedition. The ill fortune of the affair breaks through all the coloring that is given to it. 'Tis said one hundred Indians have been killed. But two hundred of our own people have certainly perished in the expedition.

---

*Note.—The certificates were those which John Harris, the founder of Harrisburg, received for the £3,000 he lent to the Government immediately after the declaration of independence. They were sold for about seventeen shillings and six pence for the pound, the interest from 1776 thus being lost.

General St. Clair.

†Note.—After the defeat of General Harmar, General Arthur St. Clair became commander-in-chief of the army designed to operate against the Miami Indians. General Harmar had been, but a short time before, defeated. When St. Clair was about to leave to take command of the expedition, Presi-

Levee Day.

This was levee day, and I accordingly dressed and did the needful. It is an idle thing, but what is the life of man but folly, and this is, perhaps, as innocent as any of them, as far as respects the persons acting. The practice, however, considered as a feature of royalty, is certainly anti-republican. This certainly escapes nobody. The royalists glory in it as a point gained. The republi-

---

dent Washington had a parting interview with him, in which he observed, you have had your instructions from the Secretary of War. I had an eye to them. I will add, "beware of surprise." You know how Indians fight. I repeat, "*beware of surprise.*" But St. Clair was surprised and was defeated, Washington refused to convene a court of inquiry, and St. Clair resigned. Congress, however, appointed a committee of investigation, which exonerated him. He afterwards applied to Congress to remunerate him for moneys advanced by him while in the revolutionary service. Whilst his matter was before Congress, *General Ogle,* of the Somerset district, in western Pennsylvania, earnestly and eloquently remarked: "This was a subject not to be mentioned in the House in the face of day; the treatment of that man ought to be spoken of here only *in the night.* For his part, if there was a statute as strong as brass, or as solid as the pillars of the Capitol, he would blow it to powder to do justice to a soldier of the Revolution."

The above has been taken from a memoir relative to John Smilie, long a member of Congress from the Fayette district, in Western Pennsylvania, by the late James Veech, Esquire, of Pittsburgh.

A memoir of General Ogle, by Doctor William Elder, will be found in Putnam's Magazine for June, 1853, page 661, &c. The following is a part of that memoir in reference to a public address by General Ogle, and which is here cited as illustrative of his strong common sense, and rude, impassioned eloquence:

"I tell ye, my dear fellows, we have had the wool pulled over our eyes by the European writers, which we are all the time reading. Of course they know no better than to call Bonaparte a hero, and Wellington another for conquering him. That will do for tother side of the water, for everything is great or small by comparison. But comparing themselves with themselves they are not wise; and they don't know enough to discern the true standard. Heaven help them to better doctrine and diet. They will have such generals as Washington and Jackson, when they have the same occasion for them; and when they go to fighting for progress, instead of power, and organize their civil institutions in the faith of the people's honesty and capacity for self-government, fully, fairly, and faithfully, they may put their achievements down upon the page of history in parallel columns with us."

In relation to General St. Clair, it is added that the act of Congress in his behalf failed by a vote of fifty to forty-eight, but the Legislature of Pennsylvania at length, in his old age and poverty, came to his relief so far as to pass an act granting him $200, to be paid immediately, and an annuity of $350 during life, to be paid half yearly. The act was approved by Governor Snyder on 10th March, 1817. The old General did not live long to enjoy the benefit of the enactment. He died in August, 1818.

In 1794, the Indians on the Miami were defeated by General Wayne, and in the next year a treaty was made with them.

cans are borne down by fashion, and a fear of being charged with a want of respect to General Washington.

December 15. This day was really a blank in the Senate. Two petitions were presented, which being only counterparts of what were expected to be acted upon in the lower House, were laid on our table. Mr. Morris was called often out by our own citizens. The door-keeper named the people who sent in for him. P. Muhlenburg was one. Col. Hartley was another. This day certificates raised four pence in the pound.

December 18. Being Saturday, and excessively cold, stayed at home all day. Was visited by Madison, Bishop, and White, and many other respectable characters.

Monday paid some visits. Attended at the Hall. Congress were engaged until about three, with the reading of a long and most *imprudent* memorial from the public creditors.

Tuesday, 21. The memorial and remonstrance of the public creditors engaged us some time. I saw, or at least thought I saw, a storm gathering in the countenances of the Senators yesterday, and moved an adjournment. I told Mr. Morris of it, and he agreed it was so, and for fear of this same storm, he moved an adjournment this day. But Schuyler had a long motion ; it concluded with the *danger and inexpediency* of any innovation in the funding. A variety of opinions were now offered as to the time of proceeding to-morrow. Thursday agreed to take it up. This day the Governor of our State was proclaimed. Mr. Morris spoke early to me. His words were : I expect every moment to hear from the delegation who are now meeting to fix a time to wait on the Governor, and I will let you know of it. I waited, but heard nothing from him.

December 22. I called this morning on the Comptroller, and he was obliging enough to send for Mr. Smilie, and did my character justice in respect to sundry aspersions cast on it by Mr. Finley and *Smiley.*

I cannot help wishing myself honorably quit of this enviable station. What an host of enemies has it not raised about me, with calumny and detraction in every corner. Fate but grant me this, that their dissentions and cabals may protract the election until my period be expired ; and if you find me in this city twenty-four hours longer, inflict what insult you please on me. Placed on an eminence, slander and defamation are the hooks applied to pull me down. It is natural to make some efforts to disengage oneself from such grapplings, yet even the slightest endeavor of this kind is reprobated as an attempt to procure votes.

December 23. Attended at the Hall. Mr. Morris was late in coming. And now the resolution respecting the public creditors, or rather in answer to their memorial, was taken up. Every mode was tried to let them down easy, as the phrase is. Great accommodation was tried to get Mr. Morris to come into the measure, and it really seemed more than once that he was satisfied with Ellsworth's modification of the resolution. King offered a second, or, perhaps, I might say a fourth one, which was adopted. Mr. M. told me he would agree to it. But a number rose for the yeas and nays. Mr. Monroe, of Virginia, desired to be excused, and was so. Mr. Morris was the only nay. I was in good humor myself, although I considered the vote of this day as waging a war with the public creditors, in which I will most probably lose my reëlection, and was sorry to see my colleague manifest such a degree of peevishness. He left the Senate chamber immediately after the vote.

A vote for the inexpediency of altering the funding system at this time from a person who uniformly opposed the system in its passage into a law may seem to require some apology.

My vote proceeds, not from an approbation of the funding system, but from a total disapprobation of the memorial now before us. Upon republican principles, I hold the voice of the majority to be sacred. That the funding law has obtained that majority is undeniable, and acquiescence is our duty; but I never will subscribe to a blind and unalterable one. The making debts irredeemable and perpetual is a power that I am convinced posterity will spurn at. The western lands are the natural fund for the redemption of our national debt. It is now unproductive. Perhaps, the fault is ours that it is so. As soon as it is otherwise, I would be happy to see all stock made strictly personal, unalienable, and incapable of descent, or any negotiation, save commutation into lands; and let it die with the obstinate speculator who refuses such commutation. The stockholder to any amount is an unproductive character. Worse; he is the tool of a bad administration. A good one needs none. It is enough that we have seen one generation of them. Let us not perpetuate the breed. Their children, cut off from such expectations, will be restored to industry.

It is a fact, that the six per cent.'s are now nearly at par, or at least this appearance is kept up among the speculators. An act, passed hastily just at the close of the last session, directed the borrowing two millions of dollars, with design of buying in the public debt, and lessening it. The real object was the increasing it, by raising the value. Three millions of florins have been borrowed, in pursuance of this law. The board of purchase, named in the law, completed their purchase of November at about 12/4d on the face, and 7/3 arrears. It was natural to expect this would be about the standing value; but by one effort of impudence, par was demanded in three days on the appearance of the Treasurer's advertisements.

December 24. The papers full of advertisements this day, of stock of every kind for sale, and there is no doubt but the show of sales nearly at par will be kept up, in order to save appearances, and cover the advanced prices which are daily given by the board of purchases, through the medium of the Treasury.

This whole matter of purchasing in stock, to sink the debt, ostensibly, has really no other object but to raise the value of it, and so to make immense fortunes to the speculators, who have amassed vast quantities of certificates for little or nothing. I did not think it possible that mankind could be so easily duped, and yet there never was a vainer task than to attempt to undeceive them.

Very little done in the Senate this day. Sundry communications were made from the Representatives, relating to the settlement of post St. Vincennes, on the Wabash. Which were laid on our table.

Relative to a National Bank.

Yesterday, the Secretary's report on the subject of a national bank was handed to us, and I can readily find that a bank will be the consequence. Considered as an aristocratic engine, I have no great predilection for banks. They may be considered, in some measure, as operating like a tax in favor of the rich, against the poor, tending to the accumulating in a few hands; and under this view, may be regarded as opposed to republicanism. And yet, stock, wealth, money, or property of any kind whatever accumulated, has a similar effect. The power of incorporating may be inquired into. But the old Congess enjoyed it. Bank bills are promissory notes, and of course not money. I see no objection in this quarter. The great point is, if possible, to prevent the making of it a machine for the mischievous purposes of bad ministers; and this must depend more on the vigilance of future legislators, than on either the virtue or foresight of the present ones.

December 25. I was this day assured that the six per cent.'s were above par. The law for purchases allows the overplus money in the Treasury, after satisfying the appropriations, to be laid out in the purchase of certificates, as well as the two millions of dollars to be borrowed abroad. It was originated and passed after I left New York, and is certainly the most impudent transaction that I ever knew in the political world. I regret my being absent when it passed, although my presence could have had no effect whatever on the progress of it, further than I would have borne my testimony against it. This nominal reduction, is a virtual raising of the whole value of the debt. Something of this kind, I have heard, is common in England. When Governments attempt a purchase of any kind of stock, the holders of that kind of stock never fail to raise the residue. Hamilton must have known this well. Our speculators or stockholders knew all this. They have a general communication with each other. They are actuated by one spirit, or I should rather say by Hamilton. Nobody (generally speaking) but them buys; it is easy for them, by preconcert, to settle what proposals they will give in; and these being filed, the commissioners are justified in taking the lowest. I cannot, however, help predicting that when the florins are out there will be a crash, and the stocks will fall.

December 26. Being Sunday, my brother agreed with me that we would visit Doctor Logan. This man has every testimony, both of practice and profession, in favor of his republicanism. He has been in the Assembly of Pennsylvania, and there had it in his power to have formed a coalition with the city interest. He has, however, continued firmly attached to the rural plans and arrangements of life, and the democratic system of government. His motto is *vox populi, vox Dei*. But mottoes and professions now-a-days are as the idle wind, which no one ought to regard unless supported by practice; and scarce can you depend on practice, unless you see it embracing interest. This has been, in some degree, his case. We had been but a little while with him, when we were joined by Judge Burke, of South Carolina. This is the very man who, while in New York, railed so tremendously against the Quakers, and against Philadelphia, and indeed all Pennsylvania, for having Quakers. But behold a wonder. Now he rails against slavery, extols Quakers, and blazes against the attentions showed to General Washington, which he calls idolatry; and that a party wish as much to make him a king, as ever the flatterers of Cromwell wished to raise him to that dignity.

Doctor Logan has Oswald's paper at his devotion, and I can foresee that Burke will discharge many of his sentiments through this channel. Burke said many just things, but he is too new a convert to merit confidence. I find, however, on examination, that this is the same man who wrote against the Cincinnati.

Monday, 27. Just as I came out of the door of the Hall, Hartley had fallen, and broke his arm. I was among the first to show

him every attention that his situation required, and the more especially as I have reason to consider him as inimical to my re-appoint-
ment to the Senate of the United States.

This day produced nothing of consequence in the Senate. My
attention to Hartley prevented my returning into the Senate
Chamber.

Tuesday, 28. Attended the Senate as usual. A slight debate
took place respecting a law for continuing to the States of Rhode
Island, Maryland, and Georgia the *power* to levy certain duties of
tonnage for the purpose of repairs on their respective ports. The
bill was re-committed, with two additional members added to the
committee.

Levee Day.

This being levee day, I attended in a new suit. This piece of duty
I have not omitted since I came to town, and, if there is little harm
in it, there cannot be much good. A reëlection might be among my
misfortunes.

December 29. This day a blank in the Senate with respect to
any business of importance. Mr. Morris told me I was blamed for
not going among the members, and speaking to them. One party
watch and ridicule me, if I am seen speaking a word to a member.
In order to avoid the censure of them, I have rather secreted myself from the members, and the fault is fixed on me.

I called this evening at the lodging of some of the members who
were out. Fitzsimmons had often said he was at home in the evening, and desired me to call. I drank tea with him and the family.
Sat a good while. The chat was various. He did not touch the
subject of my reëlection. He did not come with me to the door
when I took leave. As much as to say, I want no private communication. Be it so. If I want help, I need not look to him for it.
Whatever is, is best ; and I have little doubt that my rejection, if
it takes place, will be best.

December 30. Attended at the Hall at the usual time. A communication from the President respecting the prisoners at Algiers,
fourteen of whom only are alive, was delivered to the Senate. Read,
and committed to the Committee on the Mediteranean Navigation.

Did some business about the offices. Called and sat a good part
of the evening with White, who had two of the Lancaster members
with him. I need say nothing more to them. They now know me.
From White I had much information of the whispers, inuendoes,
and malevolent remarks made respecting me. It was painful, and
I could not refrain demanding of him what or whether any charge

was made against me. No, no, nothing in particular; but everybody says *the people don't like you.* The people won't hear of your reëlection. Who are they that say so? *The leading members of the Assembly.* Officers of the Land Office. Citizens of Philadelphia, and others.

Quere. Is not the same spirit that dictated the ostracism at Athens, the petalism at Syracuse, and similar measures in other places, still prevalent in the human mind and character? The true cause of these banishments, whether by the oyster shell or olive leaf, was really to remove a blameless rival out of the way of less deserving competitors for office, by the name and clamor of the people, when no other cause could be alleged against him. In this way is there not, in every free country, where the competition for office is laid open, a constant ostracism at work on the character of every man eminent for worth or talents? These arts will no doubt prevail on many occasions, but they will not be universally successful. When they do, we must submit to them as in some measure inseparable from republicanism.

December 31. Attended the Senate this day, where nothing was done of any consequence. Sundry papers relating to the inhabitants of post Vincent or Vincennes, on the Wabash, were committed. I was of the committee.

I went a visiting with Langdon. Dined this day with Mr. Morris. I can observe in general rather a coolness of the citizens towards me. Be it so. I will endeavor not to vex myself much with them. This is the last day of the year, and I have faithfully noted every political transaction that has happened to me in it. And of what avail has it been? I thought it possible that I would be called on with respect to the part I had acted in Senate, by the Legislature of Pennsylvania, or at least by some of them. But is there a man of them who has thought it worth while to ask me a single question? No. Are they not, every man of them, straining after offices, posts, and preferments? At least every one of them who has the smallest chance of success? Yes, verily; nor is there a man who seems to care a farthing how I acted, but wish me out to make a vacancy. Reward from men it is in vain to look for. It is, however, of some consequence to me that I have nothing to charge myself with.

31. Having some leisure on hand, I have looked over my minutes for the last month. It is with shame and contrition that I find the subject of my reëlection has engaged so much or, indeed, any of my thoughts. Blessed with affluence, domestic in my habits and manners, rather rigid and uncomplying in my temper, generally op-

posed in sentiments to the prevailing politics of the times, no place-man, speculator, pensioner, or courtier, it is equally absurd for me to wish a continuance in Congress, as to desire to walk among briars and thorns rather than on a beaten road. It may be said a love for the good of my country should influence my wishes. Let those care to whom the trust is committed ; but let me never beg for that trust when, in my own opinion, I have been of so little service, and have sacrificed both health and domestic happiness at the shrine of my country. Nothing that I could do, either by conversation or writing, has been wanting to let men see the danger which is before them. But *seeing* is not the sense that will give them the alarm. Feeling only will have this effect ; and it is hard to say how callous even this may be. Yet when the seeds of the funding system ripen into taxation of every kind, and upon every article ; when the general judiciary, like an enforcing engine, follows them up, seizing and carrying men from one corner of a State to another, and, perhaps, in time, through different States, I should not at all be disappointed if a commotion, like a popular fever, should be excited, and at least attempt to throw off these political disorders. Ill, however, will that government be, under which an old man cannot eke out ten or a dozen years of an unimportant life in quiet ; and may God grant peace in my day.

But as to the point in hand, let me now mark down some rules for my future conduct.

First, then, let me avoid anything that may seem to savor of singularity or innovation ; call on and speak to my acquaintances as formerly ; but avoiding, with the utmost care, the subject of senatorial election, and everything connected with it. If any other person introduces it, he must be either a real or pretended friend. Hear him, therefore, with complacence and even with a thankful air ; avoid every wish or opinion of my own, especially of the negative kind, for everything of the sort will hazard my sincerity.

Should an election come on while I am in town, stay in my place during the time of it ; and if it should be adverse, a thing I can scarce doubt of, immediately send in my resignation, as the appointment of another person must be considered as unequivocal proof of my having lost the confidence of the State. For this purpose, let my letter of resignation be ready, all to the filling the date ; and revise it while I am cool, for it is not unlikely that, with so many eyes upon me, I may undergo some perturbation at the time. Lastly, have my mare in readiness ; and let the first day of my liberty be employed in my journey homewards. A determination of this kind is certainly right ; for I have tried, and feel my own insignificance and total inability to give the smallest check to the torrent which is pouring down upon us. A system is daily developing itself, which must gradually undermine and finally destroy our so much boasted equality, liberty, and republicanism. High wages, ample compensations, great salaries to every person connected with the Government of the United States. The desired effect is already produced; the frugal and parsimonious appointments of the individual States are held in contempt. Men of pride, ambition, talents, all press forward to exhibit their abilities on the theater of the General Government. This, I think, may be termed grade the first; and to a miracle has it succeeded. The second grade or stage is to create and multiply offices and appointments under the General Government, by every possible means, in the diplomacy, revenue, judiciary, and military. This is called giving the President a respectable *patronage*—a term, I confess, new to me in the present sense of it, which I take to mean neither more or less than that the President should always have a number of lucrative places in his gift, to reward those members of Congress who may promote his views, or support his measures; more especially, if by such conduct they should forfeit the esteem of their constituents. We talk of corruption in Britain. I pray we may not have occasion for complaints of a similar nature here. *Respice finem*, as to the third.

January 1, 1791. Neither Congress nor the Legislature of the State met this day. I went to settle some business with the Comptroller of the State, but he was equally complaisant to the day or the Government. I determined to do something since I was out. I visited Hartley, who lies ill with his broken arm. Just as I passed the President's, Griffin called to me, and asked whether I would not pay my respects to the President. I was *in boots* and had on my worst clothes. I could not prevail on myself to go with him. I had, however, passed him but a little way, when Osgood, the Postmaster General, attacked me warmly to go with him. I was pushed forward by him; bolted into the presence; made the President the compliments of the season; had a hearty shake by the hand. I was asked to partake of the punch and cakes, but declined it. I sat down, and we had some chat. But the diplomatic gentry and foreigners coming in, I embraced the first vacancy to make my bow and wish him a good morning.

I called next on the Governor of the State, and paid my compliments, and so came home to my dinner; and thus have I commenced the year 1791.

January 2. Being Sunday, I stayed at home in the forenoon and attended at meeting in the afternoon. To worship once on the day devoted to the Deity is as small a compliment as decency can pay to the religion of any country, and a regard to health will prefer the after to the forenoon service, at this season of the year, as the fire in the stoves has had then time to produce a general effect in warming the house. I saw nobody this day, but received a letter from home by Col. Cook.

January 3. Being Monday, I attended at the Hall early, on a committee respecting the settlers on the Wabash and Mississippi. The business being tedious, the committee agreed to meet to-morrow, at ten o'clock. . . . We had a communication from the President, with some nominations, and one from the Representatives, respecting the Algerines.. It was from Jefferson. It held out that we must either go to war with these piratical States, compound and pay them an annual stipend and ransom our captives, or give up the trade. The report seemed to breathe resentment, and abounded with martial estimates in the naval way. We have now fourteen unhappy men in captivity at Algiers. I wish we had them relieved and the trade to the Mediterranean abandoned. There can be no chance of our wanting a market for our produce. At least nothing of the kind has yet happened.

This day the bank bill reported. It is totally in vain to oppose this bill. The only useful part I can act is to try to make it of some benefit to the public, which reaps none from the existing banks.

January 4. Tuesday, attended early on the committee on the Wabash business. I could not help remarking the amazing predilection of the New England people for each other. There was no room for debate, but good sense, and even demonstration herself, if personified, would be disregarded by the wise men of the East, if she did not come from a new England man.

Several bills were read this day, and business proceeded in the usual routine without any debate of consequence.

Levee Day.

It was levee day. I dressed, and did the duty of it. Handed a petition of Mr. Adlum's to Major Jackson. Nothing else of consequence happened. This petition business carried me there, and now, I think, unless I am somehow called on, I will never see them more.

January 5, Wednesday. Attended early at the Hall to meet the committee, but they let me sit an hour without attending me. Strong had not made his draft of a report, and was busy at it in the Secretary's office, and Ellsworth would do nothing without him. But, at last, both drafts, Strong's and mine, were produced. I was ready to condemn my own when there was a shadow of objection, but even this conduct would not excite a particle of candor. I, however, cared but little, and was so well guarded that the smallest semblance of discontent did not escape me. General Dickerson came in. He took me to one side. You have, said he, enemies in this place. I dined yesterday with the Governor. He is your enemy. He said: You will be hard run, and mentioned Smiley as being your competitor. I thanked him for the communication, nor could I do less, however indifferent I might be as to the event.

Thursday, 6. Nothing of consequence to the continent was transacted this day, unless it was the report of the committee on the Algerine business. The amount of it was : First, the trade of the American States in the Mediteranean cannot be supported without an armed force, and going to war with them. Secondly, this ought to be done as soon as the Treasury of the United States will admit of it. It is evident that war has been engaged in with the Indians on the frontiers in rather an unadvised manner, and it is also evident that there is a wish to engage us in this distant war with these pirates. All this goes to increase our burden and taxes, and these, in a debate of this day, were called the only bonds of our Union. I will certainly oppose all this.

Dined this day with Mr. Bingham. I cannot say that he affects to entertain in a style beyond everything in this place, or, perhaps, in America. He really does so. There is a propriety, a neatness, a cleanliness, that adds to the splendor of his costly furniture and elegant apartments. I am told he is my enemy. I believe it. But let not malice harbor with me. It is not as William Maclay that he opposes me, but as the object that stands in the way of his wishes and the dictates of his ambition.

January 7. Attended Senate as usual. We reported a bill for the Wabash and Illinois donation. Sundry other things were done in the usual routine of business. The Kentucky bill was taken up. I considered it as so imperfectly drawn with respect to what was to be the boundaries of the new State, that I opposed it, and there was much altercation on the subject, but entirely in the gentlemanly way. It ended in a postponement, with the consent of the Virginia member, Mr. Monroe.

Mr. Morris stayed out all the time of the debate. When the Senate adjourned, he asked me to go and eat *pepper-pot* with him. I agreed, and accordingly dined with him *en familie*. I cannot believe that he is my enemy with respect to my reëlection—the thing is impossible. I chatted with the family till near dark, and came home, as I had an opportunity, with Mr. Hanna.

The human heart, really a strange machine. I certainly have severely felt the inconvenience of being from home these two years past, and my judgment plainly tells me that I am wrong in having submitted to it. Further, I cannot help knowing that my reëlection, with no friends and many enemies, is impossible; and yet, under all these circumstances, the man who expresses favorable wishes is by far the most acceptable to me. But, upon the whole, this is right. Good will ought to beget gratitude; but, oh, what a recollection is it, that under such circumstances I am independent; or, in other words, that my manner of living has always been within my means.

Monday, 10. Attended the Hall as usual. The bank bill was the order of the day. I did not embark deeply, but was up two or three times. The debates were conducted rather in a desultory manner. The objectors were Izard, Butler, and Monroe. A postponement took place.

Tuesday, 11. The bank bill taken up, and the debates became rather more close and interesting. I was up several times, but the debates rather on collateral points than on the substance of the bill. The ostensible object held out by Butler and Izard were, that the public should have all the advantages of the bank; but showed no foundation for this—no system—no plan or calculation. They were called on to show any, and were promised support if they could show any practicability in their system. Till after three o'clock was the matter agitated, and a postponement broke up the business of the day.

Wednesday, 12. The bank was the business of this day; but Monroe called for a postponement of the subject, and succeeded.

A bill was now called up respecting consuls and vice consuls. This bill was drawn and brought in by Ellsworth, and, of course, he hung like a bat to every particle of it. The first clause was a mere chaos—style, preamble, and enacting clause, all jumbled together. It was really unremendable—at least the shortest way to amend it was to bring in a new one.

This same Ellsworth is a striking instance how powerful a man may be in some departments of the mind, and defective in others. All powerful and eloquent in debate, he is, notwithstanding, a miserable draughtsman. The habits of the bar and the lists of litigation have formed him to the former; the latter is, in a great degree, the gift of nature.

I dined this day with Mr. Nicholson. The company, Mr. Montgomery, Smiley, B. McClenahan, T. Smith, Kittera, Hamilton, and others. Desultory conversation on a variety of subjects. I left them soon, for from some hints it seemed as if they meant to discourse of the appointment of a Senator, &c. But I will not disgrace myself in this business. Circumstanced as I am, all the caballing and intrigue I could exercise would not be effectual. And suppose me successful, what am I to gain? Pain, remorse, vexation, and loss of health; for I verily believe that my political wrangles have affected my corporeal feelings, so as to bring on, in degree, my rheumatic indisposition. It is a melancholy truth, but I see plainly that even the best men will not emerge to office in republics without submitting, either directly or indirectly, to a degree of intrigue. It is not, perhaps, so much the case in monarchies, for even tyrants wish to be served with fidelity. *Sed ubi plurima notent non ego pancis offendar maculis.*

Thursday, January 13. This day the bank bill was debated, but in so desultory a manner as not to merit the commitment of anything to paper.

This day I dined with General Dickinson. As I went there, I fell in with Mr. Morris. He told me that great discontents prevailed in the General Assembly, and that they were about to instruct their Senators.

The dinner was a great one, and the ladies, three only of whom attended, were richly, or at least fashionably, dressed. Nothing remarkable. I sat between two merchants of considerable note. I broached the subject of the bank, and found them magnetically drawn to the contemplation of the moneyed interest.

Friday, 14. This day, the bank engaged us to the hour of adjournment. It was limited to twenty years. Mr. Morris had yesterday declared, that the public ought to subscribe on the same terms as other individuals. It was not so in the bill. I showed him an amendment to this purpose, and asked him to support me in it. He said Schuyler had told him that Hamilton said it must not be altered, but concluded, I will speak to Hamilton about it. Adjourned over till Monday.

Saturday, 15. This a very disagreeable day. I stayed at home, and read Price on Annuities. I find he establishes an opinion which I had long entertained, that women are longer lived than men. This I used to charge to accidents and intemperance. But he goes further, and seems to place it in nature—as more males than females die in infancy.

Sunday, 16. Went to meeting, and caught some cold, as usual. Spent the residue of the day in reading.

Monday, 17. This day Mr. Morris stayed very late. Langdon came, and complained of him: "This always his way. He never will come when there is any debate." He, however, came. I asked him whether he had called on Hamilton. No. I said I had a mind to move a re-commitment, that the Secretary of the Treasury might be consulted, and furnish the committee with calculations on the subject, as I had no doubt but he had such. He said he would move such a thing, but did not. The question was put on the clause. Several said aye. I got up—spoke longer than I intended —and made such a motion, but my colleague did not second me. I was seconded by Butler.

And now such a scene of confused speeches followed, as I have seldom heard before. Everyone affected to understand the subject, and undervalue the capacities of those who differed from himself. If my mental faculties and organs of hearing do not both deceive me, I really never heard such conclusions attempted to be drawn. I wanted some advantage to the United States. They were to subscribe two millions specie. Ellsworth repeatedly said, they were to do this only as a deposit, and I am convinced he wanted to deprive the public of all advantage, save that of safe-keeping, and convenience in collecting, which they could derive from the banks in existence, as well as from any new one. All other persons had the power of subscribing three fourths, in public securities. It was contended that this was nothing against the public, although, it was admitted on all hands, that the six per cent.'s were now at 16/ in the pound. King, Ellsworth, and Strong, all harped on this string.

I am now more fully convinced than ever I have been, of the propriety of opening our doors. I am confident some gentlemen would have been ashamed to have seen their speeches of this day, reflected in a newspaper of to-morrow. We sat till a quarter after three, and adjourned without any question being put.

I know not whether this fear of taking the question did not arise from some pointed expressions which fell from me. I told them plainly that I was no advocate for banking systems. That I considered them as machines for promoting the profits of unproductive men. That the business of the United States, so far as respected deposits, could be done in the present banks. That the whole profit of the bank ought to belong to the public, provided it was possible to advance the whole stock on her account. I was sorry that this at present was not possible. I would, however, take half, or I should rather, in the present case, say one fifth, of the loaf rather than no bread. But I must remark that the public was grossly imposed on in the present instance. While she advanced all specie, individuals advanced three fourths in certificates, which were of no more value in the support of the bank than so much stubble. To make this plain: Suppose the vaults empty, and a note presented for payment, would the bearer take *certificates* as *specie?* No; verily. Besides, the certificates were all under interest already, and it was highly unjust that other paper should be issued on their credit which bore a premium, and operated as a further tax on the country.

Tuesday, 18. This day the bank bill was taken up again. I feel much reluctance to minute anything on this subject. I never saw the spirit of speculation display itself in stronger colors. Indeed, the guise of regard for the interest of the public was not preserved. Two millions of specie is to be subscribed by the public. This is to be the basis of the bank; and the other subscribers, who are to draw dividends according to their subscriptions, are to pay three fourths in certificates. King evidently wanted, by a side wind, to exclude the public from any dividend, under an idea which he strongly inculcated, that the subscription of the public was to be over and above the capital—ten millions—of the bank; and was to be considered as deposit. A position which resolves itself into this : That the public should find the specie to support the bank, whilst the speculators, who subscribe almost wholly in certificates, receive the profits of the dividends.

January 19. This day the bank bill passed all through. The last clause was caviled at. I supported it, on the principle that any law containing a grant of any kind, should be irrepealable. Laws touching the *regulation* of morals, manners, or property, are all made on the principle of experiment, and accommodation to time and place; but when legislators make grants, the deed should remain inviolate. Three opinions prevailed in Senate respecting this bill; or rather, I should say, three motives of action. The most prevalent seemed to be, to accommodate it to the views of the stockholders, who may subscribe. The Potomac interest seemed to regard it as a machine, which, in the hands of the Philadelphians, might retard the removal of Congress. The direction of it was their object. I really wished to make it as subservient to the public interest as possible. Though all professed this, yet I thought few gave themselves any trouble to promote it. I cannot help adding a sincere wish, that the integrity of the directors may make amends for the want of it in many of the legislators who enacted it. For in the hands of bad men, it may be made a most mischievous engine. But, indeed, so may even the best of human institutions.

January 20. The business of this day was the third reading of the bank bill. The same questions were agitated over again, but without heat. It was moved to reduce the limitation to *ten* years. I at one time thought this long enough, but I conversed on the subject with every moneyed man I could find, and they uniformly declared that they would not subscribe on so short a period; and the consequence would be that they would all join in supporting the old banks and bearing down the national one. I sincerely wish to derive a benefit to the public from the bank; and considering that the public are, in this respect, in the hands of the moneyed interest, I thought it best to agree to such bargain as we could make, and accordingly voted against this, viz., the motion to limit the term of the bank to the year 1801, instead of 1811. Accident threw me in company with these men, but I abhor their design of destroying the bank altogether. Mr. Morris came very late this day, indeed not until all the business was over, but he desired leave to have his vote inserted on the minutes, which was granted to him. .

Dinner with the President.

Dined with the President this day. Sundry gentlemen met me at the door, and though I rather declined, they pushed me forward. After I had made my bows, and was inclining toward a vacant seat, the President, who rose to receive me, edged about on the sofa, as he sat down, and said, here is room; but I had put myself in motion for another vacant seat. A true courtier would have changed, but I am not one, and sat on the opposite settee or sofa with some New England men. At dinner, after my second plate had been taken away, the President offered to help me to part of a dish which stood before him. Was ever anything so unlucky. I had just before declined being helped to anything more, with some expression that denoted my having made up my dinner. Had, of course, for the sake of consistency, to thank him negatively. But when the dessert came, and he was distributing a pudding, he gave me a look of interrogation, and I returned the thanks positive. He soon after asked me to drink a glass of wine with him. This was readily accorded to, and what was remarkable, I did not observe him drink with any other person during dinner. But I think this must have been owing to my inattention.

Giles, the new member from Virginia, sat next me but one. I saw a speech of his in the papers, which read very well, and they say he delivers himself handsomely. I was, therefore, very attentive to him. But the frothy manners of Virginia were ever uppermost. Canvass back ducks, ham, and chickens, old Madeira, the glories of the ancient dominion, all amazingly fine, were his constant themes. Boasted of personal prowess, more manual exercise than any man in New England; fast, but fine, living in his country, wine or cherry bounce from twelve o'clock to night, every day. . .

Declared for the assumption and excise, &c.   He is but a young man, and seems as if he always would be so.

But, after this digression, let me turn to the unexpected incident of dining with the President, and to his marked attention to me. He knows the weight of political odium under which I labor.   He knows that my uniform opposition to funding systems, (at least, to ours,) assumptions, high compensations, and expensive arrangements have drawn on me the resentment of all the speculators, public creditors, expectants of office, and courtiers in the State.   There is another point which, I presume, he does not know, viz : That I will receive no support from the republican or opposition party, for there is not a man of them who is not aiming at a six dollar prize, and my place is the best chance in the wheel.   But he knows enough to satisfy him that I will be no Senator after the 3d of March, and to the score of his good nature must I place these extra attentions. Be it so.   It is, at least, one amiable trait in his character.

The Appearance of the President.

I have, however, now seen him for the last time, perhaps.   Let me take a review of him as he really is.   In stature, about six feet, with an unexceptionable make, but lax appearance.   His frame would seem to want filling up.   His motions, rather slow than lively, though he showed no signs of having suffered either by gout or rheumatism.   His complexion, pale—now, almost cadaverous.   His voice, hollow and indistinct, owing, as I believe, to artificial teeth before in his upper jaw, which occasioned a flatness of——

The rest of this description wanting.

Friday, January 21.   This was a day of no great business in the Senate.   Colonel Gunn, of Georgia, wanted copies of the secret journal.   Much talk passed about his application.   He was, however, gratified.   In fact, we have never kept our journal agreeable to the constitution.   All the executive part has been kept secret without any vote for it.   A committee is, however, appointed, and the matter will hereafter be under better regulation.

We received some lengthy communications from Captain O'Brien and the prisoners at Algiers.   A committee of the Senate some time ago recommended a war with them.   War is often entered into to answer domestic, not foreign, purposes.   I fear such was the design of the present report.   It was even talked how many ships should be fitted out, and of what force.   But O'Brien seems to show plainly that a peace may be obtained on easy terms by furnishing them with naval stores.   We have it plainly also from his letters that the French, Danes, and, above all, the British have done us all the injury in their power with the Algerines. In fact, all who are at peace with them are decidedly against us, and have done us all the disservice they could. The former report was re-committed, and these papers referred to them.

Mr. Morris came late, and left us soon. We adjourned at about half after two o'clock. George Robinson, one of the clerks of the Treasury, returned from New York, where he had been sent by the Secretary. Among his letters he pointed to a packet, and said it contained ninety thousand dollars. How can I help believing that speculation was the object of his journey.

Saturday, 22. The Speaker of the House of Representatives (of Pennsylvania) called on me yesterday, asked me to go and visit with him this day. I agreed, and called at his house about ten. He was, however, gone. His House sat this day, and this will be his excuse. I went to the Chamber of the State Representatives. The resolutions against the *excise* were the order of the day, and were passed by a great majority. The arguments were not important, nor striking. Some ill-nature was expressed by Mr. Finley, against a Mr. Evans. I feel sincere pleasure that so much independence has been manifested by the yeomanry of Pennsylvania. Indeed I am fully satisfied that if a spirit of this kind was not manifested from some quarter or another, our liberties would soon be swallowed up. I trifled away the rest of the day. Much as was said in the Chamber of Representatives, they seem totally ignorant of the principle that seems to actuate the adherents of Hamilton. Taxes originally flowed from necessity. Ways and means follow unavoidable expense. Here the system seems reversed. The ways and means are obvious to every reader of a register of European taxes. We have lands, slaves, and cattle, and every article of European or Asiatic convenience or luxury is used among us. The difficulty is to find plausible pretext for extending the arm of taxation, and ways and means to consume the collected treasures; and the reigning party seem to consider themselves as wanting in duty, if the fiscal rent-roll should fall short of the royal revenues of England.

Sunday, 23. I had firmly devoted this day to my family, in the way of writing letters, but just as I had adopted the resolution, a message was brought me from Governor Langdon, to go with him to meeting. This I could not refuse. Before I was half dressed, I received a polite note from Mr. Morris, to be one of his friends at a family dinner, and this I could not refuse; and before I had quite dressed, Langdon called on me. We attended at Arch Street Meeting.

Dined with Mr. Morris. The company, Judge Wilson, Governor St. Clair, General Butler. General Irwin was expected, but did not come. We were sociable, and I sat later than I usually do.

Monday, 24th January. This day voluminous communications were introduced by Secretary Lear. A volume of a letter from Doctor O'Fallon to the President, avowing the raising a vast body of men in the Kentucky country to force a settlement in the Yazoo country; the state of Indian affairs, both in the southern and government northwest of the Ohio; the translation of all which was a want of more troops.

The Ten Miles Square.

But the most singular of all was a proclamation for running lines of experiment for the ten miles square. The message accompanying the proclamation calls for an amendatory law, permitting the President to locate lower down, and to lay half of the square in Virginia. This seems like unsettling the whole affair. I really am surprised at the conduct of the President. To bring it back, at any rate, before Congress is certainly the most imprudent of all acts. To take on him to fix the spot by his own authority, when he might have placed the three commissioners in the post of responsibility, was a thoughtless act. I really think it not improbable that opposition may find a nest to lay her eggs in, from the unexpected manner of treating this subject. The general sense of Congress certainly was that the commissioners should fix on the spot, and it may be a query whether the words of the law will warrant a different construction. The commissioners now are only agents of demarcation, mere surveyors to run four lines of fixed courses and distances.

Sold my stock: six per cent.'s at seventeen shillings four; deferred and three per cent.'s at nine.

Mr. Brown, of Northampton, called on me, and told me that Muhlenberg was very busy in giving oyster suppers, &c., and seemed to think that I should go more among the members, &c. I find that I will offend him and some others if I do not. But it is a vile commerce, and I detest this beast worshipping. How melancholy a thing is it that the liberties of men should be in the hands of such creatures—I cannot call them men. But Brown seemed to think that Muhlenberg had made an impression on the Governor or some of them. Be it so.

I went and called on a number of the members of Assembly, and Senators—all seemed fair and smooth. Some of them, indeed, said expressly that they would support me at the ensuing election, believing that to be the object of my visit, as it, in some measure, was. *Sed nulla fides fronti* may be applied to many of them.

The bill regulating consuls and vice consuls had the second reading this day.

A letter from the National Assembly of France on the death of Doctor Franklin was communicated from them, and received with a coldness that was truly amazing. I cannot help painting to myself the disappointment that awaits the French patriots, while their warm fancies are figuring the raptures that we will be thrown into on the receipt of their letters, and the information of the honors which they have bestowed on our countryman, and anticipating the complimentary echoes of our answers, when we, cold as clay, care not a fig about them, Franklin, or freedom. Well we deserve—what do we deserve?

January 27. This day communications were received from the President of the United States, relating to Indian depredations. A post on the Muskingum cut off. The wishes of many people are gratified to involve us in war. To involve us in expense, at any rate, seems to be the great object of their design. It, perhaps, would be unjust—perhaps, cruel—to suppose it. But had a system been needed to involve us in the depth of difficulties with the Indians, none better could have been devised.

Last year, at New York, much altercation happened whether a discrimination in the duties of tonnage should not be made in favor of foreign nations in treaty with us. This measure was lost, although, in my opinion, a just one. The court of France remonstrates against the duties, expecting favors as a nation in treaty. Some gentlemen, on the receiving the communications, affected recantation publicly, and, by these very means, obtained themselves to be put on the committee. This day they report against the claims of France.

When the matter of no discrimination was carried in Congress in our first session, I could hardly suppress a thought, which I felt ready to spring up in my mind, that some persons wished to destroy the confidence between us and France, and bring us back to the fish (or flesh) pots of British dependence. This I charge to the influence of the city of New York, but Philadelphia has not altered the tenor of their political conduct.

Ellsworth could not rest a moment all this day. He was out, and in and out, all on the fidgets. Twice or thrice was an adjournment hinted at, and as often did he request that it might be withdrawn, expecting the excise bill to be taken out. But he had to bear his impatience. Three o'clock came before the bill. I can see that he will stand foremost in the gladiatorial list.

Friday, 28. The excise bill came up; but, oh, what a mistake. It is only a bill for discontinuing certain duties, and laying others in their stead. The odious name is omitted, but the thing is the same. It was read and ordered to the press.

The report of the committee on the difference with the Court of France was taken up. Almost everybody gave it against the French demands. I differed from them on some points; but as I could not obtain a sight of the papers, I joined in the motion for postponement, which was carried.

Saturday, 29. Called twice this day at the office of our Secretary to get the French papers. Otis says Carroll took them away. Went to hear the debates in the State Senate. The resolutions for instructing the Senators had been postponed yesterday, expressly for the purpose of obtaining a sight of the bill, which is in its passage through Congress. But the same men pushed for a decision this day. The State has now an opportunity of seeing the benefit of two Houses. The division was nine to eight. The yeas and nays were called. Graff, of Lancaster, was going home. This was the reason of pushing the vote this day. Assemblymen and Senators may be equally considered as Representatives of the people. From the division of the two Houses, the voice of the people appears to be unequivocally against an excise.

Sunday, 30. Not well this day, and stayed at home most of the day. Went, in the evening, to the funeral of Judge Bryan. This man rests from his labors. He had the qualities of industry and love of freedom. He was the father of the *abolition law.**

Monday, the excise bill read a second time; but the bill not being in our hands, it was made the order of the day for Wednesday.

The affair of the French discontents taken up. God forgive me if I wrong some people; but there certainly have been more censorious conclusions than to charge some people with a design of breaking our connexion with France.

When or how will all these mad measures lead us? We hear it ever in our ears, that the present General Government, with respect to the persons who compose it, contains the collected wisdom and learning of the United States. It must be admitted that they have generally been selected on account of their reputation for knowledge, either legal, political, mercantile, historical, &c. Newspapers are printed in every corner. In every corner ambitious men abound, for ignorance or want of qualification is no bar to this view.

---

* Note.—Meaning the Pennsylvania act of 1st March, 1780, for the abolition of slavery.

Friday, 28.   He states that the excise bill for discontinuing certain duties, and laying others in their stead, was taken taken up; was read ; and ordered to the press.

Tuesday, 1st February.   This day I had much to say against the report of a committee which went to declare war against the Algerines.   It is not suspicion that the designs of the court are to have a fleet and army.   The Indian war is forced forward to justify our having a standing army, and eleven unfortunate men, now in slavery in Algiers, is the pretext for fitting out a fleet to go to war with them.   While fourteen of these captives were alive, the barbarians asked about $35,000 for them ; but it is urged that we should expend half a million of dollars rather than redeem these unhappy men.   I vociferated against the measure, and, I suppose, offended my colleague.   This thing of a *fleet* has been working among our members all the session.   I have heard it break out often.

Wednesday.   The excise bill read over, and remarked on, and committed to five members.   I gave notice that I would endeavor to show that a much lower duty would answer the demand of the Secretary.   I spoke to sundry of the members to second a general postponement for the session, but not a man approved of any such thing.

Thursday, 3d February.   This day was unimportant in the Senate.   No debate of consequence took place.   I was called off the street to dine with a Quaker at about two o'clock.   As he seemed very friendly, I eat heartily of a good dinner, and was perfectly easy ; much more than I could say of the great dinners where the candles are ready to be brought in with the going out of the last dishes.   This high life is really very distant from nature.   All is artificial.

Friday, 4th February.   This day we had a large report from the Secretary of State transmitted to us from the House of Representatives respecting the fisheries of New England.   The great object seems to be the making them a nursery for seamen, that we, like all the nations of the earth, may have a navy.   We hear every day distant hints of such things as these.   In fact, it seems we must soon forego our republican innocence, and, like all other nations, set apart a portion of our citizens for the purpose of inflicting misery on our fellow mortals.   This practice is felony to posterity.   The men so devoted are not only cut off, but a proportionate share of women remain unmatched.   Had the sums expended in war been laid out in meliorating the kingdom of England or any other modern government, what delightful abodes might they have been made.   Whereas, war leaves only traces of desolation.

Saturday, 5th February. No report from the committee. It was agreed to that the powers of the inspectors should extend only to importations and distillations, but I find Hamilton will have even this modified to his mind.

7th February. There certainly is a design of quarreling with France, and that Jefferson should seem to countenance this. What can this mean? I am really astonished at all this. I think I must be mistaken, and yet to think so is to disbelieve my senses. And what can I do? I have attempted everything and effected nothing, unless it be to render myself an object of aversion. For well indeed speaks the poet:

> Truths would you teach, or save a sinking land,
> All fear, none aid you, and few understand.

Tuesday, 8th February. The Senate met. The appropriation bill had the last reading.

There was a pause about taking up the excise bill, like people pausing on the brink of a precipice, afraid to take the dangerous leap. However, it was at length attempted, and we blundered along to the fourth section. Objections had been made to this section, and it was expected the committee would alter it. They have done so with a vengeance. It now runs that there shall be an inspector general over a district, the district to be divided into surveys and an inspector to be set over each survey, who shall appoint people under him to do the business. As many of them to be appointed as the President shall think proper, and he shall pay them, too. The members, by degrees, stole away. The men who did so showed their disapprobation in their looks. It is in vain. Our Government cannot stand. All my opposition has been considered as vain babbling. But to get quit of it, in some degree, the business of commitment has taken place, and now the majority have a kind of scape goat in the committee, and a pretext for following them and disregarding opposition, under the idle idea of their knowing best, having consulted Hamilton, &c., &c.

Wednesday 9th February. The excise bill has passed, and a pretty business it is. The ministry foresee opposition, and are preparing to resist it by a band, nay a host, of revenue officers. It is put in the power of the President to make as many districts, appoint as many general surveyors and as many inspectors of survey as he pleases, and thus multiply force to bear all down before him. War and bloodshed is the most likely consequence of all this. Congress may go home. Mr. Hamilton is all powerful, and fails in nothing which he attempts. Little avail as I was sure it would be of, I nevertheless endeavored not to be wanting in my duty, and told them plainly of the precipice which I considered them as having approached; that the Legislature of Pennsylvania had been obliged to wink at the violation of her excise laws in the western parts of the State, ever since the Revolution; that, in my opinion, it could not be enforced by collectors or civil officers of any kind, be they ever so numerous, and that nothing short of a permanent military force could effect it. This, for aught I knew, might be acceptable to some characters. I could only answer for myself, that I did not wish it and would avoid every measure that tended to make it necessary.

Thursday, 10th February. Some letters, however, have come in since yesterday, from New England; and Strong was willing to move the reductions which we wanted. After the bill was read over and ready for the question, Foster, from Rhode Island, moved a reduction of three cents on the distillations from molasses, &c. I rose and seconded him, on condition of his extending the motion through all the distillations in the United States, and a reduction to forty cents on the contents of stills.

King objected to the lessening of the ratio, as productive of deficiencies in the revenue demanded. I showed, in answer, that the importations into the port of Philadelphia, and the sum expected from the stills in this State, would go a great way towards raising one half of the $826,000 demanded by the Secretary.

Ellsworth answered, with rudeness, that I was mistaken—that the Secretary demanded a million and a half. I replied by reading part of the Secretary's report, which confirmed the position I had made, and repeated my other arguments. He did not reply.

At half after three, the question was ready to be put. Henry, of Maryland, told me he had a bet depending with Butler on the division of the House, and desired the yeas and nays. I needed not this excuse, and called sharply for the yeas and nays. With all their strength, they were startled; and up got King, and round and round, and about and about; one while commit; then recommit; then postpone. Ellsworth, too, had the world and all to say; and now, in fact, they are afraid of the figure they have raised; and the fourth section was recommitted.

11th February. I find this day that the reason of recommitting the excise bill was to enable Hamilton to come forward with some new schemes. Three new clauses were brought forward, and all from the treasury. The obnoxious one (at least to me) was the putting it in the power of the President to form districts by cutting up States, so as to pay no respect to their boundaries. This was curiously worded. For fear of the little States taking any alarm, it stood, by adding, " from the great to the lesser States." This thing they got adopted. And having been successful so far, King got up and talked about it and about it. He wanted the United States divided into a number of districts, independent of any of the State boundaries. Like an Indian at the war post, he wrought himself into a passion—declared that we *had no right to pay any more attention to the State boundaries than to the boundaries of the Cham of Tartary.*

Up got Ellsworth and echoed most of what he said ; but said he wished only three great districts, and the President might subdivide each into six.

When he had done, up got Mr. Morris, and declared himself in sentiment with Mr. King, and spoke against the conveniency of the State boundaries.

King rose again, repeated his old arguments, and wished for an opportunity for taking a question on the principle of dividing the United States, without any regard to their boundaries. At length, out of his pocket comes a resolution. It imported that the United States should be divided into six districts—two east of the Hudson, two from that to the Potomac, and two from that southwestward, or words to that import ; and that the President should sub-divide these into surveys, &c. This pretty system was, after all, negatived.

Annihilations of the State governments, is undoubtedly the object of these people. The late conduct of our State Legislature, has provoked them beyond all bounds. They have created an Indian war, that an army may spring out of it, and the trifling affair of our having eleven captives at Algiers, (who ought long ago to have been ransomed,) is made the pretext for going to war with them, and fitting out a fleet. With these two engines, and the collateral aid derived from an host of revenue officers, farewell freedom in America. Gently, indeed, did I touch it in argument ; but is not a motion for the destruction of the individuality of the States, treason against the duty of a Senator, who, from the nature of his appointment, ought to be guardian of the State's rights. The little I said, however, I believe raised a goblin that frightened them from the project, at least for this time.

February 12. This day we passed the excise law, and a pretty piece of business it is. I found there was an unwillingness in many of the members to have the yeas and nays. I, however, called them sharply, and enough rose, and I had the pleasure of giving my decided negative against what I considered the box of Pandora, with regard to the happiness of America.

The communications came in this morning respecting the Indian affairs, and the bill was ordered to be printed.

As we came down stairs, Dr. Johnson spoke with great joy. Now, said he, all is over, the business is complete. We have a revenue that will support the government, and every necessary measure of government. We have now the necessary support for national measures, &c., &c. I told him, perhaps we might undo all—that the high demands we had made would raise opposition, and that opposition might endanger the government. He seemed a little struck. I repeated that the government might, and perhaps would, fall by her over-exertion to obtain support.

13. Sunday. A large party down stairs, speaking on the subject of religion. One position I thought not tenable, that man was but the first animal in nature. That he became so by the feelings of his fingers, and hence all his faculties. Give, said they, only a hand to a horse, he would rival all the human powers.

This I know to be groundless. The opossum, from its feeble, harmless, and helpless faculties, is almost extinct in Pennsylvania; and yet one that I killed on the island at Juniata, had as complete a hand, with four fingers and a thumb, as one of the human species.

February 14. 'Tis done. I doubt no longer. This day came in bulky communications from the President. The amount was the result of a negotiation, carried on by his order with the Court of Great Britain, through the agency of Governeur Morris. From the letters of Governeur Morris, it appears that the vote against discrimination, which has involved us in difficulties with France, was the work of the President, avowedly procured by his influence; and that he did it to facilitate a connection with Great Britain; thus offering direct offense to France, and incurring the contempt of Britain, for she has spurned every overture made to her; and now the result is, I suppose, a war with Great Britain; at least these troops are, as I suppose, meant to wrest the posts from her. She will resist. Reprisals at sea will take place, and all the calamities of war ensue. It is with difficulty, that I refrain from giving the most severe language to some of our Senators. King said the opponents of the constitution did not see the ground on which to attack it. The business was now complete. We need not care for opposition. Henry, of Maryland, joined with him. King said the constitution of the United States implied everything. It was a most admirable system.

The system laid down by these gentlemen, was avowedly as follows, or rather the development of the designs of a certain party:

The general power to carry the Constitution into effect by a constructive interpretation, would extend to every case that Congress may deem necessary or expedient. Should the very worst thing supposable happen, viz : The claim of any of the States to any of the powers exercised by the General Government, such claim will be treated with contempt. The laws of the United States will be held paramount to all their laws, claims, and even constitutions. The supreme power is with the General Government, to decide in this, as in everything else, for the States have neglected to secure any umpire or mode of decision in case of difference between them. Nor is there any point in the Constitution for them to rally under. They may give an opinion, but the opinion of the General Government must prevail, &c. This open point, thus unguarded, has rendered the General Government completely uncontrollable. With a fleet and army, which the first war must give us, all future opposition will be chimerical.

I ventured to dissent from these political heroes, by declaring that the people themselves would guard the pass ; that the right of judging with respect to encroachments still remained with the people ; it was originally with them, and they never had divested themselves of it.

With all their art, however, since they now confess their views, I think they have made but a bungling hand of it. The old Congress had no power over individuals ; and, of course, no system of consolidation could take place. Their legislative or recommendatory powers were over States only. The new Constitution, by the instrumentality of the judiciary, &c., aims at the government of individuals ; and the States, unless as to the conceded points, and with regard to their individual sovereignty and independence, are left upon stronger ground than formerly ; and it can only be by implication or inference that the General Government can exercise control over them as States. Any direct and open act would be termed usurpation. But whether the gradual influence and encroachments of the General Government may not gradually swallow up the State governments, is another matter.

February 15. This day was rather unimportant in the Senate. Mr. Morris labored, in private, with me, this day, to get me to join in postponing the complaints of the French Court. The President, although it is undeniable that it was through his instrumentality the offense was given to France, yet now wishes all this done away— the breach made up with France, and the resentment shown to England. The measure is right, but his motives wrong. Never should the paths of rectitude be forsaken. Had the President left Congress to themselves, the discrimination would have obtained, and as the discrimination had heretofore obtained by the State laws, England would have taken no umbrage, and we should have experienced no interruption of harmony with France. Unless we repeal the law, we lose, forever, the friendship of France. And even after repealing it, the confidence of France in us will be impaired, as she may attribute our first motives to ingratitude, and our last to fear. Continuing the law will have no effect on Britain, as she has already treated General Washington's application with contempt; but a repeal of it will be followed with resentment. This we will have to submit to, and ought not to regard.

February 16. Mr. Carroll moved for leave to bring in a bill supplementary to the residence bill. The matter, I believe, stands thus, in fact: Virginia is not fully satisfied without having half the ten miles square. She gives the $120,000, perhaps, on this very principle of having Alexandria included. This cannot be done without the supplementary law, which is now applied for.

I spoke to Mr. Morris, and gave him my thoughts on the matter. He made a just observation: " There will be people enough to manage this matter, without our taking an active part in it."

The rule demands one day's notice to be given for bringing in a bill. Carroll withdrew his motion, on being told of this; but afterwards hoped the Senate would indulge him by common consent.

Ellsworth, however, said it had better lay over one day.

I returned to the Senate. Found the draughts of General Harmar's expedition before the committee. They look finely on paper, but were we to view the green bones and scattered fragments of our defeat on the actual field, it would leave very different ideas on our minds.

February 17. This day Mr. Carroll's motion for the amendatory act respecting the Potomac, was to be taken up. Mr. Morris was very late in coming. I, however, wish he had stayed away, for he voted for leave to bring in the bill.

The military bill was reported, with amendments much longer than itself. They were ordered to be printed.

February 18. A number of communications were handed in, respecting the appointment of David Humphreys, resident at the court of Portugal. The President sends first, and asks for our advice and consent afterwards.

Now Carroll's amendatory bill was called up. It was debated with temper, but a good deal of trifling discourse was had upon it. I had determined to say nothing on the subject. I, however, changed my mind, and made the following remarks :

So far as I had an opportunity of knowing the public mind, the expectations of the people had been disappointed.   A belief had obtained, that the President would appoint three commissioners, who, under his direction, would lay out the ten miles square.   I did r⸍t arraign his authority.   I did not call it in question ; but he had d⸍ne himself what should have been done by others, under his direction. I would neither pull down nor build up.   Let the measure rest upon the law.   If all was right it would support itself; if wrong, our mending it was improper, &c., &c.

Mr. Morris followed me.   I could not well collect his drift ; but he said, with pretty strong emphasis, that if any one would move a postponement, he would be for it.

This hint was laid hold of by Langdon and Schuyler, and a postponement moved, which was carried.

Mr. Morris sustained a small attack, from Gunn, for this, as an indirect way of getting rid of the measure.

Oh, I should note that Mr. Jefferson, with more than Parisian politeness, waited on me in my chamber this morning.   He talked politics, mostly, the French difference, and the whale fishery ; but he touched the Potomac, too, as much as to say, there, oh, there.

Wednesday, 23.   A bill was committed to General Dickenson, Wingate, and myself.   It was for paying off at par $186,000 due to foreign officers.   This was domestic debt beyond a doubt.   The bill went to pay it out of the funds appropriated to foreign debt.

Tuesday, my report was read, and on Wednesday it was agreed to, or, at least, the resolution subjoined was adopted, that the bill should not pass to a third reading.

Business crowded much, and I have almost determined to pass all.   The difference, however, on the new impost law, between the two House, explains so fully the trim of the Senate, that I must have a word or two on the subject.

The bill commonly called the excise law, though the term is carefully avoided in the law, puts it in the power of the President to appoint as many inspectors as he chooses, and to pay them what he pleases, so that he does not exceed five per cent. on the whole sum collected.   This check is a mere nullity, and depends on a point arising posterior to the appointments.   The reason given for vesting the power in the President, is the want of knowledge of the subject—how many, what duties they will have to discharge.   The House of Representatives seem to say that experience will dispel this ignorance in two years, and, therefore, they amend, limiting this power of paying, &c., to two years.   No, say our Senate, we will not trust the new Congress, &c., &c.   In fact, the object is to throw all possible power into the hands of the President, even to the stripping of the Senate. A conference appointed.

It is believed that any measure that can be fairly fixed on the President will be submitted to by the people, thus making him the scapegoat of unconstitutional measures, and leading them, by their affection to him, into an acquiescence in these measures that flow from him. To break down the boundaries of the States has been a desideratum. This was attempted at the time of the impost. The geographical situation of Maryland, with respect to the Chesapeake bay, afforded a pretext to do something of the kind, under the plea of convenience, by adding the eastern shore to the State of Delaware, and indemnifying Maryland out of Virginia. Clouds of letters reprobated the measure. It would not do. The President is now put upon something of this kind. To alter the lines of States, by taking from the larger and adding to the smaller, in his arrangement for collecting the excise.

The Subject of Instructions.

Thursday, 24th February. This day nothing of moment engaged the Senate, in the way of debate, until the Virginia Senators moved a resolution that the doors of the Senate chamber should be opened on the first day of the next session, &c. They mentioned their instructions. This brought the subject of instructions from the different Legislatures into view.

Ellsworth said they amounted to no more than a wish, and ought to be no further regarded.

Izard said no Legislature had any right to instruct at all, any more than the electors had a right to instruct the President of the United States.

Mr. Morris followed—said Senators owed their existence to the Constitution; the Legislatures were only the machines to choose them; and was more violently opposed to instruction than any of them. We were Senators of the United States, and had nothing to do with one State more than another. Mr. Morris spoke with more violence than usual.

Perhaps, I may be considered as imprudent, but I thought I would be wanting in the duty I owed the public, if I sat silent, and heard such doctrines, without bearing my testimony against them.

I declared I knew but two lines of conduct for legislators to move in: The one, absolute volition; the other, responsibility. The first was tyranny. The other was inseparable from the idea of representation. Were we chosen with dictatorial powers, or were we sent forward as servants of the public to do their business? The latter clearly, in my opinion. The first question, then, which presented itself was : Were my constituents here, what would they do ? The answer, if known, was the rule for the representative. Our governments were avowedly republican. The question now before us had no respect to what was the best kind of government, but this I considered as genuine republicanism. As to the late conduct of the Legislature of Pennsylvania, I spoke with but few of them. I had no instruction from them, and, all things considered, I was happy that I had given my voice on a former occasion for it. The reasons which I gave then operated still in full force on my mind.

The first was : That I knew of no reason for keeping the door of any legislative assembly open that did not apply with equal force to us.

The second was : That I thought it a compliment due to the smallest State in the Union to indulge them in such request.

The objections against it, viz : That the members would make speeches for the gallery and for the public papers, would be the fault of the members. If they waged war in words and oral combats ; if they pitted themselves like cocks ; or played the gladiator for the amusement of the idle and curious, the fault was theirs. That let who would fill the chairs of the Senate, I hoped discretion would mark their deportment. That they would rise to impart knowledge, and listen to obtain information. That while this line of conduct marked their debates, it was totally immaterial whether thousands attended, or there were not a single spectator.

This day Butler handed forward a resolution for augmenting the salaries of all Federal officers of the different departments one fourth.

It is a great object to increase the Federal officers and salaries as much as possible to make them marks for the ambitious to aim at. This single stratagem has carried the new government on so far with increased rapidity.

Friday, 25th February. This was a busy day in Senate. We had a long communication from the President respecting the loan of three millions of florins, which, it seems, came at five and one fourth per cent., the expense of negotiation being between four and five per cent.

Up now was taken a bill for altering the time of the meeting of Congress. The title was the same with that of a bill rejected the other day. But the former had the first Monday in November ; *this* had the fourth Monday in October. The President declared that as the day was different, the bill was a different bill. There might be as many different bills as days in the year. It passed, but I confess I thought him wrong. Mr. Morris' vote carried the bill. I spoke against it, but without effect.

Now we had the resolution for opening the doors. Nine votes were given for it, and it was lost.

And now came the Potomac amendatory act. A postponement was moved, but Langdon, Schuyler, Elmer, Morris, and Reed voted against the postponement, and finally for the bill.

Saturday, February 26. The last hand was put to the detested excise law.

For weeks has the report of the committee on the French complaints lain dormant. Shame, I believe, had some hand in keeping them back. But now a steady phalanx appeared to support the report. I opposed it, what I could, and contended against the alternatives in the report of the Secretary of State as exceptionable, and opposed the whole. But all in vain. The report, with some variation, was adopted. I was the only one who voted boldly and decidedly against it.

That there has been a design to sacrifice the French interest as a peace offering to the British Court, I cannot doubt; but that this should be persisted in after the disappointment attending Governeur Morris' management, is strange, indeed. They however hope, or affect to hope, to carry their point. Mr. Morris, a few days ago, asserted that we would early this spring have a minister from Great Britain, and the papers have many accounts to the same purpose.

As to Our Relations with France.

Mr. Maclay made a series of observations in relation to the French treaty, concluding with : I have ever thought that a liberal and manly policy, being most conformable to the genius of the people, was the surest method of engaging and preserving the esteem of that magnanimous nation, and the alternative might be war and confusion.

A burst of abuse now flowed forth against the French, by Ellsworth, in the most vituperative language that fancy could invent. Selfishness, interested views, their motive. To dismember the English empire; *divide et impera*, their motto. Nay, slay British subjects with the sword of their fellows. No gratitude in nations, no honor in politics. None but a fool would expect it. Serve yourself, the first article in the creed of politics. No return due to them. Ridicule, not thanks, would attend acknowledgments.

He fell on me with the most sarcastic severity. No confusion anywhere but in the Speaker's head. Alas, how shall I write it, I lost my temper, and finding no protection from the Chair, left the room.

A moment's reflection restored me. I recollected that I had the volume of Congress of 1783, which I had looked up for this occasion, before my seat, where the greatest encomiums were bestowed on the French. I returned. King was up; and although he was in the same sentiments as Ellsworth, he said *Mr. Jay* had given a similar construction with me, or, at least, I so understood him. I did not hear one of the statements which I made answered or attempted to be answered. I happened to turn round, and the full length portrait of the King and Queen of France caught my eye. I really seemed to think they would upbraid me if I was silent. I knew the disadvantage I labored under. But up I got.

Nations being composed of individuals, the virtue, character and reputation of the nation must depend on the morals of individuals, and could have no other basis. Gratitude, generosity, sensibility of favors, benignity, and beneficence, had not abandoned the human breast; in fact these were the conditions on which the human race existed. That these passions, so far as they respected the French nation, were deeply engraved on the bosom of every American revolutionist. I knew there were characters of a different kind in America; but for them we cared not. That I was convinced the sense of America had been fairly expressed by Congress, on the resignation of General Washington, when the epithet of *magnanimous nation* was applied to them.

What were the expressions of Congress, as reported by a committee, some of whom are now within my hearing, in the year 1783, with respect to that now vilified nation? *Exertions of arms—succours of their treasury—important loans—liberal donations—magnanimity, &c.* Yes, all this, and more; for I have the book before me. In fact, language labored and seemed to fail in expressions of gratitude to our ally.

But here is a reverse, indeed. If right then, we must be wrong now; and my heart tells me it is so. Vituperation and abuse, more especially in the national way, are of the reflective kind, and attach disgrace rather to the assailants than to the assailed.

Ellsworth took a great deal of snuff about this time. He mumped and seemed to chew the cud of vexation. But he affected not to hear me; and, indeed, they were all in knots, talking and whispering. Mr. Adams talked with Otis, according to custom. The committee alluded to were Madison, Ellsworth, and Hamilton. I am too sparing—I should have read that part of the report, with their names. Vol. 8, page 200

I cannot help adding a remark or two. A war, in some shape or other, seems to have been the great object with Hamilton's people At first they would have war with the northern Indians. That failed. They have succeeded in involving us with the northwestern Indians. Britain, at one time, seemed their object. Great efforts were made to get a war with the Algerines. That failed. Now it seems to be made a point to differ with the French. That lively nation do not seem to have been aware that ours was merely a civil war with Britain; and that the similarity of language, manners, and customs, will, in all probability, restore our old habits and intercourse; and that this intercourse will revive, indeed, I fear it has already revived, our ancient prejudices against France. Should we differ with France, we are thrown, inevitably, into the hands of Britain; and should France give any occasion, we have thousands and tens of thousands of anti-revolutionists ready to blow the coals of contention.

March 1. Attended this morning the eulogium in honor of Dr. Franklin, pronounced by Dr. Smith. People say much of it; I thought little of it. It was trite and trifling. Perhaps I am censorious.

Much business was hurried through the Senate this day. Now is the time for designing men to crowd on and hurry through, under some spurious pretext, the deep laid plots of speculation. The immature resolve and ill-digested law, often escapes examination, while nothing but home occupies the minds of the departing members.

Few days happen in which I do not meet with something to fret my political temper, but this day I met with something that really roused every feeling of humanity about me. The President was directed, some time ago, to take measures to ransom eleven Americans, who are slaves at Algiers. Money was appropriated for this purpose, out of the Dutch loan, in 1788. The President, however, sent us back a message to appropriate money for the purpose, and now a committee who had the African business committed to them, reported $20,000 to treat with the Emperor of Morocco, but not a cent for the poor slaves. I said and did what I could, but all in vain, and we will not only confine to slavery, but murder with the plagues of that deleterious climate these unhappy men.

Izard came over, made a long complaint against Hamilton. Here, said he, have we been waiting, nobody knows how long, and Hamilton has promised to send us a bill for the mint. And now, at last, he sends us a resolution to employ workmen.

Bassett this day laid on the table a resolution for a committee of both Houses to wait on the President, to request him to take measures with the Indians, &c.

March 2. The resolution of the mint was smuggled through. I am at no loss now to ascertain the reasons why the *mint* business has been delayed, and finally came forward under the form of a *resolution*, rather than a *bill*. *Bills* cannot be read out of order but by unanimous consent.

It has been usual with declamatory gentlemen, in their praises of the present government, by way of contrast, to paint the state of the country under the old Congress, as if neither wood grew, nor water run in America before the happy adoption of the new Constitution. It would be well, for the future, in such comparisons, to say nothing of national credit, (which, by the by, I never considered as dependent on the prices current of certificates in the hands of speculators,) for the loan of 1788 was done in Holland, at five per cent., only postponed.

March 3. As well might I write the rambles of Harlequin Ranger, or the vagaries of a pantomime, as attempt to minute the business of this morning. What with the exits and the entrances of our Otis, the announcings, the drawings and withdrawing of Beckley and Lear, and the comings and goings of our committees of enrollment, &c., and the consequent running of doorkeepers, opening and slamming of doors, the House seemed in a continual hurricane. Speaking would have been idle, for nobody would or could hear. Had all the business been previously digested, matter of form would have been of little consequence. This, however, was not the case. It was patching, piecing, altering, and amending, and even originating new business. It was, however, only for Ellsworth, King, or some of Hamilton's people to rise, and the thing was generally done. But they had overshot themselves; for, owing to little unforseen impediments, there was no possibility of working all through, and there was to be a great dinner, which must absolutely be attended to. Terrible, indeed, but no alternative, the House must meet at six o'clock.

March 3. In the evening, by candle-light. When I saw the merry mood in which the Senate assembled, I was ready to laugh. When I considered the occasion, I was almost disposed to give way to very different emotion. I did, however, neither the one nor the other; and feeling myself of as little importance as I had ever done in my life, I took pen and paper and determined, if possible, to keep pace with the hurry of business, as it passed, which I expected would now be very rapid, as I had no doubt that Hamilton's clerks had put the last hand to everything.

1. Mr. Beckley, (Clerk of the House of Representatives,) announced that he brought a *new* resolve, for the safe-keeping of prisoners, &c.

2. A bill for compensation to commissioners of loans, for extra expenses.

3. A salary bill for the executive officers, their clerks, and assistants.

4. Resolve for the President to lay before Congress an estimate of lands not claimed by Indians.

5. The mint resolve.

These obtained the signature of the President of the Senate, and were sent off for the deliberation and approbation of the President.

The prisoner resolve was agreed to, and sent back to the Representatives, by Otis.

6. Mr. Beckley—Second message. A *new* bill, to carry into effect the convention with the French, &c. This business has been neglected. I had often spoken on the subject, but my influence was gone. I had, however, spoken lately to sundry members of the House of Representatives, and even at this late hour, was happy to see the bill.

To speak in the present uproar of business, was like letting off a pop-gun in a thunder storm. But this was the merest matter of form possible. It was only giving the authority of law to a convention solemnly entered into with the French. My colleague cried no, on a second reading. I called for the ayes and nays, not out of resentment, but merely with an exculpatory view, if this conduct should draw on us the resentment of France; for I consider it disrespectful (to say no more) towards her and dishonorable in us.

7. Mr. Beckley—Third message, with the pension, invalid, and light-house bills.

The committee reported the enrollment of the following acts:

8. For the continuance of the post office.

9. For granting lands to the settlers at Vincennes, Illinois.

10. Supplementary act for the reduction of the public debt.

11. For granting compensation to judicial officers, witnesses, and jurymen.

These bills received the signature of the President of the Senate, after being brought up by Mr. Beckley in his fourth message.

12. Who brought, at the same time, a new bill for the relief of David Cook. Twice heretofore has there been an attempt to smuggle this bill through in the crowd. It happened, however, to be smoked, and rejected.

13. Mr. Beckley's fifth message brought a bill for making further provision for collection of duties on teas, &c., which received the signature, &c.

14. And an enrolled resolve, which also received the signature, &c.

There now was such confusion with Otis, Beckley, and Lear, our committee of enrollment, &c., that I confess I lost their arrangement. Indeed, I am apt to believe, if they had any, they lost it themselves. They all agreed, at last, that the business was done. The President left the chair, and the members scampered down stairs. I stayed a moment to pack up my papers. Dalton alone came to me, and said he supposed we two would not see each other soon. We exchanged wishes for mutual welfare. As I left the Hall, I gave it a look with that kind of satisfaction which a man feels on leaving a place where he has been ill at ease, being fully satisfied that many a culprit has served two years at the wheelbarrow without feeling half the pain and mortification that I experienced in my honorable station.

End of the journal.

APPENDIX.

Mr. Maclay, in his journal, on some occasions, speaks somewhat disparagingly of Washington. This was owing to an imperfect estimate of the character of Washington, who he seemed to suppose to be favorable to extravagant display in conducting the Government, and of a leaning towards the exercise of arbitrary power in its administration. He seemed also to suppose that Washington was favorable to an additional *title*, the opposition of Washington to that measure being not then generally known; and he also believed that undue influence over Washington was possessed by Mr. Hamilton, towards whom Mr. Maclay entertained strong repugnance. His term in the Senate (being but for two years) was of too short duration to enable him to manifest, *in that position*, a change of opinion in regard to that distinguished person.

WASHINGTON.

Over all the great men of our revolutionary times, and there were great men about him and conspicuous in the public service, at that important period, Washington was preëminent. Of him it may be truly said, that his public character requires neither justification or panegyric. Acting in so many and in such important positions, it would scarcely be reasonable to suppose that he would escape obloquy, the usual attendant upon high official position in possession of extensive patronage but the soundness of his judgment, his disinterestedness, his humanity and benevolence of character, his patriotism, his justice, his honesty and sincerity of purpose, and his deep sense of moral and religious obligation, are proclaimed throughout the country.

He was not, like Cæsar or Napoleon, possessed of brilliant genius, but he was possessed of superior qualities of mind which enabled him to discharge, with signal ability, and with distinguished credit to himself and advantage to the country, the duties of the various positions in which he acted, and he occupied the highest, both military and civil, which the nation could bestow.

20

Whether, as a military man, he would have been equal to the command of a large military force, such as has appeared on European battle-fields, is, of course, for conjecture; but he proved to be sufficient for all the command he had. He was a soldier not from choice, but from motives of patriotism. He did not act in his high position, as commander-in-chief, with a view to his own credit or glory, for he was ever ready to furnish portions of his own troops to his subordinates in command, when he considered the public service to require it. He did not envy them their military successes, but welcomed such fortunate results as advancements of the common cause. In his battles with the enemy he was not always successful, but his defeats were never disheartening to himself, his army, or the people. He was prudent in his command, for the enemy was powerful and his own resources often very insufficient or precarious, for he carried on the war under a government which had no real power, but whose efficiency depended on the *voluntary* action of the States. But he was not wanting in *enterprise*, as Trenton, and Princeton, and Yorktown can testify. His military means were small, considering the magnitude of the stake, the power of his adversary, and the extent of the territory to be defended; but he managed them wisely, and, in the adverse stages of the war, bearing, with a degree of moral courage truly heroic, reproach and obloquy for apparent inefficiency, the cause of which it would have been highly impolitic, as it respected the enemy and the people, to explain or acknowledge, he finally effected the deliverance of the country. And when the great result was accomplished, unlike many other military chief, he sought not to maintain himself in power, but, to use his memorable words, he *"retired from the great theater of action;* * and this without reluctance or regret;

---

* Note.—After Washington had resigned his commission, at Annapolis, on the 23d December, 1783, he returned to Mount Vernon. With the exception of two days, when he paid it a flying visit with Count Rochambeau, in 1781, he had not enjoyed its comforts for eight years.

Washington's letter to Lafayette, on the first of February following, gives a perfect view of the philosophic geniality of temper, superinduced by his retirement from the "bustle of the camp," and return to his "domestic walks." "At length, my dear Marquis," he writes, "I can become a private citizen on the banks of the Potomac, free from the bustle of the camp, and the busy scenes of public life. I am solacing myself with those tranquil enjoyments of which the soldier, who is ever in the pursuit of fame—the statesman, whose watchful days and sleepless nights are spent in devising schemes to promote the welfare of his own, perhaps the ruin of other countries—as if this globe was insufficient for us all; and the courtier, who is watching the countenance of his prince, in hopes of catching a gracious smile, can have little conception. I have not only retired from all public employment, but I am retiring within myself, and shall be able to view the solitary walks, and tread the paths of with not a feigned, but a real desire to enjoy, in a private condition, the beneficial results of the great struggle in which he had been so conspicuous an actor.

He is not entitled to peculiar credit, as has been alleged, for making no effort to maintain himself in power by military aid; for it is not probable that the army would have supported such an effort, or that the people would have endured it. But he is entitled to the credit of not having *desired* it. The great end for which he had been appointed having been attained, he willingly descended from the pedestal which he had long occupied, disposed to enjoy the blessings of free government, with his fellow-citizens, on the same political plane with them.

But his public career was not yet ended. He was called upon to participate in forming a national government, not depending on the capricious and dilatory action of the States, but one acting by its own vital energy; and there was framed a constitution, republican in form, supreme as to national matters within its provisions, but not interfering with those interests, either of the realty or personalty local, simply to the States; containing power for its own preservation; absolute power, as in the Parliament of England, not being permitted to the Government, National or State, but checks and limitations being imposed on both, and both subjected to *judicial* restraint; a constitution not conferring especial privileges or honorary titles on any particular class, and susceptible of peaceful alteration when required by the public exigency or the national will. The constitution thus created formed a system of government capable of wide expansion and of general utility, and was submitted to the public with the recommendation of Washington, which, it has been supposed, contributed materially to its general adoption. He was subsequently elected to the chief executive office under it, the important duties of which he discharged with wisdom and efficiency during two presidential terms, when he voluntarily retired, leaving the Government, which he had done so much to establish, to pursue, under other direction, its triumphant course; having issued to the country his celebrated farewell address,* earn-

---

private life with heartfelt satisfaction. Envious of none, I am determined to be pleased with all ; and this, my dear friend, being the order of my march, I will move gently down the stream of life, until I sleep with my fathers. Come and view me in my domestic walks."

* Oliver Wolcott, who was Secretary of the Treasury under General Washington and Mr. Adams, wrote: "The principles which governed President Washington's administration are perspicuously detailed in the final address to the people, which he personally prepared, and which passed through my hands to and from General Hamilton."—*Gibbs' Wolcott, Vol. I, p. 381.*

estly urging, *with almost prophetic foresight*, the importance of *union*. He soon after died, leaving to the nation the recollection of his elevated character, his eminent services, and his bright example.

Few public men have, for so long a time, enjoyed the public confidence and real regard. From Braddock's defeat, in '55, till his own death, in December, '99, notwithstanding the various fortunes of the revolutionary war, the carping and detraction of short-sighted, impatient, or of malevolent, ambitious, or disappointed men, and the distracting political elements existing during his presidential career, his patriotism and judgment were confided in *by the mass of the people ;* and when he died, in the fullness of his fame, the public regret and respect for his memory were significantly manifested throughout the whole country.

Of all the great men prominent in our revolutionary times, his public character is freest from imperfection. He was not devoid of ambition, for that would have been unnatural; but in him it was an ambition to be of service to his country, and to mankind. He had not even the common desire of pecuniary acquisition, for he served throughout the revolutionary war with no other demand than the discharge of the economical expenses incident to his public position. He had no merely selfish views ; he never intrigued for, or even solicited, office or station; the official positions bestowed on him being the voluntary homage of his country ; and on his election to the presidency, on both occasions, the office was not only unsought by him, but the choice was unanimous. In the exercise of the duties of that important position, no public clamor or personal invective diverted him from the course of which his judgment approved; and in every act of his political administration he seemed to be actuated by an earnest desire to discharge his duty. What political errors he committed were not those of intention, but were attributable to the imperfection of humanity. We hold him up to the world as a great and a shining light, worthy of the admiration and commendation of mankind.

If he had died immediately after the resignation of his military command, his character, though illustrious, would have been incomplete. His ability, as a *statesman*, would not have been displayed. Though he was not active on the floor of the convention during the formation of our national constitution, it is not to be supposed that he did not exert an important influence on the conclusions of that distinguished body; for Patrick Henry has said that "in the first revolutionary congress, though Adams, and Rutledge, and others were distinguished as orators, yet, for solid information and sound judgment, Washington was unquestionably the greatest man on the floor." When he had assumed the presidency, his selection of Jefferson and Hamilton as heads of departments—of Jay and Ellsworth as chief justices—his tender of office to Marshall, afterwards distinguished as chief justice, evinced his knowledge of men; and the admirable judgment which he displayed in keeping the country aloof from foreign complications, and on the various important questions of foreign and domestic policy arising during his presidential career, evinced high powers of intellect and clear perception of the interest and welfare of the country. In acting in that high position, he evaded no just responsibility or official duty; not seeking to extend the executive authority beyond its legitimate limits, but acting in all respects with no other disposition than the proper discharge of the official obligation which he had assumed. In his political career he set an example worthy of imitation by his successors in the presidential office, and by rulers throughout the world.

His physical seemed to be in harmony with his mental characteristics. In stature he was somewhat above six feet, of large frame, of great strength, and of " unexceptionable make." He was of a dignified, imposing presence, inviting to confidence, but not to familiarity; of a sedate, grave countenance, seldom indulging in mirth, never boisterous, but not repressing good humor in others. He was not vain or assuming, but was affable in manner and respectful in his intercourse with all, and he excited, in an eminent degree, the regard and veneration of those, from the child to the aged, with whom he was intimately associated, and the respect and admiration of other persons of distinction with whom he came into contact. He was a signal honor to our country and to humanity. His fame is co-extensive with the civilized world, as a friend to political and personal liberty, and his name will descend in great and honorable renown to remote posterity.

We subjoin the following lines by Lord Byron relative to the distinguished subject of these remarks:

"Where may the wearied eye repose,
  When gazing on the great,
Where neither guilty glory glows,
  Nor despicable state?
Yes, one—the first, the last, the best—
The Cincinnatus of the West,
  Whom envy dared not hate,
Bequeathed the name of Washington;
To make man blush there was but one."

J. R. Ingersoll, of Philadelphia, in an address, remarked as follows :

" The late Lord Chancellor Erskine, when in the enjoyment of reputation more elevated than rank and power could confer, the fearless and successful advocate of the liberty and constitution of England, addressed a voluntary letter to General Washington, of which a copy was found among the papers of Lord Erskine, after his decease. It was as follows :

" LONDON, *March 15, 1795.*

" I have taken the liberty to introduce your august and immortal name in a short sentence, which will be found in the book I send you. I have a large acquaintance among the most valuable and exalted classes of men ; but you are the only human being for whom I ever felt an awful reverence. I sincerely pray God to grant a long and serene evening to a life so gloriously devoted to the universal happiness of the world.

" T. ERSKINE."

From a literary address at Edinburgh, by Lord Brougham :

" In Washington, we may contemplate every excellence, military and civil, applied to the service of his country and of mankind ; a triumphant warrior, unshaken in confidence when the most sanguine had right to despair ; a successful ruler in all the difficulties of a course wholly untried ; directing the formation of a new government, for a great people, the first time so rash an experiment had ever been tried by man ; voluntarily and unostentatiously retiring from supreme power, with the veneration of all parties, of all nations, of all mankind, that the rights of men might be conserved, and that his example might never be appealed to by vulgar tyrants.

" It will be the duty of the historian and the sage, in all ages, to omit no occasion of commending this illustrious man ; and until time shall be no more, will a test of the progress which our race has made in wisdom and virtue be derived from the veneration paid to the immortal name of Washington."

Letter from Governeur Morris.

In a letter of Governeur Morris to General Washington, from Philadelphia, October 30, 1787 it is remarked: "I have observed that your name to the constitution has been of infinite service. Indeed, I am convinced that if you had not attended the convention, and the same papers had been handed out to the world, it would have met with a colder reception, with fewer and weaker advocates, and with more and more strenuous opponents. As it is, should the idea prevail that you will not accept the presidency, it would prove fatal in many parts. The truth is, that your great and decided superiority leads men willingly to put you in a place which will not add to your personal dignity, nor raise you higher than you already stand; but they would not readily put another in the same situation, because they feel the elevation of others as operating, by comparison, the degradation of themselves; and however absurd the idea may be, yet you will agree with me that men must be treated as men, and not as machines, much less as philosophers, and least of all things as reasonable creatures, seeing that, in effect, they reason not to direct but to excuse their condition. Thus much for the public opinion on these subjects, which is not to be neglected in a country where opinion is everything.—*Page 289–90, vol. I, of Life of Governeur Morris, by Sparks.*

Speech of Mr. Webster.

The father of Daniel Webster was a member of the convention in New Hampshire, which assembled in February, 1788, to act upon the national constitution. A majority of the delegates had instructions from their towns to vote *against* the adoption of the Constitution. This was the case with Colonel Webster. But the convention was adjourned to meet again in June, and, in the meantime, Col. Webster obtained from his constituents permission to vote according to his own judgment. When the vote was about to be taken, he rose, and said:

"Mr. President, I have listened to the arguments for and against the constitution. I am convinced such a government as that constitution will establish, if adopted—a government acting directly on the people of the States—is necessary for the common defense and the general welfare. It is the only government which will enable us to pay off the national debt—the debt which we owe for the Revolution, and which we are bound in honor fully and fairly to discharge. Besides, I have followed the lead of Washington through seven years of war, and I have never been misled. His name is subscribed to this constitution. He will not mislead us now. I shall vote for its adoption."— *Note to pages 9, 10 of George Ticknor Curtis' Life of Daniel Webster. New York, Appleton & Co., 1870.*

As to the Farewell Address.

D. C. Claypool, former editor of the newspaper, the *Daily Advertiser*, published in Philadelphia, wrote from Philadelphia, February 22, 1826, relative to the first publication, in the year 1796, of the valedictory or farewell address by President Washington, stating that, a few days before the appearance of this memorable document in print, he received a message from the President, by his private secretary; and when he waited on the President, he stated that he had, for some time, contemplated retiring from public life, and had, at length, concluded to do so at the end of the (then) present term: that he had some thoughts and reflections on the occasion, which he deemed proper to communicate to the people of the United States, in the form of an address, and which he wished to appear in the *Daily Advertiser*, of which I was editor. After some conversation, the following Monday was fixed on as the time of its appearance; and he told me that his secretary would call on me, with a copy of the address, on the next (Friday) morning.

After the *proof sheet* had been compared with the copy, and corrected by myself, I carried another *proof*, and then a *revise*, to be examined by the President, who made but few alterations from the original, except in the punctuation, in which he was very minute.

The publication of the address, dated United States, September 17, 1796, being completed on the 19th, I waited on the President, with the original; and, in presenting it to him, expressed my regret at parting with it, and how much I should be gratified by being permitted to retain it : upon which, in an obliging manner, he handed it back to me, saying that, if I wished for it, I might keep it; and then I took my leave of him. I may say that his handwriting was familiar to me. The manuscript copy consists of thirty-two pages of quarto letter paper, sewed together as a book, and with many alterations; as, in some places, whole paragraphs are erased, and others substituted ; in others, many lines struck out ; in others, sentences and words erased, and others interlined, in their stead. The tenth, eleventh, and sixteenth pages are almost entirely expunged, saving only a few lines ; and one half of the thirty-first page is also effaced. A critical examination will show that the whole, from first to last, with all its numerous corrections, was the work of the same hand ; and I can confidentally affirm, that no other pen ever touched the manuscript now in my possession than that of the great and good man whose signature it bears.

D. C. CLAYPOOL.

PHILADELPHIA, *February 22, 1826.*

See the whole of the letter of Mr. Claypool, vol. I, p. 265-266-267, of the Memoirs of the Historical Society of Pennsylvania, published in 1864.

The original manuscript of the farewell address was, upon Mr. Claypool's death, sold at auction, in Philadelphia, by his representatives, and purchased by Mr. James Lenox, of New York, who printed an edition of a limited number of copies for private distribution, following the text as hitherto published, but noting from the manuscript the alterations and corrections of the illustrious author.— *Editor.*

Also, see *ante,* p. 307, as to the farewell address.

General Washington was born on 22d of February, 1732.

His farewell address was published September 17, 1796.

His second term expired on 4th March, 1797.

He died on 4th December, 1799, aged above 67 years.

JOHN ADAMS.

To *Mr. Adams* the country is deeply indebted. He was among the foremost in opposition to the aggressions of the King and Parliament. He was the early advocate for independence, and he supported the measure strenuously by his voice and his vote. Being subsequently in England, in an important diplomatic position, he imbibed a desire, or had his predilection strengthened for *titles*, as giving dignity to official position. He entertained an extravagant idea of the dignity or personal importance of the presidential office, and was in favor of surrounding it with striking marks of distinction. The official etiquette first established was maintained till the inauguration of Jefferson, when the coach and four, and other official paraphanalia, were omitted, with the attendance of members of both Houses on the President, in their answer to his inaugural or address, at the commencement of each session.

Mr. Adams was possessed of much vanity or self-esteem, and the exhibition of that quality in the Senate, and his interference there in matters not pertaining to his office, and as to which such action in the Vice President would not now be tolerated, caused repugnance towards him on the part of Senators.

After the declaration by Washington of his design to retire from office, Mr. Adams was nominated by the Federal party, without material opposition, and pretty much, as a matter of course; but his administration in that position manifested that, though possessing much ability and unquestionable patriotism and integrity, yet he was considered as deficient in the judgment, discretion, and temper, material to the proper discharge of the duties of that elevated station. He was charged with a want of discretion relative to the French complication, and his distrust of other distinguished men of his party, his repugnance to Mr. Hamilton, especially, and, perhaps, a desire to be considered as administering the government mainly by his own volition, without material influence by his cabinet officers, or other leading members of the Federal party, dissatisfied many, and a change in the presidential nomination was desired. It being difficult to accomplish such a result, he was continued at the helm, and was defeated; and Washington being dead, the party could not be rallied; and this defeat, with the abortive and discreditable attempt to elect Burr over Jefferson, and thus disappoint or violate the known wishes of the people, overwhelmed the Federal party, and under that name it passed out of existence. The constitution was soon after altered, requiring electors to designate the office for which their votes are intended.

Mr. Jefferson and Mr. Adams acted in harmony in the early stage of the revolutionary struggle, and then became especially distinguished, the first as the draughtsman of the Declaration, and the other as its advocate on the floor of the convention. They became for a time, from the force of political circumstances, estranged from each other; but, towards the end of their lives, their friendship revived and continued till their death. They were, at its conclusion, but for a brief space of time in this world, divided. They died on the same day, the 4th of July, 1826, the anniversary of that day which they had done so much to commemorate.

Mr. Jefferson was also the writer of the resolutions adopted by the *Kentucky* Legislature in November, 1798, which were construed or defined by that Legislature, in 1799, as follows: *Resolved*, That . . . . the several States who formed the constitution, being sovereign, and, of course, independent, have the unquestionable right to judge of its infraction, and that a nullification by those sovereignties of all unauthorized acts, done under color of that instrument, is the rightful remedy.*

Mr. Madison, in a letter in April, 1787, proposing a plan of a constitution of the United States, was in favor of giving to the General Government an absolute and unqualified veto on all acts whatever of the State Legislatures. But he afterwards drew up the resolutions adopted by the *Virginia* Legislature, in December, 1798, which were to the same effect as the resolutions adopted in Kentucky, which were drawn by Mr. Jefferson, in November, of the same year. Mr. Webster combatted the doctrine above referred to, in his celebrated speech in 1830, in reply to the speech of Mr. Hayne, of South Carolina, contending that the constitution was established not by the States, but by the people. This opinion is the prevailing one in the northern States, the other is the prevalent one in the southern States of the Union.—*Editor*.

NOTE.—General Washington, in a letter to Lafayette, December 25, 1798, declared, "The constitution, according to their (the Anti-Federalists) interpretation of it, would be a mere cipher." He also wrote, "We are to-day one nation, and to-morrow thirteen.—*See Conts., page 151.*

* See the Constitutional History of the United States, by Von Holst, p. 147.

As to Mr. Adams, Mr. Sullivan in his "Public Men of the Revolution," wrote: Mr. Adams, on the day of his inauguration, March 4, 1797, was in his sixty-second year. He was dressed in a full suit of pearl-colored broadcloth; with powdered hair. He was then bald on the top of his head. He was of middle stature, and full person; and of slow, deliberate manner, unless he was excited; and when this happened, he expressed himself with great energy.

Mr. Adams was a man of strong mind, of great learning, and of eminent ability to use knowledge, both in speech and writing. He was ever a man of purest morals, and is said to have been a firm believer in Christianity, not from habit and example, but from diligent investigation of its proofs. He had an uncompromising regard for his own opinion; and was strongly contrasted with Washington in this respect. He seemed to have supposed that his opinions could not be corrected by those of other men, nor bettered by any comparison. * * Mr. Adams came to the presidency at the time when more forbearance and discretion were required than he is supposed to have had. He seems to have been deficient in the rare excellence of attempting to see himself as others saw him; and he ventured to act as though everybody saw as he saw himself. He considered only what was right in his own views, and that was to be carried by main force, whatever the obstacles.

There was great difference of opinion among the Federal party whether to seek the election of John Adams or Thomas Pinckney. As the Constitution then was, both were voted for by that party, expecting that one of them would be President and the other Vice President. Mr. Jefferson and Mr. Clinton, of New York, were the two opposing candidates. Most unexpectedly the result was that Mr. Adams stood highest—*Mr. Jefferson* next, and Mr. Pinckney third. It was supposed that so many of the eastern electors as preferred Mr. Adams to Mr. Pinckney, placed the latter candidate lower than they intended to do, and thereby gave a result which was exceedingly unwelcome as to the *Vice President.—Sullivan.*

MR. JEFFERSON.

When Mr. Jefferson came to Philadelphia in March, 1797, he was about fifty years of age. His *personnel*, as now recollected, was this : He was a tall man, over six feet in stature, neither full nor thin in body. His limbs were long and loosely jointed. His hair was of a reddish tinge, combed loosely over the forehead, and at the sides, and tied behind. His complexion was light or sandy. His forehead rather high and broad. His eyebrows long and straight, his eyes blue, his cheek bones high, his face broad between his eyes, his chin long and his mouth large. His dress was a black coat and light under clothes. He had no polish of manners, but a simplicity and sobriety of deportment. He was quiet and unobtrusive, and yet a stranger would perceive that he was in the presence of one who was not a common man. His manner of conversing was calm and deliberate and free from all gesticulation ; but he spoke like one who considered himself entitled to deference, and as though he measured what he said by some standard of self-complacency. The expression of his face was that of thoughtfulness and observation ; and certainly, not of that of openness and frankness. When speaking he did not look at his auditor, but cast his eyes toward the ceiling or anywhere but at the eyes of his listener. He had already become a personage of some distinction and an object of curiosity, even to a very young man. These personal descriptions are from memory, after the lapse of many years and may not accord with those of persons who had more or better opportunities to observe ; and are not, therefore, offered with confidence that Mr. Jefferson is here, in all respects, justly described.

During his Vice Presidency, (during the administration of Mr. Adams,) Mr. Jefferson was employed, as usual for that officer, in the Senate. It does not appear that the Vice President was ever called to cabinet meetings in Washington's time; or that Mr. Jefferson was ever called to such meetings in the presidency of Mr Adams, or advised with him in any way.—*Sullivan.*

As to the Declaration.

Mr. Everett, speaking of the Declaration of Independence, says: " This trust devolved on Thomas Jefferson, and with it rests on him the imperishable renown of having penned the Declaration of Independence. To have been the instrument of expressing, in one brief, decisive act, the concentrated will and resolution of a whole family of States, of unfolding in one all-important manifesto, the causes, the motives, and the justification of this great movement in human affairs; to have been permitted to give the impress and peculiarity of his own mind to a charter of public rights, destined, or rather let me say already elevated to an importance, in the estimation of many, equal to anything human ever borne on parchment or expressed in the visible signs of thought. This is the glory of Thomas Jefferson."

ALEXANDER HAMILTON.

Towards Mr. Hamilton Mr. Maclay seemed to entertain strong repugnance. This appeared to be owing mainly to hs originating and supporting the provision for the assumption of the *State debts*. To the funding of the domestic debts of the *General Government*, contracted during the revolutionary war, and of the *foreign* debts, no opposition existed ; but Mr. Hamilton recommended the assumption, by the General Government, of the debts of *the States*. To this proposition Mr. Maclay and others objected, at least until a settlement was had between the States, by which the States which were in advance in appropriations during the war should be paid their advancements ; and it was alleged by Mr. Maclay that Pennsylvania was in advance to the amount of a million of dollars. But Mr. Hamilton, having little confidence in the patriotism and intelligence of the mass of the people, and in the sufficiency of the Constitution, not perceiving the vitality since manifested to exist in it, and which, so late as 1802, in a letter to Governor Morris, he pronounced to be " a frail and worthless fabric," and as a means of establishing and supporting the public credit, and, perhaps, with a desire to have an interested body of loan or stockholders to support the Government, as Secretary of the Treasury recommended such assumption,* and he urged the matter so far as to barter away the permanent seat of government, in order to effect it. This was an improper expedient, and deserving of reprobation. He was charged, through the funding measure, with a desire of advancing his private fortune ; but it does not appear that he was influenced by such a motive ; and it is alleged that to guard against such an imputation,

---

*Wolcott, in April, 1790, wrote that the assumption of the State debt was necessary for the existence of the National Government. If the State governments are to prove for their payment, these creditors will oppose all national provisions as being inconsistent with their interest.—*Gibb's Wolcott, 1, p. 45.*

Van Holst, in his Constitutional and Political History of the United States, has observed that the good opinion of foreign nations could be regained only on condition that the credit of the Union was restored ; that the funding of the debt of the Union, and the assumption by the Union of the debts of the States, were the two principal pillars on which the new political structure could be made to rest.—*Van Holst, pp. 84–88.*

he advised his immediate family connections to refrain from such speculation, then much practiced, as the probability of assumption increased. The provision in the funding bill for the assumption of purchased claims *to their full value at the time of the assumption*, without regard to the amount paid to the original creditors, was also made a ground of objection to the funding bill. The report of Mr. Hamilton on the subject of the public credits, giving the reasons for the assumption, will be found in the second volume of the Annals of Congress.

It is much to the credit of Mr. Hamilton, that notwithstanding the opinion he entertained of the constitution as giving to the General Government too little force or power, he nevertheless supported it by his articles in the *Federalist*, and in the convention in New York.

The plan of government submitted by him to the constitutional convention, recommending a Chief Executive and Senate, to serve during good behavior—the President to have an absolute negative on the acts of Congress; the Senate to have the sole power of declaring war; Senators not to be liable to expulsion, and to be capable of voting by proxy; the President to be chosen by citizens having an estate of inheritance, or for three lives, in land, or clear personal estate of the value of one thousand Spanish milled dollars, was deficient in wisdom, and not calculated to receive the public support.

Mr. Hamilton, in his much celebrated report, in December, 1791, on the subject of " Domestic Manufactures," (see third volume of the Annals of Congress, pp. 1011–12,) first gave prominence to the clause in the constitution relative to *the general welfare*, as a subject or element, for the promotion of which Congress had power to raise taxes and appropriate money. This construction of Mr. Hamilton gave strong offense to Mr. Jefferson, who was for limiting the collection and appropriation of public money to carrying out the express powers conferred on Congress by the constitution. This provision has been recently called into requisition in the Senate of the United States, in support of an appropriation in aid of the centennial celebration.

Mr. Hamilton's view of the constitutional provision on the subject of *treason* was extreme. From an opinion of the importance or necessity of the case, an opinion not confined to him, but entertained by others—that in order to manifest the strength of the constitution, an example of severity was important, he was in favor of the execution of Fries, who had been convicted, in Pennsylvania, of *treason*, for mere opposition to the execution of an act of Congress, (the excise act,) without any design of "levying war against the United States, or of adhering to their enemies—giving them aid and comfort," which is the only mode in which treason against the Government can be committed ; and he made the pardon of Fries a subject of complaint against Mr. Adams, who, from the belief that the conduct of Fries would not warrant a conviction of treason, or was not deserving of death, or from some other motive, made him the subject of clemency.

This criticism as to *treason* will apply to Mr. Hamilton's views relative to the riotous proceedings in western Pennsylvania, commonly termed the Whisky Insurrection, a disturbance on account of the attempted enforcement of a particular law, (the excise law,) which was considered as especially grievous in that remote district, where whisky was used as an article of commerce with the east for their necessary articles, on account of the facility of its transportation. These violent proceedings were liable to indictment as misdemeanors, but they were not liable to the penalty of treason, as it is defined in the Constitution.

Mr. Hamilton was a man of probity in the common affairs of life, of patriotic impulses, of eminent and varied ability, Jefferson styling him " a Colossus to the Anti-Republican party ; a host in himself ; " nobody but Mr. Madison " that can meet him ; " and he exercised much influence over many of the public men of his day, and he certainly rendered important services, both military and civil, to the country during his eventful career. But in the full tide of life he fell a victim in a duel. He had not the moral courage to avow unfavorable opinions of Burr which he had honestly entertained and expressed, and, relying on an enlightened public opinion for his justification, refused the arbitrament of arms. He was not required, even by the false code of honor, to contend in moral combat with a man who, to use his own terms, he considered to be " one of the worst men in the community, who private character is not defended by his most partial friends ;" " whose public principles have no other spring or aim than his own aggrandizement *per fas et nefas*, the Cataline of America." His own courage had been signally manifested at Yorktown, the closing battle-field of the revolution. He acted otherwise, and fell in the contest, thus depriving the country of a valuable life, and leaving to the youth of the nation a pernicious example.—*Editor.*

The duel occurred on the 11th of July, 1804, and Mr. Hamilton died on the next day.

As to Hamilton, Mr. Sullivan wrote: Alexander Hamilton, when appointed Secretary of the Treasury, was about thirty-three years of age. He resumed the practice of the law in the city of New York, in the year 1795, at the age of thirty-eight. In December of that year his appearance was this: He was under middle size; thin in person, but remarkably erect and dignified in his deportment. His hair was turned back from his forehead, powdered, and collected in a club behind. His complexion was exceedingly fair, and varying from this only by the almost feminine rosiness of his cheeks. His might be considered, as to figure and color, an uncommonly handsome face. When at rest, it had rather a severe and thoughtful expression; but when engaged in conversation, it easily assumed an attractive smile.—*Sullivan.*

As to Treason.

The third section of the third article of the Constitution of the United States is in part as follows: " Treason against the United States shall consist only in levying war against them, or in adhering to their enemies, giving them aid and comfort."

In the convention which formed the Constitution, Luther Martin, of Maryland, proposed the following: " Provided that no act or acts done by one or more of the States against the United States, or by any citizen of any one of the United States under the authority of one or more of the said States, shall be deemed treason or punished as such; but in case of war being levied by one or more of the States against the United States, the conduct of each party toward the other and their adherents respectively, shall be regulated by the laws of war and of nations." This provision was not adopted. *See Elliott's Debates, Vol. I, p. 382.*

AARON BURR.

Though Aaron Burr is not mentioned in this journal, yet as his fortunes were so intimately associated with Hamilton, a brief description by the same person is given as he appeared in December, 1795. He was probably about Hamilton's age. He was of about the same stature as Hamilton ; a thin man, but differently formed. His motions in walking were not, like Hamilton's, erect, but a little stooping, and far from graceful. His face was short and broad ; his black eyes uncommonly piercing. His manner gentle and seductive. But he had a calmness and sedateness, when these suited his purpose ; and an eminent authority of manner, when the occasion called for this. He was said to have presided with great dignity in the Senate ; and especially at the trial of Judge Chase. Though eminent as a lawyer, he was said not to be a man of distinguished eloquence, nor of luxuriant mind. His speeches were short and to the purpose.—*Sullivan, 262.*

ROBERT MORRIS.

Robert Morris was born at Liverpool, England, in 1733. After the death of his father, which happened from a casualty, he was placed in the counting house of Charles Willing, a merchant in Philadelphia. After he had arrived at full or legal age, he became a partner with Thomas Willing, a son of his patron. This mercantile connection continued for nearly forty years. After difficulties had arisen with England, he and his partner, though largely engaged in business, signed the non-importation agreement of 1765, and sustained other patriotic measures. After the Revolutionary war had begun, Mr. Morris was elected a member of the Assembly of Pennsylvania; and in 1775, he was elected by it a delegate to the Continental Congress. He was opposed to Independence when the proposition was made, and voted against Mr. Lee's resolution on the 1st of July, 1776. This was from an opinion that it was premature; and he was absent from the convention on the 2d and 4th of July, with Dickinson, Biddle and Allen; so that the vote of the State on the 4th was carried by Franklin, Morton and Wilson against Humphreys and Willing. The new convention of the State retained Mr. Morris, but superseded Dickinson, Humphreys, Willing and Allen, and appointed, in their stead, Messrs. Ross, Smith, Rush, Clymer and Taylor; and when the Declaration had been engrossed, Mr. Morris, on the 2d of August, signed it. He remained in Congress until the end of the session of 1787-8, and served upon important committees, the principal one being the committee charged with the spending of money *in the secret service;* and during his service in Congress on various occasions, he pledged his individual credit, to a considerable extent, for the public service. His service in that respect continued throughout the war, and specially after appointment as Superintendent of Finance on the 20th of February, 1781. He performed a service of special importance in procuring the pecuniary means to enable General Washington to move his forces to the South, where at Yorktown occurred the last important battle scene of the Revolution. Mr. Morris was a member of the convention to frame the National Constitution; and was subsequently elected one of the Senators in the first Senate. He there drew the longer term, and was a member of it from 1789 till the 4th of March, 1795.

He was, for many years, prosperous as a merchant, and was considered as having acquired very considerable wealth. He subsequently became embarrassed. He attributed his first embarrassment to the failure of two commercial houses in Dublin and London in the year 1793, by which he suffered largely.

He was seized with the then prevailing mania for speculation *in lands*. The country called the Genessee country, lying west of *the Seneca Lake* in New York, was originally claimed against New York by the State of Massachusetts, under an unreasonable claim that her charter bounds extended to the western sea or the Pacific ocean. As to the claim see remarks hereafter.

In the year 1786 commissioners were appointed by the States of Massachusetts and New York to settle their respective claims both as to soil and jurisdiction; and, on the 16th of December of that year, the soil west of the Seneca Lake was ceded by Massachusetts and the jurisdiction over it to New York. In 1787 or '88 Messrs. Gorham and Phelps purchased from Massachusetts the whole territory which had been ceded to it. Subsequently, however, the Legislature of Massachusetts took back from Gorham & Phelps the four million of acres west of the *Genessee river*. In November, 1790, Mr. Morris purchased, from Gorham & Phelps, twelve hundred thousand acres of the territory *which they had retained,* and to which the Indian title had been extinguished. The purchase money is supposed by his son to have been seventy thousand pounds. In 1791 Mr. Morris sold to Pulteney and another the land which he had bought from Gorham & Phelps for about seventy thousand pounds *sterling*. In 1791 Mr. Morris, for himself and others, who subsequently disappointed him, purchased from Massachusettes the four million of acres which that State had received back from Gorham & Phelps. The purchase money is supposed to have been one hundred thousand pounds in *Massachusetts money*.

In the year 1792–3 and 4, Mr. Morris entered warrants in the Land Office of Pennsylvania for about 160,000 acres. In April, 1794, he entered into an association with John Nicholson, then Controller of the State of Pennsylvania, for the purchase of about a million of acres of land in Pennsylvania—the association being called *The Asylum Company*. In February, 1795, the North American Land Company was formed between Morris, Nicholson & Greenleaf, which was designed to dispose of about six millions of acres of land in Pennsylvania, Virginia, Kentucky, North and South Carolina and Georgia. These extensive purchases and arrangements and

other monetary engagements led to the bankruptcy of Mr. Morris.
It may also be noted that in the year 1791 he purchased the whole
square of ground on Chestnut street, Philadelphia, extending from
Seventh to Eighth street, and from Chestnut to Walnut, except a lot
of about fifty feet front on the corner of Seventh street, and extending in depth about 250 feet on Seventh street.   For this ground he
was to pay £10,000.   He engaged C. Enfant, a French architect, to
erect for him a splendid dwelling house on Chestnut street on this
ground, and it has been said that his expenditure in the erection of
this house contributed materially to his subsequent embarrassment; but *Mr. Westcott,* in his book entitled, *The Historic Mansions
of Philadelphia,* contradicts this opinion, and states that the expenditure on the building of this house did not much exceed thirty
thousand dollars.

Among the first of his creditors in instituting suit against Mr.
Morris was the Bank of Pennsylvania, and levy was made on the
lot on Chestnut street previously described, and it was sold at a sacrifice.   Mr. Morris was arrested, and was confined in prison.   The
first bankrupt law was passed on the 4th of April, 1800, and was
to take effect on the 1st of July following.   John Nicholson was
also arrested and died in prison; but subsequently two thirds in
number and amount of the creditors of Mr. Morris agreed to his
discharge, and he was released from imprisonment in the latter end
of 1801.   It is stated that he was imprisoned on process to June
term, 1798, and, if so, he was in prison for more than three years.
The amount of debts proved against Mr. Morris, according to the
report of the commissioners of bankruptcy, was nearly three millions of dollars.   He died on the 7th of May, 1806, aged seventy-
three years.   During the life of Mrs. Morris she received from the
Holland Land Company an annuity of $2,000, in consideration of
her release of dower in certain lands sold by Mr. Morris to that
company.   One of the sons of Mr. Morris was elected sheriff of
Philadelphia in 1841, but died before he had been a year in office.

Mr. Sullivan, in his book relative to " Public Men of the Revolution," describes Mr. Morris as follows : In his person (as now recollected) he was nearly six feet in stature ; of large, full, well-formed,
vigorous frame, with clear, smooth, florid complexion.   His loose
gray hair was unpowdered.   His eyes were gray, of middle size, and
uncommonly brilliant.   He wore, as was common at that day, a full
suit of broadcloth, of the same color, and of light mixture.   His
manners were gracious and simple, and free from the formality which
generally prevailed.   He was very affable, and mingled in the common conversation even of the young.

Note as to the Claim from Sea to Sea.

Massachusetts was not the only Province or State which claimed such an extreme boundary. Connecticut, or a portion of its citizens, claimed under it a part of the upper portion of Pennsylvania under a similar provision in its charter, and Virginia also claimed extension to the western sea. The land beyond the Mississippi did not belong to the English Government, and where the western sea was, was not known in England at the dates of these charters. Some of Chaplain's men in the early part of the last century, who had been a few days' march west from Quebec, reported that they had seen it from a high mountain. In or about the year 1607 when the company were soliciting a charter for Virginia, it designed a search for the western sea, and had a barge constructed, which, for convenience, might be taken to pieces. Captain Newport, who was afterwards Deputy Governor, was instructed to ascend the *James river in Virginia* as far as the falls thereof; and then, carrying the barge beyond the falls, he was to proceed *to the South sea;* and he was ordered not to return *without a lump of gold, or a certainty of the said sea.* John Smith, the pioneer of Virginia, advised against the expedition; but Captain Newport set off with 120 men, and went about forty miles above the falls of the James river, and then returned without having dug a lump of gold or having seen the western sea, more than 2,000 miles away.—*See Paine's Essay Public Good, p. 282–3; also 1 Bancroft, 129.—Editor.*

AS TO OTHER MEMBERS OF THE FIRST SENATE.

JOHN LANGDON. He was educated for mercantile pursuits. He was one of the party who removed the powder and military stores from Fort William and Mary in 1774. In 1775–6 he was a delegate to Congress. In 1783 he was again elected. In November, 1788, he was elected a member of the United States Senate. From 1805 to 1808, and in 1810 and 1811, he was Governor of New Hampshire. He died in August, 1819, aged seventy-eight.—*Blake.*

PAINE WINGATE was born in Stratham, in New Hampshire, May 14, 1739, and graduated at Harvard college in 1759. He was a clergyman for several years ; but in 1789 was a Senator in Congress, and probably was the last surviving member of that body. In 1798 he was appointed a judge of the Supreme Court of New Hampshire and held this office until 1809, being then seventy years of age. For many years he was the oldest graduate of Harvard college. He died in 1838, aged ninety-nine years. He was highly esteemed by his contemporaries.—*Blake.*

CALEB STRONG.—When Thomas Jefferson first became President, Caleb Strong was Governor of Massachusetts. He was born in Northampton in 1744 ; educated at Harvard University ; by profession a lawyer ; and was actively engaged in the first scenes of the Revolution. As early as 1775, when he was only thirty-one years of age, he was a member of the committee of public safety. He was in public service during the whole of revolutionary times ; a member of the convention which framed the Federal Constitution and of that which adopted it in his native State. He was a Senator in Congress from 1789 to 1797 ; Governor of Massachusetts from 1800 to 1807 ; and again elected in 1812, and continued in that office during the war. He refused to give up the militia called for at the beginning of the war, because, in his opinion, the call was not warranted by the Constitution. In this opinion he was sustained by that of the Supreme Judicial Court.

Governor Strong was a tall man, of moderate fulness, of rather

long visage, dark complexion and blue eyes. He wore his hair
loose, combed over his forehead, and slightly powdered. He had
nothing of the polish of cities in his demeanor, but a gentle complaisance and kindness. He was a man of strong mind, calm, cool
judgment, and of purest character throughout his life. He died in
November, 1819, aged seventy-four years.—*Sullivan.*

TRISTRAM DALTON was born at Newburyport, Massachusetts, in
1738, and graduated at Harvard in 1755. He was Speaker of the
House of Representatives of Massachusetts, and a member of the
Senate. Afterwards a member of the United States Senate. He
was subsequently appointed surveyor of the ports of Boston and
Charleston, which office he held until his death in 1817. He was
noted for gentleness and elegance of manners—for mental cultivation and integrity.—*Blake.*

OLIVER ELLSWORTH graduated at Princeton in 1766. In 1777 he
was chosen a delegate in Congress. In 1784 he was appointed a
judge of the Supreme Court of Massachusetts. In 1787 he was a
member of the convention which framed the Federal Constitution,
and was afterwards a member of the State convention and favored
its ratification by that State. In 1789 he was a member of the
United States Senate. In 1796 he was appointed by Washington
Chief Justice of the Supreme Court of the United States ; but, on
account of ill health he resigned the office in 1800. In 1799 he was
appointed by President Adams envoy extraordinary to France to
negotiate a treaty. He died in 1807, aged sixty-five.—*Ben Perley
Poore.*

WILLIAM SAMUEL JOHNSON graduated at Yale in 1744. He studied
law, and in 1765 he was a delegate to the Congress which met at
New York; and in 1766 an agent of Connecticut in England.
While there he formed acquaintance with eminent men, and for years
was a correspondent of Doctor Johnson. He returned in 1771, and
in 1772 he was appointed a judge of the Supreme Court of Connecticut, which office he relinquished in 1774. In 1785 he was a
delegate to Congress, and in 1787 a member of the convention
which framed the Federal Constitution. He was one of the first
Senators in Congress from Connecticut, and it is said assisted Mr.
Ellsworth in drawing the judiciary bill. From 1792 till 1800, he
was the president of Columbia college ; after which period he resided in his native village until his death in 1819, aged ninety-two.—
Blake.

RUFUS KING was graduated at Harvard college in 1777 and was admitted to the bar in 1780.   In 1784 he was a delegate from Massachusetts in Congress, and whilst there, in March 1785, he brought forward and advocated the passage of the resolution by which slavery was prohibited in the territory northwest of the Ohio.   In 1787 he was a member of the convention which framed the Constitution of the United States and bore a considerable part in its formation, and was one of the committee to report a final draft of it.   In 1788 he removed to New York, and in 1789 he and General Schuyler were elected Senators to the first Senate.   In 1796 he was appointed by President Washington minister to England, but returned in 1803.   In 1813 he was elected by the Democrats of New York to the United States Senate.   In 1825 he was again appointed minister to England, but was prevented by disease contracted during his passage from the active discharge of his duties.   He remained abroad about a year, when he returned.   As an orator he was rather distinguished in Congress.   In person he was above the middle size. His countenance was manly and denoted intelligence of a high order.   He died in 1827 aged seventy-two.—*Blake and National Portrait Gallery, and Biographica Americana.*

As to Mr. King, Mr. Sullivan wrote : Rufus King, at this time, was about thirty-three years of age.   He was an uncommonly handsome man in face and form, and he had a powerful mind, well cultivated, and was a dignified and graceful speaker.   He had the appearance of one who was a gentleman by nature, and who had well improved all her gifts.   It is a rare occurrence to see a finer assemblage of personal and intellectual qualities, cultivated to the best effect, than were seen in this gentleman.—*See Vol. III of the National Portrait Gallery.*

PHILIP SCHUYLER was a Major General in the American army during the Revolution, to which office he was appointed in 1775, and was despatched to the fortifications in the north of New York for the purpose of preparing for an invasion of Canada.   His health became impaired and the command devolved upon General Montgomery.   After his recovery he was employed in directing the military operations in that section ; and on the approach of Burgoyne, in 1777, he made efforts to obstruct his progress.   In consequence of the evacuation of Ticonderoga by General St. Clair, he became unreasonably suspected and was superseded in the chief command by General Gates.   He subsequently rendered important services in the operations at New York, though not in command.   He was a member of Congress previous to the formation of the Federal Constitution, and afterwards twice a Senator. He died at Albany in 1804, in his seventy-third year. He possessed a mind of great vigor and enterprise, and was characterized by integrity and amiability.— *Blake.*

WILLIAM PATERSON. He graduated at Princeton in 1763 in the same class with Tapping Reeve. He was Attorney General of New Jersey from 1776 to 1786. He was a member of the convetion which framed the Federal Constitution. In 1789 he was chosen a Senator of the United States, but resigned in 1790. In 1791 he was elected Governor of New Jersey, and held the office for two years. In 1793 he was appointed a justice of the Supreme Court of the United States, which position he held until his death. He died September 9, 1806, aged sixty-four years.—*Blake.*

PHILEMON DICKINSON.—Mr. Dickinson was born near to Dover, Delaware, in 1739. He was an officer in the Revolutionary army, and commanded the New Jersey militia in the battle of Monmouth. He was elected a Senator of the United States from New Jersey in place of William Paterson, appointed judge, and served from December 6, 1790, till March, 1793. He died in February, 1809.— *Blake.*

JONATHAN ELMER.—Dr. Jonathan Elmer and Judge Paterson were the Senators from New Jersey in the first Senate of the United States. In a notice by William Maclay in his Journal, under date of September 3, 1789, Dr. Elmer is quite favorably spoken of. Dr. Elmer was born in Cumberland county, New Jersey, in November, 1745. He studied medicine and practiced extensively in Jersey, and it is said was regarded by *Dr. Rush* as a distinguished physician. He was, during the Revolution, an ardent Whig, and in the year 1774 approved of the destruction of the tea which had been stored at Greenwich in Jersey. He held various offices in that State, and in November, 1776, he was chosen by the Legislature of that State a member of the General Congress, in which body he served for several years, and for a while in conjunction with Richard Stockton and Dr. Witherspoon. After the adoption of the Constitution of the United States he was, as a Federalist, chosen a member of the first Senate, in which he drew the shorter term of two years, which expired on the 4th of March, 1791.

He did not confine his studies to the science of medicine, but also directed his attention to the law, and he became a judge of the court of common pleas. Whilst acting in that capacity he, as he alleged, following the example of English judges during the prevalence of the plague in London, directed a prisoner in confinement to be removed from the prison, where he was in danger of or was affected by disease, to the house of his mother, where he died. The creditor inhumanly brought suit against the sheriff for an escape ; and when the case came up for trial, objection was made to Judge Elmer's sitting on the case ; but he maintained his position and the plaintiff lost his suit. On account of his age and failing health he declined in 1814 to remain longer on the bench. In the year 1798 he united himself with the Presbyterian church at Bridgeton, and subsequently became a ruling elder and an active member of the church. He died in September, 1817.—*Editor.*

RICHARD BASSETT.—Mr. Bassett was born in Delaware, and received a liberal education. He studied law, and was admitted to the bar and practiced. He was a delegate from Delaware to the convention which framed the Constitution of the United States ; and was a United States Senator from Delaware in the first Senate, serving from March 4, 1789, till March 3, 1791. He was a Presidential elector in 1797, voting for Mr. Adams as President ; was Governor of Delaware from 1798 till 1801, and was a United States circuit judge in 1801–2. He died in September, 1815.—*Poore's Directory.*

GEORGE READ was born in Cecil county, Maryland, in 1733. He was admitted to the bar in 1752. He was Attorney General of the three lower counties in Delaware from 1763 till 1774. He was a delegate in the Continental Congress from 1774 to 1777, and a delegate to the State Constitutional Convention of 1776, and was its president ; and was a delegate from Delaware to the convention which framed the Constitution of the United States. He was a United States Senator from 1789 to 1793 ; was the Chief Justice of Delaware from 1793 till his death in September, 1798. A notice of his life and correspondence, by his grandson, William Thompson Reed, has been published.—*Poore's Directory.*

CHARLES CARROLL, of Carrollton.—The charter of Maryland was obtained from Charles I by Lord Baltimore, in June, 1632. Lord Baltimore was a Roman Catholic, and it is said his avowed intention was to erect an asylum in America for persons of the Catholic faith. By the charter, Lord Baltimore was created absolute proprietary, saving allegiance to the crown. But license was given to all British subjects to transport themselves thither, and they and their posterity were declared to be entitled to the liberties of Englishmen, as if born within the kingdom, with power to make laws for the province " not repugnant to the jurisprudence of England." At an early period the proprietary had declared in favor of *religious toleration*, and in 1649 the Assembly adopted that principle by declaring " that no persons professing to believe in Jesus Christ should be molested in respect to their religion, or in the free exercise thereof." The State thus became *the first* of the American States in which religious toleration was established by law.

In 1702 Charles Carroll, the father of Charles Carroll, of Carrollton, was born. It is stated that " he took an active part in the affairs of the Provincial Government; and in the religious disputes of the time, stood prominent as one of the leading and most influential members of the Catholic faith." In September, 1737, his son, Charles Carroll, surname of Carrollton, was born. At eight years of age he was taken to France to be educated. He remained there until 1757, when he visited London, and there commenced the study of law. In 1764 he returned to Maryland. In 1765 the stamp act caused much excitement in the country, and Charles Carroll, the subject of this sketch, took a zealous part on the side of the colonists. The stamp act was at length repealed. Mr. Carroll became distinguished as a writer on the popular side. The delegates of the Province at length prohibited the importation of tea. After this had been done, a vessel arrived at Annapolis with a quantity of tea on board. Popular violence was threatened, and the owner of the vessel applying to Mr. Carroll, was advised to burn the vessel and the tea in it, which was done, with the sails of the vessel set and its colors displayed, amidst the acclimations of the multitude.

In February, 1776, Mr. Carroll, then a member of the Maryland Convention, was appointed by the Continental Congress to visit Canada, in conjunction with Dr. Franklin, Samuel Chase, and the Rev. John Carroll, to endeavor to influence the Canadians to unite their efforts with those of the United Provinces in the political struggle; but the defeat of General Montgomery's army, and the opposition of priests, rendered the mission abortive. Mr. Carroll arrived at Philadelphia from this mission when the subject of independence was under discussion in the convention. The delegates from Maryland had been instructed to refuse their assent for it; but Mr. Carroll proceeded to Annapolis, and in the convention advocated independence; and, on the 28th of June, new instructions were given, and on the 4th of July, 1776, the votes of the Maryland delegates were given for independence. Mr. Carroll was appointed a delegate to the convention, and took his seat in it on the 18th of July. On the next day a resolution was adopted for engrossing the Declaration on parchment, and he was one of those who signed it.   He assisted in framing the Constitution of Maryland, and continued in Congress until 1778.   He was a member of the Senate of the State for several years, and was a member of *the first Senate of the United States* from 1789 till 1791.   Subsequently he was without public position.   After the death of Jefferson and Adams he was the sole survivor of those who signed the Declaration.   He died on the 14th of November, 1832, in the ninety-sixth year of his age.   He was descended from an Irish family, and inherited a large estate.   Mr. Sullivan stated of him that he was a small, thin person, of gracious, polished manners—that at the age of ninety he was still upright, and could hear and see as well as men commonly do.   He had a smiling expression when he spoke ; and that he had none of the reserve which usually attends old age.   He was said to have preserved his vigor by riding on horseback, and by daily bathing in cold water.

Oliver Wolcott, who was Secretary of the Treasury under the administration of Washington and Adams, wrote of him, that Mr. C.'s opinions are such as were to have been expected from a wise, virtuous, firm and experienced man.   I have long considered this gentleman as one of the most distinguished props of society in our country." (See Gibbs Wolcott, vol. 2, p. 446.)

Charles Carroll, the father of Charles Carroll, of Carrollton, was an agent of Lord Baltimore ; and it is probable that the wealth of the latter was mainly owing to lands obtained by his father from Lord Baltimore.—*Editor.*

JOHN HENRY was born at Easton, Maryland, and graduated at Princeton in 1760, and studied law.   He was a delegate from Maryland to the Continental Congress in 1778 till 1781, and from 1784 till 1787.   He was a United States Senator from Maryland from March 4, 1789, till December, 1797, when he resigned, having been elected Governor of Maryland. He died in December, 1798.—*Poore's Directory.*

RICHARD HARRY LEE was born in Virginia in 1732, and was sent to England to be educated.   He returned in 1751.   In 1758 he tendered his services to General Braddock as captain, but they were declined.   He was elected a delegate to the House of Burgesses in 1757 and took an active part in Revolutionary movements.   He was a member of the first Congress in 1774.   On June 10, 1776, he introduced the motion to declare *independence*, and when it was adopted he would have been of course the chairman of the committee to draw up the Declaration ; but sickness in his family induced his absence, and Jefferson was fortunately appointed to prepare the Declaration.

Mr. Lee was reëlected to Congress in 1778, but retired in 1780. He served in the State Legislature and as colonel in the militia. He was again in Congress in 1784, and was chosen its President, but retired at the end of the year. On the adoption of the Federal Constitution he was elected a Senator of the United States. He took his seat in April, 1789; was at one time its President, but resigned on account of ill health in 1792. He died in Virginia in June, 1794.— *Poore's Directory.*

Resolution from Virginia.

The convention of Virginia on the 15th of May, 1776, passed a resolution by which, *inter alia*, they decreed : " That their delegates in Congress be instructed to propose to that body to declare the United Colonies *free and independent States*, absolved from all allegiance or dependence upon the crown or Parliament of Great Britain ; and that they give the assent of the Colony to such declaration and to measures for forming foreign alliances and a confederation of the Colonies, providing that the power of forming governments for and the regulation of the internal concerns of each Colony be left to the respective Colonial Legislatures."—*Bancroft, Vol. VIII, p. 378.*

In conformity with this resolve Mr. Lee, on the 10th of June, 1776, submitted the resolution, " That these Colonies are and of right ought to be free and independent States—that they are absolved from all allegiance to the British crown ; and that all political connection between them and the State of Great Britain is and ought to be totally dissolved."

WILLIAM GRAYSON was born in Virginia. He received a classical education in England, graduating at the University of Oxford, and studied law at the Temple in London. After his return he practiced law at Dumfries, Virginia ; and in August, 1776, he was appointed an aid-de-camp to General Washington. He entered the Revolutionary army as colonel of a Virginia regiment, in January, 1777, and was distinguished at the battle of Monmouth. He was appointed a delegate to the Continental Congress, serving from 1784 to 1787. He was a member of the Virginia Convention, and on the question of adopting the Federal Constitution, he opposed its adoption. He was appointed a Senator in the first Congress, and took his seat in May, 1789, and served until his death at Dumfries, Virginia, on his way to New York, then the seat of the General Government, in March, 1790.—*Poore's Directory.*

NOTE.—As to Mr. Grayson, see page 71 of the sketches. James Monroe was the successor of William Grayson.

RALPH IZARD was born near to Charleston, South Carolina, in 1742. He was educated at Cambridge, England. He inherited an ample fortune, and in 1771 settled in London ; but the troubled condition of American politics induced him, in 1774, to retire to the Continent. In 1780 he returned to the United States, where he was instrumental in procuring the appointment of General Greene for the command of the Southern army. He pledged his whole estate as security for funds needed in the purchase of ships of war in Europe. In 1781 he entered the Continental Congress ; and upon the adoption of the Federal Constitution, he was elected a United States Senator from South Carolina, and he served there from March 4, 1789, till March 3, 1795. He died near to Charleston May 30, 1804.—*Poore's Directory and American Cyclopedia.*

PIERCE BUTLER was born in Ireland in July, 1744, and it is said that he was descended from the family of the Dukes of Ormond. Before the Revolution he was a major in a British regiment in Boston, but resigned before the Revolution and settled in Charleston, South Carolina. In 1787 he was a delegate from South Carolina to the Continental Congress, and was a member of the convention which framed the Constitution of the United States. He was elected as a Democrat, United States Senator from South Carolina, serving from March, 1789, till 1796. He was again elected to the United States Senate in place of J. C. Calhoun, deceased, serving from October, 1803, till 1804, when he resigned. He died in Philadelphia on February 15, 1822.—*Poore's Directory.*

WILLIAM FEW was born in Maryland in 1748. In 1758 his father removed to North Carolina. He received an academic education ; studied law, and was admitted to the bar at Augusta. He served as colonel in the Revolutionary war ; was a delegate to the Continental Congress in 1780, and from 1785 till 1788. He was a delegate to the convention which framed the Constitution of the United States, and was a United States Senator from 1789 till 1793. He removed to the city of New York in 1799. He was a member of the House of Representatives of New York from 1802 till 1808 ; and died in New York July 16, 1828.—*Poore's Directory.*

JAMES GUNN was born in Virginia. He received an academic education ; studied law ; was admitted to the bar and commenced practice at Savannah, Georgia. He was elected a United States Senator from Georgia in the first Congress, and was reëlected, serving from March 4, 1789, till March 3, 1801.—*Poore's Directory.*

BENJAMIN HAWKINS.—North Carolina was not represented in the Senate during the first session, but adopted the Constitution on the

14th of January, 1790.   At the second session of the Senate Benjamin Hawkins appeared on the 13th of January, 1790, as a Senator from North Carolina, and on the 29th of the same month Samuel Johnson appeared as a Senator from the same State.   Benjamin Hawkins was born in North Carolina in August, 1754.   He received a classical education , was at Princeton college, but 'the Revolutionary war suspended the college exercises whilst he was in the senior class.   Having acquired a knowledge of the French language he was placed on the staff of General Washington as interpreter, and was at the battle of Monmouth and other engagements.   He was a delegate to the Continental Congress from 1781 to 1784, and from 1786 to 1787.   He was appointed by Congress as commissioner to negotiate treaties with the Creeks and Cherokees in 1785.   He was elected a Senator in the first Congress, serving from January 13, 1790, till March 3, 1795.   He was appointed by General Washington in 1796 agent for all of the Indian tribes south of the Ohio river, and held the office by successive appointments until his death at the Creek agency, June 6, 1816.—*Poore's Directory.*

SAMUEL JOHNSTON was born in Scotland in 1733, and immigrated, in early life, to Chowan county, North Carolina.   He was a dele_ gate to a State meeting in North Carolina in 1755, and its moderator; and was the chief magistrate in North Carolina between the time of the abdication of the last of the royal governors and the accession of the first State Governor.   He was elected a delegate to the Continental Congress from 1780 to 1782, and was president of the State Convention in 1788 to consider the Federal Constitution, which was then rejected.   He was also the president of the convention in 1789, which ratified the Constitution.   He was elected a Senator to the first Congress as a Federalist, serving from January 29, 1790, till March 2, 1793.   He was appointed judge of the Superior Court of North Carolina in February, 1800, which position he resigned in November, 1803.   He died near to Edenton, in North Carolina, in August, 1816.—*Poore's Directory.*

JAMES MONROE, of Virginia.—James Monroe, appointed by the Legislature, appeared as a Senator from Virginia, on December 6, 1790, William Grayson, a former Senator, having died.   James Monroe was born in Westmoreland county, Virginia, on April 28, 1758.   He received a liberal education, graduating at William and Mary College, in Virginia, in 1776.   He joined the Revolutionary army as a cadet, became a captain, and participated in several engagements.   He studied law under Thomas Jefferson.   He was a member of the House of Representatives of Virginia in 1782, and a delegate, from

Virginia, to the Continental Congress from 1783 to 1786. He was a member of the United States Senate from 1790 to 1794; was minister to France from May, 1794, to December, 1796 ; was Governor of Virginia from 1799 to 1802 ; was again minister to France from January till July, 1803 ; was minister to England in 1803, and to Spain in 1805. He returned home in 1808, and again became Governor of Virginia. He was Secretary of State of the United States from November, 1811, till March 3, 1817. He was elected and reelected President of the United States, serving from 4th March, 1817, till March 3, 1825. He retired to his own farm in Loudon county, Virginia, and resided there till 1831, when he removed to the city of New York, where he died on the 4th of July, 1831.—*Poore's Directory.*

JOSEPH STANTON.—Rhode Island did not adopt the United States Constitution until 1790, and was not represented in the Senate during the first and second sessions ; but at the third session of the Senate, which was held at Philadelphia, Mr. Stanton and Mr. Foster, in December, 1790, appeared as Senators from that State. Joseph Stanton was born at Charleston, Rhode Island, in July, 1739. He served as second lieutenant in a Rhode Island regiment raised for the expedition to Canada in 1759 ; was a member of the General Assembly of Rhode Island from 1768 till 1774 ; was a member of the Committee of Safety in January, 1775, and was colonel of a Rhode Island regiment in 1776. He was a delegate to the State Convention of 1790, which in or about May, 1790, adopted the Federal Constitution. He was elected a United States Senator from Rhode Island as a Democrat, serving from the 15th of December, 1790, till March 3, 1793. He was elected a Representative to the Seventh Congress as a Democrat, and was elected to the Eighth Congress and to the Ninth, serving till March 3, 1807. He died at Charleston, Rhode Island.—*Poore's Directory.*

THEODORE FOSTER was born at Brookfield, Massachusetts, in April, 1752. He received a classical education, graduating at the Rhode Island college, (now Brown's university,) 1770, and again at Dartsmouth college, in New Hampshire, in 1786. He studied law, and commenced practice at Providence, Rhode Island. He was a member of the House of Representatives of Rhode Island from 1776 to 1782 ; was appointed a judge of the admiralty court in May, 1785, and was elected a United States Senator from Rhode Island, serving from December 17, 1790, till March 3, 1803. He was a member of the House of Representatives of Rhode Island from 1812 to 1816, and died at Providence January 13, 1828.—*Poore's Directory.*

MISCELLANEOUS.

Notices of other persons not members of the first Senate, but who were distinguished either in the civil or military service in the course of the Revolution.

SAMUEL ADAMS.—Jefferson wrote, in 1819, of Samuel Adams: I can say that Samuel Adams was truly a great man; wise in council, fertile in resources, immovable in his purposes, and had, I think, a greater share than any other member in advising and directing our measures in the Northern war. As a speaker he could not be compared with his living colleague and namesake, whose deep conceptions, nervous style, and undaunted firmness, made him truly our bulwark in debate. But Mr. Samuel Adams, although not of fluent elocution, was so vigorously logical, so clear in his views, abundant in good sense, and master always of his subject, that he commanded the most profound attention whenever he rose in an assembly, by which the froth of declamation was heard with the most profound contempt.—*Randall's Jefferson, vol. 1, page 182.*

And according to Mr. Trist's memoirs, Jefferson, on another occasion, remarked: " If there was any Palinurus to the Revolution, Samuel Adams was the man. Indeed, in the Eastern States, for a year or two after it began, he was truly the *Man of the Revolution.* He was constantly holding caucuses of distinguished men, (among whom was R. H. Lee,) at which the generality of the measures pursued were previously determined on, and at which the parts were assigned to the different actors, who afterwards appeared in them. *John* Adams had very little part in these caucuses; but ̄as one of the actors in the measures decided on in them, he was a *Colossus.*"—*Randall, 182.*

Galloway afterwards wrote: " Samuel Adams eats little, sleeps little, thinks much, and is most indefatigable in the pursuit of his object. It was this man who, by superior application, managed at once the factions in Congress at Philadelphia, and the factions of New England."—*Galloway, vol. 4, p. 356, quoted in 4th Grahame's History U. S., p. 389.*

Samuel Adams was of common size, of muscular form, light-blue eyes, light complexion, and erect in person. He wore a tie wig, cocked hat, and red cloak. His manner was very serious. At the close of his life, and probably from early times, he had a tremulous motion of the head, which probably added to the solemnity of his eloquence, as this was, in some measure, associated with his voice. He was in favor of adopting the Federal Constitution, but became an opponent to the administration. Though he and Hancock were the only two men excepted in the British proclamation of amnesty, they were, at one time, on very ill terms with each other from differences of opinion. He died in 1803.—*Sullivan, 142-3.*

Samuel Adams died in 1803, aged seventy. He was a poor man at his death. He left scarcely property enough to pay the expenses of his funeral.—*Hawthorn, 241, Grandfather's Chair.*

JAMES MADISON.—Mr. Madison was a man of small stature and grave appearance. At the close of his presidency he seemed to be a care-worn man, and seemed, by his face, to have attained to a more advanced age than was the fact. He had a calm expression, a penetrating blue eye, and looked like a thinking man. He was dressed in black, was bald on the top of his head, powdered, of rather protuberant person in front, small lower limbs, slow and deliberate in speech. Mr. Madison was a warm advocate for the Union, and the associate of Jay and Hamilton in the effort to make it acceptable to the public. But he early became an opponent of the administration, and closely allied to Mr. Jefferson.—*Sullivan, 140.*

There was much opposition in Virginia, as well as in New York, to the Federal Constitution without the amendments proposed in their several conventions. This opposition was strongly manifested in Virginia in the choice of the first Senators. Mr. Madison, who had been instrumental in its formation and adoption, was a candidate for the Senate, but was defeated. Richard Henry Lee and William Grayson were elected. Mr. Grayson, with Patrick Henry and others, had opposed its ratification without amendments.—*Pitkin, 332-375.*

Mr. Madison is thus described by Fisher Ames, in a letter dated May 3, 1789: (See Ames' Works, 1, 35-6.)

Madison is a man of sense, reading, address and integrity—as 'tis allowed, very much *Frenchified* in his politics. He speaks low, his person is little and ordinary. He speaks decently as to manner, and no more. His language is very pure, perspicuous and to the point. Pardon me, if I add, I think him too much of a book politician, and too timid in his politics, for prudence and caution are opposites of timidity. He is not a little of a Virginian, and thinks that State the land of promise ; but is afraid of their State politics, and

of his popularity there, more than, I think, he should be. * * *
He is our first man.

In a subsequent letter, dated May 18, 1789, he remarks further :
Madison is cool and has an air of reflection which is not very distant from gravity and self-sufficiency. In speaking he never relaxes
into pleasantry, and discovers little of that warmth of heart which
gives efficacy to George Cabot's reasoning, and to Lowell's. His
printed speeches are more faithful than any other person's, because
he speaks very slow, and his discourse is strongly marked. He states
a principle and deduces consequences with clearness and simplicity.
Sometimes declamation is mingled with argument, and he appears
very anxious to carry a point by other means than addressing the
understanding. He appeals to popular topics and to the pride of
the House—such as, that they have voted before and will be consistent. I think him a good man and an able man, but he has rather
too much theory, and wants that discretion which men of business
commonly have. He is also very timid, and seems evidently to want
manly firmness and energy of character.—*Ames' Works, vol. 1, 41–42.*

GENERAL HENRY KNOX.—General Knox was a bookseller and
bookbinder at Boston, when the war began, at which time he was
twenty-five years of age. He had been a captain of a grenadier
company, and was a volunteer at the battle of Bunker Hill. He met
Washington at Cambridge, in 1776, and was immediately made chief
of artillery, in which relation he continued during the war, and always near headquarters. He served throughout the war, and left
the service with the rank of Major General. He was nominated for
the War Department by General Washington on the 11th of September, 1789. When he resigned that office at the close of the year
1794, he removed to Boston, and for some years resided there. He
was a large man, above middle stature ; his lower limbs inclined a
little outward, as though they had taken a form from the long continued use of the saddle. His hair was short in front, standing up,
powdered and queued. His forehead was low ; his face large and
full below ; his eyes rather small, gray and brilliant. The expression of his face altogether, was a very fine one. When moving along
the street he had an air of grandeur and complacency. He carried
a large cane, not to aid his steps, but usually under his arm, and
sometimes, when he happened to stop and engage in conversation
with his accustomed ardor, his cane was used to flourish with in aid
of his eloquence. He was usually dressed in black. In the summer
he commonly carried his light silk hat in his hand when walking in
the shade. His left hand had been mutilated, and a part of it was

gone. He wore a black handkerchief wrapped around it, from which the thumb and forefinger appeared. When engaged in conversation he used to unwind and replace the handkerchief, but not so as to expose his disfigured hand. His voice was strong. His mind was powerful, rapid and decisive, and he could employ it continuously and effectively. His natural propensity was highly social, and no man better enjoyed a hearty laugh. He said that he had through life left his bed at the dawn, and had been always a cheerful, happy man.

His hospitality, generosity, and too confident a calculation on the productiveness of sales of extensive tracts of land in Maine, led him into embarrassment towards the close of his life. He died at his splendid mansion at Thomaston, in Maine, in the year 1806.—*Sullivan, 130–1.*

Mr. Sullivan further remarks that when living in his splendid mansion in Maine, it was not unusual for General Knox, in the summer when numbers of his friends visited him, to have killed an ox and twenty sheep on every Monday morning; and to have made up daily an hundred beds, in his own house. He kept for his own use and that of his friends, twenty saddle horses and several pairs of carriage horses. This style of living was too much for his means, and he became embarrassed, as before observed.

BENJAMIN LINCOLN, a Revolutionary officer, Secretary of War, and first collector of the port of Boston. In 1794 he was about sixty years of age. He had received only an inferior education, but had done much to compensate its defects. Before the war he had been a member of the Legislature and a militia colonel. He was about five feet nine inches in stature, and of so uncommonly broad person as to seem to be of less stature than he was. His gray hair was combed back from his forehead, unpowered and gathered in a long queue. His face was round and full; his eyes blue, and his complexion light. He was usually dressed in a blue coat and light underclothes, and wore a cocked hat. He always appeared in boots, in consequence of a deformity of his left leg, occasioned by a wound received at the capture of Burgoyne. His speech was with apparent difficulty, as though he were too full. The expression of his countenance was exceedingly kind and amiable. His manner was very gracious; and like those of all the high officers of the Revolution, his deportment was dignified and courteous. He wrote essays on several subjects, commercial, agricultural and philosophical. He employed some one to read these essays, and assigned as a reason that being entirely ignorant of the grammatical construction of language, he could judge only, by the sound, of its correctness. He was afflicted with somnolency. This was not occasioned by age, but was constitutional. In the midst of conversation, at table, and when driving himself in a chaise, he would fall asleep. When he commanded the troops against the Massachusetts insurgents he dictated dispatches and slept between the sentences. His sleep did not appear to disturb his perception of circumstances that were passing around him. He was a man of exemplary morals, and of sincere piety, carrying fully into practical life the ethics of the religion he professed. He enjoyed the high respect and confidence of Washington, and the affectionate regard of his fellow officers. He performed his various trusts with ability and integrity. He was president of the Cincinnati. He died in 1810 at an advanced age. He was collector of the port of Boston, and was one of the few whom Jefferson did not turn out of office. He at length retired from the office.—*Sullivan, 128–9.*

JOHN JAY was the first Chief Justice of the United States. Whilst occupying that position he was appointed by President Washington minister to England, where he negotiated the treaty known as Jay's treaty, and which was the subject of bitter contest before its confirmation by precisely the constitutional majority (two thirds) of the Senate.

Mr. Jay was descended from one of the Protestant families usually called Huguenots. This name, which appears to be of uncertain derivation, like Puritan, was given to a certain class of Christians. In 1598, after Henry the Fourth, of France, had fought his way to the throne, he issued the edict of Nantes, by which he assured to all his Protestant subjects the rights and privileges enjoyed by those who were Catholics. In 1685 this edict was revoked by Louis XIV. Many of the Huguenots escaped from France and established themselves elsewhere; their skill, talents and industry being thus lost to France. The parents of Mr. Jay settled in New York. He was born in this country. He was forty-four years of age when appointed Chief Justice in 1790. His height was a little less than six feet; his person thin, but well formed. His complexion was without color; his eyes black and penetrating; his nose aquiline, and his chin pointed. His hair came over his forehead, was tied behind, and lightly powdered. His dress was black. The expression of his face was exceedingly amiable. When standing he was a little inclined forward. His manner was gentle and unassuming. This impression of him was renewed in 1795, in New York. He had returned from his mission to England, in that year, and had been chosen Governor of New York, which office he assumed in July.

He was then about fifty. His deportment was tranquil and unassuming, and one who had met him, not knowing who he was, would not have been led to suppose that he was in the presence of one eminently gifted by Nature with intellectual power, and who had sustained so many offices of high trust and honor. * * * *
Throughout his useful and honorable life he was governed by the dictates of an enlightened Christian conscience. He thought and acted under the conviction that there is an accountability far more serious than any which men can have to their fellow men.—*Sullivan, 90–2.*

As to Dress.

About the year 1760 dress was much attended to by both sexes. Coats of every variety of color were worn, not excepting red. Sometimes the cape and collar were of velvet, and of a different color from the coat.—*Sullivan, 67.*

About the end of the century the forms of society underwent a change. The leveling process of France began to be felt. Powder for the hair began to be unfashionable. A loose dress for the lower limbs was adopted. Wearing the hair tied was given up, and short hair became common. Colored garments were out of use, and dark or black were substituted. Buckles disappeared. The style of life had acquired more of elegance as means had increased. Crowded evening parties were not as common then as they are now. There was more of sociability and less form of display than there is now.—*Sullivan, 145.*

Articles of Provisions in the Constitution of the United States, to which Reference is made on pages 13–14 of the Preface; or in Sketches of Debate Relative to Power in the President to Remove from Office without the Sanction of the Senate—and as to the Judicial Power.

The Preamble to the Constitution of the United States.

We, the people of the United States, in order to form a more perfect union, establish justice, insure domestic tranquility, provide for the common defense, promote *the general welfare*, and secure the blessings of liberty to ourselves and our posterity, do ordain and establish this Constitution for the United States of America.—*1 Wheaton, 324; 4 Wheaton, 403.*

Article First of the Constitution.

SECTION 8. Congress shall have power to lay and collect taxes. duties, imports and excises to pay the debts, and provide for the

---

NOTE.—The *italics* are not used in the Constitution.

common defense and *general welfare* of the United States; but all duties, imposts, and excises shall be uniform throughout the United States, &c.

As to the Power of the President.

ARTICLE II, SECTION 2. He shall have power, by and with the advice and consent of the Senate, to make treaties, provided two thirds of the Senate present concur; and he shall nominate, and by and with the advice and consent of the Senate, shall appoint ambassadors, other public ministers and consuls, judges of the Supreme Court, and all officers of the United States, whose appointments are not herein otherwise provided for, and which shall be established by law. But Congress may, by law, vest the appointment of such inferior officers, as they think proper, in the President alone, in the courts of law, or in the heads of department.

SECTION 3. The President shall have power to fill up all vacancies that may happen during the recess of the Senate, by granting commissions, which shall expire at the end of their next session.

SECTION 3. He shall, from time to time, give to Congress information of the state of the Union, and recommend to their consideration such measures as he shall judge necessary and expedient; he may, on extraordinary occasions, convene both houses, or either of them; and in case of disagreement between them with respect to the time of adjournment, he may adjourn them to such time as he shall think proper; he shall receive ambassadors and other public ministers; *he shall take care that the laws be faithfully executed*, and shall commission all the officers of the United States.

SECTION 4. The President, Vice President, and all civil officers of the United States, shall be removed from office on impeachment for, and conviction of, treason, bribery, or other high crimes and misdemeanors.

As to the Judiciary.

ARTICLE III, SECTION 2. The judicial power of the United States shall be vested in one Supreme Court, and in such inferior courts as Congress may, from time to time, ordain and establish. The judges, both of the Supreme and inferior courts, shall hold their offices during good behavior; and shall, at stated times, receive for their services a compensation which shall not be diminished during their continuance in office.

2. The judicial power shall extend to all cases, in law and equity, arising under this Constitution, the laws of the United States, and

NOTE.—The *italics* used above are not in the Constitution.

treaties made, or which shall be made, under their authority ; to all cases affecting ambassadors or other public ministers and consuls ; to all cases of admiralty and maritime jurisdiction, to controversies to which the United States shall be a party ; to controversies between two or more States ; between a State and citizens of another State ; between citizens of different States ; between citizens of the same State claiming lands under grants of different States, and between a State, or the citizens thereof, and foreign States, citizens, or subjects.

Third Congress, Second Session, December 2, 1793.

ARTICLE XI. The judicial power of the United States shall not be construed to extend to any suit in law or equity, commenced or prosecuted against one of the United States, by citizens of another State, or by citizens or subjects of any foreign State.

Essay on Imprisonment for Debt, by Mr. Maclay.

Imprisonment for debt having been introduced, with other British customs, at the first settlement of the country, public prejudice was in its favor. Great was the grief and misery attendant on it ; but it seemed to be classed with the ills inseparable from the lot of humanity, and the result of British wisdom and experience. Investigation will remove this veil of prejudice and predilection for ancient custom. To the person who will cast his eye back on British practice it will be found that no such thing existed at *common law.* Jurisprudence, both civil and criminal, was in the earliest times administered in a common court, called the *Regia aula,* or Royal Hall. Distinctions naturally presented themselves, and this great court was sub-divided into a number of others, the principal of which were the King's Bench and the Common Pleas. Offenses against the peace, order and regularity of society were considered as committed against the *Government,* and, of course, fell to the cognizance of the King's Bench. Actions between man and man, of a pecuniary nature respecting property, fell to the court of Common Pleas. In the proceedings of the first or King's Bench, where personal liberty was used to exercise violence and injure the liberty of another, arrests were allowed, more especially as offenses of this kind could and often were committed by persons who had no property. The demands prosecuted in the Common Pleas were against property only, and, of course, personal liberty was not considered as the proper object of process. Great competition took place between these courts, and the utmost stretch of ability was exerted to try who should engross the business. In order to this the King's Bench, under the law maxim that *in fictione juris consistat equitas,* feigned trespasses where none existed; and, of course, all their process was by arrest. When dispute happens between two persons it is easy to conceive that a law case or suit is the consequence; but to feign a trespass, which implies violence to be committed in such case, after such case had happened, is absolute nonsense. Yet the thing obtained, and trespass on the case, trespass in debt, are common law terms. It is true practice has assigned a kind of meaning to them, and you can guess by them whether the demand is on a note or bond, as different ingredients will sometimes produce a third something by mixture. But nothing can be more absurd than the terms so applied in their original meaning; and yet by such absurdity was the liberty of freemen lost. The feigned trespass was *first* set forth in the proceedings; then came the *ac etiam* clause, stating the debt after he was in custody for the trespass, &c. All these petty proceedings were carried on by what lawyers call the *trinum in lege;* and by such tricks the King's Bench obtained a superiority.

But the Common Pleas also fell to fictions, and they tried their *clausum fregit*—their *etiams,* &c., too, for they found they must gratify the vengeance of creditors as well as the King's Bench, or they would have no business. And thus imprisonment for debt became general.

Such a picture is not very pleasing, and ought certainly to be rejected unless better reasons can be adduced than arise from the origin or practice of it. But if ancient precedent is to fix the matter, let us inquire how it was in Athens while ancient Greece was in all her glory? The liberty of the citizen was so precious that its exercise could be suspended by the law alone. He could not engage it for *debt* on any pretext whatever.

Let us, however, endeavor to settle this question on principle, abstract from all practice and custom whatever.

Debt, then, appears to be the child of *credit.* What, then, are the objects which have influence upon or from which credit is generated? Not liberty and personal freedom certainly, for in that case our Indians would have more credit than any people we know. Does it flow from accomplishments, elegance of manners or personal beauty? No such thing is known in men, (female beauty excepted.) Property and personal honor will be considered as the fullest answer that can be given to the question. But honor without property is will without power. We trust a man not because we know him to be willing, but because we believe him to be able to pay. Original traffic proceeded on the principle of benevolence and accommodation. The wants of one were supplied by the superfluities of the other, and both were obliged. But is it the case in the present mercantile system? Far from it. Commerce is now a game of abilities, and the outwitted dealer is often the best man of the two; for whether it is that the benevolent qualities of the heart impede the activity of the head, or from whatever cause, it is a common remark that the best men are generally the most unlucky in trade. Shall then the loss of liberty be added to the misfortunes of such a one? Certainly no. There is no treating a subject of this kind without bringing into view the profession of the law, and a class of men of whom all the good and all the evil that could be imagined has been said with some appearance of reason. What more amiable than the man of legal abilities, exerting his utmost powers for the protection of innocençe and relief of distress? What more detestable than the wretch who glories in the miseries and preys upon the distress of his fellow citizens? You behold in one the good Samaritan with his wine and oil. In the other the Alpine wolf attacking the distressed wanderer, depriving him of life, and rending his carcass in pieces. Here we find the fabled figure realized, where the superior parts are adorned with all the charms and attractions of female beauty, but the inferior end in the fins of a filthy fish or the claws of a griping lobster.

Having said so much on the character of the bar, it will be superfluous to add that they are divided on this question. While some reprobate the measure in the strongest terms, others support it and blush not to declare that the confined client always gives the most generous fees. " Skin for skin—all that a man hath will he give for life." Liberty is the soul of life. Life without it is misery. Gaols are the man traps of the hunters of the law. Once shut up, the prisoner's property is sure game. He regards it not. Liberty is his only wish, and all his substance is generally cast at the feet of some mighty Nimrod of the bar to procure his enlargement. Thus while some chase the devoted game into the toils of the law and the pitfall of a gaol, others strip them completely in the taking out; and the spoils of their property, instead of paying their creditors or supporting their families, fall often, in great proportion, into the hands of those who have hunted them.

NOTE.—In the year 1787, when a bill was depending in Parliament for the relief of insolvent debtors, the Chancellor opposed it and said: "The general idea that humanity requires the intervention of the legislature between the debtor and the creditor is a false notion, founded in error and dangerous in practice. A much greater evil than the loss of liberty is the dissipation and corruption that prevail in our prisons. To these your Lordships had better direct your attention than to defrauding the creditor of the chance of recovering his property by letting loose his debtors, and taking from him the very hope of payment." Lord Campbell observes that so blinded was he, "the chancellor," by prejudice as not to see that the "dissipation and corruption" of which he complains were produced by the very power of imprisonment which he defended.—*Lord Campbell's Lives of Lord Chancellors, vol. 7, p. 96–7.*

In 1759 Dr. Johnston computed the number of imprisoned debtors in England at not less than 20,000; and asserted that one in four died every year from the treatment they underwent. He afterwards admitted that he had found reasons to question the accuracy of this calculation. But cases were proved of debtors *unable to pay their fees,* who were locked up with prisoners suffering from small-pox, and thus destroyed. Of others who were reduced almost to skeletons by insufficient food ; of sick women who were left without beds, without attendance, and without proper nourishment until they died of neglect ; of men who were tortured by thumb screws, or who lingered in slow agony under irons of intolerable weight.—*Page 542–4 of the History of England in the Eighteenth Century, by Lecky.*

Imprisonment for mere debt was not abolished in Pennsylvania till 1842. It still exists, we believe, against certain classes of persons in *England.*

The Alleged Mecklenburg Declaration of the *twentieth* of May, seventeen hundred and seventy-*five*.

That whosoever directly or indirectly abetted, or in any way, form, or manner countenanced the unchartered and dangerous invasion of our rights, as claimed by Great Britain, is an enemy to this country, to America, and to the inherent and inalienable rights of man. That we, the citizens of Mecklenburg county, do hereby dissolve the political bands which have connected us to the mother country, and hereby absolve ourselves from all allegiance to the British crown, and abjure all political connection, contract, or association with that nation, who have wantonly trampled on our rights and liberties, and inhumanly shed the blood of Ameriɡan patriots at Lexington.

That we hereby declare ourselves a free and independent people; are and of right ought to be a sovereign and self-governing association, under the control of no power other than that of God, and the general government of Congress; to the maintenance of which independence, we solemnly pledge to each other our mutual coöperation, our lives, our fortunes, and our most sacred honor, &c., &c.

(Signed)   ABRAHAM ALEXANDER, *Chairman.*
JOHN MCNITT ALEXANDER, *Secretary.*

Resolution submitted by Richard Henry Lee.

The resolution submitted by Mr. Lee on the 10th of June, 1776, in conformity to the resolution from Virginia, was: That these colonies *are and of right ought to be* free and independent States, that they are *absolved from all allegiance to the British crown*, and that *all political connection* between them and the State of Great Britain is and ought to be totally dissolved.*

In the Declaration of Independence Mr. Jefferson wrote: When, in the course of human events, it becomes necessary for one people to *dissolve the political bands which have connected* them with another, &c. We hold these truths to be self-evident—that all men are created equal; that they are endowed by their Creator with certain *inalienable rights*, that among these are life, liberty, and the pursuit of happiness, &c.; and concluding, that these colonies solemnly publish and declare, That these united colonies " *are and of right ought to be* free and independent States " " that they are absolved *from all allegiance to the British crown*," and that " *all political connection* between them and the State of Great Britain is and ought to be

---

* The words italicized in the above are in the *Mecklenburg* declaration.

totally dissolved," and that as free and independent States they have full power to levy war, conclude peace, contract alliances, establish commerce, and do all other acts and things which independent States may of right do. And for the support of this declaration, with a firm reliance on the protection of Divine Providence, we mutually *pledge to each other our lives, our fortunes, and our sacred honor.*

The words between quotation marks are in the resolution offered by Mr. Lee. The only other expressions used by Mr. Jefferson and which are in the alleged Mecklenburg declaration, are " inalienable rights," " political bands which have connected," and " our lives, our fortunes, and our sacred honor."

It would seem that the Mecklenburg declarations, if they existed, had been seen in Virginia before the Virginia resolution was adopted; and they may have been also seen by Mr. Jefferson without his special recollection where he had seen them.

For the resolution adopted in Virginia on 15th of May, 1776, see antea, page 333.

NOTE.—The words in italics are in the Mecklenburg declaration of 20th May, 1775, if it existed.

Declaration of Independence of the United States, adopted on the fourth of July, 1776.

[NOTE.—The words italicized in this copy of the Declaration are in the *alleged* Mecklenburg Declaration of 20th May, 1775, if it existed.]

When, in the course of human events, it becomes necessary for one people to *dissolve the political bands which have connected* them with another, and to assume, among the powers of the earth, the separate and equal station to which the laws of nature and nature's God entitle them, a decent respect to the opinions of mankind requires that they should declare the causes which impel them to the separation.

We hold these truths to be self-evident, that all men are created equal ; that they are endowed by their Creator with certain *inalienable rights ;* that among these are life, liberty, and the pursuit of happiness. That, to secure these rights, governments are instituted among men, deriving their just powers from the consent of the governed ; that, whenever any form of Government becomes destructive of these ends, it is the right of the people to alter or to abolish it, and to institute a new Government, laying its foundation on such principles, and organizing its powers in such form, as to them shall seem most likely to effect their safety and happiness. Prudence, indeed, will dictate that Governments long established, should not be changed for light and transient causes; and accordingly, all experience hath shown, that mankind are more disposed to suffer, while evils are sufferable, than to right themselves by abolishing the forms to which they are accustomed. But, when a long train of abuses and usurpations, pursuing invariably the same object, evinces a design to reduce them under absolute despotism, it is their right, it is their duty, to throw off such Government, and to provide new guards for their future security. Such has been the patient sufferance of these colonies, and such is now the necessity which constrains them to alter their former systems of Government. The history of the present King of Great Britain is a history of repeated injuries and usurpations, all having, in direct object, the establishment of an absolute tyranny over these States. To prove this, let facts be submitted to a candid world :

He has refused his assent to laws the most wholesome and necessary for the public good.

He has forbidden his Governors to pass laws of immediate and pressing importance, unless suspended in their operation till his assent should be obtained ; and, when so suspended, he has utterly neglected to attend to them.

He has refused to pass other laws for the accommodation of large districts of people, unless those people would relinquish the right of representation in the Legislature ; a right inestimable to them, and formidable to tyrants only.

He has called together legislative bodies at places unusual, uncomfortable, and distant from the depository of their public records, for the sole purpose of fatiguing them into compliance with his measures.

He has dissolved representative Houses repeatedly, for opposing, with manly firmness, his invasions on the rights of the people.

He has refused, for a long time after such dissolutions, to cause others to be elected ; whereby the legislative powers, incapable of annihilation, have returned to the people at large for their exercise ; the State remaining, in the meantime, exposed to all the danger of invasion from without, and convulsions within.

He has endeavored to prevent the population of these States ; for that purpose, obstructing the laws for naturalization of foreigners ; refusing to pass others to encourage their migration hither, and raising the conditions of new appropriations of lands.

He has obstructed the administration of justice, by refusing his assent to laws for establishing judiciary powers.

He has made judges dependent on his will alone, for the tenure of their office, and the amount and payment of their salaries.

He has erected a multitude of new offices, and sent hither swarms of officers to harass our people, and eat out their substance.

He has kept among us, in times of peace, standing armies, without the consent of our Legislature.

He has affected to render the military independent of, and superior to, the civil power.

He has combined, with others, to subject us to a jurisdiction foreign to our Constitution, and unacknowledged by our laws ; giving his assent to their acts of pretended legislation :

For quartering large bodies of armed troops among us.

For protecting them, by a mock trial, from punishment, for any murders which they should commit on the inhabitants of these States.

For cutting off our trade with all parts of the world.

For imposing taxes on us without our consent.

For depriving us, in many cases, of the benefits of trial by jury.

For transporting us beyond seas to be tried for pretended offenses.

For abolishing the free system of English laws in a neighboring province, establishing therein an arbitrary Government, and enlarging its boundaries, so as to render it at once an example and fit instrument for introducing the same absolute rule into these colonies.

For taking away our charters, abolishing our most valuable laws, and altering, fundamentally, the powers of our Governments.

For suspending our own Legislatures, and declaring themselves invested with power to legislate for us in all cases whatsoever.

He has abdicated Government here, by declaring us out of his protection, and waging war against us.

He has plundered our seas, ravaged our coast, burnt our towns, and destroyed the lives of our people.

He is at this time transporting large armies of foreign mercenaries to complete the works of death, desolation and tyranny, already begun, with circumstances of cruelty and perfidy scarcely paralleled in the most barbarous ages, and totally unworthy the head of a civilized nation.

He has constrained our fellow-citizens, taken captive on the high seas, to bear arms against their country, to become the executioners of their friends and brethren, or to fall themselves by their hands.

He has excited domestic insurrections among us, and has endeavored to bring on the inhabitants of our frontiers the merciless Indian savages, whose known rule of warfare is an undistinguished destruction of all ages, sexes, and conditions.

In every stage of these oppressions, we have petitioned for redress, in the most humble terms; our repeated petitions have been answered only by repeated injury. A prince, whose character is thus marked by every act which may define a tyrant, is unfit to be the ruler of a free people.

Nor have we been wanting in attention to our British brethren. We have warned them, from time to time, of attempts made by their Legislature to extend an unwarrantable jurisdiction over us. We have reminded them of the circumstances of our emigration and settlement here. We have appealed to their native justice and magnanimity, and we have conjured them, by the ties of our common kindred, to disavow these usurpations, which would inevitably interrupt our connections and correspondence. They, too, have been deaf to the voice of justice and consanguinity. We must, therefore, acquiesce in the necessity which denounces our separation, and hold them, as we hold the rest of mankind, enemies in war, in peace, friends.

We, therefore, the representatives of the UNITED STATES OF AMERICA, in GENERAL CONGRESS assembled, appealing to the Supreme Judge of the world for the rectitude of our intentions, do, in the name and by the authority of the good people of these colonies, solemnly publish and declare, That these United Colonies *are and of right ought to be* FREE AND INDEPENDENT STATES; that they are absolved from all *allegiance to the British crown*, and that all *political connection* between them and the State of Great Britain is, and ought to be, totally dissolved; and that, as FREE AND INDEPENDENT STATES, they have full power to levy war, conclude peace, contract alliances, establish commerce, and to do all other acts and things which INDEPENDENT STATES may of right do. And, for the support of this declaration, with a firm reliance on the protection of Divine Providence, we mutually *pledge to each other, our lives, our fortunes, and our sacred honor.*

INDEX.

For an account of Tammany, see Harper's Magazine of April and May, 1872, where are photographs of distinguished political characters, viz: of Aaron Burr, Morgan Lewis, George Clinton, DeWitt Clinton, Daniel D. Tompkins, Martin Van Buren, Silas Wright, William L. Marcy, A. Oakey Hall. Richard B. Connolly, William M. Tweed, Peter B. Sweeny, and Fernando Wood.